The A to Z of
Classical Music

The Great Composers and Their Great Works

Keith A

NAXOS

First published by HNH International Ltd. 1996

© 1996 HNH International Ltd.

ISBN 9-6263-4499-7

The A to Z of Classical Music

Adam, Adolphe (1803 - 1856)

The son of a distinguished Paris Conservatoire piano-teacher, Adolphe Adam was born in Paris in 1803. He won popular success with his many compositions for the stage, much of his later work necessitated by the failure of a theatre venture in the revolution of 1848 and the consequent need to pay off heavy debts, cleared by the time of his death in 1856.

Stage Works

Adam wrote some eighty works for the stage. Of these the best known is the ballet Giselle or Les Wilis, based on a legend according to which the ghosts of unmarried girls return to seek revenge on the living. His opera Si j'étais roi was among the most successful, and the overture remains in international concert repertoire.

☛ **Recommended Recordings**

Giselle (Suite)
Naxos 8.550081

Giselle (Complete Ballet) (2 CD's)
Naxos 8.550755-6

Overture: Si j'étais roi
Naxos 8.550473

Aguado, Dionysio (1784 - 1849)

A Spanish guitar virtuoso, Dionysio Aguado was born in Madrid and in 1825 settled for the next thirteen years in Paris, where he won great popularity as a teacher and performer. Unlike his distinguished older contemporary Fernando Sor he favoured the use of the finger-nails in plucking the instrument, ensuring a more incisive tone.

Guitar Music

Aguado is still remembered for his famous Escuela de guitarra and his studies, published in Madrid in 1820, Colección de estudios para guitarra.

☛ **Recommended Recording**

Menuett, Andante, 6 Etudes
Naxos 8.553007

Aichinger, Gregor (1564-5 - 1628)

A fellow student of Jakob Fugger, of the banking family, the German organist and composer Gregor Aichinger was appointed organist to an older member of the Fugger family in Augsburg. His patron allowed him study in Venice with Giovanni Gabrieli, followed by further visits to Italy, where it is probable he was ordained a priest. At his return to Augsburg in 1601 he continued his association with the Fugger family in addition to church benefices, with a series of compositions now exclusively sacred.

Church Music

Aichinger published three volumes of Sacrae cantiones, in 1590, 1595 and 1597 respectively. These choral and polychoral collections were followed in 1607 by the first of Aichinger's published works that included a basso continuo, the first example of such a publication in Germany. These represent part of an extensive series of sacred vocal works.

Alaín, Jehan (1811 - 1940)

Son of the composer Albert Alain and brother of the famous organist Marie-Claire Alain, the French composer and organist Jehan Alain left a fascinating body of music for piano and for organ, much of it published after his premature death in action in 1940. A pupil of Marcel Dupré, Paul Dukas and Roger-Ducasse, Alain wrote music of originality, within the French tradition to which he belonged.

Organ Music

Jehan Alain's music for organ, collected for publication in 1943 in three volumes, contains music of profound religious inspiration, as well as exploring traditional forms of prelude, fugue, fantasy and variations.

Piano Music

Alain's music for piano was again published posthumously in 1944 in three volumes and is similar in its inspiration to the music he wrote for organ.

Choral Music

Choral music by Jehan Alain includes a Nuptial Mass for four voices and string quartet, a Requiem Mass and a Messe brève.

Albéniz, Isaac (1860 - 1909)

A pianist and composer, the Spanish musician Albéniz was a leading figure in the creation of a national style of composition in Spain. Although he wrote operas, including a King Arthur to English words, songs and orchestral music, he is best known for his piano music, some of which has been arranged by others for orchestra.

Piano Music

The music for piano includes the four books of the Suite Iberia, the Suite Española, Op. 47, Twelve Characteristic Pieces (12 piezas caracteristicas), Op. 92 and Recuerdos de viaje, Op. 71. Some of the piano pieces by Albéniz have been orchestrated. These include three pieces from the Suite Iberia, and Navarra, left unfinished at the composer's death, orchestrated by Arbos, and other colourful arrangements.

☞ **Recommended Recording**
Iberia (orch. Arbos)
Naxos 8.550174

d'Albert, Eugen (1864 - 1932)

The German composer Eugen d'Albert was born in Glasgow and had his early musical training in London, where his father had formerly been ballet-master at the King's Theatre and at Covent Garden. He enjoyed a career as a virtuoso pianist, later turning his attention to opera, a form in which he won immediate, if ephemeral success. He died in Riga in 1932.

Stage Works

The best known of d'Albert's stage works is his music-drama Tiefland, based on a Portuguese original and first staged in Prague in 1903. This was followed by a musical comedy on the subject of the flautist king Frederick the Great, Flauto solo. His final work for the stage, Mister Wu, was left unfinished at his death.

Orchestral Music

D'Albert left two piano concertos, a cello concerto and a symphony. Better known is his Symphonic Prelude to Tiefland.

Piano Music

D'Albert made the usual transcriptions and arrangements for piano, expected of any virtuoso. Original compositions include a Suite, Op.1, a Sonata and a large number of shorter genre pieces.

☞ **Recommended Recording**
Prelude and Intermezzo from Tiefland
Naxos 8.550240

Albinoni, Tomaso (1671 - 1750)

A contemporary of Vivaldi in Venice, Albinoni's compositions include 53 operas, now generally neglected and a variety of instrumental works, many of which remain in chamber orchestra repertoire.

Orchestral Music

The most popular work associated with the name of Albinoni is the spurious but delightful Adagio of Giazotto, apparently based on a genuine fragment by Albinoni himself. Albinoni wrote some 54 concertos. Of these the set of twelve for strings, Op. 5, the twelve Oboe

Concertos, Op. 7, the set of a dozen varied concertos, Op. 9 and the Violin Concertos, Op. 10, repay attention.

☞ **Recommended Recordings**

Oboe Concerti Op. 7, Nos. 1, 2, 3, 8 & 9
Sinfonia
Naxos 8.553002

Oboe Concerti Op. 7, Nos. 4, 5, 6, 11 & 12
and Op. 9, No. 12
Naxos 8.553035

Oboe Concerti Op. 9, Nos. 2, 3, 5, 8, 9 and 11
Naxos 8.550739

Adagio (Giazotto)
Naxos 8.550014

Chamber Music

Chamber music by Albinoni includes two attractive works written for trumpet and strings, the Sonata a 6, and the Sonata di concerto a 7, as well as four sets of trio sonatas.

Albrechtsberger, Johann Georg (1736 - 1809)

Johann Georg Albrechtsberger gave lessons to Beethoven and succeeded Mozart, at the latter's request, as assistant to the Kapellmeister of St Stephen's Cathedral in Vienna, with right of succession, a promotion realised two years after Mozart's death, in 1793. He won contemporary distinction as an organist, composer and teacher, and displayed a particular mastery of counterpoint, reflected in his own 240 fugues and in the later work of his pupil Beethoven.

Organ Music

Albrechtsberger published an enormous quantity of fugues and preludes and fugues, many for either organ or harpsichord. He left some 278 keyboard works, which, in general, show his technical skill.

Chamber Music

Equally prolific in chamber music for various groups of instruments, Albrechtsberger based many of his instrumental compositions on the church sonata of the Baroque period, with its contrapuntal content.

Orchestral Music

While Albrechtsberger's four symphonies may be forgotten, his concertos for jew's harp have occasionally made their way into the modern trumpet repertoire. He also wrote concertos for trombone, for harp and for organ.

☞ **Recommended Recording**

Prelude and Fugue in C
Naxos 8.550964

Alfonso el Sabio (1221 - 1284)

Alfonso el Sabio (Alfonso the Wise) became king of Castile and León in 1252. As a patron of the arts and of learning he was responsible for a number of important publications, among them the Cantigas de Santa Maria, a varied collection of songs in honour, in one way or another, of the Blessed Virgin. His court was an artistic and scholarly centre, where Jewish, Islamic and Christian met. Politically he was less successful, his patronage of the arts leading to accusations of weakness.

Vocal Music

The Cantigas de Santa Maria are songs that celebrate the Blessed Virgin, whether in songs of praise or in anecdotal accounts of miracles, probable or improbable. Alfonso el Sabio may have been both poet and musician, but the Cantigas represent a collection that he ordered and by which he set great store rather than his own original creative work.

☛ **Recommended Recording**

Cantigas de Santa Maria
Naxos 8.553133

Alfvén, Hugo (1872 - 1960)

A Swedish composer, conductor and violinist, Alfvén was born and had his musical training in Stockholm. He wrote a considerable amount of orchestral, choral, vocal and chamber music.

Orchestral Music

Alfvén is probably best known abroad for his Swedish Rhapsody No. 1, Midsummer Vigil (Midsommarvaka), rather than for the five symphonies, the Swedish vocal music or chamber music.

☛ **Recommended Recordings**

Polka from Roslagen / Gustavus
Adolphus II Suite / Midsummer Vigil
Naxos 8.553115
Swedish Rhapsody No. 1
Naxos 8.550090

Alkan, Charles-Valentin (1813 - 1888)

Alkan, born Morhange in Paris in 1813, was among the most gifted piano virtuosi of his time. Much of his life, in particular from 1853 onwards, was spent in eccentric isolation. His remarkable abilities as a pianist, in later years only intermittently displayed, were coupled with an equally remarkable body of keyboard compositions, neglected until recent years. In addition to his musical interests, he maintained his classical and biblical studies, the latter reflecting the Jewish faith into which he had been born and to which he remained loyal throughout his life.

Piano Music

While Alkan's piano music includes the operatic fantasias and transcriptions fashionable in his time, his more remarkable works must be his virtuoso Etudes, notably the set in all minor keys, containing a Scherzo diabolique, Symphony, Concerto, Ouverture and final Festin d'Esope variations. The four movement Symphony includes a sober Marche funèbre. There are Préludes in all keys, major and minor, many with idiosyncratic titles, Impromptus, Etudes in all major keys and a set of 48 Esquisses, the last as original as anything else he wrote. Much of Alkan's piano music makes fierce technical demands on any performer and the larger works are massive in scale and conception.

☞ **Recommended Recordings**

25 Préludes, Op. 31
Marco Polo 8.223284

Esquisses, Op. 63
Marco Polo 8.223352

Etudes from Opp. 35 and 39
Marco Polo 8.223351

Grand Duo concertant, Op. 21
Sonata de concert, Op. 47
Marco Polo 8.223383

Préludes, dans tous les tons majeurs et mineurs,
Op. 3 / Deuxième recueil d'impromptus, Op. 32
Le chemin de fer, Op. 27
Etudes (dans tous les tons majeurs), Op. 35
Marche funèbre, Andantino, Op. 39, No. 6
Esquisses, Op. 63
Scherzo diabolique, Op. 39, No. 3
Naxos 8.553434

Quartre impromptus, op. 32 (1)
Deuxième recueil d'impromptus, Op. 32 (2)
Variations, Op. 1
Rondeau chromatique, Op. 12 / Alleluia, Op. 25
Salut, cendre du pauvre!, Op. 45
Paraphrase on Psalm 137, Op. 52
Marco Polo 8.223657

Seven Etudes from Op. 39
Marco Polo 8.223285

Trois Etudes de Bravoure, Op. 12
Trois Grandes Etudes, Op. 76
Marco Polo 8.223500

Allegri, Gregorio (1582 - 1652)

In a career largely centred on Rome, Allegri provided music for the papal choir.

Church Music

Allegri's most famous work is his setting of the Miserere for five-part choir, with a second four-part choir of soloists. The work was kept secret, but the 14-year-old Mozart wrote it out from memory, after he had heard it sung in Holy Week in the Sistine Chapel in 1770.

☞ **Recommended Recording**

Miserere
Naxos 8.550827

Anglebert, Jean-Henri d'

(1635 - 1691)

Jean-Henri d'Anglebert succeeded Chambonnières as harpsichordist to Louis XIV, a position later held by his son. At Versailles he collaborated, inevitably, with Lully, excerpts from whose operas and ballets he transcribed for keyboard.

Keyboard Music

The four keyboard suites of d'Anglebert, including dances, transcriptions and opening unmeasured preludes, represent a significant element in French keyboard music between Chambonnières and Couperin. His published music also includes fugues for organ.

Arensky, Anton Stepanovich

(1861 - 1906)

The Russian composer, conductor and pianist Arensky was a pupil of Rimsky-Korsakov at St. Petersburg Conservatory and later taught at the Moscow Conservatory, where his pupils included Rachmaninov and Scriabin. His compositions often reflect the influence of other composers, more particularly that of Tchaikovsky. He was musical director of the Imperial Chapel in St. Petersburg from 1895 until 1901 and thereafter continued his career as composer, pianist and conductor, travelling widely in the last two capacities. He died in 1906.

Orchestral Music

Arensky wrote two symphonies and a violin concerto, as well as a set of variations for strings on a theme by Tchaikovsky, a work originally for string quartet.

Chamber Music

The best known of Arensky's compositions is his Piano Trio in D minor, the first of two such works. This was written in 1894 and shows something of the influence of Mendelssohn.

☛ **Recommended Recordings**

Piano Suites Nos. 1-5
Marco Polo 8.223497

Piano Trio in D Minor
Naxos 8.550467

String Quartets, Opp. 11 and 35
Piano Quintet, Op. 51
Marco Polo 8.223811

Arne, Thomas (1710 - 1778)

One of the leading English composers of his time, and also a violinist, Arne wrote a great deal of theatre music, attempting to establish English opera, as well as composing instrumental and vocal music.

Vocal Music

Above all Arne is remembered popularly for his patriotic composition Rule, Britannia, written for the dramatic work Alfred of 1740 and for his settings of Shakespearean songs, including Where the bee sucks from The Tempest, When daisies pied from Love's Labour's Lost and Blow, blow, thou winter wind from As You Like It. The comic opera Thomas and Sally or The Sailor's Return followed a 1760 revival by Arne of Gay's enduringly popular The Beggar's Opera.

Arnold, Malcolm (1921 -)

The English composer Malcolm Arnold made his early career as a trumpet-player, principally with the London Philharmonic Orchestra. Since 1948 he has concentrated on his work as a composer, writing music that shows his thorough understanding of the orchestra and in a style that is tonal and often attractive to a wider audience than is usual in contemporary music. He has written a large number of film scores, including the music for The Bridge on the River Kwai and The Inn of the Sixth Happiness.

Orchestral Music

Malcolm Arnold's symphonies have not always received the attention that is their due. Frequently heard, however, are the comedy overture Beckus, the Dandipratt, and the overture Tam o'Shanter. He has written concertos for a variety of instruments, including two flute concertos, two clarinet concertos and a concerto for organ, two trumpets and strings.

☛ **Recommended Recordings**

Dances
(English Dances, Set 1, Op. 27 & Set 2, Op. 33
Four Scottish Dances, Op. 59
Four Cornish Dances, Op. 91
Four Irish Dances, Op. 126
Four Welsh Dances, Op. 138)
Naxos 8.553526

Chamber Music

Malcolm Arnold's chamber music provides interesting and attractive additions to wind repertoire in particular, among which the Three Shanties for wind quartet have found a popular place. A series of Fantasies for various solo wind instruments, for guitar and for harp demonstrate his technical command of instrumental resources.

Auber, Daniel-François-Esprit

(1782 - 1871)

Daniel-François-Esprit Auber was a leading composer of French opera from the 1820s onwards, collaborating from then for some thirty years with the librettist Augustin- Eugène Scribe. He is particularly known for his contributions to the genre of opéra- comique, although one of his most famous works is Masaniello or La muette de Portici (The Dumb Girl of Portici), of which the first title is preferred in English. This work, staged in Paris in 1828, began the era of French grand opera. Auber wrote a considerable quantity of music, vocal and instrumental, sacred and secular. He was respected by Rossini and Wagner, and much honoured by the state in his life-time.

Operas

Auber's most popular operas are Fra Diavolo, Le cheval de bronze (The Bronze Horse), Les diamants de la couronne (The Crown Diamonds), and the seminal grand opera Masaniello or La muette de Portici (The Dumb Girl of Portici).

- ☛ **Recommended Recording**
  Overtures: Masaniello / The Bronze Horse
  The Crown Diamonds
  Naxos 8.550473

Aubert, Louis (1877 - 1968)

Unduly neglected, Louis Aubert, a pupil of Gabriel Fauré, in the first performance of whose Requiem he took part as a boy, was a composer of considerable distinction, showing some affinity with both Debussy and Ravel.

Stage Works

Aubert's lyrical tale La forêt bleue brings to the stage the fairy world of children's stories. His Cinéma: Tableaux symphoniques, a ballet, shows episodes in the development of the cinema.

Orchestral Music

Dryade, Tableau symphonique, originally written in 1924 as a score for a film, is similar in its inspiration to Ravel's Daphnis et Chloé or the work of Debussy that has its source in pagan antiquity. Aubert's Tombeau de Chateaubriand pays tribute to his fellow-countryman, also a native of Saint-Malo. His moving Offrande of 1952 is dedicated to the memory of those who suffered in the war.

☞ **Recommended Recording**

"Cinéma", six tableaux symphoniques
"Dryade", tableau symphonique
"Feuille d'Images", cinq pièces enfantines
"Tombeau de Chateaubriand"
Marco Polo 8.223531

Bach, Carl Philipp Emanuel
(1714 - 1788)

The second son of the great Johann Sebastian Bach by his first wife, C.P.E. Bach was recognised as one of the greatest harpsichordists of his time. After study at university, a privilege denied his father, he became harpsichordist to the Crown Prince of Prussia, later Frederick the Great, and left his service in 1767, after the death of his godfather Telemann, whom he succeeded as director of music of the five city churches of Hamburg.

He was greatly respected both as a composer and as a friend of some of the most distinguished writers and thinkers of his time. In 1755 he published his influential Essay on the True Art of Playing Keyboard Instruments. From his very considerable output his sonatas for flute and harpsichord remain an attractive part of chamber music repertoire, with the symphonies written for Baron van Swieten, arbiter elegantium in Vienna, a man whose taste was generally trusted in artistic matters. Music by C.P.E. Bach is often listed with a reference number from the catalogue of his works by Wotquenne (Wq).

Orchestral Music

C.P.E. Bach wrote a set of six String Symphonies, Wq. 182, for Baron van Swieten, Court Librarian and associate of Haydn and Mozart. Four Flute Concertos, Wq. 166 - 169, are arranged from the composer's own harpsichord concertos, of which the set of six, listed as Wq. 43, are an excellent example.

☞ **Recommended Recordings**

Sinfonias Wq. Nos. 1-4
Naxos 8.553289

Oboe Concertos Wq. 164 & 165
Oboe Sonata Wq. 132
Naxos 8.550556

Chamber Music

The varied chamber music of C.P.E. Bach includes a set of Sonatas for flute & harpsichord, Wq. 83 - 87, five Trio Sonatas for flute, violin and basso continuo, Wq. 143 - 147, and an unusual Sonata for solo flute, Wq. 132.

☞ **Recommended Recording**

Sonatas for Flute & Harpsichord, Wq. 83-87
Naxos 8.550513

Keyboard Music

C.P.E. Bach wrote a great deal of music for the instruments on which he was acknowledged to be pre-eminent as a performer, the harpsichord and the gentler clavichord. These include Six Sonatas, Wq. 49, and 12 Variations on the best known of contemporary themes for variations, La Folia, Wq. 118/9.

Bach, Johann Christian

(1735 - 1782)

The youngest son of Johann Sebastian Bach by his second wife, Johann Christian Bach was born in Leipzig in 1735 and on the death of his father in 1750 moved to Berlin to live with his brother C.P.E. Bach. He later travelled to Italy, where he studied with the famous Padre Martini, became a Catholic and was employed for a short time as organist at Milan Cathedral. In 1762 he moved to London as a composer of Italian opera, like Handel fifty years before him, and enjoyed a considerable reputation there for a number of years, establishing a series of subscription concerts with his colleague Abel. His fame extended both to Mannheim and to Paris, but by the time of his death his popularity in London had waned. His influence on the young Mozart was considerable, and they met both in London and in Paris. He is sometimes known as "the London Bach".

Orchestral Music

Johann Christian Bach wrote a number of orchestral works, some for the concerts that he organised in the Hanover Street concert rooms in London. These compositions included Six Grand Overtures, Op. 18, and Six Harpsichord Concertos, Op. 7.

☞ **Recommended Recordings**

Sinfonias Op. 3, Nos. 1-6
Naxos 8.553083

Sinfonias Op. 6, Nos. 1-6
Naxos 8.553084

Sinfonias Op. 9, Nos. 1-3
Sinfonie concertanti
Naxos 8.553085

Sinfonias Op. 18, Nos. 1-6
Naxos 8.553367

Bach, Johann Sebastian

(1685 - 1750)

Johann Sebastian Bach belonged to a dynasty of musicians. In following inevitable family tradition, he excelled his forebears and contemporaries, although he did not always receive the respect he deserved in his own life-time. He spent his earlier career principally as an organist, latterly at the court of one of the two ruling Grand Dukes of Weimar. In 1717 he moved to Cöthen as Court Kapellmeister to the young Prince Leopold and in 1723 made his final move to Leipzig, where he was employed as Cantor at the Choir School of St. Thomas, with responsibility for music in the five principal city churches. In Leipzig he also eventually took charge of the University Collegium musicum and occupied himself with the collection and publication of many of his earlier compositions. Despite widespread neglect for almost a century after his death Bach is now regarded as one of the greatest of all composers.

Bach-Werke-Verzeichnis numbers, abbreviated to BWV, are generally accepted for convenience of reference.

Choral & Vocal Music

Bach wrote a very large amount of choral music, particularly in connection with his employment at Leipzig, where he prepared complete cycles of cantatas for use throughout the church year, in addition to the larger scale settings of the Latin Mass and the accounts of the Passion from the gospels of St. Matthew and of St. John. These works include the Mass in B minor, BWV 232, the St. Matthew Passion, BWV 244, the St. John Passion, BWV 245, the Christmas Oratorio, BWV 248, and the Easter Oratorio, BWV 249, with the revised setting of the Magnificat, BWV 243. Cantatas include, out of over 200 that survive, Herz und Mund und Tat und Leben, BWV 147 (from which the pianist Dame Myra Hess took her piano arrangement under the title Jesu, Joy of Man's Desiring, making this the most popular of all), Ein feste Burg ist unser Gott, BWV 80, Ich habe genug, BWV 82, Jesu, meine Freude, BWV 358, Mein Herze schwimmt im Blut, BWV 199, Wachet auf, BWV 140 and Jauchzet Gott in allen Landen, BWV 51, for soprano, trumpet, strings and basso continuo. The rather more formal half dozen or so Motets include a memorable version of Psalm CXVII, Lobet den Herrn, alle Heiden, BWV 230.

Secular Cantatas include the light-hearted Coffee Cantata, BWV 211, a father's attempt to stem his daughter's addiction to the fashionable drink, the Peasant Cantata, BWV 212, in honour of a newly appointed official, two Wedding Cantatas, Weichet nur, BWV 202, and O holder Tag, BWV 210. Was mir behagt, ist nur die muntre Jagd, BWV 208, was written in 1713 to celebrate the birthday of the hunting Duke Christian of

Saxe-Weissenfels and later reworked for the name-day of August III, King of Saxony, in the 1740s. The Italian Non sa che sia dolore, BWV 209, apparently marked the departure of a scholar or friend from Leipzig.

➤ Recommended Recordings

Mein Herze schwimmt im Blut, BWV 199
Weichet nur, betrübte Schatten BWV 202
Non sa che sia dolore BWV 209
Naxos 8.550431

Schweigt stille, plaudert nicht
(Coffee Cantata), BWV 211
Mer hahn en neue Oberkeet
(Peasant Cantata), BWV 212
Naxos 8.550641

Ein feste Burg ist unser Gott, BWV 80
Herz und Mund und Tat und Leben, BWV 147
Naxos 8.550642

Jauchzet Gott in allen Landen, BWV 51
Was mir behagt, ist nur die muntre Jagd,
BWV 208
Naxos 8.550643

Christmas Oratorio (3 CD's)
Naxos 8.550428-30

Magnificat / Cantata "Ich habe genug"
Naxos 8.550763

Mass in B Minor (2 CD's)
Naxos 8.550585-6

St. John Passion (2 CD's)
Naxos 8.550664-5
St. Matthew Passion (3 CD's)
Naxos 8.550832-4

Organ Music

Much of Bach's organ music was written during the earlier part of his career, culminating in the period he spent as court organist at Weimar. Among many well known compositions we may single out the Chromatic Fantasia & Fugue in D minor, BWV 903, the Dorian Toccata & Fugue in D minor, BWV 538, the Toccata, Adagio and Fugue, BWV 564, Fantasia & Fugue in G minor, BWV 542, Passacaglia & Fugue in C minor, BWV 582, Prelude & St. Anne Fugue, BWV 552, (in which the fugue theme resembles a well known English hymn), Toccata & Fugue in D minor, BWV 565, and the Toccata & Fugue in F, BWV 540.

The Chorale Prelude is a composition for organ that consists of short variations on simple hymn tunes for all seasons of the church year. Better known melodies used include the Christmas In dulci jubilo, BWV 508, Puer natus in Bethlehem, BWV 603, the Holy Week Christ lag in Todesbanden, BWV 625, and Easter Christ ist erstanden, BWV 627, with the moving Durch Adam's Fall ist ganz verderbt, BWV 637, and the familiar Wachet auf, ruft uns die Stimme, BWV 645, and Nun danket alle Gott, BWV 657.

☛ Recommended Recordings

Chorales BWV 651-658
Toccata, Adagio and Fugue BWV 564
Naxos 8.550901

Chorales BWV 659-668
Canonic Variations BWV 769
Naxos 8.550927

Clavierübung BWV 669-681
Prelude BWV 552
Naxos 8.550929

Clavierübung BWV 682-689, 802-805
Fugue BWV 552
Naxos 8.550930

Kirnberger Chorales BWV 690-701
Naxos 8.553134

Kirnberger Chorales BWV 702-713
Naxos 8.553135

The Little Organ Book Vol. 1
Naxos 8.553031

The Little Organ Book Vol. 2
Naxos 8.553032

Organ Chorales
from the Leipzig Manuscript Vol. 1
Naxos 8.550901

Organ Chorales
from the Leipzig Manuscript Vol. 2
Naxos 8.550927

Organ Recital (BWV 535, 550, 584,
588, 589, 736, 740 & 767)
Naxos 8.553033

Organ Transcriptions
BWV 585-587, 592-597
Naxos 8.550936

Organ Works
(Preludes & Fugues, Toccata, Pastorale etc.)
Naxos 8.550184

Preludes and Fugues BWV 536, 541, 542,
544 and 546
Naxos 8.550652

Schübler Chorales, BWV 645-650
Fantasia & Fugue, BWV 537
Toccata & Fugue, BWV 538
Prelude & Fugue, BWV 545
Pièce d'orgue, BWV 572
Naxos 8.553150

Trio Sonatas BWV 525-527
Naxos 8.550651

Trio Sonatas BWV 528-530
Naxos 8.550653

The Art of Fugue, Vol. 1
Naxos 8.550703

The Art of Fugue, Vol. 2
Naxos 8.550704

Other Keyboard Music

Important sets of pieces are the six English Suites, BWV 806 - 811; the six French Suites, BWV 812 - 817; the Goldberg Variations, BWV 988, written to soothe an insomniac patron; the Italian Concerto, BWV 971, the six Partitas, BWV 825 - 830, suites of dance movements, and the monumental two books of preludes and fugues in all keys, The Well-Tempered Clavier, BWV 846 - 893, the so-called '48'.

☞ **Recommended Recordings**

The Well-Tempered Clavier Book 2
Naxos 8.550970-1

Keyboard Favourites (Italian Concerto
Chromatic Fantasia & Fugue / Toccata
Fantasia / Capriccio / French Suite No. 6)
Naxos 8.550066

Goldberg Variations
Naxos 8.550078

Italian Concerto / Fantasia & Fugue
12 Little Preludes
Naxos 8.550571

Inventions and Sinfonias
Naxos 8.550960

Partitas Nos. 1 & 2, BWV 825-6
Naxos 8.550692

Partitas Nos. 3 & 4, BWV 827-8
Naxos 8.550693

Partitas Nos. 5 & 6, BWV 829-30
Naxos 8.550694

English Suites, BWV 806-808
Naxos 8.553012

English Suites, BWV 809-811
Naxos 8.553013

Toccatas
Naxos 8.550708

French Suites, BWV 812-813
Naxos 8.550709

French Suites, BWV 814-817
Naxos 8.550710

Chamber Music

During the period Bach spent at Cöthen he was able to devote his attention more particularly to instrumental composition for solo instruments, smaller groups or for the small court orchestra.

Particularly important are the three Sonatas and three Partitas for unaccompanied violin, BWV 1001 - 6, works that make great technical demands on a player, and the six Suites for unaccompanied cello, BWV 1007 - 1012. There are six Sonatas for violin and harpsichord, BWV 1014 - 1019, and an interesting group of three Sonatas for viola da gamba and harpsichord, sometimes appropriated today by viola-players and cellists, BWV 1027 - 1029.

- **Recommended Recordings**

  Violin Sonatas Nos. 1 & 2 / Partita No. 1
  Naxos 8.550569

  Violin Sonata No. 3 / Partitas Nos. 2 & 3
  Naxos 8.550570

  Cello Suites Nos. 1-3
  Naxos 8.550677

  Cello Suites Nos. 4-6
  Naxos 8.550678

Orchestral Music

The six Brandenburg Concertos, BWV 1046 - 1051, dedicated to the Margrave of Brandenburg in 1721, feature a variety of forms and groups of instruments, while the four Orchestral Suites or Overtures, BWV 1066 - 1069, include the famous Air on the G string, a late 19th century transcription of the Air from the Suite in D major, BWV 1068.

- **Recommended Recordings**

  Brandenburg Concertos (2 CD's)
  Naxos 8.550047-8

  Orchestral Suites (2 CD's)
  Naxos 8.550244-5

Concertos

Three of Bach's violin concertos, written at Cöthen between 1717 and 1723, survive in their original form, with others existing now only in later harpsichord transcriptions. The works in original form are the Concertos in A minor and in E major, BWV 1041 and 1042, and the Double Concerto in D minor, for two violins, BWV 1043.

Bach wrote or arranged his harpsichord concertos principally for the use of himself and his sons with the Leipzig University Collegium musicum between 1735 and 1740. These works include eight Concertos for a single solo harpsichord and strings, BWV 1052 - 1059, and others for two, three and four harpsichords and strings.

- **Recommended Recordings**

  Violin Concertos
  (A minor, E major & Double Concerto)
  Naxos 8.550194

  Piano Concertos BWV 1052-1054
  Naxos 8.550422

  Piano Concertos BWV 1055-1058
  Naxos 8.550423

  Concerto for Violin & Oboe, BWV 1060
  Naxos 8.553028

Bach, Wilhelm Friedemann

(1710 - 1784)

The eldest son of Johann Sebastian Bach, Wilhelm Friedemann was born in 1710 in Weimar and was taught by his father, after 1723, when the family moved to Leipzig, becoming a pupil at the Thomasschule. He spent four years at the University of Leipzig, before finding employment as organist at the Sophienkirche in Dresden and subsequently, with unhappy results, at the Liebfrauenkirche in Halle. From 1764 until his death twenty years later he held no official position, although he had been widely recognised as one of the most distinguished organists of his time and had mastered very thoroughly the lessons taught him by his father. His own tendency to the freedom of thought of the Enlightenment had not endeared him to his Pietist superiors in Halle and independence of character rendered him gradually less employable, within the restrictive circumstances of his time.

Keyboard Music

W.F.Bach wrote a number of harpsichord sonatas, fantasias and shorter dance pieces. His contrapuntal command was shown in a series of fugues that also reflect something of his known distinction in organ improvisation. His Concerto for two harpsichords combines the Baroque and the newly developing classical style of his time.

Orchestral Music

Bach left a number of harpsichord concertos and sinfonias.

Chamber Music

Chamber music by W.F.Bach includes a set of flute duets and trio sonatas.

Church Music

The exigencies of his employment led Bach to the composition of a number of church cantatas.

☞ **Recommended recording**
Sinfonia in F Major
Naxos 8.553289

Balakirev, Mily Alexeyevich

(1837 - 1910)

Balakirev was the self-appointed leader of the Five or Mighty Handful, a group of Russian Nationalist composers in the second half of the 19th century, including César Cui, Mussorgsky, Borodin and Rimsky-Korsakov. His own success as a composer was intermittent, largely owing to eccentricites of character and a tendency to make enemies through his own overwhelming enthusiasm and intolerance of other ideas. He was particularly opposed to the establishment of Conservatories of Music in Russia by the Rubinstein brothers and was accused in his turn of amateurism.

☛ Recommended Recordings

Symphony No. 1 / Islamey / Tamara
Naxos 8.550792

Symphony No. 2 / Russia
Naxos 8.550793

Chopin Suite / In Bohemia / King Lear Overture on a Spanish March Theme
Marco Polo 8.220324

Scherzi and Mazurkas (Complete)
Marco Polo 8.220447

Piano Music

Balakirev's best known work today is his oriental fantasy, Islamey.

☛ Recommended Recording

Islamey (1869 rev.1902)
Naxos 8.550044

Barber, Samuel (1910 - 1981)

Samuel Barber is widely known for his famous Adagio for Strings, the slow movement of a string quartet he wrote in 1936. Born in West Chester, Pennsylvania, in 1910, he was one of the first students at the Curtis Institute in Philadelphia, where he studied piano, conducting,

singing and composition. Awards allowed subsequent study in Rome. He taught briefly at the Curtis Institute, but soon withdrew, sharing a house with his former fellow student Menotti. His music remained neo-romantic in idiom, although not without contemporary influences.

Orchestral Music

The Adagio for Strings was arranged for string orchestra from the slow movement of Barber's string quartet of 1936 and played in this form by the NBC Symphony Orchestra under Toscanini in New York two years later, in a programme that included his first Essay. Other orchestral compositions include an overture, The School for Scandal, which had won him an award in 1933, concertos for violin, for cello and for piano, a Capricorn Concerto for solo wind instruments and two symphonies.

☛ Recommended Recording

Adagio for Strings
Naxos 8.551149

Stage Works

Barber wrote three operas, Vanessa, with a libretto by Menotti, A Hand of Bridge, for four singers and chamber orchestra, and Antony and Cleopatra, with a libretto by Zeffirelli. His two ballet scores are Medea and Souvenirs.

Vocal and Choral Music

Barber's songs include a setting of Matthew Arnold's Dover Beach, Knoxville: Summer of 1915 and Hermit Songs, settings of Irish texts from the 13th to 18th centuries. Choral works include an arrangement of the Adagio as an Agnus Dei, Prayers of Kierkegaard and the 1971 Neruda setting The Lovers, for baritone, chorus and orchestra.

Chamber Music

In addition to the String Quartet, Barber wrote sonatas for violin and for cello.

Piano Music

Barber's Piano Sonata touches in passing on twelve-note technique, although generally tonal in conception. Other compositions for piano are Excursions, four pieces, and Nocturne, a homage to the originator of the form, John Field.

Bartók, Béla (1881 - 1945)

Béla Bartók was one of the leading Hungarian and European composers of his time, proficient also as a pianist. He joined his friend Zoltán Kodály in the collection of folk-music in Hungary and neighbouring regions, including, in his case, Anatolia. His work in this field deeply influenced his own style of composition, which is, however, very much more astringent in its apparent mathematical organisation than much of what Kodály wrote. He was out of sympathy with the government that replaced the immediate post-1918 republic in Hungary, where he was held in less official esteem than abroad, and moved in 1940 to the United States, dying there in relatively straitened circumstances in 1945.

Orchestral Music

Probably the best loved of Bartók's orchestral compositions is the Concerto for Orchestra, commissioned by Koussevitzky for the Boston Symphony Orchestra. The two Violin Concertos are important additions to the solo violin repertoire, as is the Viola Concerto for players of that instrument. This last, with the Third Piano Concerto, were left in various stages of incompleteness when Bartók died. Both are moving works, while the earlier two Piano Concertos have much to offer. Other important orchestral works that form not infrequent parts of concert programmes are the Divertimento for strings and the challenging Music for Strings, Percussion and Celesta. The energetic Romanian Dances appear in various versions, including one for solo violin and string orchestra, arranged from an original piano composition.

Concerto for Orchestra
Music for Strings, Percussion & Celesta
Naxos 8.550261

Piano Concertos Nos. 1-3
Naxos 8.550771

Divertimento
Naxos 8.550979

Chamber Music

Bartók's six string quartets are a significant and important part of repertoire, extending the musical and technical range of the form. The 44 Duos for two violins are primarily educational compositions, but make attractive concert pieces in various groupings suggested by the composer.

A work of greater importance is the spectacular Sonata for two pianos and percussion, later rescored by the composer for two pianos and orchestra. The original version makes use of three kettle-drums, a xylophone, two side-drums, cymbals, suspended cymbal, bass drum, triangle and tam-tam, with the two pianos. It has an extended first movement, a night-music second and a tautly rhythmic third. Written in 1937, the sonata experiments fruitfully with the varied percussive sonorities of pianos and percussion instruments.

☛ **Recommended Recordings**

Rhapsodies Nos. 1 & 2
Andante / Piano Quintet
Naxos 8.550886

Sonata for Solo Violin
Duos for 2 Violins
Naxos 8.550868

Violin Sonatas Nos. 1 & 2 / Contrasts
Naxos 8.550749

Piano Music

Mikrokosmos consists of six books of pieces of progressive difficulty, intended to be used for teaching, with the last two volumes including more demanding pieces possible for concert use. Folk melodies form the basis of 85 Pieces for Children, while the Allegro barbaro shows the composer in a more aggressive mood.

☛ **Recommended Recordings**

Romanian Folk Dances
Naxos 8.550052

Mikrokosmos (Selection)
Romanian Folk Dances
Naxos 8.550451

Piano Transcriptions
Marco Polo 8.223663

Bax, Arnold (1883 - 1953)

Arnold Bax, English by birth, found, through reading the poet W.B.Yeats, a latent affinity with things Irish, with which he thereafter closely identified. The Celtic element, in consequence, plays a large part in his work and thought. He occupied an important place in English music in his own time and was knighted in 1937. At its best his music has a compelling charm and power.

Film Music

Bax wrote scores for the films Oliver Twist, the war-time Malta GC and Journey into History.

Orchestral Music

In addition to his seven symphonies Bax wrote a series of evocative tone poems of Celtic implication, including The Garden of Fand, November Woods and Tintagel. There are concertos for cello, for viola and for violin and Symphonic Variations for piano and orchestra in addition to a Concertante for piano left hand and orchestra, written for Harriet Cohen, with whom he had a long relationship.

Chamber Music

Bax wrote string quartets and quintets, an interesting Viola Sonata, three Violin Sonatas and works for larger instrumental groups, including a Nonet for wind and string instruments and an Octet for horn, piano and string sextet.

Vocal and Choral Music

Bax's choral works include settings of traditional carols, while his solo songs allow him to explore more Celtic ground in a variety of settings, ranging from A Celtic Song Cycle to settings of poems by James Joyce, J.M. Synge, and by the English writers A.E. Housman and his brother, the writer Clifford Bax.

Piano Music

Bax wrote seven piano sonatas, some unpublished, and a number of pieces for piano solo or duo, many with evocative titles.

☛ **Recommended Recording**
Sinfonietta / Overture, Elegy and Rondo
Marco Polo 8.223102

Beethoven, Ludwig van
(1770 - 1827)

Born in Bonn in 1770, the eldest son of a singer in the Kapelle of the Archbishop- Elector of Cologne and grandson of the Archbishop's Kapellmeister, Beethoven moved in 1792 to Vienna, where he had some lessons from Haydn and others, quickly establishing himself as a

remarkable keyboard-player and original composer. By 1815 increasing deafness made public performance impossible and accentuated existing eccentricities of character, patiently tolerated by a series of rich patrons and his royal pupil the Archduke Rudolph. Beethoven did much to enlarge the possibilities of music and widen the horizons of later generations of composers. To his contemporaries he was sometimes a controversial figure, making heavy demands on listeners both by the length and by the complexity of his writing, as he explored new fields of music.

Stage Works

Beethoven wrote only one opera, eventually called Fidelio after the name assumed by the heroine Leonora, who disguises herself as a boy and takes employment at the prison in which her husband has been unjustly incarcerated. This escape opera, for which there was precedent in contemporary France, ends with the defeat of the evil prison governor and the rescue of Florestan, testimony to the love and constancy of his wife Leonora.

Beethoven contemplated other operas, but eventually only wrote the one, first staged in 1805 and mounted again in a revised performance in 1814, under more favourable circumstances. The ballet The Creatures of Prometheus was staged in Vienna in 1801, and he wrote incidental music for various other dramatic productions, including Goethe's Egmont, von Kotzebue's curious The Ruins of Athens, and the same writer's King Stephen.

Choral and Vocal Music

Beethoven's most impressive choral work is the Missa Solennis, written for the enthronement of his pupil Archduke Rudolph as Archbishop of Olmutz, but finished too late for that occasion. An earlier work, the oratorio The Mount of Olives, is less well known. In common with other composers, he wrote a number of songs. Of these the best known are probably the settings of Goethe, which did little to impress the venerable poet and writer, who ignored their existence, and the cycle of six songs known as An die ferne Geliebte (To the Distant Beloved). The song Adelaide is challenging but not infrequently heard.

Orchestral Music

(a) Symphonies

Beethoven completed nine symphonies, works that influenced the whole future of music by the expansion of the traditional classical form. The best known are the Third, "Eroica", originally intended to celebrate the initially republican achievements of Napoleon, the Fifth, the Sixth, "Pastoral", and the Ninth, "Choral". The less satisfactory Battle Symphony celebrates the earlier military victories of the Duke of Wellington.

☛ Recommended Recordings

Symphonies Nos. 1 & 6 "Pastoral"
Naxos 8.553474

Symphonies Nos. 2 & 5
Naxos 8.550177

Symphonies Nos. 3 "Eroica" & 8
Naxos 8.553475

Symphonies Nos. 4 & 7
Naxos 8.550180

Symphony No. 9 "Choral"
Naxos 8.550181

Battle Symphony
Naxos 8.550230

(b) Overtures

For the theatre and various other occasions Beethoven wrote a number of Overtures, including four for his only opera, Fidelio, one under that name and the others under the name of the heroine, Leonora. Other Overtures include Egmont, Coriolan, Prometheus, The Consecration of the House and The Ruins of Athens.

☛ Recommended Recordings

Overtures Vol. 1 (Egmont / Coriolanus
Leonora No. 3 / Fidelio / Prometheus
Ruins of Athens / Consecration of the House)
Naxos 8.550072

Overtures Vol. 2 (Consecration of the House
Namensfeier / Leonora Nos. 1 and 2
King Stefan / Music from a Ritterballett
Marches from Tarpeja)
Naxos 8.553431

(c) Concertos

Beethoven completed one violin concerto and five piano concertos, as well as a triple concerto for violin, cello and piano, and a curious Choral Fantasia,for solo piano, chorus and orchestra. The piano concertos were for the composer's own use in concert performance. The Fifth, the so-called "Emperor" Concerto, is possibly the most impressive. The single Violin Concerto is part of the standard repertoire, with two Romances, possible slow movements for an unwritten violin concerto.

☛ Recommended Recordings

Violin Concerto / Romances Nos. 1 & 2
Naxos 8.550149

Piano Concerto No. 1 / Rondo
Naxos 8.550190

Piano Concertos Nos. 2 & 5 "Emperor"
Naxos 8.550121

Piano Concertos 3 & 4
Naxos 8.550122

Chamber Music

Beethoven wrote ten sonatas for violin and piano, of which the "Spring" and the "Kreutzer" are particular favourites with audiences. He extended very considerably the possibilities of the string quartet, even with his first, Opus 18 set of quartets, but it is possibly the named quartets, the group of three dedicated to Prince Razumovsky and known, therefore, as the Razumovsky Quartets, Opus 59, that are best known. The later string quartets offer great challenges to both players and audience, and include the remarkable Grosse Fuge (Great Fugue) a gigantic work, discarded as the final movement of the String Quartet, Opus 130, and published separately. Other chamber music includes a number of Trios for violin, cello and piano, with the "Archduke" Trio pre-eminent and the "Ghost" Trio a close runner-up, for very different reasons. The Cello Sonatas and sets of Variations for cello and piano, including one set based on Handel's See here the conqu'ring hero comes and others on operatic themes from Mozart, are a valuable part of any cellist's repertoire. Chamber music with wind instruments and piano include a Quintet, Op. 16, for piano, oboe, clarinet, horn and bassoon.

☛ **Recommended Recordings**

Violin Sonatas Op. 12 Nos. 1-3
Naxos 8.550284

Violin Sonatas Op. 30 Nos. 1-3
Naxos 8.550286

Violin Sonatas Nos. 5 "Spring" & 9 "Kreutzer"
Naxos 8.550283

Violin Sonatas Opp. 23 & 96
Mozart Variations
Naxos 8.550285

Cello Sonatas Op. 69 & Op. 102 Nos. 1 & 2
Naxos 8.550478

Cello Sonatas Op. 5 Nos. 1 & 2
Mozart and Handel Variations
Naxos 8.550479

Piano Trios Op. 1, Nos. 1-2
Naxos 8.550946

Piano Trios Op. 1, No. 3, Op. 44,
WoO 38, Hess 48
Naxos 8.550947

Piano Trios Op. 70, No. 1 "Ghost" & No. 2
Naxos 8.550948

Piano Trio Op. 97 "Archduke"
Kakadu Variations, Op. 121a
Allegretto, WoO 39
Naxos 8.550949

"Archduke" Trio & "Ghost" Trio
Naxos 8.550442

String Quartets, Op. 18, Nos. 1 & 2
Naxos 8.550558

String Quartets Op. 18, Nos. 3 and 4
Naxos 8.550559

String Quartets Op. 18, Nos. 5 and 6
Naxos 8.550560

Quintet for Piano & Wind, Op. 16
Naxos 8.550511

Piano Music

Beethoven's 32 numbered piano sonatas make full use of the developing form of piano, with its wider range and possibilities of dynamic contrast. There are also interesting sets of variations, including a set based on God save the King and another on Rule, Britannia, variations on a theme from the Eroica Symphony and a major work based on a theme by the publisher Diabelli. The best known of the sonatas are those that have earned themselves affectionate nicknames, the Pathétique, Op. 13, Moonlight, Op. 27/2, Waldstein, Op. 53, Appassionata, Op. 57, Les Adieux, Op. 81a, and the Hammerklavier, Op. 106. Less substantial piano pieces include three sets of Bagatelles, and the all too well known Für Elise, with the Rondo a capriccio, known in English as Rage over a Lost Penny.

☛ **Recommended Recordings**

Piano Sonatas (Complete) Vol. 1 (5 CD's)
Naxos 8.505002

Piano Sonatas (Complete) Vol. 2 (5 CD's)
Naxos 8.505003

Piano Sonatas Nos. 14 ("Moonlight"),
21 ("Waldstein") & 23 ("Appassionata")
Naxos 8.550294

Piano Sonatas Nos. 8 ("Pathétique"),
14 ("Moonlight") & 23 ("Appassionata")
Naxos 8.550045

Bagatelles, Opp. 33, 119, 126
Naxos 8.550474

Für Elise
Naxos 8.550168

Piano Variations Opp. 34 & 35 "Eroica"/
Paisiello Variations WoO 70
32 Variations WoO 80
Naxos 8.550676

Dance Music

Famous composers like Haydn and Mozart were also employed in the practical business of providing dance music for court and social occasions. Beethoven wrote a number of sets of Minuets, German Dances and Contredanses, ending with the so-called Mödlinger Dances, written for performers at a neighbouring inn during a summer holiday outside Vienna.

☛ **Recommended Recording**

Mödlinger Dances / Contredanses
German Dances / Minuets
Naxos 8.550433

Bellini, Vincenzo (1801 - 1835)

Vincenzo Bellini was one of the most important composers of Italian opera in the earlier years of the 19th century. He died in Paris in 1835 at the height of his success. Bellini's influence was not confined to opera and Chopin owes much to him, particularly in his handling of melody. Although Bellini is known primarily as a composer of opera, his Oboe Concerto enjoys some popularity.

Operas

Bellini's first great success was in 1827 when Il Pirata was staged at La Scala, Milan. The six further operas that he wrote include a version of Shakespeare's Romeo and Juliet, I Capuletti i Montecchi, the famous and complicated La Sonnambula produced in Milan in 1831, the demanding opera set in Roman Gaul, Norma, staged at La Scala at the end of the same year, and the final work, I Puritani, mounted in Paris in 1835.

☛ **Recommended Recording**

Soprano Opera Arias from I Puritani
Capuletti e Montecchi / La Sonnambula
Naxos 8.550605

La Sonnambula (2 CD's)
Naxos 8.660042-3

Benjamin, Arthur (1893 - 1960)

The Australian composer Arthur Benjamin eventually established himself in London, where he made his career as a teacher, composer and pianist. His piano pupils at the Royal College of Music included Benjamin Britten.

Orchestral Music

Among a number of attractive compositions, Arthur Benjamin's Jamaican Rumba remains the most popular, with his charming oboe concerto, based on the work of the Italian 18th century composer Cimarosa.

☛ **Recommended Recording**

Symphony No. 1 / Ballade
Marco Polo 8.223764

Bennet, John (?1575 - 1614?)

The exact dates of the birth and death of the English madrigal composer John Bennet are unknown, although his first collection of madrigals was published in 1599. The English madrigal, derived from earlier Italian models, is a significant element in the vocal music of the later 16th century, the age of Queen Elizabeth I.

Vocal Music

Bennet's most popular madrigals are Weep, o mine eyes, apparently based on John Dowland's famous Flow, my teares, one of the most internationally famous of all songs of the period, and All creatures now, part of the collection of madrigals by a number of composers in praise of Queen Elizabeth I, under the guise of Oriana, Queen of the Shepherds.

Bennett, William Sterndale

(1816 - 1875)

With musical gifts much admired by his friend Robert Schumann, Bennett (who never used the name Sterndale) briefly enjoyed popularity as a composer, although his obvious abilities were later submerged in the demands of public life, as Professor of Music at the University of Cambridge and later as Principal of the Royal Academy of Music. Interest in his music is now growing, with the occasional revival in particular of his piano music and five Piano Concertos. His songs remain an important example of the genre in mid-19th century England.

Orchestral Music

The third and fourth piano concertos are a good introduction to Sterndale Bennett's music, the first with a romantic slow movement and the latter with a Barcarole (Gondolier's Song) slow movement, inserted at the suggestion of Mendelssohn.

☛ Recommended Recordings

Piano Works Vol. 1
4 Pieces / Allegro grazioso / Geneviève
Rondo piacevole / Scherzo
3 Musical Sketches / The Maid of Orleans
Marco Polo 8.223512

Piano Works Vol. 2
Suite de pièces Op. 24
Piano Sonata No. 1, Op. 13
Marco Polo 8.223526

Piano Works Vol. 3
Capriccio / 3 Romances / 3 Impromptus
30 Preludes and Lessons
Marco Polo 8.223578

Sextet, Op. 8 / Duo Sonata, Op. 32
Marco Polo 8.223304

Berg, Alban (1885 - 1935)

The so-called Second Viennese School of Arnold Schoenberg has exercised a strong influence over the course of music in the 20th century. Schoenberg's pupils Alban Berg and Anton Webern, each with an individual musical language, put into practice the general principles of atonality, music without tonality or key-centre, and twelve-note music or serialism, music based on a series of the twelve semitones or half-steps of the modern scale.

Opera

Berg wrote two important operas, Wozzeck, a study of insanity, based on the play by Büchner, and the unfinished Lulu, based on Wedekind.

Orchestral Music

Berg's Violin Concerto and Chamber Concerto are an important part of 20th century repertoire. His Lyric Suite, for string quartet, was later orchestrated in part, while the delicately orchestrated Three Pieces of 1914-1915 form an occasional part of modern concert repertoire.

Berio, Luciano (1925 -)

Luciano Berio occupies a leading position in 20th century music, a pioneer in the use of electronic and avant-garde techniques of composition. He was married for some years to Cathy Berberian, a singer well known for her performances of contemporary music.

Instrumental Music

Berio's works include a series of nine compositions under the title Sequenza for a series of solo instruments, some of them the basis of later elaboration.

Vocal Music

A number of vocal works were written for Berio's wife, Cathy Berberian. These include Circles, a setting of poems by E.E. Cummings and Sequenza III.

Bériot, Charles-Auguste de
(1802 - 1870)

A pupil of the Italian violinist Viotti, Bériot became one of the most distinguished players of his time, the creator of the Franco-Belgian school of violin-playing that was so important in the 19th century. He spent much of his teaching career in Brussels, where he died in 1870.

Concertos

Beriot's ten Violin Concertos are known to most players, in the practice studio if not in the concert hall. The so-called Military Concerto, No. 1 in D major, is of particular interest, with his popular Spanische Weisen for violin duet.

☞ **Recommended Recording**
Violin Concertos Nos. 1, 8 and 9
Marco Polo 8.220440

Berlíoz, Hector (1803 - 1869)

In his own time Hector Berlioz was something of an outsider, as far as the French musical establishment was concerned. Nevertheless he remains the outstanding figure in French romantic music, typical of the period particularly in his literary interests. At first a medical student, he eventually entered the Paris Conservatoire, but encountered some difficulty in his subsequent career, as he strove for a hearing of his music. He earned his living in part as a critic and writer, and his Mémoires remain a fascinating if prejudiced account of musical life in Paris in his time.

Orchestral Music

The Symphonie fantastique of 1830, an orchestral work that contains autobiographical elements, suggested new paths in composition. This was followed four years later by Harold in Italy, for viola and orchestra, with a narrative programme of literary origin, written for but never performed by the great violinist Paganini. Concert overtures include a Shakespearean King Lear and two overtures based on the work of Sir Walter Scott, Waverley and Rob Roy. The overture Le carnaval romain (Roman Carnival) was derived from his opera Benvenuto Cellini, while Le corsaire has at least Byronic overtones. His interest in Shakespeare, increased by his love affair and later unsuccessful marriage with the Shakespearian actress Harriet Smithson, had a further result in the dramatic symphony Romeo and Juliet.

☛ **Recommended Recordings**

> *Symphonie fantastique*
> *Naxos 8.550093*

> *Harold in Italy / Franc-Juges Overture*
> *Rêverie et Caprice*
> *Naxos 8.553034*

> *Overtures*
> *(Benvenuto Cellini / Waverley*
> *Beatrice and Benedict / King Lear*
> *Roman Carnival / Rob Roy / Le Corsaire)*
> *Naxos 8.550999*

> *Roméo et Juliette (excerpts)*
> *Les Troyens à Carthage (excerpts)*
> *Naxos 8.553195*

Choral Works

Other important works by Berlioz include the Eight Scenes from Faust, later revised as The Damnation of Faust, one of the most original of a number compositions based on Goethe's drama. The Christmas oratorio L'enfance du Christ (The Childhood of Christ) is a significant and characteristic work, with the remarkable and extravagantly orchestrated Grande Messe des morts (Requiem) with its brass bands and massed choirs.

Operas

Equally extravagant is the opera Les Troyens (The Trojans), later divided into two parts, The Capture of Troy and The Trojans. Excerpts from the opera, the music for the Royal Hunt and Storm, in which the Carthaginian Queen Dido and her Trojan lover Aeneas realise their love for each other, can be heard in concert programmes.

Bernstein, Leonard (1918 - 1990)

The American conductor and composer Leonard Bernstein had a strong influence on American musical taste, particularly in his championing of Mahler. In some works, notably in West Side Story, a modern American version of Romeo and Juliet, he attempted a synthesis of American musical styles.

Stage Works

Popular compositions of Bernstein include the ballet-score Fancy Free and the overture to his comic opera Candide, in addition to West Side Story.

Orchestral Works

Bernstein wrote three symphonies, his second symphony, The Age of Anxiety, based on the work of the English poet W.H. Auden. The Jeremiah Symphony of 1943, with its mezzo-soprano solo, represents a religious vein in Bernstein's music.

Choral Works

The Jeremiah Symphony was followed twenty years later by another overtly Jewish work, the so-called Kaddish Symphony. The Chichester Psalms were commissioned for Chichester Cathedral in the South of England. His theatrical setting of the Roman Mass may be mentioned by the side of his later Missa brevis, based on his own incidental music for a play by Jean Anouilh.

Berwald, Franz (1796- 1868)

Franz Berwald, descended from a family of Swedish musicians of remoter German origin, was the most important figure in Swedish music of the 19th century.

Orchestral Works

Of Berwald's four surviving symphonies the third, the Sinfonie singulière, remains the most popular. Like the symphonies of his Danish contemporary Carl Nielsen, Berwald's symphonies have idiosyncratic titles, the first known as Sinfonie sérieuse, the second Sinfonie capricieuse and the fourth originally as Sinfonie naïve.

Symphonies No. 1 "Sinfonie sérieuse"
and No. 2 "Sinfonie capricieuse"
Overture to Estrella de Soria
Naxos 8.553051

Symphonies No. 3 "Sinfonie singulière"
and No. 4
Piano Concerto
Naxos 8553052

Piano Trios Vol. 1
(Nos. 1-3)
Marco Polo 8.223170

Piano Trios Vol. 2
C Major / E Flat Major (Fragment)
C Major (Fragment) / C Major
Marco Polo 8.223430

Biber, Heinrich (1644 - 1704)

The Bohemian virtuoso violinist and composer Heinrich Biber spent the last 24 years of his life at the court of the Archbishop of Salzburg, after earlier service with the Prince-Bishop of Olmutz.

Instrumental Music

Among a number of interesting compositions are Biber's fifteen Rosary Sonatas, for violin and basso continuo, with its unaccompanied violin Passacaglia, and the curious string orchestra Battalia (Battle), with its imitation gunfire and drunken soldiers. In the first he makes considerable use of scordatura, with the violin retuned to provide different sonorities and unusual chordal effects.

Binchois, Gilles de Bins
(c. 1400 - 1460)

In a period when Franco-Flemish composers were of the greatest importance, Binchois was one of the three most influential, with Dufay and the English Dunstable, associated with the court of the Duke of Burgundy, with its widespread dynastic connections throughout Europe. His setting of the Te Deum, the earliest polyphonic setting to survive, was particularly well known, with a series of vocal compositions both sacred and secular.

Bishop, Henry (1786 - 1855)

The reputation of Sir Henry Bishop has diminished with time, although in his own lifetime he occupied a commanding position in England as a conductor and composer of opera.

Vocal Music

Bishop's song Home, Sweet Home remains generally known, even if its composer's name may occasionally be forgotten, with the song Lo, Hear the Gentle Lark, for coloratura soprano and flute accompaniment, the latter written for Shakespeare's Comedy of Errors.

Bizet, Georges (1838 - 1875)

Bizet won early success as a composer and initially as a pianist. His later career in Paris was more variable, and a number of stage works remained unfinished at the time of his early death, which took place as his most famous opera, Carmen, was enjoying increasing favour.

Operas and Stage Works

Bizet's last opera, Carmen, is among the most famous of all operas, with its realistic Spanish setting and strongly dramatic story. Concert audiences are familiar with two concert suites drawn from the opera. His melodrama L'Arlésienne, a collaboration with the writer Alphonse Daudet, was coolly received in the theatre. The two suites from the work are well known, the second arranged by Bizet's friend Ernest Guiraud.

☛ Recommended Recordings

Carmen (3 CD's)
Naxos 8.660005-7

L'Arlésienne Suites Nos. 1 & 2,
Carmen Suites Nos. 1 & 2
Naxos 8.550061

Symphony in C / Jeux d'enfants
Scenes Bohémiennes
Naxos 8.553027

Orchestral Music

Bizet's only surviving symphony, written in 1855, was rediscovered and first performed in 1935.

Piano Music

Popular piano works include the two-piano Jeux d'enfants, Children's Games.

Blacher, Boris (1903 - 1975)

Boris Blacher was born in China but returned to Germany, working as a composer and teacher in Berlin and later in Dresden, a career interrupted by the intervention of National Socialism, but resumed in 1945.

Orchestral Music

Among 20th century compositions, the works of Boris Blacher remain approachable, in particular his Variations on a Theme of Paganini, an orchestral work based on the theme from the 24th Caprice of the great virtuoso violinist Paganini, a melody used by Brahms, Rachmaninov and others for a similar purpose.

Bliss, Arthur (1891 - 1975)

Sir Arthur Bliss, Master of the Queen's Music in Great Britain from 1953 until his death, eventually followed the late romantic tradition of Elgar in English music, after a more controversial period of composition in youth. In accordance with the perceived duties of his official position, he wrote various ceremonial pieces, in addition to music for the concert-hall, theatre and cinema.

Film Music

Familiar music by Bliss includes excerpts from his film-score for H.G. Wells's Things to Come, and the patriotic march Welcome the Queen, also written for a film.

☛ **Recommended Recordings**
Christopher Columbus / Seven Waves Away Baraza / Men of Two Worlds
Marco Polo 8.223315

Colour Symphony
Naxos 8.553460

Concerto for Cello and Orchestra Music for Strings / Two Studies Nos. 2 & 3
Naxos 8.553383

Ballets

The ballets Checkmate, an allegorical game of chess, with choreography by Ninette de Valois and Miracle in the Gorbals, a morality play set in the slums of Glasgow with choreography by Robert Helpman, made a strong impression on ballet audiences.

☛ **Recommended Recording**
Adam Zero
Naxos 8.553460

Bloch, Ernest (1880 - 1959)

Essentially a Jewish composer, Ernest Bloch was born in Switzerland and later took out American citizenship, serving as director of the Cleveland Institute from 1920 to 1925 and later of the San Francisco Conservatory.

Orchestral Music

Bloch's most characteristic compositions are of Jewish inspiration, in particular his Suite hébraïque (Hebrew Suite) for viola or violin and orchestra, Baal Shem for violin and piano, later orchestrated, and Schelomo for cello and orchestra. His Concerto Grosso No. 1 and Concerto Grosso No. 2 represent another, neo-classical aspect of Bloch's music.

☛ **Recommended Recordings**
Schelomo
Naxos 8.550519

Piano Works (Complete) Vol. 1
Poems of the Sea / Nirvana / In the Night /
Five Sketches in Sepia / Enfantines
Four Circus Pieces
Marco Polo 8.223288

Piano Works (Complete) Vol. 2
Ex-voto / Sonata / Danse sacrée
Visions and Prophecies
Marco Polo 8.223289

Symphony in C Sharp Minor
Marco Polo 8.223103

Blow, John (1649 - 1708)

John Blow was the most significant English composer in the generation before Henry Purcell, ten years his junior, whom he outlived by thirteen years. Born in 1649, the year of the execution of King Charles I, he was young enough to benefit from the restoration of the monarchy in 1660, with the revival of church music.

Dramatic Works

Blow's masque Venus and Adonis, a charming masque designed for the king's entertainment, influenced Purcell's better known short opera Dido and Aeneas, by the side of which it deserves a place.

Sacred and Secular Vocal Music

Like Purcell Blow wrote music mourning the death of Queen Mary, a monarch for whom he had six years earlier written coronation music, when, with her Dutch husband William of Orange, she had succeeded her Catholic father, King James II. His works include a quantity of vocal music, sacred and secular, the former including a well known setting of the Lord is my shepherd. Anthems include the distinguished I beheld, and lo! a great multitude, a verse anthem, with the customary instrumental accompaniment. For the coronation of King James II in 1685 he wrote the anthem God spake sometime in visions.

Boccherini, Luigi (1743 - 1805)

The reputation of Boccherini rivalled that of Haydn, if the nick-name "the wife of Haydn" may be accepted as evidence of contemporary fame. He was a virtuoso cellist and worked first in his native Lucca and then in Vienna, before moving to Paris and thence to Spain, where he seems to have remained from 1768 until his death. There he was in the service of the Infante Don Luis and various other patrons, and was appointed court composer to King Friedrich Wilhelm II of Prussia, himself a cellist, although there is no evidence of his actual presence at Potsdam. He died in apparent poverty in 1805.

Chamber Music

Boccherini is popularly known as the composer of the famous Minuet, taken from one of his quintets, written for a string quartet with an additional cello. The set of Quintets for string quartet and guitar includes a thoroughly Spanish Fandango.

☞ **Recommended Recordings**

Flute Quintets, Op. 17
Naxos 8.553739

Guitar Quintets Vol. 1
Naxos 8.550551

Guitar Quintets Vol. 2
Naxos 8.550552

Guitar Quintets Vol. 3 / String Quintet
Naxos 8.550731

Cello Concertos

Of Boccherini's eleven surviving cello concertos the Concerto No. 7 in G major is probably the best known, closely rivalled by a B flat Cello Concerto arranged by the 19th century cellist Grützmacher.

☞ **Recommended Recording**

Cello Concerto in B flat major
Naxos 8.550059

Boëllmann, Léon (1862 - 1897)

The name of Léon Boëllmann is known to all organists above all because of his brilliant Toccata for the instrument, the final movement of a Suite gothique. Born in Alsace in 1862, he served as organist at the church of St. Vincent-de-Paul in Paris from 1881 until his early death in 1897.

Organ Music

In addition to the Toccata from the Suite gothique, Op. 25, the Douze Pièces (Twelve Pieces), Op. 16, and Heures mystiques, Opp. 29 & 30, are well enough known.

☞ **Recommended Recordings**

Suite Gothique
Naxos 8.550581

Piano Quartet, Op. 10 / Piano Trio, Op. 19
Marco Polo 8.223524

Boïeldieu, François-Adrien
(1775 - 1834)

The principal composer of French opera in the first quarter of the 19th century, Boïeldieu was born in Rouen in 1775 and had his first theatrical success in 1793. Success in Paris was followed by failure in marriage and a period as director of French opera at the Russian court in St. Petersburg, whence he returned to Paris in 1811, after some eight years of absence. By the time of his death in 1834 he had gone some way towards upholding French comic opera traditions against the inroads of the more popular Italian comedy of Rossini.

Operas

The overture to the opera Le calife de Bagdad (The Calif of Baghdad) remains a popular concert item, with La dame blanche (The White Lady), based on Sir Walter Scott.

Boíto, Arrígo (1842 - 1918)

Arrigo Boito is probably better known as a librettist than as a composer, especially for his texts for Verdi's Simon Boccanegra, and the Shakespearian Otello and Falstaff, as well as the libretto of Ponchielli's La Gioconda.

Opera

Boito's only completed opera, for which he wrote both words and music, was Mefistofele, based on Goethe's Faust, a work to which he made considerable alterations. The Prologue, Ave, Signor, for Mephistopheles and the prison scene for the soprano Margaretta (Gretchen) remain familiar recital items.

Borodín, Alexander Porfir'yevích (1833 - 1887)

The Five, the Mighty Handful, so named by the Russian critic and librarian Vladimir Stasov, were the principal nationalist composers in later 19th century Russia, following the example of Glinka, their forerunner. Borodin, like some of his musical colleagues, followed another profession than music, winning distinction as a professor of chemistry. His output was limited by the amount of attention he was able to give to composition and at his death he left a number of works unfinished, to be completed by his friend Rimsky-Korsakov and others.

Operas

Borodin's most famous opera, Prince Igor, was completed by Rimsky-Korsakov and Glazunov. It includes the famous choral dances, the Polovtsian Dances, with which the captive Prince is entertained by Khan Konchak.

☞ **Recommended Recordings:**

Polovtsian Dances
Naxos 8.550051

Prince Igor Overture
Naxos 8.550085

Orchestral Music

The best known example of Borodin's orchestral music is the musical picture In the Steppes of Central Asia, a vivid evocation of an exotic region. The second of his three symphonies, the last unfinished, occupied him intermittently for seven years, and is an attractive and very Russian work, the three forming an important addition to nationalist symphonic repertoire.

☛ **Recommended Recordings**

In the Steppes of Central Asia
Naxos 8.550051

Symphonies Nos. 1-3
Naxos 8.550238

Piano Quintet / String Quintet / Cello Sonata
Marco Polo 8.223172

String Quartets Nos. 1 & 2
Naxos 8.550850

Bottesini, Giovanni (1821 - 1889)

Giovanni Bottesini was not only among the most famous double bass players of his time, but was also a conductor of some distinction and a composer. He conducted the first performance of Verdi's opera Aida in Cairo in 1871 and won success with some, at least, of his own ten operas. Known to some as the Paganini of the double bass, he significantly extended the technical possibilities of the instrument.

Double Bass Music

Bottesini's compositions include a number of double bass concertos, some for double bass and piano, as well as works for solo violin and double bass and for two double basses. His Metodo completo per contrabasso is an important addition to the pedagogical literature of the instrument.

Chamber Music

In 1849 Bottesini played the cello part in London in a quintet by George Onslow. His own chamber music includes a Gran Quintetto for two violins, viola, cello and double bass. He wrote eleven string quartets and arranged his Second Double Bass Concerto for solo instrument and string quartet.

Boulanger, Lili (1893 - 1918)

Encouraged by her elder sister Nadia, the French composer Lili Boulanger was the first woman to win the Prix de Rome and was prolific, during her short life, writing music very much in the prevailing style of the period.

Orchestral Music

Lili Boulanger's compositons for orchestra include Pièce, Sicilienne and Marche gaie for small orchestra and a fuller Poème symphonique.

Chamber Music

In addition to pieces for piano and for organ, Lili Boulanger wrote a violin sonata and pieces for cello, for oboe and for flute and piano.

Choral and Vocal Music

Choral and vocal music by Lili Boulanger includes a group of psalm settings, with the moving Du fond de l'abîme, and the Vieille prière bouddhique of 1917. Other vocal settings include a Pie Jesu for mezzo-soprano, string quartet, harp and organ and settings of poems by Jammes and by Maeterlinck, whose La princesse Maleine had been intended as the subject of an opera, left unfinished at the composer's death in 1918.

Boulanger, Nadia (1887 - 1979)

Nadia Boulanger is better known as a teacher and conductor than as a composer. In the first capacity she was responsible for the musical training of a generation of distinguished composers from Europe and America. Her work as an interpreter influenced many, not least by the part she played in the revival of interest in Monteverdi.

Vocal Music

Nadia Boulanger's few compositions include Les heures claires, settings of poems by Verhaeren completed in 1912, after which she wrote little, although in 1908 she had won the second Prix de Rome.

> ☛ **Recommended Recording**
> *Lux aeterna / Pieces for Cello and Piano*
> *Marco Polo 8.223636*

Boulez, Pierre (1925 -)

Pierre Boulez is among the most influential contemporary musicians, both as a composer and as a conductor. He is known principally for his extension of the techiques of serialism beyond the limits of the Second Viennese School of Schoenberg, under the strong influence of his teacher Messiaen, into a logical style that brings with it a paradoxical freedom. His career as a conductor has brought him engagements with the most famous orchestras in a relatively wide repertoire, from Rameau to Wagner and to the contemporary.

Piano Music

The music Boulez has written for piano includes three sonatas, the last involving an element of chance in the possible choices of order offered to performers. The first part of Structures I, for two pianos, was first performed by Messiaen with the composer in 1952 and Structures II by Yvonne Loriod and Boulez at Donaueschingen in 1961.

☛ **Recommended Recording**

Piano Sonatas Nos. 1-3
Naxos 8.553353

Instrumental Music

The compositions of Boulez include works for various groups of instruments. Le marteau sans maître is scored for flute, guitar, vibraphone, xylorimba, percussion and viola, and Improvisation sur Mallarmé I for soprano, harp, tubular bells, vibraphone, four percussion, while Improvisations II adds celesta and piano. Improvisation sur Mallarmé III is for soprano and orchestra. The choice of instruments here, as in Eclats and other works is seemingly eclectic, certainly unusual, but logical in its relation to the music, much of which remains open to further development.

Boyce, William (1711 - 1779)

William Boyce is among the most important English composers of the late Baroque period, 25 years younger than Handel, whom he outlived by twenty years. He was a rival of Arne and in 1757 became Master of the King's Music. His works include a variety of music for both church and theatre.

Instrumental Music

Boyce's instrumental music includes a set of Eight Symphonies in eight parts, published in 1760, compositions that reflect the changing tastes of the time. His set of Twelve Trio Sonatas followed a fashion that had started with Corelli in the previous century and was now coming to an end.

Vocal and Choral Music

One of Boyce's best known songs is the patriotic Heart of Oak. His church music still retains a place in Anglican cathedral repertoire, strengthened by the appearance of his collected Cathedral Music.

Brahms, Johannes (1833 - 1897)

Born in Hamburg, the son of a double-bass player and his older seamstress wife, Brahms attracted the attention of Schumann, to whom he was introduced by the violinist

Joachim, and after Schumann's death he maintained a long friendship with his widow, the pianist Clara Schumann, whose advice he always valued. Brahms eventually settled in Vienna, where to some he seemed the awaited successor to Beethoven. His blend of classicism in form with a romantic harmonic idiom made him the champion of those opposed to the musical innovations of Wagner and Liszt. In Vienna he came to occupy a position similar to that once held by Beethoven, his gruff idiosyncrasies tolerated by those who valued his genius.

Orchestral Music

Brahms wrote four symphonies, massive in structure, and all the result of long periods of work and revision. The two early Serenades have their own particular charm, while the Variations on a Theme by Haydn, in fact the St. Anthony Chorale, used by that composer, enjoy enormous popularity, examples of a form of which Brahms had complete mastery. A pair of Overtures, the Academic Festival Overture and the Tragic Overture, with arrangements of his Hungarian Dances, completed the body of orchestral music without a solo instrument. His concertos consist of two magnificent and demanding Piano Concertos, a Violin Concerto and a splendid Double Concerto for violin and cello.

☞ Recommended Recordings

Symphony No. 1 / Haydn Variations
Naxos 8.550278

Symphony No. 2 / Serenade No. 2
Naxos 8.550279

Symphony No. 3 / Serenade No. 1
Naxos 8.550280

Symphony No. 4
Academic Festival & Tragic Overtures
Naxos 8.550281

Violin Concerto
Naxos 8.550195

Hungarian Dances (orchestrated)
Naxos 8.550110

Piano Concerto No. 2
Naxos 8.550506

Double Concerto for Violin and Cello
Naxos 8.550938

Chamber Music

Brahms completed some two dozen pieces of chamber music and almost all of these have some claim on our attention. For violin and piano there are three sonatas, Opp. 78, 100 and 108, with a separate Scherzo movement for a collaborative sonata he wrote with Schumann and Dietrich for their friend Joachim. For cello and piano he wrote two fine sonatas, Opp. 38 and 99. There are two late sonatas, written in 1894, for clarinet or viola and piano, Op. 120, each version deserving attention, with a

Trio for clarinet, cello and piano, Op. 114 and a Quintet for clarinet and string quartet, Op. 115, written three years earlier. In addition to this mention must be made of the three Piano Trios, Opp. 8, 87 and 101, the Trio for violin, horn and piano, Op. 40, three Piano Quartets, Opp. 25, 26 and 60, a Piano Quintet, Op. 34 and three String Quartets, Opp. 51 and 67. Two String Sextets, Opp. 18 and 36, and two String Quintets, Opp. 88 and 111, make up the list.

☞ Recommended Recordings

Clarinet Quintet Op. 115
Clarinet Trio Op. 114
Naxos 8.550391

Piano Quintet
Naxos 8.550406

String Sextets Nos. 1 & 2
Naxos 8.550436

String Quintets Nos. 1 & 2
Naxos 8.553635

Horn Trio
Naxos 8.550441

Cello Sonatas, Opp. 38 & 99
Naxos 8.550656

Piano Trios Nos. 1 and 2
Naxos 8.550746

Piano Trio No. 3 / Trio in A Major
Naxos 8.550747

Hungarian Dances for Violin and Piano
(tr. Joachim)
Naxos 8.553026

Piano Music

If all the chamber music of Brahms should be heard, the same may be said of the music for piano. Brahms showed a particular talent for the composition of variations, and this is aptly demonstrated in the famous Variations on a Theme of Handel, Op. 24, with which he made his name at first in Vienna, and the Paganini Variations, Op. 35, based on the theme of the great violinist's Caprice No. 24. Other sets of variations show similar skill, if not the depth and variety of these major examples of the art. Four Ballades, Op. 10, include one based on a real Scottish ballad, Edward, a story of parricide. The three Piano Sonatas, Opp. 1, 2 and 5, relatively early works, are less well known than the later Piano Pieces, Opp. 118 and 119, written in 1892, and the Fantasias of the same year, Op. 116. Music for four hands, piano duets, include the famous Hungarian Dances, often heard in orchestral arrangement.

☞ Recommended Recordings

Piano Sonatas Nos. 1 & 2
Naxos 8.550351

Piano Sonata No. 3 / Ballades
Naxos 8.550352

Handel, Schumann & Paganini Variations
Naxos 8.550350

Klavierstücke Opp. 76, 79 & 116
Naxos 8.550353

Klavierstücke Opp. 117, 118 & 119
Scherzo Op. 4
Naxos 8.550354

Hungarian Dances / Waltzes Op. 39
Naxos 8.550355

Fifty One Exercises, WoO 6
Naxos 8.553425

Variations on an Original Theme
Variations on a Hungarian Song
Five Studies for Piano
Naxos 8.550509

Waltzes, Op. 39 (second version)
Four Song Transcriptions
from "Die schöne Magelone" / Cadenzas
Naxos 8.553426

Vocal and Choral Music

There is again great difficulty of choice when we approach the large number of songs written by Brahms, important additions to the repertoire of German Lied (art song). The Liebeslieder Waltzes, Op. 52, for vocal quartet and piano duet, are particularly delightful, while the solo songs include the moving Four Serious Songs, Op. 121, reflecting preoccupations as his life drew to a close. Wiegenlied (Cradle Song), is one of a group of Five

Songs, Op. 49; the charming Vergebliches Ständchen (Vain Serenade) appears in a later set of Five Romances and Songs, Op. 84, and there are two particularly wonderful songs for contralto, viola and piano, Gestillte Sehnsucht (Tranquil Yearning) and the Christmas Geistliches Wiegenlied (Spiritual Cradle-Song), based on the carol Josef, lieber Josef mein, Op. 91 (Joseph dearest, Joseph mine).

Major choral works by Brahms include the monumental German Requiem, Op. 45, a setting of biblical texts, the Alto Rhapsody, Op. 53, with a text derived from Goethe, and the Schicksalslied (Song of Destiny), Op. 54, a setting of Hölderlin.

☛ **Recommended Recordings**
Four Serious Songs (Vier ernste Gesänge)
Naxos 8.550400

A German Requiem
Naxos 8.550213

Bridge, Frank (1879 - 1941)

The work of the English composer and viola-player Frank Bridge is now beginning to enjoy some favour, not least through the fact that he was the teacher of Benjamin Britten, one of whose earlier works is based on a composition by Bridge.

Orchestral Music

Bridge's orchestral works bring useful additions to the string orchestra repertoire. These include his Lament of 1915, an earlier Suite and a Christmas dance, Sir Roger de Coverley, and versions of Sally in Our Alley and Cherry Ripe, originally designed for string quartet.

☛ **Recommended Recording**
   Lament
   Naxos 8.550331

☛ **Recommended Recording**
   Works for String Quartet
   (Phantasie Quartet / Novelletten / Three Idylls /
   An Irish Melody: London Air /
   Sir Roger de Coverley / Sally in Our Alley /
   Cherry Ripe / Three Pieces)
   Naxos 8.553718

Brito, Estêvâo de (c. 1575 - 1641)

Estêvâo de Brito was appointed maestro de capella at Badajoz Cathedral in 1597 and was ordained priest in 1608, in 1613 becoming maestro de capella at Málaga Cathedral, subsequently to be offered and to refuse a similar position at the royal chapel. He died in Málaga in 1641.

Church Music

The church music of de Brito represents a particularly late flowering of the Renaissance, tempered by Baroque innovations. His setting of the Lamentations of Jeremiah, from the Holy Week liturgy, is characteristic of his style.

☛ **Recommended Recording**
   Lamentation
   Naxos 8.550572

Britten, Benjamin (1913 - 1976)

Benjamin Britten must be accepted as the most outstanding English composer working in the mid-20th century, winning a significant international reputation, while remaining thoroughly English in inspiration, a feat his immediate predecessors had been unable fully to achieve.

Operas

Britten won a triumph in 1945 with his opera Peter Grimes, first staged when the Sadler's Wells in London re-opened after the 1939-1945 war. The aspirations of the central character, the fisherman Peter Grimes, a man at odds with the community in which he lives, are frustrated by a combination of social pressure and sheer chance, leading to the suicide of the protagonist. The drama is set against the background of the sea, in various moods, summarised in the Four Sea Interludes that form an evocative part of concert repertoire. Britten's subsequent operas, including the Church Parables that draw inspiration from Japan and the remarkable operatic version of Thomas Mann's Death in Venice, Britten's last opera, constitute a very significant element in dramatic and operatic repertoire.

Orchestral Music

The best known of all Britten's orchestral music must be the Variations and Fugue on a Theme of Purcell, more generally known under its popular title The Young Person's Guide to the Orchestra, a work that is both a tribute to the great 17th century English composer Henry Purcell and a useful teaching instrument. Lachrymae, subtitled Reflections on a Theme of Dowland, a tribute to a still earlier predecessor, the lutenist John Dowland, arranged by the composer shortly before his death from its original viola and piano version is immensely moving, while the early Matinées Musicales, based on the music of Rossini, is at once attractive. Britten's Simple Symphony, for string orchestra, based on tunes written by the composer in childhood, is a useful element in string orchestra repertoire.

- **Recommended Recording**

  A Young Person's Guide to the Orchestra
  Naxos 8.550335

  Sinfonia da Requiem Op. 20
  Four Sea Interludes Op. 33a
  Passacaglia Op. 33b / An American Overture
  Naxos 8.553107

Vocal & Choral Music

Britten was strongly influenced in his music and in his life by the tenor Peter Pears. For him he wrote a quantity of songs, including the splendid Serenade for tenor, horn and strings, and the evocative Nocturne, incomparable settings of the words of various English poets, with a number of other settings of poets from Michelangelo to Thomas Hardy, for tenor and piano. His folk-song arrangements have pleased a wide audience. Major choral works include the War Requiem, a work that combines the text of the Latin Requiem with the war poems of Wilfred Owen, an expression of Britten's own pacifism.

- **Recommended Recording**

  War Requiem (2 CD's)
  Naxos 8.553558-9

Chamber Music

Britten's chamber music includes a Cello Sonata and three Cello Suites for his friend the Russian cellist

Mstislav Rostropovich, a fine Suite for the Welsh harpist Osian Ellis and a Nocturnal after John Dowland for the guitarist Julian Bream. Of his three numbered string quartets, Quartet No. 2 was written to mark the 250th anniversary of the death of Purcell, the quartet's inspiration.

- **Recommended Recording**
  Cello Suites Nos. 1-3
  Naxos 8.553663

Brouwer, Leo (1939 -)

A guitarist and composer, Leo Brouwer was born in Havana and has made his career in his native country, with support from the government. An overt nationalist in his early music, he later turned his attention to more advanced contemporary techniques of composition.

Guitar Music

Brouwer's compositions for guitar include La espiral eterna, Per sonare a tre, a Suite and a Guitar Concerto, in addition to the relatively early three Dansas concertantes for guitar and string orchestra.

Bruch, Max (1838 - 1920)

Max Bruch was born in Cologne, where he had his early musical training, going on to a career as a teacher, conductor and composer that included a short spell as conductor of the Liverpool Philharmonic Society. From 1891 he was principally occupied in Berlin as professor of composition at the Berlin Academy. Known in his lifetime as a composer of choral works, he is now remembered chiefly for a handful of orchestral compositions.

Orchestral Music

By far the best known of all Bruch's works must be the Violin Concerto, Op. 26, to which the Scottish Fantasia for solo violin and orchestra is a relatively modest pendant. Kol Nidrei, for cello and orchestra, based on Hebrew themes, is a major item in cello repertoire, making use of themes from an external source, as Bruch did on other occasions to good effect.

- **Recommended Recordings**
  Violin Concerto No. 1
  Naxos 8.550195
  Kol Nidrei
  Naxos 8.550519
  Symphony No. 3 / Suite on Russian Themes
  Marco Polo 8.223104

Bruckner, Anton (1824 - 1896)

Bruckner, born near Linz in 1824, is known chiefly as a symphonist. He was trained as a school-teacher and organist, and served in the second capacity in Linz until moving in 1868 to Vienna to teach harmony, counterpoint and organ at the Vienna Conservatory. His success as a composer was varied in his life-time, his acceptance hampered by his own diffidence and his scores posing editorial problems because of his readiness to revise what he had written. He was nine years the senior of Brahms, who outlived him by six months. Bruckner continued Austro-German symphonic traditions on a massive scale, his techniques of composition influenced to some extent by his skill as an organist and consequently in formal improvisation.

Orchestral Music

Bruckner completed nine numbered symphonies, ten, including the so-called Symphony No. 0, Die Nullte. The best known is probably Symphony No. 7, first performed in Leipzig in 1884, a work that includes in its scoring four Wagner tubas , instruments that were a newly developed cross between French horn and tuba. Symphony No. 4, "Romantic", has an added programme, a diffident afterthought. All the symphonies, however, form an important element in late 19th century symphonic repertoire.

☞ **Recommended Recording**

Symphony No. 4 "Romantic"
Naxos 8.550154

Choral Music

Bruckner wrote a number of works for church use, both large and small scale. Among the former are the Te Deum, completed in 1884 and various settings of the Mass, including the well known Mass No. 2 in E minor.

☞ **Recommended Recording**

Motets
Naxos 8.550956

Bruneau, Alfred (1857 - 1934)

The French composer Alfred Bruneau enjoyed a long friendship with Zola, resulting in a series of operas that continued after the writer's death in 1902. Bruneau was respected as a critic and was the author of a life of Zola. As a composer he inherited the lyrical tradition of his teacher Massenet, mingled with the realism implicit in his literary sources.

Operas

Bruneau's operas range from Le rêve (The Dream), staged at the Opéra in 1891 to Angelo, tyran de Padoue (Angelo, Tyrant of Padua), based on Victor Hugo, in

1928 and the comic opera Virginie two years later. Other operas based on Zola include Naïs Micoulin, L'ouragan (The Hurricane), and Messidor. the last two with libretti by Zola himself.

Choral and Vocal Music
Bruneau wrote a number of orchestral works that include a choral element, including the choral symphony Léda: poème antique and the symphonic poem Penthésilée. His important Requiem has much of the drama of the setting by Berlioz. Some of his songs also have orchestral accompaniment.

Orchestral Music
Bruneau's orchestral music includes a symphonic poem, La belle au bois dormant (Sleeping Beauty).

☛ **Recommended Recording**

Orchestral Highlights
(Messidor / Naïs Micoulin /
L'attaque du moulin - Suite)
Marco Polo 8.223498

Bull, John (?1562-3 - 1628)
John Bull was among the most distinguished English keyboard-players of his time, and his career forms a link with the developing keyboard tradition of the Netherlands. Bull was in the service of Queen Elizabeth and her successor, before taking refuge in the Netherlands to avoid various charges levelled at him in England. He was known as an organist and a virginalist and as a maker of both instruments, the second a form of keyboard instrument with a mechanism for plucking rather than hammering the strings.

Keyboard Music
Bull wrote keyboard compositions based on both sacred and secular models. The best known of his works must be The King's Hunt, with a series of dance movements, fantasias and song-variations, some of which make considerable demands on the performer.

Busoni, Ferruccio (1866 - 1924)
The son of an Italian musician father and a German pianist mother, Ferruccio Busoni represented a remarkable synthesis of two differing attitudes to music, while winning an outstanding reputation as a piano virtuoso. Busoni composed operas, including Turandot and Doktor Faust, a series of orchestral works, including a piano concerto that also uses a male chorus in the finale, and various pieces of chamber music.

Piano Music

Of the various works Busoni composed or transcribed for the piano one of the most impressive is the famous arrangement of Bach's Chaconne for unaccompanied violin, one of a number of works based on Bach. His Fantasia after Bach and the much revised Fantasia Contrappuntistica demonstrate something of his musical preoccupations.

Buxtehude, Dietrich (c. 1637 - 1707)

Buxtehude belongs to the generation of organists before Johann Sebastian Bach, who, like Handel, once travelled to Lübeck to hear the master perform at the Marienkirche, where he served as organist for forty years, from 1667 until his death in 1707. He wrote a considerable quantity of music, choral and instrumental, for church use, as well as chamber music and keyboard music of a more secular kind.

Organ Music

Buxtehude's many surviving compositions for the organ include some twenty Preludes and a larger number of chorale preludes, variations on Lutheran chorale melodies.

☞ **Recommended Recording**
Prelude and Fugue BuxWV 139
Naxos 8.550964

Byrd, William (1543 - 1623)

The greatest English composer of his generation, comparable in stature to his most distinguished continental contemporaries, William Byrd was a versatile composer. Although remaining a Catholic, loyalty that cost him considerable trouble in times of persecution in England, he served as a member of the Chapel Royal, providing music for the liturgy of the Church of England and, on a more private scale, for his fellow-Catholics.

Church Music

Byrd's compositions for the church may be separated into those for the Catholic liturgy and those designed for the officially recognised Church of England. The first category includes settings of the Mass for three, four and five voices, and a large quantity of other works for the various seasons of the church year.

For the Church of England Byrd wrote a Great Service and three other service settings, using the texts of the Anglican liturgy.

In addition to these compositions there are a number of anthems and psalm-settings, and consort songs with sacred texts of one sort or another.

☞ Recommended Recording
Masses for Four and Five Voices / Infelix Ego
Naxos 8.550574

Vocal Music

Byrd also wrote a number of secular consort songs, songs with accompaniment entrusted to varying numbers of instruments.

Consort Music

Following the popular fashion of the time, Byrd provided music for various groups of instruments, usually performing in homo- genous ensembles, generally on viols, bowed and fretted string instruments that were held in higher social esteem than the lowly violin. Byrd's consort music includes a number of In nomines, a curious English form of music based on a fragment taken from a setting of the Benedictus by the 16th century composer Taverner. To these consort pieces may be added a series of Fantasias, contrapuntal music, as the title then implied.

☞ Recommended Recording
Works for Viols
Naxos 8.550604

Keyboard Music

Byrd was well known as a keyboard-player. He wrote a wealth of music for the virginals, Fantasias, Pavans and Galliards, the fashionable paired dances of the time, and song variations. The Earl of Salisbury Pavan and Galliard is a familiar recital piece as are the variations on Sellinger's Round and The Carman's Whistle.

Cabezón, Antonio de (1510 - 1566)

Antonio de Cabezón had much of his musical training in Palencia, where his uncle was vicar-general of the diocese. He became organist in the chapel of Queen Isabella in 1526, later serving Philip II, before and after his accession to the throne, accompanying the king on journeys abroad, including that involved in the king's marriage to Queen Mary of England. He was among the leading keyboard players of his day. His three sons and two daughters also served the royal family, two of the former as organists and composers.

Keyboard Music

Antonio de Cabezón was distinguished as an organist and clavichord player. His music for keyboard consists of 29

Tientos, pieces varied in technique and mood, Diferencias, sets of variations on secular tunes, Versillos, harmonized versions of the eight psalm tones, and Magnificats, as well as Glosas, compositions based on polyphonic works by other composers.

☞ **Recommended Recording**

Tiento I-Diferencias on the Italian Pavane
- Diferencias on the Milanese Galliard
- Tiento on Qui la dira
Naxos 8.550705

Cage, John (1912 - 1992)

A leading American avant-garde musician, John Cage won notoriety for his famous silent work, 4'33", for any instrument or instruments. Equally controversial was 0'0", ten years later, performed by the composer and consisting of the slicing of vegetables, then put into a blender, with the performer concluding by drinking the juice. Cage has had a considerable influence on younger composers, with his use of chance and indeterminacy, electronic techniques and every possible experimental device, whether musical or dramatic. He combined his interest in music with considerable knowledge of mushrooms and a fondness for bridge and other card and board games.

Compositions

Cage's compositions are not easily classified. His early use of percussion was a natural corollary of his work with dance groups. Devices used included the prepared piano, pioneered in his 1938 Bacchanale, and followed by a number of other compositions in which various objects are inserted into the piano to create different effects, largely percussive in quality. An interest in Zen and the I Ching resulted in Music of Changes, where chance dictated the choice of notes. Dramatic actions dominate Water Music, for a pianist, who must empty pots of water and perform other feats, while later music makes considerable use of tapes or calls for undetermined forces.

Campra, André (1660 - 1744)

André Campra occupied a leading position in French music of the early 18th century. After an earlier career in Toulon and Toulouse, he moved to Paris, where he became maître de musique at Notre Dame and finally won distinction in the opera-house, composing for the Académie Royale de Musique and employed also by the chapelle royale.

Stage Works

Campra's first success in the theatre came in 1697 with L'Europe galante, an opéra-ballet with entrées for

France, Spain, Italy and Turkey. He continued to write opéra-ballets and tragédies lyriques, generally to be staged at the Paris Opéra.

Church Music

Campra wrote a number of motets and, in 1722, a setting of the Requiem Mass.

Campion, Thomas (1567 - 1620)

The English poet, composer and doctor Thomas Campion established his reputation as a poet in the 1590s and published his first songs in 1601. He wrote and composed masques for royal entertainment, particularly after the succession of King James of Scotland to the throne of England as James I, and was unusual in that he wrote both words and music for his many songs with lute accompaniment.

Vocal Music

Campion's musical legacy consists entirely of some 119 lute-songs. Many of these were published in a series of four Bookes of Ayres. They include the vivid "Fire, fire, fire fire loe here I burne, Never weather-beaten saile" and "Woo her, and win her, he that can", among a rich collection.

Canteloube (de Calaret), Marie Joseph (1879 - 1957)

Born in the Auvergne, Canteloube was a pupil of Vincent d'Indy in Paris, but won a reputation primarily in the musical evocation of his native region.

Vocal Music

Canteloube has enjoyed considerable popularity for his arrangements of a delightful series of Auvergnois folk-songs, to which he later added further collections of folk-song arrangements, from Languedoc, Touraine and the Basque country.

Cardoso, Manuel (1566 - 1650)

The Portuguese composer Manuel Cardoso was trained as a chorister at the cathedral in Évora, an important musical centre, and became a Carmelite, spending much of his career at the Convento do Carmo in Lisbon. He enjoyed royal patronage from both King John IV of Portugal and Philip IV of Spain.

Church Music

Cardoso followed the example of Palestrina, whose contrapuntal practices he mastered. His surviving church music, published in his lifetime, includes three books of

Masses, a Cantica to the Blessed Virgin and a collection of various motets, music for Holy Week and other pieces.

☛ Recommended Recordings
Lamentatio / Magnificat secundi toni
Naxos 8.553310

Missa pro defunctis
Naxos 8.550682

Carissimi, Giacomo (1605 - 1674)

Carissimi occupies an important position in Italian music of the 17th century. Ordained priest, he spent the greater part of his life as director of music at the German College in Rome, an important Jesuit educational establishment.

Church Music
Carissimi's many compositions include various works for church performance, Mass settings, cantatas and motets. Of particular interest are his Latin oratorios, important in the development of the genre. These include Belshazzars' Feast, under the title Baltazar and a dramatic musical version of the story of Jephtha.

Carulli, Ferdinando (1770 - 1841)

Carulli is a composer whose name is well known chiefly to guitarists, both as the author of a useful teaching manual and as a composer. Born in Naples, he was at first a cellist, but turned as a young man to the guitar. He moved in 1808 to Paris, where he remained until his death in 1841.

Guitar Music
Carulli's compositions for the guitar include two concertos, musically insubstantial, but both effective vehicles for the instrument.

☛ Recommended Recording
Guitar Sonatas Op. 21, Nos. 1-3 / Op. 5
Naxos 8.553301

Castelnuovo-Tedesco, Mario
(1895 - 1968)
A composer and pianist, Castelnuovo-Tedesco was born in Florence into an Italian Jewish family. In 1939 he moved to the United States, where, in common with other European composers in exile, he turned his hand to film music. He died in Los Angeles in 1968.

Vocal Music

Castelnuovo-Tedesco was a very prolific composer. His songs include 33 attractive settings of Shakespeare which have won wide approval.

Guitar Music

Castelnuovo-Tedesco made particularly useful additions to the solo guitar repertoire, notably in two concertos for solo guitar and one for two guitars, as well as a Capriccio diabolico, a tribute to the demon violinist Paganini.

☞ **Recommended Recordings**

Guitar Concerto
Naxos 8.550729

Catalani, Alfredo (1854 - 1893)

Occupying a position of importance in Italian opera before the rise to fame of Puccini, Alfredo Catalani is now chiefly remembered for one opera, La Wally.

Operas

Catalani's opera La Wally, first staged at La Scala Milan in 1892, is set in Switzerland and makes use of local colour from its village setting.

☞ **Recommended Recording**

Ebben, ne andrò lontana from La Wally
Naxos 8.550606

Cavalli, Francesco (1602 - 1676)

The Italian composer Cavalli was possibly the most important composer of Italian opera in the third quarter of the 17th century. Recent revivals of his work in the theatre have served to bring his name before a more general public. He became a choir-boy at St. Mark's in Venice in 1616 and enjoyed a subsequent close working relationship with Monteverdi, maestro di musica of the basilica. He wrote music for the theatre and the church.

Operas

Cavalli wrote over 40 operas including a version of the legend of Medea, Giasone, and the operas Egisto and Serse, among a series of works chiefly relying on ancient Greek or Roman legend or history, some of which have enjoyed successful modern revival.

Chabrier, Emmanuel (1841 - 1894)

Intended by his parents for a more conventional career than that of a musician, the French composer Emmanuel Chabrier was from 1861 employed in the

Ministry of the Interior in Paris, only devoting himself fully to music from 1880. His compositions include some colourful orchestral compositions and piano music that had a marked influence on his immediate successors.

Orchestral Music

Chabrier's most popular composition is his Spanish rhapsody España. To this one may add the occasional Joyeuse marche and his Suite pastorale, an arrangement of some of his own piano pieces.

☞ **Recommended Recordings**

> España
> Naxos 8.550501
>
> Marche joyeuse
> Naxos 8.550088

Piano Music

The ten Pièces pittoresques, some of which were orchestrated by Chabrier in his Suite pastorale, are inventive in harmony and melody and attractive in form. They range from a simple landscape, Paysage, to a Menuet pompeux and a final Scherzo-valse.

☞ **Recommended Recordings**

> Piano Works Vol. 1
> Bourrée fantasique / Feuillet d'album
> Ballabile / Caprice / Petite valse / Habanera
> 10 Pièces pittoresques
> Naxos 8.553009
>
> Piano Works Vol. 2
> Marche des Cipayes / Julia / Impromptu
> Aubade / Ronde champêtre / Capriccio
> Souvenir de Brunehaut
> Naxos 8.553010
>
> Piano Works Vol. 3
> España / Trois Valse romatiques
> Prélude et marche française
> Cortège burlesque / Souvenirs de Munich
> Air de ballet / Suite de Valses
> Naxos 8.553080

Chambonnières, Jacques Champion (1601-2 - 1672)

Chambonnières may be regarded as the founder of the school of French keyboard music that led to François Couperin and Rameau. A member of the minor nobility, he entered the royal service and enjoyed a career of varied material success, while nevertheless winning a considerable reputation as a performer and composer. At the least he exercised a strong influence over the father and two uncles of François Couperin le grand, Charles, Louis and François.

Keyboard Music

The keyboard music of Chambonnières includes dances, a collection of which was published in 1670, assembled into suites by key, although not originally so conceived.

Charpentier, Gustave (1860 - 1956)

After Bohemian distractions in Paris, Gustave Charpentier eventually became a composition pupil of Massenet at the Conservatoire, winning the important Prix de Rome two years later. His chief activity as a composer took place before 1914 and he is remembered principally for his opera Louise.

Operas

Charpentier wrote four operas, the first of them, the roman musical (musical novel) Louise, with its seamstress heroine and her Bohemian lover Julien, rejected by her family. One aria from the opera, Depuis le jour, has remained a frequent recital item.

Charpentier, Marc-Antoine

(? 1643 - 1704)

Less materially successful than his Paris contemporary Lully, Marc-Antoine Charpentier nevertheless won considerable esteem. A prolific composer, he wrote extensively for the church and with slightly less fecundity for secular purposes. He was in the service of the Dauphin and held important positions at the Jesuit Church of St. Louis and later at the Sainte-Chapelle.

Church Music

From a very large number of compositions, the Messe de Minuit pour Noël may be singled out, with the second of Charpentier's Te Deum settings, impressively scored for forces that include woodwind, trumpet, timpani and strings.

☛ **Recommended Recordings**

Messe des morts / Litanies à la Vierge
Confitebor tibi / Nisi Dominus
Transfige dulcissime Jesu
Laudate pueri Dominum
Naxos 8.553173

Vespres à la Vierge
Naxos 8.553174

Chausson, Ernest (1855 - 1899)

After a sheltered childhood in a cultured family and subsequent study of law, Chausson became a pupil of Massenet at the Conservatoire, also attending the classes of César Franck. He led a generally peaceful life, shortened by a cycling accident, and echoed in his music the developments of the period, from Massenet to Debussy.

Orchestral Music

Chausson wrote relatively little orchestral music. Of the four surviving works, Poème, for solo violin and orchestra, is an important item in violin repertoire. He completed a single symphony, in B flat, with two surviving symphonic poems.

Cherubini, Luigi (1760 - 1842)

The Italian composer Cherubini came to occupy a dominant position in French musical life. He was employed at the Conservatoire in Paris on its foundation and from 1822 was director of the institution, retaining this position until the year of his death. His works include compositions for the stage, the church and for political purposes, a requirement of the turbulent revolutionary years.

Operas

Cherubini wrote some 30 operas and of these Les deux journées, now seldom heard, had influence on Beethoven's only opera, Fidelio. The opera Médée, first staged in Paris in 1797, remains in occasional repertoire, with the aria Ah, nos peines, providing a popular soprano operatic recital item.

Chopin, Frédéric (1810 - 1849)

Born near Warsaw in 1810, the son of a French émigré and a Polish mother, Chopin won early fame in the relatively limited circles of his native country, before seeking his fortune abroad, in Paris. His departure from Warsaw coincided with the unsuccessful national rising against Russian domination and Chopin found himself in Paris in the company of a number of other Polish exiles. He was able to establish himself as a pianist and as a teacher of the piano, primarily in fashionable society.

For some ten years Chopin enjoyed a liaison with the writer George Sand, but broke with her during the last years of his life, brought to a close by the tuberculosis from which he had long suffered. His compositions, principally for the piano, make a remarkable use of the newly developed instrument, exploring its poetic possibilities while generally avoiding the more obvious ostentation of the Paris school of performers.

Orchestral Music

As a young musician embarking on a career as a pianist, Chopin provided himself with half a dozen works for piano and orchestra, a form for which he later found no necessity. These include two piano concertos, three works based on Polish themes, a Fantasia, a Krakowiak and a Grand polonaise, and a set of variations on a theme by Mozart.

☛ Recommended Recordings

Piano Concertos Nos. 1 & 2
Naxos 8.550123

Piano Concerto No. 1 / Fantaisie
Andante spianato & Grand Polonaise
Naxos 8.550368

Piano Concerto No. 2 / Krakowiak
Mozart Variations
Naxos 8.550369

Chamber Music

Chopin wrote an Introduction and Polonaise for cello and piano for an early patron and towards the end of his life a Cello Sonata. His G minor Piano Trio is a valuable addition to recital repertoire.

☛ Recommended Recording

Cello Sonata / Polonaise brillante / Grand Duo
Naxos 8.553159

Piano Music

Chopin created or developed a number of new forms of piano music, vehicles for his own poetic use of the instrument, with its exploration of nuance, its original harmonies and its discreet but often considerable technical demands. He used the popular form of the Waltz in a score of such compositions, of which the so-called Minute Waltz is probably the best known of many of almost equal familiarity. The Polish dance, the Polonaise, elevated from village to ball-room, provided the basis of another characteristic form, in sixteen such works, written between 1817, when Chopin was seven, and 1846. The best known, among generally familiar works, are the Polonaise in A major, Opus 40 No. 1, the Polonaise in A flat, Opus 53, and the Polonaise-Fantaisie, Opus 61. Other Polish dances used by Chopin include the 62 Mazurkas. The four Ballades are supposedly based on patriotic poems by Chopin's friend Mickiewicz, evocative narrative works with no precise extra-musical association. The 21 Nocturnes continue an evocative form initiated by the Irish pianist John Field. Chopin wrote 26 Preludes, 24 of them completed during an ill-fated winter with George Sand in Mallorca and 27 Studies, of which the Revolutionary Study is perhaps the best known. Other compositions include four Scherzos, expansions of the earlier form into a more extended virtuoso piece, three Sonatas, a Berceuse, a

Barcarolle, four Impromptus and a number of other works. The whole body of Chopin's music is of the greatest musical and technical importance, melodies often of operatic inspiration and harmonies and forms of considerable originality.

☞ Recommended Recordings

Ballades / Berceuse / Fantasie etc.
Naxos 8.550508

Etudes Opp..10 & 25
Naxos 8.550364

Impromptus and Scherzi
Naxos 8.550362

Mazurkas (Complete) Volume 1
Naxos 8.550358

Mazurkas (Complete) Volume 2
Naxos 8.550359

Nocturnes (Complete) Volume 1
Naxos 8.550356

Nocturnes (Complete) Volume 2
Naxos 8.550357

Polonaises (Complete) Volume 1
Naxos 8.550360

Polonaises (Complete) Volume 2
Naxos 8.550361

Preludes (Complete) / Bourrees
Naxos 8.550366

Sonatas Nos.1-3
Naxos 8.550363

Variations / Rondos etc.
Naxos 8.550367

Waltzes (Complete)
Naxos 8.550365

Cilea, Francesco (1866 - 1950)

Francesco Cilea was trained at the Naples Conservatory and won his principal reputation with the opera Adriana Lecouvreur in 1902. He had a career as a teacher in Florence, in Palermo and finally in the Conservatory in Naples, a position he retained until he retired in 1936.

Operas

Cilea's opera Adriana Lecouvreur, with a libretto based on the play by the French writers Scribe and Legouvé, with a plot concerning the stage actress Adriana Lecouvreur and her lover Maurizio, Count of Saxony and ending in her death. The best known arias from the opera are for the soprano Adriana, her Io son' l'umile ancella (I am the humble handmaid), in which she expresses her humility as an interpreter of the words of Corneille, and her tragically ironic Poveri fiori, as she receives from Maurizio the flowers that she had given him, now withered, and poisoned by her rival.

Cimarosa, Domenico (1749 - 1801)

Trained in Naples, Cimarosa became one of the more important composers of Italian comic opera in the last quarter of the 18th century. He spent some years from 1787 as maestro di cappella to Catherine the Great in St. Petersburg and at the court of the Emperor Leopold II in Vienna in 1791, the year of Mozart's death. His later association with republicans in Naples led to a brief period of imprisonment before his death in Venice in 1801.

Operas

Cimarosa composed a very large number of operas, of which the best remembered is Il Matrimonio Segreto, based on the English comedy The Clandestine Marriage by David Garrick and George Colman.

Clarke, Jeremiah (c. 1674 - 1707)

The English composer Jeremiah Clarke belongs to the generation following that of Henry Purcell. He was a member of the Chapel Royal and later a vicar-choral at St. Paul's Cathedral. In 1704 he became joint organist with Dr. Croft of the Chapel Royal, but went out of his mind and shot himself in 1707. He wrote a quantity of music for the church and songs and incidental music for the theatre, as well as various instrumental pieces.

Instrumental Music

Jeremiah Clarke's best known composition is his Trumpet Voluntary, once attributed to Purcell. It forms part of a suite for wind instruments with the original title of The Prince of Denmark's March.

☛ **Recommended Recording**

Trumpet Voluntary
Naxos 8.550790

Clementi, Muzio (1752 - 1832)

The piano music of Muzio Clementi, or at least his pedagogical Gradus ad Parnassum, has in part been well enough known to generations of ambitious keyboard-players. Clementi himself, born in Rome in 1752, was taken as a boy to England by Peter Beckford, cousin of the eccentric William Beckford. There he developed his abilities as a performer. His subsequent career brought success as a composer, teacher and pianist, and later as a manufacturer of pianos. He died at Evesham in 1832.

Piano Music

Clementi wrote a great deal of music for the piano, including more than a hundred sonatas. He published a number of pedagogical works, of which the Introduction to the Art of Playing the Piano Forte and Gradus ad Parnassum are the best known.

☞ **Recommended Recording**

Six Progressive Sonatinas, Op. 36
Sonata Op. 24 No. 2 / Sonata Op. 37 No. 2
Sonatas Op. 25 Nos. 2 & 5
Naxos 8.550452

Coleridge-Taylor, Samuel

(1875 - 1912)

The reputation of Samuel Coleridge-Taylor, son of an English mother and a father who was a doctor from Sierra Leone, has suffered in recent years, although at one time his music enjoyed considerable popularity in England, while as a conductor visiting New York he was hailed by one critic as "the black Mahler".

Choral Music

Coleridge-Taylor's best known composition is the cantata Hiawatha's Wedding Feast, later extended as Scenes from the Song of Hiawatha, based on the poem by Longfellow.

Orchestral Music

The ballet music from Hiawatha was later arranged as an orchestral suite. The Petite Suite de concert of 1910 has retained a measure of popularity also in a piano arrangement.

☞ **Recommended Recording**

Hiawatha Overture / Petite Suite
Four Waltzes / Gipsy Suite / Romance
Othello Suite
Marco Polo 8.223516

Copland, Aaron (1900 - 1990)

The son of immigrant Jewish parents from Poland and Lithuania, Aaron Copland was born in Brooklyn in 1900 and lived to become the doyen of all American composers. He studied with Nadia Boulanger in Paris. His wider popular reputation in the United States was founded on his thoroughly American ballets, Billy the Kid, Rodeo and Appalachian Spring, and, less overtly, on his film scores, while a great variety of other compositions won him an unassailable position in American concert-life.

Ballet Music

Copland's three ballets Billy the Kid, Rodeo and Appalachian Spring are quintessentially American, the first two dealing with familiar elements of the Wild West and the third turning to Shaker country in the farm-lands of Appalachia. All three works are well known also in the concert-hall.

Orchestral Music

Unquestionably the best known of all Copland's orchestral works must be Fanfare for the Common Man, followed by An Outdoor Overture and El salón Mexico and Quiet City, the last originally incidental music for a play by Irving Shaw.

- ☛ **Recommended Recording**
  Rodeo / Billy the Kid / Appalachian Spring
  Fanfare for the Common Man
  Naxos 8.550282

Corelli, Arcangelo (1653 - 1713)

The work of the Italian violinist-composer Arcangelo Corelli exercised incalculable influence over the following generation of composers, not least over Handel, who worked briefly with him in Rome in 1707. Corelli was born at Fusignano in 1653 and studied in Bologna, an important musical centre. His later career was chiefly in Rome, where he served the exiled Catholic Queen Christina of Sweden, Cardinal Pamphili and the young Cardinal Ottoboni, in whose palace he lived for a number of years. He died in January 1713 and was buried in the Pantheon, a sign of the respect in which he was held.

Instrumental Music

Corelli's influence depended largely on his published instrumental music, notably 48 Trio Sonatas for two violins and basso continuo (generally harpsichord and cello), twelve sonatas for violin and continuo and twelve Concerti grossi, works for string orchestra with a solo group of two violins, cello and harpsichord. The Violin Sonatas include a particularly well known set of variations on the popular dance-tune La Follia, a melody used by many composers of the period. Concerto grosso No. 8 is the famous Christmas Concerto, which includes a pastoral movement setting the scene for Christmas, to be played on the night before the festival.

- ☛ **Recommended Recordings**
  Concerti Grossi, Op. 6 Nos. 1-6
  Naxos 8.550402
  Concerti Grossi, Op. 6 Nos. 7-12
  Naxos 8.550403

Couperin, François (le grand) (1668 - 1733)

François Couperin, known as le grand to distinguish him from an uncle of the same name, was the most distinguished of a numerous family of French musicians, officially succeeding his uncle and father as organist of

the Paris church of St. Gervais when he was eighteen. He enjoyed royal patronage under Louis XIV and in 1693 was appointed royal organist and belatedly royal harpsichordist. As a keyboard-player and composer he was pre-eminent in France at the height of his career. He died in Paris in 1733.

Church Music

Couperin composed church music for the royal chapel under Louis XIV. The surviving Leçons de ténèbres are possibly the best example of this form of composition, the first of the three for soprano solo and continuo and the third for two sopranos, settings of the Lamentations of Jeremiah for the Holy Week liturgy.

Chamber Music

Couperin's chamber music includes L'apothéose de Lully (The Apotheosis of Lully), a tribute to the leading composer in France in the second half of the 17th century Jean-Baptiste Lully, a tribute to the Italian composer Corelli, L'apothéose de Corelli, part of a larger collection of ensemble pieces under the title Les goûts réunis (Tastes United), an exploration of the rival French and Italian tastes in music, a quarrel in which Couperin remained neutral. The Concerts royaux represent another important element in Couperin's music for instrumental ensemble.

Harpsichord Music

Couperin's compositions for the harpsichord occupy a very important position in French music. In 27 suites for the harpsichord, most of them published between 1713 and 1730, Couperin offered a series of harpsichord pieces, many of them descriptive in one way or another. These richly varied suites or "ordres" represent the height of Couperin's achievement as a composer and arguably that of the French harpsichord composers.

☛ **Recommended Recordings**

> Suites for Harpsichord Nos. 6, 8 & 11
> Naxos 8.550460
>
> Suites for Harpsichord Nos. 13, 17, 18 & 21
> Naxos 8.550461
>
> Suites for Harpsichord Nos. 22, 23, 25 & 26
> Naxos 8.550462

Couperin, Louis (c. 1626 - 1661)

Louis Couperin, uncle of François Couperin le grand, inherited musical ability and interests from his father. His serenading of Chambonnières, with his two brothers, François and Charles, at the Chambonnières property, not far distant from Chaume, where the Couperins had settled, led, it is said, to wider recognition in Paris, where Louis Couperin became organist at St Gervais. He later refused the royal position of joueur d'espinette (harpsichordist), from which Chambonnières was to be dismissed. His brothers seem to have left no compositions, although he was succeeded at St Gervais, on his death in 1661, by his youngest brother, Charles, father of the great Couperin.

Keyboard Music

Louis Couperin's keyboard music, an important element in the French keyboard tradition, consists of preludes and dance movements, with versets, fugues and other works for organ.

Harpsichord Music

Louis Couperin wrote a number of harpsichord pieces in the usual forms of his day, preludes, allemandes, courantes, sarabandes and gigues, chaconnes and passacailles, with other dance-forms, as well as variations on the music of other composers.

☛ **Recommended Recording**

Harpsichord Suites
(D Major / A Minor / C Major / F Major)
Naxos 8.550922

Organ Music

Louis Couperin's organ compositions include a number of fantaisies (fugues) and plainsong versets in a traditional French form, designed for liturgical use.

There are six division basses, a varied bass-line, for trompette or cromorne stops, with harmonic accompaniment in the upper parts. His two Carillons imitate the sound of the bells of St Gervais.

Cras, Jean (1879 - 1932)

A native of Brest, Jean Cras had a distinguished naval career, with final promotion to the position of rear-admiral. He was a pupil of Duparc and, within the limitations of his career, a prolific and varied composer.

Orchestral Music

In his suite Journal de bord Cras reflected his interest in the sea. His 1931 Piano Concerto was written for his daughter, who gave the first performance, and works for solo instrument and orchestra include a Légende for cello.

Opera

Cras wrote one opera, Polyphème, based on a drama by Albert Samain. This was staged at the Opéra-Comique in 1922.

Chamber Music

Chamber music by Jean Cras includes a string trio, Suite for flute and harp and a piano quintet.

Vocal Music

Songs by Cras include La flûte de Pan, Fontaines and L'offrande lyrique.

Cui, César (1835 - 1918)

César Cui, one of the group of five nationalist Russian composers of the second half of the 19th century known as the Mighty Handful or the Five, was the son of a French officer who had remained in Russia after the retreat of Napoleon in 1812. In common with other composers of his generation and background, he had a career apart from music, in his case as a professor at the Academy of Military Engineering, an expert in fortification. This did not prevent him from ambitious activity as a composer and an important career as a critic, often harsh and intolerant in his judgements. He is best known for his colourful short piano pieces.

Operas

Cui's first opera was A Prisoner in the Caucasus, with a libretto based on Pushkin. Particularly pleasing to his friends and supporters was the opera William Ratciff, based on the play by Heine. Further operas followed, enjoying varying success, followed by four final children's operas.

Orchestral Music

In his four orchestral Suites Cui demonstrates his ability in the handling of attractive smaller forms, belying contemporary accusations of lack of skill in orchestration. Suite No. 4 offers orchestral arrangements of piano pieces written originally for his Belgian patroness, the Countess of Mercy-Argenteau. The Suite concertante for violin and orchestra makes an unusual addition to solo violin repertoire.

☛ Recommended Recordings

Suite Concertante Op. 25
Suite Miniature Op. 20
Suite Op. 43 "In Modo Populari"
Marco Polo 8.220308

Suite No. 2, Op. 38 / The Buccaneer
Suite No. 4 "A Argenteau", Op. 40
Marco Polo 8.223400

Chamber Music

Cui's chamber music includes various shorter pieces for violin and piano or cello and piano, notably two sets of Miniatures for violin and piano, as well as three string quartets.

Piano Music

In his piano music Cui again shows his gifts as a miniaturist, exhibited in a large number of attractive short pieces.

☞ **Recommended Recording**
25 Preludes, Op. 64
Marco Polo 8.223496

Vocal and Choral Music

Cui claimed that he was compelled, in general, in his operas to avoid Russian subjects, since he was himself half French and half Lithuanian. His songs, of course, do treat Russian texts and include settings of Pushkin, Nekrasov and A.K. Tolstoy, while his choral music is generally on a more ambitious scale.

Czerny, Carl (1791 - 1857)

Precociously gifted as a pianist, Carl Czerny studied as a ten-year-old with Beethoven and made his first public appearance in Vienna in 1800, when he played Mozart's C minor Piano Concerto. Impressed as he was by the performance style of Mozart, heard through Mozart's pupil Hummel, he nevertheless became a leading exponent of the piano music of Beethoven, with its demands for a legato style suited to the newer forms of the instrument. Czerny's principal fame, however, was as a teacher, his pupils including Thalberg, Liszt and Stephen Heller, and his pedagogical works had and continue to have wide currency.

Piano Music

Czerny's principal works were in the form of exercises and studies, of which he wrote a very large number, extending up to his Opus 861, Studies for the Left Hand. His other piano music consists of Sonatas and Sonatinas, with various medleys, variations and other shorter pieces. He wrote music for piano duet, and for up to four players, with many arrangements and transcriptions.

Organ Music

With his usual facility, Czerny wrote a certain amount of organ music, of which the Prelude and Fugue, Op. 603, No. 3, is a characteristic example.

☞ **Recommended Recording**
Prelude and Fugue Op. 603, No. 3
Naxos 8.550964

Orchestral Music

Czerny's symphonies, overtures and concertos are generally unknown, some of them remaining unpublished.

Chamber Music

Czerny wrote a certain amount of chamber music, generally in a form involving the piano in some way, whether in piano trios or piano quartets, including one work for four pianos.

Church Music

Even less known must be Czerny's church music, which includes settings of the Mass, Graduals, Offertories and other liturgical works.

Danzi, Franz (1763 - 1826)

Franz Danzi served as a cellist in the famous Mannheim orchestra, remaining in Mannheim when the Electoral court moved to Munich in 1778. In 1783 Danzi took his father's place in the Munich orchestra and now continued his career as a composer with his third German opera. Having married a singer, he enjoyed an active career in opera that led to his appointment as deputy Kapellmeister in Munich in 1798. After his wife's death he returned to Mannheim and in 1807 was appointed Kapellmeister in Stuttgart, where he met Weber. In 1812 he moved to Karlsruhe, where again he was able to stage operas by Weber. He was, at the same time, a prolific composer in many genres.

Stage Works

Danzi wrote some eighteen stage works, generally in the form of German Singspiel, with its mixture of music and spoken dialogue. Other forms used include melodrama, with its simultaneous music and speech, and grand opera in a setting of a version of the early 18th century libretto by Apostolo Zeno, Iphigenie in Aulis.

Vocal and Choral Music

Danzi wrote sacred and secular choral music, Masses, oratorios and cantatas. His songs and canzonettes are in contemporary style, but no longer regarded as an important part of German song tradition.

Orchestral Music

In orchestral music Danzi was similarly prolific, contributing principally to the Sinfonia concertante and concerto repertoire.

Chamber Music

Danzi's chamber music includes sextets, quintets, quartets and trios, some for strings, some for wind instruments and some for a combination of the two. His duo sonatas show a similar variety in their instrumentation. These works are generally in a style that reflects his own early experience in Mannheim and the influence of his teacher Abt Vogler, with whom Weber also studied.

☛ **Recommended Recording**
Wind Quintets Op. 56, Nos. 1-3
Wind Sextet in E Flat
Naxos 8.553076

Piano Music

There is a smaller amount of piano music by Danzi, including a number of works for four hands.

David, Félicien (1810 - 1876)

Félicien David was a boy chorister in Aix-en-Provence and moved to Paris in 1830 to study at the Conservatoire. There he fell under the influence of the Saint-Simonians, a revolutionary philosophical, religious and social movement that attracted other musicians and artists of the time, becoming their official musician. He travelled with the 'apostles' to the Near East, which exerted a strong influence on him, and on his return to France he gradually won a reputation for himself, notably, in 1844, with his ode-symphonie Le désert, and then by other works that continued to display the influence of the Near East.

Operas

David's operas include Lalla-Roukh, based on the poem by Thomas Moore.

Ode-Symphonies and Oratorios

The ode-symphonie Le désert, with its introductory recitations and vividly exotic scenes of desert life, is typical of David's compositions in this form, which include Christophe Colombe. His oratorio Moïse au Sinaï also finds an obvious place for exoticism.

Vocal and Choral Music

David wrote songs of all kinds, in addition to the choral works he wrote for the Saint-Simonians.

Piano Music

Piano music by David ranges from the Saint-Simonian to the exoticism of Mélodies orientales.

☛ **Recommended Recordings**

Les Brises d'Orient / Les Minarets
Marco Polo 8.223376

Piano Trios Nos. 2 and 3
Marco Polo 8.223492

Debussy, Claude (1862 - 1918)

Claude Debussy has exercised widespread influence over later generations of composers, both in his native France and elsewhere. He was trained at the Paris Conservatoire, and decided there on a career as a composer rather than as a pianist, his original intention. His highly characteristic musical language, thoroughly French in inspiration, extended the contemporary limits of harmony and form, with a remarkably delicate

command of nuance, whether in piano-writing or in the handling of a relatively large orchestra.

Operas

Debussy attempted many operas, two based on stories by Edgar Allan Poe. But he completed only one, Pelléas et Mélisande, a version of the medieval play by Maurice Maeterlinck, with its story of idealised love perfectly matched with the composer's musical idiom.

☛ **Recommended Recording**

Pelléas et Mélisande
Naxos 8.660047-9

Orchestral Music

The most influential piece of orchestral music by Debussy is the Prélude à l'après-midi d'un faune (Prelude to the Afternoon of a Faun), based on a poem by Mallarmé. This was later used for a ballet, with choreography by Nijinsky, who created a considerable scandal at the first performance. The music evokes a pagan world, as the satyr of the title takes his ease in the afternoon shade on a summer day.

The three symphonic sketches that constitute La mer (The Sea), published with a famous woodcut known as The Wave, from the Japanese artist Hokusai's views of Mount Fuji, an indication of oriental influence on Debussy, offer evocations of the sea from dawn to midday, of the waves and of the dialogue of wind and sea.

Other orchestral works by Debussy include the three movements of Nocturnes - Nuages (Clouds), Fêtes (Festivals) and Sirènes. Images, a work in three movements completed in 1912, includes Gigues, Ibéria and Ronde de printemps, the last a celebration of spring.

His Le martyre de Saint Sébastien, finally scored by André Caplet, was in origin a theatrical and choreographic collaboration with Gabriele d'Annunzio.

Debussy sketched out orchestration for his Rapsodie for saxophone and piano, completed after his death by Roger-Ducasse, an interesting addition to the repertoire of an instrument more often neglected by classical composers.

☛ **Recommended Recordings**

La mer / Nocturnes
Prélude à l'après-midi d'un faune
Naxos 8.550262

Images / Le martyre de Saint Sébastien
Berceuse héroïque / Marche écossaise
Naxos 8.550505

Chamber Music

Debussy's chamber music includes a fine string quartet, known as the first, although the second, like so much of the composer's work, existed only as a future project. Somewhat reluctantly he wrote a Rapsodie for saxophone, later orchestrated, while Syrinx, for unaccompanied flute, in which the pagan god Pan plays his flute, was originally written as incidental music for the theatre. Towards the end of his life Debussy planned a series of six chamber works, patriotically announced as by Claude Debussy, musicien français. He completed three of these projected works, a violin sonata, a cello sonata and a sonata for flute, viola and harp.

☞ **Recommended Recordings**

String Quartet No. 1
Naxos 8.550249

Violin Sonata
Naxos 8.550276

Vocal Music

Debussy made a significant addition to the French song repertoire, capturing the spirit, in particular, of the work of poets like Verlaine and Mallarmé, but also turning to earlier poets, including Villon and Charles d'Orléans. His Chansons de Bilitis, settings of verses by Pierre Louÿs, turn again to the pagan world, while the settings of the Verlaine Fêtes galantes, including Clair de lune, capture the nostalgia of the poems, yearning for an unattainable past.

Piano Music

In his writing for the piano Debussy proved himself a successor to Chopin, who had died in Paris thirteen years before Debussy's birth. His own debt to Chopin was overtly expressed in his two books of Etudes (Studies), completed in 1915. The two Arabesques, early works, enjoy continued popularity, as does the Suite bergamasque, with its all too popular Clair de lune. Estampes (Prints) evokes the Far East in Pagodes, Spain in La soirée dans Grenade (Evening in Granada), and autumnal sadness in Jardins sous la pluie (Gardens under the Rain), while L'isle joyeuse turns to Watteau for inspiration. Two sets of Images offer further delicate pictures, while the two books of Préludes offer still more varied images, from La fille aux cheveux de lin (The Girl with Flaxen Hair) and La cathédrale engloutie (The Submerged Cathedral) to the final Feux d'artifice (Fireworks). The single La plus que lente (More than slow) of 1910 and the light-hearted Children's Corner Suite form a further part of a larger series of works.

☞ **Recommended Recordings**

Images / Préludes / Suite bergamasque
Deux arabesques / La plus que lente
Naxos 8.550253

Piano Works Vol. I
(Suite bergamasque / Nocturne
Danse bohémienne / Rêverie / Mazurka
Deux arabesques / Valse romantique
Ballade / Danse / Suite: Pour le piano)
Naxos 8.553290

Piano Works Vol. 2
(Children's Corner Suite / La boite à joujoux
Epigraphes / The Little Negro)
Naxos 8.553291

Arrangements for 2 Pianos
Marco Polo 8.223378

Delalande, Michel-Richard

(1657 - 1726)

Variously known as La Lande, de La Lande or Delalande, Michel-Richard Delalande was a chorister at St Germain-l'Auxerrois in Paris and won a reputation as an organist and harpsichordist. In the former capacity he succeeded Charles Couperin at St Gervais, to hold the position until François Couperin came of age. He was later appointed court composer, gradually assuming fuller responsibilities, sharing a position with one unmusical son of Lully and succeeding another as superintendent of the royal chamber music. He enjoyed a successful and prosperous career in the service of Louis XIV and was also honoured by his successor.

Church Music

Delalande contributed significantly to the French grands motets, compositions for solo voice, chorus and instrumental ensemble that formed an important element in the music of the royal chapel at Versailles. Delalande left some seventy grands motets, representing the height of a form also used by Lully and Charpentier, in addition to other liturgical settings.

Instrumental Music

Delalande provided music for ballet and opera-ballet and from this assembled instrumental music for concert use, collected for publication in suites or Symphonies, to which were added a collection of instrumental music based on French Christmas carols, Symphonies de Noëls.

Delibes, Léo (1836 - 1891)

Delibes was trained at the Paris Conservatoire, where he achieved no particular distinction. His first major triumph came with the ballet Coppélia, based on a story by E.T.A. Hoffmann and staged at the Opéra in 1870. He excelled as a composer of operetta, his career culminating in equally successful operas of a more serious kind.

Ballets

Delibes won early success with Coppélia and its Hoffmann story of old Dr. Coppelius and his doll Coppélia, who seems to come to life. He followed this in 1876 with Sylvia, set in pagan Greece. The 1866 ballet La Source had given Delibes an earlier opportunity, in collaboration with the established composer Minkus.

Stage Works

In 1882 Delibes wrote a set of pastiche ancient airs and dances for Victor Hugo's play Le roi s'amuse, later to provide a subject for Verdi's opera Rigoletto. His opera Lakmé, dealing with the love of a British officer and the daughter of a Brahmin priest in mid-19th century India, provides the well known Bell Song for ambitious coloratura sopranos. The Flower Duet, popularised by its recent commercial use, remains singularly attractive. Delibes's last opera, Kassya, was orchestrated by Massenet after the composer's death.

☛ Recommended Recordings

Ballet Suites: Coppélia / Sylvia / La source
Le roi s'amuse: Ancient Airs & Dances
Kassya: Trepak
Naxos 8.550080

Coppelia (Complete Ballet)
Intermezzo from Naila
La Source (Suite No. 2) (2 CD's)
Naxos 8.553356-7

Sylvia (Complete Ballet) (2 CD's)
Naxos 8.553338-9

Delius, Frederick (1862 - 1934)

Born in 1862 in Bradford of German parentage, Delius was sent by his father to Florida as an orange-grower. There he developed further his earlier musical interests and eventually persuaded his father to support him during a period of musical study at Leipzig Conservatory, where he met Grieg. With continued paternal support he moved thereafter to Paris and in 1897 settled at Grez-sur-Loing with the painter Jelka Rosen, who later became his wife. His final years brought blindness and paralysis, the result of an early syphilitic infection, and his later music was dictated to the young English musician Eric Fenby, who became his amanuensis. Delius had a strong champion in the conductor Sir Thomas Beecham, who did much to bring his music before the British public. The musical language of Delius with a characteristic harmony and lyricism of its own often has a rhapsodic intensity of feeling.

Stage Works

The stage works of Delius include the lyric drama Koanga, a love- story set on a Mississippi plantation, where the heroine, the slave-girl Palmyra, rejects the advances of the overseer in favour of a prince of her own tribe, Koanga. La Calinda, from this opera, is a well known orchestral excerpt. The opera A Village Romeo and Juliet, based on a novel by Gottfried Keller, is generally known to concert-audiences because of the familiar orchestral interlude The Walk to the Paradise Garden, as the lovers walk together to a village inn. From the later opera Fennimore and Gerda comes an orchestral Intermezzo, arranged after the death of the composer by Eric Fenby. The opera Irmelin, first performed under Beecham only in 1953, offers an orchestral Prelude for concert repertoire. Incidental music for James Elroy Flecker's Hassan has again provided items for concert repertoire.

Orchestral Music

Popular orchestral works by Delius must include Brigg Fair, appropriately described as an English Rhapsody and the rhapsody In a Summer Garden. On Hearing the First Cuckoo in Spring and Summer Night on the River constitute two pieces for small orchestra, with a further work, A Song before Sunrise, for similar forces. Légende, for violin and orchestra, is a useful work for violinists,

and may also be heard in a violin and piano version. A rhapsodic Violin Concerto, a Cello Concerto and a Double Concerto for both instruments together are heard rather less frequently.

☛ Recommended Recordings

Brigg Fair / In a Summer Garden
Naxos 8.550229

Paris / Brigg Fair / Eventyr / Irmelin / La Calinda
Naxos 8.553001

Two Aquarelles
Naxos 8.550823

Choral & Orchestral Music

Music by Delius for singers and orchestra includes his variations on a traditional plantation song Appalachia and his Walt Whitman settings Sea Drift and Songs of Farewell. The remarkable A Mass of Life, based on Nietzsche, expresses the composer's own creed.

Chamber Music

Delius wrote three numbered violin sonatas, the third first performed and recorded by the violinist May Harrison with the composer Arnold Bax as pianist. The cellist Beatrice Harrison gave the first performance of Delius's Cello Sonata, accompanied by the composer Hamilton Harty.

Dittersdorf, Carl Ditters von

(1739 - 1799)

Dittersdorf had composition lessons from Giuseppe Bonno in his native Vienna and served as a violinist in the orchestra of the Prince of Sachsen-Hildburghausen, followed by a position in the imperial theatre. There followed a period as Kapellmeister to the Bishop of Grosswardein, where, in 1762, he succeeded Michael Haydn. In 1769 he became Kapellmeister to the Prince-Bishop of Breslau, at this period acquiring the patent of nobility that added to the name of Ditters the honorific von Dittersdorf. Conditions in Johannisberg, the seat of the Prince-Bishop, deteriorated in the political circumstances of the time, and on the death of his employer in 1795, he moved with his family to join the household of a nobleman in Bohemia.

Stage Works

Dittersdorf wrote a large number of stage works. The earlier Italian works written for Johannisberg were followed by a series of Singspiel primarily for Vienna, and eleven further such works in 1793 and 1794 for Duke Friedrich-August of Brunswick-Oels. These, all in all, mark an important stage in the development of the form.

Vocal and Choral Music

Dittersdorf made his due contribution to oratorio in four such works. He wrote settings of the Mass and other liturgical works, as well as cantatas and arias for church use. His secular vocal works are few.

Orchestral Music

In orchestral music Dittersdorf may be compared in some respects to his near contemporary Joseph Haydn. His 120 listed symphonies include a set of six giving musical expression to the Metamorphoses of Ovid and another 'nel gusto di 5 nazioni' (in the taste of five nations). His concertos, rather less in number, include eighteen for violin, five for viola, one for cello and one for double bass, as well as a double concerto for viola and double bass.

☛ **Recommended Recordings**

Six Symphonies on Ovid's Metamorphoses Vol. 1
Symphonies 1-3
Naxos 8.553368

Six Symphonies on Ovid's Metamorphoses Vol. 2
Symphonies 4-6
Naxos 8.553369

Chamber Music

The chamber music of Dittersdorf, with all the clarity of classical style, includes string quartets and quintets, divertimenti and compositions for groups of wind instruments.

Dohnányi, Ernő (1877 - 1960)

Ernő Dohnányi was born in Poszony (now Bratislava) in 1877 and opted for further musical study in Budapest rather than, more conventionally, in Vienna, setting an example that was followed by his younger contemporary Bartók. He played a leading part in forming the musical culture of Hungary, although there were difficulties with the régime that replaced the first republican government of the country. Due to his overt opposition to the association of Hungary with National Socialist Germany, he found it necessary to spend his final years in America, dying in New York in 1960.

As a composer Dohnányi was versatile, continuing existing traditions of music, while as a pianist he enjoyed international fame.

Orchestral Music

Although there is much in the music of Dohnányi to give pleasure, he is probably still best known abroad for his Variations on a Nursery Theme, for piano and orchestra.

Donizetti, Gaetano (1797 - 1848)

A native of Bergamo, Donizetti was, for nearly a decade after the early death of Bellini in 1835, the leading composer of Italian opera. He had his first success with Zoraida di Granata in 1822. There followed a series of nearly sixty more operas and removal to Paris, where Rossini had been induced to settle to his profit. His final illness confined him to a hospital in France for some 17 months, before his return to Bergamo, where he died in 1848. Donizetti was not exclusively a composer of opera, but wrote music of all kinds, songs, chamber music, piano music and a quantity of music for the church.

Operas

The opera Anna Bolena, which won considerable success when it was first staged in Milan in 1830, provides a popular soprano aria in its final Piangete voi ? Deserto in terra, from the last opera, Dom Sébastien, staged in Paris in 1843, has been a favourite with operatic tenors from Caruso to Pavarotti. The comedy Don Pasquale, staged in Paris in 1843, is a well-loved part of standard operatic repertoire, as is L'elisir d'amore (The Elixir of Love), from which the tenor aria Una furtiva lagrima (A hidden tear) is all too well known. Mention should be made of La Favorita and La Fille du régiment (The Daughter of the Regiment), both first staged in Paris in 1840 and sources of further operatic recital arias. Lucia di

Lammermoor, based on a novel by Sir Walter Scott, provides intense musical drama for tenors in the last act Tomba degl'avei miei (Tomb of My Forebears).

☛ Recommended Recordings

L'Elisir d'Amore
Naxos 8.660045-46 (2 CD's)

Lucia di Lammermoor:
Il dolce suono (Mad Scene)
Linda di Chamonix: O luce di quest'anima
Naxos 8.550605

Sinfonias (D Minor / A Major / D Major)
Marco Polo 8.223577

Instrumental Concerti
Marco Polo 8.223701

Allegro in C Major for Strings
Naxos 8.550621

Dowland, John (1563 - 1626)

John Dowland, of English or possibly Irish origin, was born in 1563, probably in London. He was a lutenist of distinction but failed, allegedly because he was a Catholic, to win a position in the royal service, seeking his fortune abroad at Kassel and later, in 1598, at the court of Christian IV of Denmark. He was forced by debt to return to England in 1606 and eventually won appointment as one of the King's Lutes in 1612. He performed during the funeral ceremonies of King James I and himself died the following year. Dowland was the composer, in particular, of one of the best known songs of the period, Flow my teares, music much imitated, epitomising the fashionable humour of the day, melancholy. Dowland himself provided an apt pun on his own name - Dowland, semper dolens (Dowland, always grieving) - although he had a reputation as a cheerful man, yet professionally embittered by his long failure to find employment at court.

Vocal Music

Dowland was above all the composer of lute-songs, publishing his first collection of airs in 1597, followed by a second in 1600 and a third in 1603. He left over eighty secular songs and these include Come again: sweet love doth now endite, Fine knacks for ladies and Flow my teares, among many others of moving intensity.

Lute Music

For the lute itself Dowland wrote Fantasias, and dance-movements, including Pavanes, Galliards, Almains and Jigs.

Other Instrumental Music

The best known of Dowland's instrumental compositions is his famous Lachrimae or Seaven Teares, for five viols and lute. This work includes a series of dance-movements, chiefly Galliards, and solemn Pavanes, using the theme familiar from the lute-song Flow my teares.

☞ **Recommended Recording**
Galliard a 5
Naxos 8.550331

Dufay, Guillaume (c. 1400 - 1474)

Generally regarded as the leading composer of his time, Guillaume Dufay was born in Cambrai at the beginning of the 15th century. A chorister at Cambrai Cathedral, he was briefly in the service of the Malatesta family in Italy, and after a further period at home, returned to join the papal choir in 1428. He was subsequently involved with a number of ruling families in Italy, including the d'Estes of Ferrara and the rulers of Savoy, before returning to Cambrai, where he retained a position as canon of the cathedral until his death. Dufay represents the generation influenced by the English composer John Dunstable and forming the so-called Burgundian or First Netherlands School of composers, flourishing in the territory ruled by the Dukes of Burgundy, but widespread in its own influence as the predominant Renaissance musical style.

Church Music

Dufay wrote a considerable quantity of church music. These compositions include a number of Mass settings, with one based on the most popular secular cantus firmus, L'homme armé, one on his own secular ballade Se la face ay pale and another on his Marian antiphon Ave regina caelorum. He asked for the Marian antiphon-motet Ave regina caelorum to be sung on his death-bed. His isorhythmic motet, a work using a particular rhythmic structural device developed in the previous century, Nuper rosarum flores, was performed at the dedication of the Brunelleschi dome in Florence in 1436. His motet O très piteulx / Omnes amici, a lament for the fall of Constantinople in 1453, was probably sung at the extravagant Banquet of the Oath of the Pheasant given by Philippe the Good of Burgundy at Lille in 1454, when an attempt was made to raise a Crusade to free the old Eastern capital of the Roman Empire.

☞ **Recommended Recording**
Missa l'homme armé
Supremum est mortalibus bonum
Naxos 8.553087

Secular Music

Dufay wrote more than seventy chansons setting verses in the fashionable forms of the time, the ballade, the virelai and rondeau. It would be invidious to make distinction between many of these, the majority in the form of rondeaux, although Adieu ces bons vins de Lannoys strikes a note of poetic nostalgia that may arouse sympathy.

☛ **Recommended Recording**
Chansons
Naxos 8.553458

Dukas, Paul (1865 - 1935)

A friend of Debussy at the Conservatoire and a pupil of Bizet's friend Guiraud, Paul Dukas came near to winning the Prix de Rome, but when he left the Conservatoire found an early musical career as a critic and as an orchestrator. His strong critical sense led him to destroy a number of his compositions and only to allow a relatively small number of works to be published. He remained influential and respected as a teacher.

Orchestral Music

By far the best known of the compositions of Dukas is the symphonic scherzo L'apprenti sorcier, (The Sorcerer's Apprentice), based on Goethe's poem Der Zauberlehrling. The music was later popularised by its inclusion in Walt Disney's Fantasia, with appropriate cartoon illustration. A year before, in 1896, Dukas had completed his only

symphony, a work that deserves more attention than it has generally received.

☛ **Recommended Recording**
The Sorcerer's Apprentice
Naxos 8.551148

Dunstable, John (c. 1390 - 1453)

Relatively little is known for certain about the life of the English composer Dunstable, although his influence on younger composers such as Dufay is hardly open to question. He is thought to have been in the service of the Duke of Bedford, possibly during the latter's regency of Paris and governorship of Normandy, from 1423 to 1429 and 1429 - 1435 respectively. This presence in France is based on very little evidence. Nevertheless contemporary copies of Dunstable's music appear relatively numerous on the continent of Europe, where he was held in some esteem.

Church Music

From a number of Marian compositions, one may single out Quam pulchra es and Ave regina caelorum. His motet Veni Sancte Spiritus / Veni Creator Spiritus, using the technique of isorhythm, with the application of a recurrent rhythmic pattern to a given series of notes, was intended for the Whitsunday liturgy.

Secular Music

O rosa bella has been attributed to others. With Je languis en piteux martire, Puisque m'amour, Durer ne puis and I pray you all secular music constitute the surviving body of Dunstable's secular music.

Duparc, Henri (1848 - 1933)

The French composer Henri Duparc wrote remarkably little music, leaving thirteen songs that nevertheless have some importance as part of French vocal repertoire. Although never a full-time student of music, Duparc took lessons from César Franck. He published his first five songs in 1868. His last surviving song was written in 1884. Thereafter, suffering from a nervous complaint, he gave up composition.

Vocal Music

The small number of songs by Duparc constitute an important and well enough known part of French mélodie repertoire. These include a setting of Baudelaire's L'invitation au voyage, later orchestrated, as was La vie antérieure by the same poet. Duparc made orchestrations also of the accompaniments of Chanson triste, Au pays où se fait la guerre, Le manoir de Rosemonde, Phidylé and Testament.

Duphly, Jacques (1715 - 1789)

Jacques Duphly belongs to the French harpsichordist tradition. Born in Rouen, where he was employed as an organist, he moved to Paris in 1742 and there won a reputation as a teacher, one of the best, according to the famous harpsichord-maker Pascal Taskin, and as a performer.

Keyboard Music

The harpsichord music of Duphly owes much to the example of Rameau. The greater part of it was published in his life-time in four collections, the third of which includes a possible violin accompaniment.

Durey, Louis (1888 - 1979)

Strongly influenced by Debussy's opera Pelléas et Mélisande, Louis Durey joined the informal Groupe des Six, the six young French composers under the influence of Satie and Cocteau, but soon took a divergent course that allowed increasing scope for his political affiliations. He was Secretary General of the Fédération Musicale

Populaire and later of the Association Française des Musiciens Progressistes.

Dramatic Works

Durey's music for the theatre includes the Chant des partisans coréens, incidental music, among other works.

Orchestral Music

Durey wrote a Concertino for piano, wind instruments, double bass and timpani, a Mouvement symphonique for piano and strings and a string Sinfonietta, as well as a Fantaisie concertante for cello, among other relatively large scale compositions.

Chamber Music

Chamber music by Durey includes a flute sonatina, a string trio and Les soirées de Vallère for wind quintet, in addition to his three string quartets.

Vocal and Choral Music

Durey's political affiliations are clear from his setting of two poems by Ho Chi Minh and the choral La longue marche, with words by Mao Tse Tung. There are notable settings of poems by Apollinaire, Eluard and Cocteau, among the first Le bestiaire (The Bestiary) and, with words by Cocteau, Le printemps au fond de la mer.

Piano Music

Durey wrote Carillons and Neige (Snow) for piano duet, three sonatinas and Obsession, the last later orchestrated.

Duruflé, Maurice (1902 - 1986)

The French organist and composer Maurice Duruflé was a pupil of Tournemire and Gigout and enjoyed a career as an organist both in Paris and in numerous concert tours abroad, a representative of the French tradition of organ-playing and composition inherited from his teachers, and from the example of Guilmant and Vierne.

Organ Music

Duruflé's organ music includes a Prélude, adagio and choral varié on the Veni Creator Spiritus, a Suite and a Prelude and Fugue in memory of the composer and organist Jehan Alain, killed in action in 1940.

Church Music

Duruflé's best known work is his Requiem, music firmly founded on Gregorian chant in its melodic material and treatment of the liturgical text. He also left a number of motets and a Mass setting.

Recommended Recordings

Requiem / Quatre Motets Op. 10
Scherzo Op. 2 / Notre Père Op. 14
Prélude et fugue sur le nom d' A.L.A.I.N. Op. 7
Naxos 8.553196

Messe "cum jubilo"
Prélude, adagio et choral varié Op. 4
Suite pour orgue Op. 5
Naxos 8.553197

Dussek, Jan Ladíslav (1760 - 1816)

Born and educated in Bohemia, latterly at the University of Prague, Dussek for some years led a peripatetic existence as a pianist that took him to Holland, to Russia, to Lithuania, to various cities in Germany, with possible lessons from C.P.E.Bach in Hamburg and, in 1786, to Paris. With the revolution he took refuge, in 1789, in London, where he married the singer, pianist and harpist Sophia Corri. Here he joined his father-in-law in music publishing and persauded the piano-maker Broadwood to extend the range of the keyboard. In 1799, with the failure of his business, Dussek moved to Hamburg, performed successfully in Bohemia and entered the service of Prince Louis Ferdinand of Prussia, whose death he mourned in an elegiac piano sonata. His final years were spent in the service of Talleyrand in Paris, where he died in 1812.

Orchestral Music

Dussek wrote a number of concertos for piano, piano and harp and two pianos. He makes some demands for virtuosity in music that was much admired in his own time.

Recommended Recording

Sonata No. 2 for Harp, Op. 34
Harp Concerto Op. 15
Naxos 8.553622

Chamber Music

Chamber music by Dussek includes a number of sonatas for violin and piano and some for piano trio. The harp features quite extensively in original compositions and transcriptions, there are string quartets, piano quintets and a Serenade for nonet. A topical novelty is The Naval Battle and Total Defeat of the Dutch Fleet by Admiral Duncan, scored for piano, violin, cello and percussion.

Piano Music

As a pianist, Dussek wrote a number of works for piano. These include The Sufferings of the Queen of France (The Farewell), written in 1793, and Elégie harmonique sur la mort du Prince Lous Ferdinand de Prusse (Harmonic Elegy on the Death of Prince Louis Ferdinand of Prussia), in addition to a series of less programmatic sonatas, many in an incipient romantic idiom that has some passing resemblance at times to the musical idiom of other composers.

Dutilleux, Henri (1916 -)

The French composer Henri Dutilleux, although individual in his approach, nevertheless follows the traditions of Ravel and Debussy, seeking clarity and economy in his musical language and an enjoyment of varied timbres.

Orchestral Music

In his two symphonies Dutilleux explores novel combinations of sound, in the first contrasting groups and single instruments and in the second dividing the orchestra into a smaller chamber group, separate from the larger body. His Métaboles of 1964 allows a gradual emergence of thematic material, as, in a measure, does Tout un monde lointain . . . , a work for cello and orchestra written between 1968 and 1970.

Chamber Music

Similar qualities are to be heard in the chamber music of Dutilleux, with its idiomatic use of wind instruments, and in the string quartet of 1976, Thus the Night.

Duvernoy, Frédéric Nicolas
(1765 - 1838)

An important figure in the establishment of a French school of French horn playing, Duvernoy occupied a leading position as a performer in his own time, employed as a principal player at the Opéra in Paris. He was much admired by Napoleon and retained official favour under his immediate successors, until 1830.

French Horn Music

Duvernoy's compositions are principally for his own instrument and include concertos and chamber music, in addition to an important Méthode pour le cor (Method for the Horn).

☞ **Recommended Recording**
Horn Trio
Naxos 8.550441

Dvořák, Antonín (1841 - 1904)

The later 19th century brought an increasing consciousness of national identity to various ethnic groups in Europe and elsewhere in the world. Dvořák, born in a Bohemian village, where his father was an inn-keeper and butcher, followed Smetana as the leading exponent of Czech musical nationalism, firmly within the classical traditions of Central Europe. His early musical training was followed by employment for some years as a violist, for a time under Smetana, and then, with the positive encouragement of Brahms, by a life primarily devoted to composition. Dvořák won recognition abroad and rather more grudging acceptance in Vienna. Between 1892 and 1895 he spent some time in the United States of America as director of the new National Conservatory, a period that brought compositions that combine American and Bohemian influence. At home again he was much honoured, resisting invitations from Brahms to move to Vienna in favour of a simple life in his own country. He died in 1904, shortly after the first performances of his last opera, Armida.

Orchestral Music

Dvořák wrote nine symphonies, of which the best known must be the Symphony No. 9, From the New World, written in 1893 and first performed in New York in the same year. This New World Symphony derived some inspiration from a Czech translation of Longfellow's poem Hiawatha.

Works for solo instrument and orchestra by Dvořák include an important Cello Concerto, a Violin Concerto and a slightly less well known Piano Concerto. The Romance for solo violin and orchestra, and Silent Woods

for cello and orchestra, make interesting and attractive additions to solo repertoire for both instruments.

Other orchestral works include two sets of Slavonic Dances, arrangements of works originally designed for piano duet, and three Slavonic Rhapsodies. Overtures include My Home, In Nature's Realm, Othello, Hussite and Carnival. To this one may add the Scherzo capriccioso of 1883, a Polonaise, written four years before, and the splendid Serenade for Strings of 1875. The Symphonic Variations meet the challenge of an apparently intractable theme and the ten Legends were orchestrated by the composer from his original piano duet version. To this may be added the symphonic poems The Noonday Witch, The Golden Spinning-Wheel and The Wild Dove, works that seem to explore new ground, with their narrative content.

☞ Recommended Recordings

Symphony No. 1 / Legends Nos. 1-5
Naxos 8.550266

Symphony No. 2 / Legends Nos. 6-10
Naxos 8.550267

Symphonies Nos. 3 & 6
Naxos 8.550268

Symphonies Nos. 4 & 8
Naxos 8.550269

Symphonies Nos. 5 & 7
Naxos 8.550270

Symphony No. 9 "From the New World"
Symphonic Variations
Naxos 8.550271

Symphonic Poems:
The Noonday-Witch, The Golden Spinning-Wheel and The Wild Dove
Naxos 8.550598

Serenade for Strings
Naxos 8.550419

Polonaise / Scherzo capriccioso
Slavonic Rhapsody
Naxos 8.550376

Slavonic Rhapsodies
Naxos 8.550610

Slavonic Dances Opp. 46 & 72
Naxos 8.550143

Cello Concerto
Naxos 8.550503

Overtures: Vanda / In Nature's Realm
Carnival / Othello / My Home
Naxos 8.550600

Opera Overtures and Preludes
Marco Polo 8.223272

Rhapsody Op. 14
Overtures (Vanda / Selma Sedlak / Dramatic)
Marco Polo 8.220420

Czech Suite, Op. 39 / Hussite Overture, Op. 67
Festival March, Op. 54 / A Hero's Song, Op. 111
Naxos 8.553005

Piano Concerto Op. 33 / The Water Goblin
Naxos 8.550896

Violin Concerto Op. 53
Romance for Violin and Orchestra Op. 11
Naxos 8.550758

The Wild Dove / The Noon Witch
The Golden Spinning-Wheel
Naxos 8.550598

Chamber Music

Dvořák left fourteen string quartets, of which the best known is the so-called American Quartet, No. 12 in F Major, written in 1893, the year of the Symphony from the New World. The composition of Quartets Nos. 13 and 14, in 1895, seems to have taken place over the same period. From the American period comes the G major Sonatina for violin and piano, its second movement sometimes known as Indian Lament. Of the four surviving piano trios the fourth, nick-named the Dumky because of its use of a Bohemian national dance-form, is the best known, closely rivalled in popularity by the third. Dvořák's quintets for piano and strings or strings alone offer further pleasure, with the String Sextet and the charming Terzetto for two violins and viola

Recommended Recordings

String Quartets Op. 96 "American" & Op. 105
Naxos 8.550251

String Quartets Opp. 96 and 106
Naxos 8.553371

String Quartets Opp. 61 & 80
Naxos 8.553372

String Quartet No. 9, Op. 34
Terzetto for 2 Violins and Viola, Op. 74
Naxos 8.553373

Piano Music

The best known of all the pieces Dvořák wrote for the piano must be the Humoresque in G flat major, the seventh of a set of eight. Close to this come the two sets of Slavonic Dances for piano duet.

Recommended Recording

Four-Hand Piano Music Vol. I
Legends, Op. 59 / From the Bohemian Forest
Naxos 8.553137

Operas

Dvořák wrote nine operas, the first in 1870 and the last completed and staged in 1903. Rusalka, first produced in 1900, provides a well known concert aria, O silver moon.

Songs

Dvořák wrote a number of songs and a popular set of Moravian Duets for soprano and contralto. The most popular of the songs is the fourth of Seven Gypsy Songs, Op. 55, Songs my mother taught me.

Elgar, Edward (1857 - 1934)

Edward Elgar was arguably the leading English composer of his generation and a significant figure among late Romantic European musicians. Born in the West of England in 1857, the son of a piano-tuner and owner of a music shop, he earned his earlier living as an organist, violinist and teacher in his own part of the country. After his marriage in 1889 he found himself able to move to London as a composer, but success only came later, after his return to the West Country, confirmed by the Enigma Variations, first performed in London in 1899. He wrote relatively little after the death of his wife in 1920.

Choral/Orchestral Music

Elgar wrote a number of oratorios. The Dream of Gerontius, a setting of words by Cardinal Newman, is rather different, a remarkable study of a man on his deathbed.

Orchestral Music

The Enigma Variations, with its portraits in each variation of one of the composer's friends and its unsolved musical puzzle, in the well known melody that Elgar claimed would go with the theme itself, is one of the best of his works. More familiar, if less substantial, must be the Pomp and Circumstance Marches. The concert overture Cockaigne is an evocation of London, while the Elegy, the Introduction and Allegro and the Serenade, all for string orchestra, offer music of the highest quality. Elgar's Cello Concerto, written in 1919, enjoys great popularity, not yet matched by that of the earlier Violin Concerto, composed before the war. Elgar's two completed symphonies are comparable, at least, to the work of other great symphonists of the period.

☛ Recommended Recordings

Enigma Variations
Pomp & Circumstance Marches Nos. 1 & 4
Naxos 8.550229

Elegy / Introduction & Allegro / Serenade
Naxos 8.550331

Cello Concerto
Naxos 8.550503

Violin Concerto / Cockaigne
Naxos 8.550489

Symphony No. 1 / Imperial March
Naxos 8.550634

Symphony No. 2
Naxos 8.550635

Chamber Music

Elgar wrote a number of pieces for violin and piano during the earlier part of his life. Of the smaller pieces that survive Chanson de nuit and Chanson de matin have considerable charm. Of much greater weight are the three chamber works of 1918, the Violin Sonata in E minor, String Quartet in the same key and Piano Quintet in A minor.

Piano Music

Elgar wrote relatively little for the piano, but his Salut d'amour (Love's Greeting) originally written with a German title for his wife, has proved popular both in its original form and in a multitude of arrangements.

☛ Recommended Recording

Salut d'amour (Orchestrated)
Naxos 8.550229

Emmanuel, Maurice (1862 - 1938)

A pupil of Delibes at the Paris Conservatoire, Maurice Emmanuel also studied a wide range of subjects at the Sorbonne and the Ecole du Louvre. The disapproval expressed by Delibes of an early composition led him to study with Bizet's friend Guiraud. Having specialised in a study of ancient Greek dance, he was eventually appointed to the Conservatoire as teacher of the history of music, a position he held for 25 years. His interest in earlier music is reflected in his modal musical language.

Stage Works

Emmanuel's interest in Greek drama is apparent from his two operas based on Aeschylus, Prométhée enchaîné (Prometheus Bound) and Salamine.

Orchestral Music

There is a literary basis to Emmanuel's two symphonies, as there is to his Le poème du Rhône (Poem of the Rhone), derived from the poet Mistral.

☛ **Recommended Recording**
   Symphonies Nos. 1 and 2
   Le poème du Rhône
   Marco Polo 8.223507

Chamber Music

Emmanuel's chamber music includes a trio for flute, clarinet and piano, a string quartet and the early cello sonata that earned such condemnation from Delibes.

Piano Music

Piano music by Emmanuel consists chiefly of six sonatinas, the earlier with programmatic titles and the fourth based on Hindu modes.

Enescu, George (1881 - 1955)

The greatest of Romanian musicians, George Enescu was equally remarkable as a violinist and as a composer. He contributed significantly to the development of music in his own country, although much of his activity centred on Paris, where he was a pupil of Marsick and for composition of Fauré and Massenet. His violin pupils include Grumiaux, Ferras, Gitlis and Menuhin.

Orchestral Music

Although much that he wrote may be of greater musical significance, Enescu's most popular composition is the Romanian Rhapsody No. 1.

☛ **Recommended Recording**
   Romanian Rhapsodies Nos. 1 & 2
   Naxos 8.550327

Falla, Manuel de (1876 - 1946)

The music of Spain has exercised an exotic fascination, but often in forms adapted by foreign composers. Manuel de Falla is representative of a group of Spanish composers who won international recognition. He was born in 1876 in Cádiz, where he first studied, moving later to Madrid and then to Paris, but returning to Madrid when war broke out in 1914. Strongly influenced by the traditional Andalusian cante jondo, he settled in

Granada, where his friends included the poet Federico Garcia Lorca. The Civil War of 1936 found de Falla neutral in the struggle, but in 1939 he moved to Buenos Aires, where he continued work on his ambitious stage-work Atlántida, which remained unfinished at the time of his death in 1946.

Stage Works

Manuel de Falla helped to support his family in Madrid, after a change in their fortunes, by composing zarzuelas, typically Spanish musical comedies. His first substantial stage work was the lyric drama La vida breve, completed in 1905 and first staged in Nice in 1913. The ballet El amor brujo (Love the Magician), with its ghostly story of gypsy jealousy, was first staged in Madrid two years later. The ballet El sombrero de tres picos (The Three-Cornered Hat), reached its final form for its London production under the impresario Dyagilev in 1919. The puppet opera El retablo de maese Pedro, based on an episode in the classical Cervantes novel Don Quixote, was completed in 1922. There are popular orchestral suites from the first three of these four works.

☛ **Recommended Recordings**
The Three-Cornered Hat Suites Nos. 1 & 2
El amor brujo: Ritual Fire Dance
La vida breve: Interlude & Dance
Naxos 8.550174

El Amor Brujo / El Retablo Maese Pedro
Naxos 8.553499

Orchestral Music

In addition to the concert version of El amor brujo and two suites from El sombrero de tres picos made by the composer, Manuel de Falla wrote an evocatively beautiful work for solo piano and orchestra under the title Noches en los jardines de España (Nights in the Gardens of Spain) completed in 1915.

Vocal Music

In 1915 de Falla also completed his arrangement of seven popular Spanish songs, Siete canciones populares españolas, familiar not only in the original vocal version but in arrangements, particularly an effective arrangement for violin and piano.

Chamber Music

Among chamber works by de Falla may be included the Concerto for harpsichord, with flute, oboe, clarinet, violin and cello, making use of the early keyboard instrument that had played an important part in his puppet opera El retablo de maese Pedro.

Piano Music

Piano works occupy a less important element among the compositions of Manuel de Falla, although the four

Spanish Pieces and the early Serenata Andaluza offer pieces in characteristically Spanish musical idiom.

Farnaby, Giles (c. 1563 - 1640)

A Londoner and a joiner by trade, Giles Farnaby occupies an ambivalent position in the English music of his period, lacking something of the consistency of his more distinguished contemporaries and apparently, in the long run, lacking material success either as a musician or as a joiner or virginal-maker.

Keyboard Music

Chief among Farnaby's surviving compositions are eleven Fantasias for virginals. There is a smaller number of keyboard pieces still extent by Farnaby's son Richard.

Fauré, Gabriel (1845 - 1924)

In the rigid official musical establishment of Paris in the second half of the 19th century Gabriel Fauré won acceptance with difficulty. He was a pupil of Camille Saint-Saëns at the Ecole Niedermeyer and served as organist at various Paris churches, including finally the Madeleine, but had no teaching position until 1897 at the Conservatoire, where his pupils included Ravel and Enescu. In 1905 he became director of the Conservatoire

in the aftermath of the scandal of the refusal of the Prix de Rome to Ravel and introduced a number of necessary reforms. He retired in 1920, after which he was able to devote himself more fully again to composition, notably two final chamber works, a piano trio and a string quartet. He died in Paris in 1924.

Stage Works

In 1893 Fauré wrote incidental music for a production of Molière's Le bourgeois gentilhomme. The Sicilienne for this production was later used again in incidental music for Maeterlinck's Pelléas et Mélisande and later still won popularity in a variety of arrangements, including the composer's own orchestral version and arrangement for violin or cello and piano.

There is a concert suite from Pelléas et Mélisande, orchestrated by Fauré's pupil Koechlin.

Orchestral Music

Fauré's nostalgic Pavane is an orchestral work with an optional chorus part, added at the suggestion of a patron, but generally omitted in modern performance. Music for solo instrument and orchestra includes the Ballade for piano and orchestra, the Berceuse for solo violin and the Elégie for solo cello. The piano duet Dolly Suite was arranged for orchestra in 1906 by Henri Rabaud.

Vocal

Fauré is a song composer of major importance, capturing in his settings the spirit of his time, the mood of nostalgic yearning for the unattainable. Some of the songs, such as Après un rêve (After a Dream) have achieved even wider popularity in instrumental transcription. In addition to individual songs of great beauty, Lydia, Clair de lune, Les roses d'Ispahan, Sylvia, En prière and many others, there are song cycles, including the Verlaine settings La bonne chanson and Cinq mélodies de Venise, L'horizon chimérique, La chanson d'Eve and Le jardin clos.

Church Music

Fauré's Requiem remains a standard element in choral repertoire, with its setting of funeral rites, rather than the full Requiem Mass of tradition. The earlier Messe basse (Low Mass) was originally a collaborative compositon of 1881 with Messager, but in final revision in 1906 consisting of four Mass movements by Fauré himself.

☞ **Recommended Recording**

Requiem / Messe basse
Cantique de Jean Racine
Naxos 8.550765

Chamber Music

Chamber music by Fauré includes two fine Violin Sonatas and the Piano Trio and String Quartet of his last years. There are several evocative smaller pieces, including the Romance, Berceuse and Andante for violin and piano and the Elégie, Romance and Sérénade for cello and piano.

☞ **Recommended Recording**

Violin Sonatas Nos. 1 and 2
Berceuse / Romance / Andante
Naxos 8.550906

Piano Music

Fauré made a significant addition to piano repertoire, particularly in a series of thirteen Barcarolles and a similar number of Nocturnes, with five Impomptus and a single Ballade. The piano duet Dolly Suite was written in the 1890s for the daughter of Emma Bardac, later wife of Debussy, after divorce from her banker husband, a singer for whom Fauré wrote La bonne chanson.

☞ **Recommended Recordings**

Nocturnes Nos. 1-6
Theme and Variations Op. 73
Naxos 8.550794

Nocturnes Nos. 7-13
Preludes Op. 103, Nos. 3 & 9
Trois Romances sans paroles Op. 17
Naxos 8.550795

Barcarolles Nos. 1 to 13
Ballade, Op. 19
Naxos 8.553634

Fayrfax, Robert (1464 - 1521)

Robert Fayrfax enjoyed royal favour under Henry VIII as a gentleman of the Chapel Royal. He was one of the most improtant English composers of his generation and has had the posthumous advantage that a number of his works have survived.

Church Music

Fayrfax is in particular associated wth the cyclic Mass, settings of the Mass in which related material appears in each section, generally based on a plainsong tenor. His settings of the Magnificat are of alternate verses, to be interspersed, according to common practice, by verses sung to plainchant.

Secular Music

Fayrfax wrote a number of part-songs, of which some seven survive.

Fíala, Joseph (1748 - 1816)

Cellist, oboist and player of the viola da gamba, the Czech composer Joseph Fiala joined the musical establishment of the Elector of Bavaria in Munich, where he met and impressed Mozart. He later took employment in Salzburg, moved in 1785 to Vienna and thence to the Russian imperial service in St Petersburg. He impressed the cello-playing King of Prussia by his performance on the viola da gamba and from 1792 until his death served as Kapellmeister to Prince Fürstenberg at Donaueschingen.

Orchestral Music

Orchestral compositions by Fiala include concertos for oboe and for cor anglais and a double horn concerto. He wrote a number of works for wind band.

☞ **Recommended Recording**
Concerto in E Flat for 2 Horns
Naxos 8.550459

Chamber Music

Chamber music by Fiala includes string quartets and quartets with oboe, as well as sets of duos for violin and cello.

Field, John (1782 - 1837)

To the Irish pianist and composer John Field has been credited the invention of the Nocturne, a form later adopted and developed by Chopin. Field was born in Dublin in 1782, the son of a violinist, but moved with his family to London in 1793, perhaps taking violin lessons from Haydn's friend Salomon. He became an apprentice of Muzio Clementi, appearing in a series of important London concerts, and later touring widely. After concerts in Russia, he remained in St. Petersburg, where he became a fashionable teacher and performer, moving to Moscow in 1821. Illness brought him, in 1831, to London again, a visit followed by a continental tour and a final return to Moscow, where he died in 1837.

Piano Music

Although Field wrote seven piano concertos and a series of chamber compositions for piano and strings, his chief claim on posterity lies in his eighteen Nocturnes.

Finzi, Gerald (1901 - 1956)

Of Italian Jewish ancestry, Gerald Finzi was among the most English of composers, spending much of his life in the countryside of Hampshire and later near Newbury, where the string orchestra he founded became an important vehicle for the performance of his music. His interest in earlier English music and in English literature is largely reflected in his own music, which owes something to Parry, to his older contemporary Vaughan Williams and to Elgar.

Orchestral Music

Finzi's orchestral music includes a Clarinet Concerto and a Cello Concerto, with a Grand Fantasia and Toccata for piano and orchestra.

Vocal and Choral Music

Choral music by Finzi's demonstrates his wide knowledge of English literature, with settings of poems by near contemporaries such as Edmund Blunden and Robert Bridges and by the 17th century poets Crashaw, Traherne and Vaughan. His setting of Wordsworth's Intimation of Immortality was performed at the West of England Three Choirs Festival in 1950, while his Dies natalis, for soprano or tenor and string orchestra, setting poems by Traherne, was originally intended for the same festival in 1939. The cycle Let us garlands bring, settings of Shakespearian verses for baritone and piano was also arranged for baritone and string orchestra, and other groups of songs aptly set poems by Hardy.

Flotow, Friedrich von (1812 - 1883)

The music of the German nobleman Friedrich von Flotow, nowadays enjoys much less popularity than it once did, when his opera Martha was first staged in Vienna in 1847. He had varying success in Paris and in Vienna with other stage works.

Operas

Martha or Richmond Market deals with the story of two girls, who in jest disguise themselves as countrywomen and sell themselves as servants at Richmond Market, only to find that they are legally bound to their new masters for a year. Still popular extracts from the opera include the tenor Porter Song, Lasst mich euch fragen and the even more celebrated Ach, so fromm, (M'appari in its equally well known Italian version). In the second act Martha, alias Lady Harriet, Maid of Honour to Queen Anne, sings the Irish song The Last Rose of Summer, music that somehow seems appropriate enough in this unlikely context.

☞ **Recommended Recording**

M'appari tutt'amor (from Martha)
Naxos 8.551172

Forqueray, Antoine (c. 1671 - 1745)

Antoine Forqueray, described as crabbed, crotchety and odd in character, won an unrivalled reputation as a player of the bass viol and was appointed Musicien ordinaire de la chambre du roy in 1689. His wife, a harpsichord-player, accompanied him in recitals, but the couple separated in 1710, eleven years after the birth of their son Jean-Baptiste. It is to this last that the publication and possibly the arrangement for harpsichord of music by his father is credited. By 1730 Antoine Forqueray had retired to Nantes, where he died in 1745. He had been succeeded at court by Jean-Baptiste in 1742.

Harpsichord Music

Antoine Forqueray's harpsichord suites, published by his son in 1747 as Pièces de viole mises en pièces de clavecin, explore the resonant lower register of the French harpsichord of the time, each movement bearing a characteristic title, often chosen to honour some contemporary, as in La Couperin or La Régente.

☞ **Recommended Recording**

Harpsichord Suites Nos. 1, 3 and 5
Naxos 8.553407

Viol Music

Forqueray's technique as a virtuoso of the bass viol is reflected in the 29 pieces published by his son in 1747.

Fossa, François de (1775 - 1849)

François de Fossa, born in Perpignan in 1775, fought as a soldier in Spain against the French invaders and subsequently served in Mexico. He later saw service in France. His work as a composer, generally neglected until recently, includes instrumental music that shows a clear understanding of the possibilities of the guitar.

Guitar Music

De Fossa's three Trios concertants for guitar, violin and cello, show something of the influence of Boccherini, a resident of Madrid for 37 years, until his death in 1805. This is heard particularly in the handling of the cello in the Trios, while his own knowledge of the guitar is clear from his writing for the instrument. He also wrote a set of quartets with guitar.

☛ **Recommended Recording**

Guitar Trios (Trios concertants, Op. 18)
Naxos 8.550760

Françaix, Jean (1912 -)

A composer of great facility and consistent wit, Jean Françaix, a pupil of Nadia Boulanger, has written music of charm and elegance, inventive and attractive in idiom, with instrumental works that show the characteristic French handling of woodwind instruments.

Stage Works

The fifth of the operas of Jean Françaix, La Princesse de Clèves, exemplifies his qualities as a composer, heard also in his various ballet and film scores.

Orchestral Music

The Piano Concertino of 1932, written while Françaix was a student, won immediate popularity. Other concertos include a Piano Concerto and a Two Piano Concerto, a Violin Concertino and concertos for clarinet and for flute, as well as a number of other works making use of varied groups of solo instruments.

Chamber Music

There is particularly idiomatic handling of wind instruments in a number of works for instrumental ensemble, including a Saxophone Quartet. There is a Sonatine for violin and piano and another for trumpet and piano, while the Neuf pièces charactéristiques for ten wind instruments have a particular charm.

Keyboard Music

Keyboard music by Françaix includes L'insectarium for harpsichord, Huit danses exotiques for two pianos, a Marche solennelle for organ and a Piano Sonata.

Vocal and Choral Music

Solo vocal and choral settings by Françaix range from an oratorio, L'apocalypse de St Jean, to a cantata for mezzo-soprano and strings, Déploration de Tonton, chien fidèle (Lament for Tonton, faithful dog), with settings of La Fontaine and Rabelais.

Franck, César (1822 - 1890)

Born at Liège in 1822, César Franck was originally intended by his father for a career as a virtuoso pianist. In Paris his nationality excluded him at first from the Conservatoire, where he eventually failed to achieve the necessary distinction as a performer, turning his attention rather to composition. In 1846 he left home and went to earn his living as a teacher and organist, winning particular fame in the second capacity at the newly built church of Ste. Clotilde, with its Cavaillé-Coll organ. He drew to him a loyal and devoted circle of pupils and in 1871 won some official recognition as the nominated successor of Benoist as organ professor at the Conservatoire. A man of gentle character, known to his pupils as Pater seraphicus, he exercised considerable influence through his classes and performances, although remaining something of an outsider as a composer in a Paris interested largely in opera.

Orchestral Music

Franck's best known orchestral works are the Symphonic Variations for solo piano and orchestra and the Symphony in D minor, completed in 1888 and first performed at a Conservatoire concert the following year. A brief series of symphonic poems includes the early Ce qu'on entend sur la montagne, based on Victor Hugo, Le chasseur maudit, inspired by a ballad by Burger, Les Djinns, after Hugo, and Psyché, a work that also calls for a chorus.

☞ Recommended Recordings

Symphony in D Minor
Naxos 8.550155

Variations Symphoniques
Naxos 8.550754

Sacred Music

Franck wrote a number of large scale choral works on biblical subjects, with smaller scale works for occasional or liturgical use. This last category includes the well known Panis angelicus of 1872, originally for tenor, organ, harp, cello and double bass. The Panis angelicus was later interpolated into the three-voice Mass of 1861.

Chamber Music

Franck wrote one Violin Sonata, which, like his symphony, is united by a cyclic use of thematic material that connects the movements. There is a fine Piano Quintet, completed in 1879 and a final String Quartet, written in 1890.

☞ **Recommended Recording**

Violin Sonata
Naxos 8.550417

Organ Music

As a very distinguished organist, Franck wrote remarkably little for the instrument on which his improvisations had won him fame and pupils. Organ compositions published include Trois chorals of 1890 and three pieces, Trois pièces, written a dozen years earlier. The six organ pieces of 1860-62 include a Fantaisie, Grande pièce symphonique, Prélude, fugue et variation, Pastorale, Prière and Final.

Piano Music

Franck's earlier piano music was designed for his own virtuoso performance. Two later works remain in general repertoire, the Prélude, choral et fugue of 1884 and the Prélude, aria et final completed in 1887.

Frescobaldi, Girolamo (1583 - 1643)

Frescobaldi must be accounted one of the most important keyboard composers of the first half of the 17th century. He was born in Ferrara, where the musical tastes of the ruling duke, Alfonso II d'Este, attracted musicians of great distinction. Moving to Rome at the beginning of the new century, he was under the patronage of Guido Bentivoglio, who took him in 1607 to Brussels, an important centre of keyboard music in the northern European tradition. In 1608 he became organist at St. Peter's in Rome, where he remained until his death, with a brief absence for promised employment in Mantua in 1615 and a subsequent period of six years serving the Medici in Florence.

Keyboard Music

As an important composer for the organ and other keyboard instruments, Frescobaldi published a number of collections of keyboard pieces, as well as compositions for varied groups of instruments. The keyboard works include Toccatas, Caprices, Ricercari and dance movements.

Gabrieli, Giovanni (c. 1558 - 1613)

Nephew of Andrea Gabrieli, organist at St. Mark's in Venice from 1566 until his death twenty years later, Giovanni Gabrieli was appointed to a permanent position at the same basilica in 1585, where he also served as organist until his death in 1613. His work as a composer represents the height of musical achievement in Renaissance Venice.

Church Music

Gabrieli continued the traditional cori spezzati techniques developed at St. Mark's during the century, contrasting different groups of singers and instrumentalists and making use of the spacial effects possible in the great basilica. His eight-part setting of the Jubilate, using double choir and brass, is characteristic of his style of writing.

Instrumental Music

The most widely known of Gabrieli's works is the Sonata pian' e forte, an eight-part composition for two four-part groups of wind instruments included in the Sacrae symphoniae of 1597, with a number of instrumental Canzoni for between six and sixteen parts. These works, and a quantity of compositions of a similar kind, including Toccatas and Ricercars, have provided an interesting repertoire for modern brass-players, although originally they were played by instruments that included sackbuts (the earlier form of trombone), cornetti (curved wooden instruments with a cup-shaped mouth-piece) and other instruments of the period.

Gade, Niels (1817 - 1890)

The Danish composer Niels Gade started his musical career as a violinist in the Danish Royal Orchestra. His first success as a composer came in 1840 with his overture Echoes of Ossian. His First Symphony was accepted by Mendelssohn and performed by the Gewandhaus Orchestra in Leipzig, where the composer met Mendelssohn and Schumann, succeeding the former as conductor of the Gewandhaus Orchestra in 1847. The following year he returned to Denmark, where he came to assume a leading position in the musical life of the country, writing music in a style greatly influenced by Mendelssohn and Schumann.

Orchestral Music

Gade's orchestral music includes eight symphonies, a Violin Concerto and several concert overtures, with an evocative A Summer's Day in the Country, five pieces for orchestra.

Recommended Recordings

Symphonies Nos. 1 & 2
Marco Polo DCCD 9201

Symphonies Nos. 3 & 5
Marco Polo DCCD 9004

Symphonies Nos. 4 & 6
Marco Polo DCCD 9202

Symphonies Nos. 7 & 8
Marco Polo DCCD 9301

Chamber Music

Gade's chamber music includes one mature String Quartet and two String Quintets, a String Sextet and String Octet, Fantasiestücke for clarinet and piano and three Violin Sonatas.

Recommended Recording

String Quartets Op. 63
Marco Polo 8.224015

Piano Music

Piano music by Gade, items of which once formed a general part of popular amateur repertoire, includes a Piano Sonata, Fantasy Pieces and Akvareller (Water-Colours), attractive brief sketches.

Recommended Recordings

Complete Piano Works, Vol. 1
Marco Polo DCCD 9115

Complete Piano Works, Vol. 2
Marco Polo DCCD 9116

Complete Piano Works, Vol. 3
Marco Polo DCCD 9117

Vocal and Choral Music

Gade's vocal and choral music ranges from the Wagnerian Baldur's Dream. The cantatas Zion and Psyche were written for the Birmingham Festival, testimony to the international reputation of Gade, while the earlier Comala reflects his interest in Ossian and Elverskud (Elf-King's Daughter) is Scandinavian in choice of subject and treatment. In his later music Gade's nationalism was subsumed in the German musical idiom that he had experienced in Leipzig.

Geminiani, Francesco 1687 - 1762)

The Italian violinist and composer Francesco Geminiani belongs to the generation of Bach and Handel. He studied in Rome with the violinist-composer Arcangelo Corelli and the opera-composer Alessandro Scarlatti. In 1714 he moved to London, where he soon established himself as a performer and composer, later publishing a number of theoretical works on performance techniques and on harmony. He visited Ireland on various occasions and died in Dublin in 1762.

Chamber Music

Geminiani published a number of sets of sonatas for violin and basso continuo, a chordal and a bass instrument, or for violin and harpsichord, a set of half a dozen sonatas for cello and harpsichord and twelve trio sonatas, for two violins, cello and harpsichord. These largely follow the example of his teacher Corelli.

Concertos

Again following the example of his teacher, Geminiani wrote a number of sets of Concerti grossi, works for string orchestra, with a small solo group consisting of two violins and basso continuo, with the addition of a viola, an instrument he omitted from the larger string ensemble. His arrangements of Corelli's Concerti grossi in this new form were particularly well received.

German, Edward (1862 - 1936)

Edward German, knighted in 1928 for his services to music, was the successor of Sir Arthur Sullivan in the field of English operetta. A composer of some versatility, he wrote little after 1910, feeling out of sympathy with the new age in music, which by then had dawned.

Operettas

The patriotic comic opera Merrie England was staged at the Savoy Theatre in London in 1902. The stirring Yeomen of England vies in popularity with an aria for Queen Elisabeth I of England, O peaceful England, while I my watch am keeping.

☛ **Recommended Recordings**

Piano Works
Marco Polo 8.223370

Richard III (Overture)
Theme and Six Diversions / The Seasons
Marco Polo 8.223695

Romeo and Juliet / Nell Gwyn / The Conqueror
Three Dances from Henry VIII / Gipsy Suite
Tom Jones Waltz
Marco Polo 8.223419

Symphony No. 2 "Norwich"
Valse Gracieuse / Welsh Rhapsody
Marco Polo 8.223726

Gershwin, George (1898 - 1937)

In a period in which national American music was developing with composers of the calibre of Aaron Copland and others trained in Europe, George Gershwin, the son of Russian-Jewish immigrant parents, went some way towards bridging the wide gap between Tin Pan Alley and serious music. He won success as a composer of light music, of songs and musicals, but in a relatively small number of compositions made forays into a new form of classical repertoire.

Stage Works

Gershwin has won serious attention with his opera Porgy and Bess, a drama of Black America, set at first in Catfish Row, Charleston, South Carolina. There is an effective instrumental suite, Catfish Row, derived from the opera, while the song Summertime has proved particularly attractive and memorable.

Orchestral Music

Gershwin's Rhapsody in Blue, written in 1924 for Paul Whiteman and his jazz band, marries jazz with something of the classical form, an avenue further explored in Gershwin's Piano Concerto of the following year. The tone poem An American in Paris again offers a synthesis between apparently divergent forms of music.

☞ **Recommended Recording**
Piano Concerto / An American in Paris
Rhapsody in Blue
Naxos 8.550295

Piano Music

Gershwin's piano music includes the three Preludes, written in 1926, pieces that retain a modest place in modern American piano repertoire.

☞ **Recommended Recording**
Three Preludes / Six Songs
Naxos 8.550341

Gesualdo, Carlo (c. 1561 - 1613)

Carlo Gesualdo, Prince of Venosa, murderer in 1590 of his guilty wife and her lover, later took a wife from the d'Este family, rulers of Ferrara, whose musical interests coincided with his own. He wrote a quantity of sacred and secular vocal music and a relatively small number of instrumental pieces. In style his music is unexpected in its sudden changes of tonality, its harmony and its intensity of feeling, qualities that have found particular favour among some modern theorists.

Secular Vocal Music

Gesualdo, a nobleman of melancholy reserve, published six books of madrigals, the second of them originally under an improbable pseudonym. These include some remarkable and striking compositions, such as the five-voice Moro, lasso, al mio duolo, and the earlier Ahi, disperata vita.

Sacred Vocal Music

Gesualdo's numerous sacred compositions include works intended for the liturgy of Good Friday and Holy Saturday, as well as Marian compositions such as Ave, dulcissima Maria and Ave, regina caelorum. Volumes of sacred music in a Sacrarum cantionum liber primus (First Book of Sacred Songs) of works in five parts and another of works in six and seven parts were published in Naples in 1603.

☞ **Recommended Recording**

Sacrae Cantiones (1603)
Naxos 8.550742

Gibbons, Orlando (1583 - 1625)

Orlando Gibbons belongs to the generation of English composers that followed that of William Byrd, forty years his senior, who had died in 1623. He was a chorister at King's College, Cambridge, where his elder brother was Master of the Choristers, and later became a gentleman of the Chapel Royal, which he served as an organist and to which he later added the position of organist at Westminster Abbey. He wrote music for the Church of England, madrigals, consort music and keyboard works.

Church Music

Gibbons wrote some forty anthems. Of these the verse anthem This is the record of John is one of the best known. The verse anthem, a peculiarly Anglican form of church music, contrasts a solo voice with passages for full choir. The eight-voice full anthem O clap your hands is a fine example of another form of anthem, without the use of solo voices. Other full anthems include Hosanna to the son of David and Lift up your heads, while the Christmas anthem Behold, I bring you glad tidings, with Glorious and powerful God and Sing unto the Lord, o ye saints, are fine examples of the verse anthem.

☞ **Recommended Recording**

Choral and Organ Music
Naxos 8.553130

Secular Vocal Music

The most famous of all the madrigals Gibbons wrote is The Silver Swanne, included in the only collection published by the composer, The First Set of Madrigals and Mottets, apt for Viols and Voyces, which appeared, advertised as newly composed, in 1612. Some of these have more of the form of consort songs, for solo voice and instrumental accompaniment, and could be performed in this way, rather than with each part sung. Gibbons's consort songs include a remarkable concoction, The Cryes of London, for five voices and five viols, a composition that makes use of the street cries of hawkers and vendors in London in his time.

Instrumental Music

Gibbons wrote a number of pieces for consorts of viols (bowed string instruments) the playing of which was socially acceptable. These include contrapuntal Fantasias, dance movements and examples of the traditional English instrumental form, the In nomine, a composition based on a fragment of a setting of the Benedictus in a Mass by the English composer John Taverner.

☞ Recommended Recording

Works for Viols and Voices
Naxos 8.550603

Keyboard Music

Gibbons continued the English tradition of keyboard music exemplified in the work of William Byrd, John Bull and others. Work by all three was published in 1613 under the title Parthenia or the Maydenhead of the First Musicke that ever was printed for the Virginals. Gibbons contributed a number of fantasias, one of them for double organ, and various airs and dance movements, including Lord Salisbury's Pavan and Galliard.

Ginastera, Alberto (1916 - 1983)

Alberto Ginastera occupied a leading position in the musical world of his native Argentina, where he exercised a strong influence over a younger generation of composers. He later spent much time in Europe, settling in Geneva. His style of writing develops from overt nationalism to a flexible application of the serialist principles proposed by Schoenberg.

Stage Works

The ballet Estancia is evocatively Argentinian, with its echoes of gaucho life. The opera Don Rodrigo, based on a twelve-note series, makes original use of spacial effects, while the operas Bomarzo and Beatrix Cenci draw also on Renaissance forms, set, as they are, in Renaissance Italy.

Orchestral Music

Ginastera's orchestral music includes a concerto for harp, two concertos for piano and concertos for violin and for cello. Ollantay, three symphonic movements, Pampeana No.3, a symphonic pastoral, and Overture to a Criollo Faust, have strongly Latin American elements.

Chamber Music

Chamber music by Ginastera includes the first two Pampeanas, for violin and piano and for cello and piano respectively, in addition to string quartets, the third with a soprano and texts by Lorca, Alberti and Jiménez.

Giordano, Umberto (1867 - 1948)

Umberto Giordano was trained as a musician in Naples and achieved his first great success in Milan in 1896 with the opera Andrea Chenier. His last completed opera, Il rè, was staged in Milan in 1929. In style his music bears some resemblance to that of Puccini or, still more, to that of Leoncavallo.

Operas

The opera Andrea Chenier deals with the fate of the poet of that name in the French Revolution, to which he finally fell a victim, joined in death by his beloved Madeleine. Arias from the work are popular in recital, including the tenor arias Un dì all'azzurro spazio, Si, fui soldato and Come un bel dì di maggio and the soprano aria La mamma morta. The tenor aria from the less successful opera Fedora, staged in 1898, Amor ti vieta, is popular with singers.

☞ **Recommended Recordings**
Come un bel dì di maggio from Andrea Chenier
Naxos 8.550497

La mamma morta, from Andrea Chénier
Naxos 8.551171

Giuliani, Mauro (1781 - 1829)

The Italian guitar virtuoso Mauro Giuliani settled in Vienna in 1806. There he exercised strong influence over the progress of the instrument, as a teacher, performer and composer. He left Vienna in 1819, spending some four years in Rome before retiring to Naples, where he died in 1829.

Guitar Music

Giuliani wrote three Guitar Concertos, with a number of works for solo guitar and for two guitars. Other ensemble music includes works for guitar and string quartet, guitar and violin and guitar and piano. His songs also offer the option of guitar accompaniment.

☞ **Recommended Recording**
Guitar Concerto No. 1, Op. 30
Naxos 8.550483

Glass, Philip (1937 -)

The American composer Philip Glass has enjoyed a degree of popularity unusual among contemporary composers. A pupil of Nadia Boulanger, he was influenced too by the Indian sitar player Ravi Shankar and has won a reputation as an exponent of minimalism, based on the systematic repetition of a motif, modified or extended.

Stage Works

Glass has won particular favour in some quarters for his stage works Einstein on the Beach, in collaboration with Bob Wilson, Satyagraha and Akhnaten. A more recent theatrical piece is Hydrogen Jukebox.

Glazunov, Alexander Konstantínovích (1865 - 1936)

Glazunov, a pupil of Rimsky-Korsakov, received encouragement also from Belyayev, an influential patron and publisher, whose activities succeeded and largely replaced the earlier efforts of Balakirev to inspire the creation of national Russian music. He joined the teaching staff of the St. Petersburg Conservatory in 1899 and after the student protests and turmoil of 1905 was elected director, a position he retained until 1930, although from 1928 he had remained abroad, chiefly in Paris, where he died in 1936. His music represents a synthesis between the Russian and the so-called German, the technical assurance introduced by the Rubinstein brothers in the Conservatories of St. Petersburg and of Moscow in the middle of the century.

Orchestral Music

In addition to his nine symphonies and a variety of other orchestral works, Glazunov wrote a Violin Concerto, completed in 1904, when he was at the height of his powers as a composer. The symphonies have won less popularity, but the symphonic poem Stenka Razin, written in 1885, retains a place in national repertoire.

☛ Recommended Recordings

Oriental Rhapsody / From Darkness to Light
Karelian Legend / March Op. 76
Marco Polo 8.220444

Overture on Greek Themes No. 1
Poème épique / Finnish Sketches
Spring Op. 34 / Triumphal March Op. 40
Cortège Solennel
Marco Polo 8.220309

Ruses d'amour, Op. 61 (Complete Ballet)
Marco Polo 8.220485

Serenades / Carnaval / Idylle / Rêverie
Scène dansante / Wedding March
Cortège solennel
Marco Polo 8.220487

Song of Destiny / Overture Op. 6
Salome / Intermezzo Op. 69
Marco Polo 8.220445

Stenka Rasin Op. 13 / Une fête slave Op. 26
Cortègè solennel Op. 50 / Fantaisie Op. 53
Mazurka Op. 18 / March Op. 76
Naxos 8.553538

The King of the Jews, Op. 96
Naxos 8.553575

The Kremlin / From the Middle Ages
Poème lyrique / Poème épique
Naxos 8.553537

The Seasons / Scènes de Ballet
Marco Polo 8.223136

Ballets

Glazunov's ballets include Raymonda, first staged in St. Petersburg in 1898, with choreography by Marius Petipa. Les ruses d'amour followed in 1900, with The Seasons in the same year. He orchestrated music by Chopin for Les sylphides. The choreographer Fokin also made use of Stenka Razin for a ballet of that name.

☛ **Recommended Recordings**

Raymonda (2 CD's)
Naxos 8.553503-4

Les Sylphides
Naxos 8.550324-5

The Seasons
Naxos 8.550079

'Sacha' Suite / Two Pieces / 'Sabela' Waltzes
Prelude and Two Mazurkas / Three Studies
Petite Valse / Nocturne
Grande Valse de Concert / Three Miniatures
Marco Polo 8.223151

Valse de salon / Trois morceaux
2 Impromptus / Prelude and Fugue
Theme and Variations
Deux Poèmes-improvisations
Marco Polo 8.223152

Piano Sonatas Nos. 1 and 2
Prelude and Fugue
Marco Polo 8.223153

4 Preludes and Fugues / Idylle
Fantasy for 2 Pianos
Marco Polo 8.223154

Glinka, Mikhaíl Ivanovích

(1804 - 1857)

Glinka is commonly regarded as the founder of Russian nationalism in music. His influence on Balakirev, self-appointed leader of the later group of five nationalist composers, was considerable. As a child he had some lessons from the Irish pianist John Field, but his association with music remained purely amateur, until visits to Italy and in 1833 to Berlin allowed concentrated study and subsequently a greater degree of assurance in his composition, which won serious attention both at home and abroad.

His Russian operas offered a synthesis of Western operatic form with Russian melody, while orchestral music, with skilful instrumentation, offered a combination of the traditional and the exotic. Glinka died in Berlin in 1857.

Operas

Glinka's first Russian opera, A Life for the Tsar, was well received at its first staging in 1836. His second full opera, Ruslan and Lyudmila, with a libretto by Pushkin, proved less acceptable at its first staging in St. Petersburg in 1842. The Overtures to these operas make effective curtain-raisers.

☞ **Recommended Recording**
Overtures: A Life for the Tsar
Ruslan and Lyudmila
Naxos 8.550085

Orchestral Music

Travel abroad inspired the Spanish mood of Jota aragonesa, a Capriccio brillante also known as the First Spanish Overture. The second of the series was expanded from Recuerdos de Castilla, Souvenirs of Castile, into Souvenir d'une nuit d'été à Madrid (Memory of a Summer Night in Madrid). Kamarinskaya, written in Warsaw, uses Slav thematic material.

☞ **Recommended Recordings**
Kamarinskaya
Naxos 8.550085

Jota aragonesa / Summer Night in Madrid
Naxos 8.550086

Gluck, Christoph (1714 - 1787)

Opera in Western Europe arose at the close of the 16th century in Italy. The form underwent various changes and reforms and the name of Gluck is associated with a tendency to greater operatic realism, the drama subsumed in the music, his principles expounded in his introduction to his opera Alceste in 1767. Reform opera, exemplified in the later work of Gluck, represented a reaction against the stylised forms of later Baroque opera. Gluck achieved considerable success in Vienna, Paris, and elsewhere in Europe.

Operas

Gluck wrote over forty operas. Of these Orfeo ed Euridice, staged in Vienna in 1762 in its original Italian version and in Paris in 1774 in a French version, is the best known, a treatment of the story of the legendary musician Orpheus and his journey to the Underworld to bring back again his beloved Euridice, an ancient illustration of the power of music. Alceste again turned to Greek legend as did the two tragedies Iphigénie en

Aulide and Iphigénie en Tauride, first staged in Paris in 1774 and in 1779 respectively.

By far the best known of all excerpts from operas by Gluck is the Dance of the Blessed Spirits from Orfeo, closely rivalled by the aria Che farò senza Euridice from the same opera. The soprano aria Divinité du Styx, from Alceste, is popular in recital.

☛ **Recommended Recording**
Dance of the Blessed Spirits
from Orfeo ed Euridice
Naxos 8.551131

Ballet Music

Gluck was associated with the choreographer and dancer Angiolini. Their first collaboration was on the subject of Don Juan, later used by Mozart in his Don Giovanni, based on the Spanish play by Tirso de Molina.

Godard, Benjamin (1849 - 1895)

A violist and pupil of Vieuxtemps, the French composer Benjamin Godard won a precociously early reputation as a composer of salon music, with a series of pieces that would once have found a ready place in any album of piano music. His other music, influenced by contemporary German trends, is more substantial, if neglected.

Operas

The Berceuse from Godard's opera Jocelyn proved its most popular element. Other operas were unsuccessful, although his final comic opera La vivandière, left incomplete at his death, seemed to promise more.

Orchestral Music

The four published symphonies of Godard include a Symphonie gothique and a Symphonie orientale, while his concertos consist of two Piano Concertos and two Violin Concertos, the first a Concert romantique. Other works include orchestral arrangement of the piano Scènes italiennes and Scènes écossaises.

Chamber Music

Godard wrote five Violin Sonatas and a series of other pieces for violin and piano and other ensembles.

Piano Music

Much of Godard's piano music is in the form of salon pieces of no great pretensions, designed for a lucrative popular market.

☛ **Recommended Recording**
Etudes
Marco Polo 8.223802

Goldmark, Karl (1830 - 1915)

Hungarian by birth, Karl Goldmark made his principal career in Vienna, after earlier years during which he earned his living as a violinist in theatre orchestras and as a teacher. Largely self-taught as a composer, he had his first success with his String Quartet, Op. 8, in 1860. He joined in the establishment of a Wagner Society in Vienna and gradually assumed a position of great importance in the musical life of the city.

Operas

Goldmark's opera Die Königin von Saba (The Queen of Sheba) enjoyed considerable popularity also in Italy, its musical idiom influenced to some extent by the music of the synagogue with which the composer was familiar from his childhood. Other operas were less successful, although his opera based on Shakespeare's A Winter's Tale exemplified a form of stage work more familiar from Humperdinck.

Orchestral Music

In addition to two symphonies and two violin concertos, Goldmark wrote a series of concert overtures and the popular Rustic Wedding Symphony.

☛ Recommended Recordings

Rustic Wedding Symphony
Overtures (Im Frühling & In Italien)
Naxos 8.550745

Symphony No. 2 / Penthesilea
Marco Polo 8.220417

Chamber Music

Goldmark wrote a series of works for conventional chamber ensembles, duos, trios, quartets and quintets, the later compositions showing signs of other contemporary influences, within the prescribed forms.

Górecki, Henryk (1933 -)

The Polish composer Henryk Górecki was born in Silesia in 1933 and studied in Katowice and with Messiaen in Paris. He has achieved very considerable sudden international success with the third of his symphonies, after earlier achievement that was recognised principally in his native country. His musical idiom is original and unconventional, while often drawing on the simplest of materials, whether from popular peasant sources or from the liturgy.

Orchestral, Choral and Vocal Music

Górecki's Third Symphony, the Symphony of Sorrowful Songs, with its moving soprano solo, has exercised a hypnotic fascination over recent audiences. It is a powerful work of mounting intensity, insistent in its effect. His Second Symphony, Kopernikowska, uses a solo baritone and chorus, combining texts from the Psalms and from Copernicus into a remarkable creation.

☛ Recommended Recording
Symphony No. 3 / 3 Olden Style Pieces
Naxos 8.550822

Gounod, Charles (1818 - 1893)

Gounod had a particularly strong influence on French composers from the middle of the 19th century. He was educated at the Paris Conservatoire, where he won the Prix de Rome in 1837. His return to Paris in 1843, after developing a wide knowledge of earlier and contemporary music abroad, brought a position as an organist. He achieved considerable success in the theatre, particularly with the opera Faust in 1859, but the Franco- Prussian War of 1870 and a period spent in England, brought a largely unprofitable interruption. His influence on English vocal music, however, was perceptible and not always for the best.

Operas

Goethe's drama Faust had the widest influence over artists of all kinds during the 19th century, a period when Faust might be identified by some with the heroic artist and champion of freedom from conventional restraints. Gounod's opera Faust is concerned principally with Faust's seduction of Marguerite, whose own redemption is secured, while Faust remains the prey of the devil Mephistopheles. Recital arias from Faust include the Mephistophelean Le veau d'or (The Golden Calf), the tenor Salut! demeure and Marguerite's Jewel Song, Ah! je ris. Choral societies have enjoyed the famous Soldiers' Chorus, while the Walpurgisnacht ballet music has provided orchestras with an item of concert repertoire.

Gounod's Roméo et Juliette, an operatic version of Shakespeare's play, was staged in Paris in 1867. Juliette's Waltz Song, Je veux vivre, is a familiar soprano aria, while tenors have expressed their feelings in Roméo's L'amour, l'amour.

☛ Recommended Recordings
Faust: Ballet Music
Naxos 8.550081
Faust: Salut! demeure chaste
Naxos 8.550343

Church Music

Gounod's church music has seemed to some excessively sweet, a charge that cannot justly be levelled at the Messe solennelle de Ste. Cécile (the Solemn Mass of St. Cecilia), patron saint of music. By far the most generally known of his religious music, not intended for church use, was the Ave Maria derived from the first Prelude of Bach's 48 Preludes and Fugues. Gounod himself and others transcribed the piece for various combinations of instruments.

Orchestral Music

Gounod wrote two symphonies, but it is his Petite symphonie of 1885, for ten wind instruments, that has proved more attractive.

His energetic Saltarello, an Italian dance akin to the Tarantella, was seemingly written in 1865.

☞ **Recommended Recording**
  Saltarello
  Naxos 8.550087

Vocal Music

Although Gounod happily provided music to suit English sentimental taste, in songs suitable for the Victorian drawing- room, he added music of more substance in some of his many French songs, even those of a certain sentimental piety, such as Prière du soir. There is a setting of Venise, a poem by Alfred de Musset, and Victor Hugo's Sérénade. O ma belle rebelle and D'un coeur qui aime may also be mentioned, among a considerable number of songs.

Grainger, Percy (1882 - 1961)

The Australian pianist and composer Percy Grainger, an eccentric figure, may seem of marginal importance. Nevertheless he wrote a number of works that continue to give considerable pleasure, as do some of the remarkable arrangements that he devised. He became a friend of Grieg and of Delius and took a strong interest in the active collection of folk-songs. He gave particular attention to the creation of music not bound by the traditional restraints of form and harmony. In 1918 he became an American citizen.

Instrumental Music

Grainger's original instrumental music includes the delightful Handel in the Strand, intended for piano trio, piano quartet or string orchestra, and Mock Morris, for either string sextet or violin and piano, or again in arrangements for string or full orchestra. Harvest Hymn appears in various chamber or orchestral arrangements, while Walking Tune remains in its original wind quintet form. Folk-song arrangements for various groups of instruments, sometimes idiosyncratically described as with elastic scoring, include Early One Morning, Green Bushes, Molly on the Shore, Ye Banks and Braes and Shepherd's Hey. Some of these were also arranged for large wind ensemble.

Vocal Music
Grainger wrote some original songs and choral music as well as solo and choral arrangements of folk-songs. These include the Irish Tune from County Derry, also arranged for wind band, Brigg Fair for tenor and chorus and The Men of Harlech for double chorus and drums.

Keyboard Music
Country Gardens, apparently derived from a medieval source, occurs in arrangements by Grainger for from two to eight hands. Molly on the Shore is arranged for solo piano or piano duet, with similar versions of Shepherd's Hey and Spoon River.

Granados, Enrique (1867 - 1916)
Born in Lérida in 1867, Enrique Granados studied the piano and composition in Barcelona and then in Paris, returning to Barcelona in 1889. He won distinction as a pianist and popularity in Spain with his contributions to the form of zarzuela. He was drowned in the English Channel when the boat on which he was returning home from an American tour by way of Liverpool was torpedoed.

Operas
In addition to a number of zarzuelas, Granados wrote an opera Goyescas, derived from piano pieces after paintings by Goya. This was first performed at the Metropolitan Opera in New York in 1916. An Intermezzo from the opera, either in orchestral form or as a duet for cello and piano, has proved viable in the concert hall.

Piano Music & Orchestral Arrangements
The ten Danzas españolas (Spanish Dances) are immensely effective, both in their original piano version and in various instrumental, and orchestral arrangements. The Goyescas of 1911 are more ambitious in their technical requirements. There are further compositions for piano including six pieces based on popular Spanish songs and seven Valses poeticos.

☛ **Recommended Recording**
Twelve Spanish Dances
Escenas Poeticas (Book 1)
Naxos 8.553037

Gregorian Chant

Plainchant is the general name given to the traditional chant of the Catholic liturgy, monophonic, modal and in free rhythm, that is to say, with a single melody line, using older forms of scales and with a rhythm that largely follows that of the words. Plainchant exists in various forms, although early attempts at standardisation were made, notably and probably wrongly attributed to St. Gregory the Great, Pope from 590 to 604. Gregorian chant is the official chant of the Western church, although some local variants have been permitted to survive. Plainchant itself was the basis of early developments of polyphony and remained for centuries a common and generally known core of musical experience for the Catholic world.

☞ Recommended Recordings

Gregorian Chant (Male Voices)
(Adorate Deum)
Naxos 8.550711

Gregorian Chant (Female Voices)
(Salve Festa Dies)
Naxos 8.550712

Ego sum Resurrectio (Female Voices)
(Gregorian Chant for the Dead)
Naxos 8.553192

In Passione et Morte Domini
(Gregorian Chant for Good Friday)
Naxos 8.550952

Grieg, Edvard (1843 - 1907)

Edvard Grieg is the most important Norwegian composer of the later 19th century, a period of growing national consciousness. As a child, he was encouraged by the violinist Ole Bull, a friend of his parents, and studied at the Leipzig Conservatory on his suggestion. After a period at home in Norway he moved to Copenhagen and it was there that he met the young composer Rikard Nordraak, an enthusiastic champion of Norwegian music and a decisive influence on him. Grieg's own performances of Norwegian music, often with his wife, the singer Nina Hagerup, established him as a leading figure in the music of his own country, bringing subsequent collaboration in the theatre with Bjørnson and with Ibsen. He continued to divide his time between composition and activity in the concert-hall until his death in 1907.

Stage Works

Grieg collaborated with the dramatist Bjørnson in the play Sigurd Jorsalfar, for which he provided incidental music, and still more notably with Ibsen in Peer Gynt. The original music for the latter makes use of solo

voices, chorus and orchestra, but is most often heard in orchestral form in the two suites arranged by the composer. These include Morning, Aase's Death, Anitra's Dance and In the Hall of the Mountain King in the first suite, and Ceremonial March, Arabian Dance, Peer Gynt's Homecoming and Solveig's Song in the second, the order not corresponding to the sequence of events in Ibsen's remarkable play.

☞ **Recommended Recording**

Peer Gynt Suites Nos. 1 & 2
Wedding-Day at Troldhaugen
Lyric Pieces Op. 68
Norwegian Bridal Procession
Three Orchestral Pieces from Sigurd Jorsalfar
Naxos 8.550864

Orchestral Music

In addition to the two Peer Gynt Suites and three pieces from Sigurd Jorsalfar, Grieg wrote one of the most famous of all romantic piano concertos, completed in 1868. The so-called Holberg Suite, more correctly Suite from the Time of Holberg, for string orchestra, celebrates the Scandinavian Molière, the Norwegian playwright Ludvig Holberg, an almost exact contemporary of J.S. Bach and Handel. The two Elegiac Melodies of 1881 are also for strings only, with other arrangements of piano

music, and the Lyric Suite, based on four piano pieces of 1891, was orchestrated in 1904.

☞ **Recommended Recordings**

Piano Concerto in A minor
Naxos 8.550118

Norwegian Airs / Two Melodies / Elegiac Pieces
Naxos 8.550330

Holberg Suite
Naxos 8.553106

Chamber Music

Grieg's three violin sonatas remain a part of standard romantic repertoire, revealing his mastery of harmonic colour in the clearest of textures. The third of these, in C minor, was completed in 1887 and is particularly striking.

☞ **Recommended Recordings**

Violin Sonata No. 3 in C minor
Naxos 8.550417

Cello Sonata Op. 36 / Piano Sonata Op. 7
Intermezzo
Naxos 8.550878

String Quartets (G Minor Op. 27 / F Major)
Naxos 8.550879

Piano Music

As a pianist himself, Grieg wrote extensively for the piano, excelling, in particular, in his ten volumes of Lyric Pieces, and in other sets of short compositions for the instrument, often derived directly or indirectly from Norwegian folk-music.

☛ Recommended Recordings

Piano Works Vol. 1
Four Piano Pieces / Funeral March
Humoresques, Op. 6 / I love you, Op. 41, No. 3
Moods, Op. 73 / Piano Sonata, Op. 7
Siren's Enticement
Naxos 8.550881

Piano Works Vol. 2
Ballad to Saint Olaf
Improvisations on Two Norwegian Folk-Songs, Op. 29
19 Norwegian Folk-Songs, Op. 66
The First Meeting, Op. 52, No. 2
Naxos 8.550882

Piano Works Vol. 3
Humoresques, Op. 19 /
Four Album Leaves, Op. 28
Poetic Tone-pictures, Op. 3 / Iceland
Prayer from "Sigurd Jorsalfar", Op. 56
Ballade, Op. 24
Naxos 8.550883

Piano Works Vol. 4
Holberg Suite / I went to bed so late
Six Norwegian Mountain Melodies
Morning Mood / Slåtter, Op. 72
Naxos 8.550884

Piano Works Vol. 5
Norwegian Melodies Nos. 1-63
Naxos 8.553391

Piano Works Vol. 6
Norwegian Melodies Nos. 64-117
Naxos 8.553392

Piano Works Vol. 7
Norwegian Melodies Nos. 118-152
Naxos 8.553393

Piano Works Vol. 8
Lyric Pieces Opp. 12, 38, 43 & 47
Naxos 8.553394

Piano Works Vol. 9
Lyric Pieces Opp. 54, 57 & 62
Naxos 8.553395

Piano Works Vol. 10
Lyric Pieces Opp. 65, 68 & 71
Naxos 8.553396

Piano Works Vol. 11
Sigurd Jorsalfar, Op. 22
Peer Gynt, Suite Nos. 1 and 2
Two Pieces from Olav Trygvason, Op. 50
Bergliot, Op. 42
Naxos 8.553397

Piano Works Vol. 12
Agitato, EG 106 / Norwegian Dances, Op. 35
Album Leaf, EG 109 / Waltz Caprices, Op. 37
Johan HALVORSEN (tr. GRIEG):
"The Entry of the Boyars"
Peer Gynt, Op. 23
Dance of the Mountain King's Daughter
Three Piano Transcriptions from Sigurd
Jorsalfar, Op. 56
Naxos 8.553398

Piano Works Vol. 13
Three Piano Pieces, EG 105
Two Elegiac Melodies, Op. 34
Norwegian Melodies No. 6
Two Melodies, Op. 53
Piano Transcriptions of Songs, Op. 41
Norwegian Melodies No. 22
Two Nordic Melodies, Op. 63
Three Piano Pieces, EG 110-112
Naxos 8.553399

Piano Works Vol. 14
Larvikspolka, EG 101
23 Small Pieces for Piano
At the Halfdan Kjerulf Statue, EG 167
Piano Transcriptions of Songs, Op. 52
Canon à 4 voci, EG 179
Norwegian Melodies No. 146
Piano Sonata, Op. 7 - Movements 2 and 4
Mountain Song
Piano Concerto, Fragment, EG 120
Naxos 8.553400

Hahn, Reynaldo (1875 - 1947)

Born in Caracas, Reynaldo Hahn moved with his family to Paris at the age of three. There he studied at the Conservatoire under Massenet and made a particular impression with his songs, which he sang himself, to his own piano accompaniment. His interest in the theatre led to his appointment in 1945 as director of the Paris Opéra.

Stage Works

Hahn wrote a considerable amount of music for the theatre, operas, ballets and incidental music. Of these the operetta Ciboulette remains in popular repertoire. Ballets include Le dieu bleu (The Blue God), written for Dyagilev, with a scenario by Cocteau and Madrazo.

Orchestral Music

Orchestral music by Reynaldo Hahn has proved less durable, with concertos for piano and for violin which repay study.

Chamber Music

Chamber music by Hahn includes two string quartets and a piano quintet that stands comparison with Fauré.

Vocal Music

Reynaldo Hahn's songs deserve an honoured place in French vocal repertoire, with the songs of Gabriel Fauré.

They include settings of poems from Victor Hugo to Verlaine, with a curious group of songs in Venetian dialect and the ever popular Si mes vers avaient des ailes (If my verses had wings).

Halvorsen, Johan (1864 - 1935)

Johan Halvorsen, violinist, conductor and composer, continued the nationalist Norwegian traditions established by Grieg, serving for thirty years as conductor of the Christiania National Theatre.

Orchestral Music

There is a place in popular repertoire for Halvorsen's Danses norvégiennes, for violin and orchestra, and for his Entry March of the Boyars. Less often heard are his three symphonies and two Rhapsodies on Norwegian folk-tunes.

☛ **Recommended Recording**
Danses Norvégiennes / Air Norvégien Op. 7
Naxos 8.550329

Chamber Music

Halvorsen is regarded with gratitude by viola players for his arrangements of a Sarabande and a Passacaglia by Handel for violin and viola, transcriptions that call for a measure of virtuosity in both players.

Handel, George Frideric

(1685 - 1759)

Born in the German town of Halle in 1685, Handel studied briefly at the University of Halle, before moving to Hamburg in 1703, where he served as a violinist in the opera orchestra and subsequently as harpsichordist and composer. From 1706 until 1710 he was in Italy, where he further developed his mastery of Italian musical style. Appointed Kapellmeister to the Elector of Hanover, the future George I of England, he visited London, where he composed the first London Italian opera Rinaldo, in 1710 and settled there two years later. He enjoyed aristocratic and later royal patronage, and was occupied largely with the composition of Italian opera with varying financial success until the 1740s. He was successful in developing a new form, English oratorio, which combined the musical felicities of the Italian operatic style with an increased rôle for the chorus, relative economy of production and the satisfaction of an English and religious text, elements that appealed to English Protestant sensibilities. In London he won the greatest esteem and exercised an influence that tended to overshadow the achievements of his contemporaries and immediate successors. He died in London in 1759 and was buried in Westminster Abbey in the presence of some 3000 mourners.

Operas

Handel wrote over forty Italian operas, the majority for staging in London. The operatic conventions of the time, restricting subject and form, and the major use of castrato singers in the principal male rôles, led to a general neglect of this important part of Handel's work until recent years, with the increased cultivation of male soprano and male alto voices and a growing understanding of Handel's achievement within the limitations of the genre. Arias and other operatic excerpts, however, have retained a continued place in vocal and to some extent in instrumental repertoire. In particular the aria from the opera Serse of 1738, Ombra mai fù, popularly known as Handel's Largo, has re-appeared in every possible arrangement. Other arias are familiar in something approaching their original form. These include Lascia ch'io pianga from Rinaldo, Piangèro la sorte mia from Giulio Cesare and Care selve from Atalanta.

☛ **Recommended Recording**

Acis and Galatea (2 CD's)
Naxos 8.553188-9

Lascia ch'io pianga from Rinaldo
Naxos 8.553751

Oratorios

Messiah is by far the best known of all English oratorios. Its three parts deal with the birth, passion and resurrection of Christ, using a text in part derived from the Bible and from the version of the Psalms familiar from the Church of England Book of Common Prayer. The work was completed and first performed in 1742 and later repeated annually in London in aid of the Foundling Hospital. Israel in Egypt, Judas Maccabaeus, Samson, based on Milton, and Solomon are only some of the English oratorios of Handel that are familiar in whole or in part to choirs and audiences. To these may be added the secular oratorio Semele, with a text by the dramatist William Congreve, dealing with an episode from classical mythology and including, for a disguised Jupiter, the well known aria Where'er you walk.

☛ **Recommended Recordings**

Messiah: Choruses (in English)
Naxos 8.550317

Messiah (complete original version) (2 CD's)
Naxos 8.550667-8

Messiah (Highlights)
Naxos 8.553258

Church Music

Handel wrote music for the Catholic liturgy in 1707, when he was in Rome. In England, under the patronage of the Duke of Chandos, he wrote a set of anthems, the so-called Chandos Anthems. The four Coronation Anthems, written for the coronation of George II in 1727, represent music for a royal ceremonial occasion at its most impressive. Other settings for the Anglican liturgy include the Utrecht Te Deum of 1713, celebrating the Peace of Utrecht, and the Dettingen Te Deum, a celebration of the victory of Dettingen over the French army in 1743.

Secular Vocal & Choral Music

The story of the shepherd and shepherdess Acis and Galatea and the monster Polyphemus forms the basis of the pastoral Acis and Galatea, first performed in 1718. The aria of Polyphemus O ruddier than the cherry is in popular baritone repertoire. L'allegro, il penseroso ed il moderato, based on Milton and completed in 1740, provides at least one popular soprano aria, Sweet bird. In the earlier part of his career Handel wrote a large number of solo and duo Italian cantatas, with instrumental accompaniment, as well as vocal duets and trios with the more economical accompaniment of basso continuo, a chordal and a bass instrument. This last repertoire deserves further exploration.

Orchestral Music

Since Corelli, a musician who was said to have found Handel's "French" style alien to Italian tradition, the concerto grosso had continued as the most popular Baroque orchestral form, with a small concertino group, usually of two violins, cello and harpsichord, contrasted with the whole string orchestra. Handel wrote and published in 1739 a set of twelve such concertos, Opus 6, designed originally for strings and continuo. An earlier compilation of six concerti grossi, scored also for wind instruments, had been published in London in 1734. Alexander's Feast is the name given to one of the concertos first performed with the choral work of that name, a setting of Dryden in celebration of the Feast of St. Cecilia, patron saint of music, in 1736. His sixteen Organ Concertos, the first six included in Opus 4 and a further six in Opus 7, served a practical and novel purpose as interval music, to be played at performances of oratorio. No. 13 is generally known as The Cuckoo and the Nightingale. The Water Music is a set of pieces written in 1717 to entertain George I as he was rowed up the Thames to supper at Chelsea, and the Music for the Royal Fireworks, written in 1749, preceded a firework display in Green Park, a celebration of the Peace of Aix-la-chapelle.

Recommended Recordings

Water Music / Music for the Royal Fireworks
Naxos 8.550109

Organ Concertos Op. 4, Nos. 2, 4 & 5
Op. 7, No. 1 & No. 13,
Naxos 8.550069

Concerti Grossi Op. 3, No. 3
Op. 6 Nos. 4, 5 & 6
Naxos 8.550157

Concerti Grossi Op. 6, Nos. 8, 10 & 12
Alexander's Feast
Naxos 8.550158

Chamber Music

Music for smaller groups of performers by Handel includes a number of Trio Sonatas, the majority for two violins and basso continuo, and a number of sonatas for solo instrument and continuo, six for recorder and six for violin. The publisher of the twelve sonatas of Opus 1, about 1730, described a dozen of these sonatas as for treble instrument and continuo, allowing potential performers a freedom of choice that was not altogether unusual at the time.

Recommended Recording

Recorder Sonatas Op. 1 Nos. 2,4,7 & 11
& HV. 367a
Naxos 8.550700

Keyboard Music

Handel was as versatile as any musician of his age. He excelled, however, as a keyboard-player, judged in an early contest in Rome with the harpsichordist Domenico Scarlatti, with the wisdom of Solomon, as the better organist, while Scarlatti was honoured as the better harpsichordist. Handel left a great deal of keyboard music, most of it for the harpsichord and much of it written early in his career. The first eight Suites for harpsichord were published by the composer in 1720, followed in 1733 by a second collection of eight Suites, assembled largely by the publisher.

The G major Chaconne, using a popular Baroque variation form, consists of 62 variations on a simple repeated bass pattern.

The Air from Suite No. 5, with its five following variations, has won fame under the title The Harmonious Blacksmith, a reference to an unlikely anecdote concerning the inspiration of the piece.

Recommended Recordings

Harpsichord Suites Nos. 1-5
Naxos 8.550415

Harpsichord Suites Nos. 6-8
Naxos 8.550416

Haydn, Franz Joseph (1732 - 1809)

Various paternity charges have been levelled at the composer Haydn. His career coincided with the development of classical style and forms, with the symphony, sonata, string quartet and other instrumental forms, in the moulding of which he played an important part. Born in Rohrau in 1732, the son of a wheelwright, he was trained as a chorister at St. Stephen's Cathedral in Vienna, where he made his early living, before appointment to the small musical establishment of Count Morzin in 1759. In 1760 he entered the service of the Esterházy Princes, and succeeded to the position of Kapellmeister on the death of his predecessor and immediate superior Gregorius Werner in 1766. Much of Haydn's life now centred on the magnificent palace and estate at Esterháza, where his employer Prince Nikolaus Esterházy had moved his entourage for most of the year. The death of the Prince in 1790 released Haydn and allowed travel to London. There followed further service of the successors of Prince Nikolaus, now at the former residence at Eisenstadt, and concluding retirement in Vienna, where he died in 1809, as the soldiers of Napoleon again entered the city.

Church Music

Haydn's duties as Kapellmeister to the Esterházy family involved the provision of church music, as well as music for entertainment. The Mass settings composed for the younger Prince Nikolaus include the well known Nelson Mass, celebrating the English admiral's victory at the Battle of the Nile. Between 1796 and 1802 Haydn wrote seven Masses, all with popular German nicknames, "Heiligmesse", "Paukenmesse", "Coronation Mass", "Theresienmesse", "Schöpfungsmesse" and "Harmoniemesse".

Oratorios

Haydn's visits to London suggested to him the musical possibilities of oratorio, in the form perpetuated after Handel's death by commemorative festival performances. The result was The Creation (Die Schöpfung), with a text by Baron van Swieten based on English sources, first performed in Vienna in 1798. The Seasons (Die Jahreszeiten), with a text by van Swieten based on James Thomson, was first performed in 1801. Haydn's earlier oratorios include Il ritorno di Tobia (The Return of Tobias), completed in 1775.

Stage Works

Haydn's two dozen operas have received rather less attention than many of his other works. Most of these were written for performance at Esterháza, either in the principal theatre or in the marionette theatre.

Vocal Music

Haydn wrote a number of songs, providing nearly 400 British folk-song arrangements for the Edinburgh publisher Thomson, in addition to songs and cantatas in German and English. The two sets of Canzonettas written in England in 1794 and 1795 include settings of verses by the wife of Haydn's London surgeon, Hunter.

Orchestral Music

(a) Symphonies

Haydn's 108 symphonies, written between 1759 and 1795, range from works written for the relatively modest local court orchestra of two oboes, two horns and strings, to the greater complexity of his larger scale London Symphonies, the twelve written for performance in London under the direction of the German-born violinist and impresario Salomon during the composer's two London visits. The London Symphonies include a number of works with nicknames, No. 94, "The Surprise", No. 96, "The Miracle", No. 100, "The Military", No. 101, "The Clock", No. 103, "The Drumroll", and No. 104, known as "The London" or "The Salomon". Other named symphonies that remain in regular concert repertoire include No. 92, "The Oxford" and Nos. 82, 83 and 84, "The Bear", "The Hen" and "La reine" (The Queen of France). Earlier named symphonies include the interesting Symphony No. 22,

"The Philosopher", which includes two cor anglais or English horns, tenor oboes in place of the normal higher-pitched instrument, written in 1764, three years after "Le matin", "Le midi" and "Le soir" (Morning, Noon and Evening), Nos. 6, 7 and 8. The "Farewell" Symphony, No. 45, allows players, impatient for a return from Esterháza to their families at home, to leave the platform one by one. Its immediate predecessor is the "Trauersinfonie", Mourning Symphony, while No. 49, " La Passione", reflects elements of Sturm und Drang, the Storm and Stress movement in German literature and art of the period.

☛ **Recommended Recordings**

Symphonies Nos. 6 "Le Matin",
7 "Le Midi" & 8 "Le Soir"
Naxos 8.550722

Symphonies Nos. 22 "The Philosopher",
29 & 60 "Il Distratto"
Naxos 8.550724

Symphonies Nos. 23, 24 & 61
Naxos 8.550723

Symphonies Nos. 26 "Lamentatione",
35 & 49 "La Passione"
Naxos 8.550721

Symphonies Nos. 30, 55 "The Schoolmaster"
& 63 "La Roxelane"
Naxos 8.550757

Symphonies Nos. 44 "Trauer", 77
& 104 "London"
Naxos 8.550287

Symphonies Nos. 45 "Farewell",
48 "Maria Theresia" & 102
Naxos 8.550382

Symphonies Nos. 53 "L'Impériale", 86 & 87
Naxos 8.550768

Symphonies Nos. 64 "Tempora Mutantur",
84 & 90
Naxos 8.550770

Symphonies Nos. 69 "Laudon", 89 & 91
Naxos 8.550769

Symphonies Nos. 72, 93 & 95
Naxos 8.550797

Symphonies Nos. 82 "The Bear",
96 "The Miracle" & 100 "Military"
Naxos 8.550139

Symphonies Nos. 83 "The Hen",
94 "Surprise" & 101 "The Clock"
Naxos 8.550114

Symphonies Nos. 85, 92 & 103
Naxos 8.550387

Symphonies Nos. 97 and 98
Naxos 8.550780

(b) Concertos

Of Haydn's concertos, the work written in 1796 for the newly developed and soon to be obsolete keyed trumpet, is the best known, closely rivalled by the two surviving Cello Concertos, in D and in C. Three genuine Violin Concertos remain, in G, in C and in A, and one Horn Concerto. The keyboard concertos have recently entered popular repertoire, in particular the Concerto in D major. They were originally designed either for organ or harpsichord and were written in the earlier part of Haydn's career, before his employment by the Esterházys.

☞ **Recommended Recordings**

Cello Concertos in D & C Major
Naxos 8.550059

Trumpet Concerto in E flat
Naxos 8.550243

Piano Concertos Nos. 4, 7, 9 & 11
Naxos 8.550713

Chamber Music

Haydn was a prolific composer of chamber music, with a considerable number of compositions for his principal patron, Prince Nikolaus Esterházy, who played the baryton, a bowed string instrument resembling a viola da gamba, with sympathetic strings that could also be plucked. The English scholar Dr. Burney suggested it as only useful on a desert island, where a player could accompany a bowed melody with plucked accompaniment, without other assistance.

For the more conventional string quartet Haydn wrote some 83 works, described originally as divertimenti, but later dignified by the more serious title by which they are generally known. Once again nicknames reflect the continued popularity of many of these works. Sets of named quartets include the Sun Quartets of 1772, Op. 20, the Russian Quartets written in 1781, Op. 33, and including "The Joke" and "The Bird", the Prussian Quartets of 1787, Op. 50, much influenced by Mozart and including "The Frog". There are three sets of Tost Quartets, Opp. 54, 55 and 64, bearing the name of the Esterháza violinist turned business-man Johann Tost. The Tost Quartets include "The Razor" and "The Lark". Further sets of quartets were issued in 1793 and 1797, the "Apponyi", Opp. 71 and 74, including "The Rider", and the "Erdödy", Op. 76, including the "Fifths", "Emperor" and "Sunrise", both groups bearing the names of aristocratic patrons. The Opus 1 Quartets were seemingly written between 1757 and 1761. The Seven Last Words of Christ on the Cross was arranged in string quartet form from the original work for full orchestra, amplified with the addition of choral parts. It was written for performance in Cádiz on Good Friday 1787.

In addition to a number of works for two violins and cello and 126 baryton trios, Haydn wrote a number of attractive piano trios between 1784 and 1797. The best known of these last is the G major Trio with its so-called Gypsy Rondo.

☛ Recommended Recordings

String Quartets "Emperor", "Fifths" & "Sunrise"
Naxos 8.550129

String Quartets, Op. 1, Nos. 1-4
Naxos 8.550398

String Quartets, Op. 1, Nos. 5 & 6
Op. 2, Nos. 1 & 2
Naxos 8.550399

String Quartets Op. 2, Nos. 4 & 6 and Op. 42
Naxos 8.550732

String Quartets Op. 9, Nos. 1, 3 & 4
Naxos 8.550786

String Quartets Op. 9, Nos. 2, 5 & 6
Naxos 8.550787

String Quartets, Op. 20, Nos. 1-3
Naxos 8.550701

String Quartets, Op. 20, Nos. 4-6
Naxos 8.550702

String Quartets Op. 33, Nos. 1, 2 & 5
Naxos 8.550788

String Quartets Op. 33, Nos. 3, 4 & 6
Naxos 8.550789

String Quartets Op. 54 Nos. 1-3
Naxos 8.550395

String Quartets Op. 55 Nos. 1-3
Naxos 8.550397

String Quartets Op. 64 Nos. 1-3
Naxos 8.550673

String Quartets Op. 64 Nos. 4-6
Naxos 8.550674

String Quartets Op. 71 Nos. 1-3
Naxos 8.550394

String Quartets Op. 74 Nos. 1-3
Naxos 8.550396

String Quartets Op. 76 Nos. 1-3
Naxos 8.550314

String Quartets Op. 76 Nos. 4-6
Naxos 8.550315

String Quartets Op. 77, Nos. 1-2
Naxos 8.553146

String Quartets Op. 103
Op. 51 Seven Last Words
Naxos 8.550346

Keyboard Works

Haydn composed nearly fifty keyboard sonatas, the earlier intended for harpsichord and the last for the newly developed hammer-action fortepiano. The final works in this form include the so-called English Sonata in C major, written in 1795 during Haydn's second visit to London.

☛ Recommended Recordings

Piano Sonatas Nos. 36-41
Naxos 8.553127

Piano Sonatas Nos. 42-47
Naxos 8.550844

Piano Sonatas Nos. 48-52
Naxos 8.553128

Piano Sonatas Nos. 53-56 & 58
Un Piccolo Divertimento
Naxos 8.550845

Piano Sonatas Nos. 59-62
Naxos 8.550657

Haydn, Michael (1737 - 1806)

Joseph Haydn's younger brother Michael has earned less fame. His earlier career followed that of his brother, as a chorister and then earning a living from music as best he could in Vienna. He became Kapellmeister in 1757 to the Bishop of Grosswardein and in 1762 moved to Salzburg, home of the Mozart family, serving there as Konzertmeister to the ruling Archbishop and to his successor, while earning a not inconsiderable reputation beyond the confines of his position. His pupils included Weber and the composer-publisher Diabelli, while his influence on Mozart cannot be discounted.

Church Music

Like his elder brother, Michael Haydn wrote music of all kinds. One of the most interesting of his liturgical works is the Requiem he wrote on the death of his first Salzburg patron, Archbishop Sigismond, in 1771.

Orchestral Music

Michael Haydn wrote a number of symphonies and concertos. His Trumpet Concerto of 1764 is a useful repertoire item for soloists, but other orchestral works are heard less frequently.

Chamber Music

Michael Haydn's instrumental music, in addition to a number of divertimenti, includes a dozen attractive string quartets.

Heinichen, Johann David

(1683 - 1729)

Johann David Heinichen was educated at the Thomasschule in Leipzig, where J.S.Bach was later to teach, serving as assistant to the then cantor, Kuhnau, and proceeding thereafter to the University of Leipzig. After an initial career as a lawyer in Weissenfels, Heinichen returned to musical activity in Leipzig, followed by a period of work and study in Italy. In 1717 he was appointed Court Kapellmeister in Dresden, a position he retained until his death in 1729.

Operas

Heinichen wrote operas in the earlier part of his career and moved to Italy with the express purpose of studying the art of Italian oepra at its source. His single opera for Dresden, Flavio Crispo, remained incomplete, abandoned, it seems, when the Italian opera company was disbanded.

Orchestral Music

Heinichen was extremely prolific as a composer. Of his instrumental music some two dozen concertos survive. These include a number of cocnertos for multiple instruments.

Vocal and Instrumental Music

Heinichen, in accordance with the demands of his employment, wrote a number of serenades and other celebratory pieces for voices and instruments.

Church Music

Heinichen's church music follows the requirements of the Catholic liturgy, with settings of the Mass, canticles and parts of the Holy Week liturgy.

Heller, Stephen (1813 - 1888)

Stephen Heller was born in Hungary but made his career in Paris, after earlier patronage from members of the Fugger family in Augsburg, from where he contributed to Schumann's Neue Zeitschrift für Musik (New Chronicle for Music). In Paris, where he settled in 1838, he earned a living as a teacher, composer and writer, in later years supported by charitable subscription arranged by Charles Hallé, Robert Browning and Lord Leighton.

Piano Music

Heller wrote a very large amount of piano music, including a quantity of studies that tended to eclipse his reputation in other genres of piano music. These latter included pieces of all kinds, variations, character pieces, operatic transcriptions and fantasies, a much smaller number of sonatas, with a larger number of dance movements and smaller forms, nocturnes, waltzes, caprices and scherzos. His career spans the period from Schumann to Massenet and Bizet, and his music suggests the paths to be taken by later Romantic composers such as Rachmaninov and Medtner.

Henze, Hans Werner (1926 -)

Hans Werner Henze is among the most prolific and successful of contemporary German composers. His systematic study of music only began after the war, with Wolfgang Fortner, and later with visits to Darmstadt and absorption of serial technique, to be used with great originality in a musical language that was also influenced by Stravinsky. In 1953 he moved to Italy and gradually developed his leaning towards the political New Left, reflected in some of his music and choices of texts and themes.

Stage Works

Henze's immensely successful operas range from the 1951 Kafka radio opera, with its Trakl settings, Der Landarzt (The Country Doctor) to König Hirsch (King Stag), the Kleist Prinz von Homburg, Elegy for Young Lovers, with a libretto by Auden and Chester Kallmann, Der junge Lord (The Young Lord), The Bassarids, with Auden and Kallmann, based on Euripides, and We Come to the River and The English Cat, with texts by Edward Bond. Henze has also provided music for a series of ballets, with incidental music for the cinema and the theatre.

Orchestral Music

An exceptionally wide range of orchestral music includes seven symphonies, with concertos for piano, for violin and, for Gary Karr, a double bass concerto, as well as a double concerto for oboe and harp for Heinz and Ursula Holliger.

Vocal and Choral Music

Vocal and choral music by Henze is equally varied and remarkable, with Novae de infinito laudes (New Praises of the Infinite) with a text from Giordano Bruno, the Virgilian Muses of Sicily and the controversial Das Floss der 'Medusa' (The Raft of the Medusa), as well as the revolutionary El Cimarrón (The Fugitive).

Hérold, Ferdinand (1791 - 1833)

A pupil of the violinist Rodolphe Kreutzer and of Adolphe Adam's father at the Paris Conservatoire, Hérold made his name as a composer of opéra comique in Paris with works that retained their popularity through the 19th century.

Stage Works

Hérold is chiefly known in concert or brass-band repertoire for his overture to the comic opera Zampa of 1831. His ballet La fille mal gardée remains in current ballet repertoire, the score making use of excerpts from Rossini and from popular French songs.

Hildegard of Bingen (1098 - 1179)

Abbess of Rupertsberg, which she herself founded, Hildegard of Bingen held an important position as a religious, a mystic, a diplomat, a writer on a wide variety of subjects and a composer. A visionary, she was highly respected, her advice widely sought by the powerful in church and state. As a poet she writes in a style replete with colourful imagery, as in her books of visions.

Religious Music

The music of Hildegard of Bingen is contained in her Symphonia armonie celestium revelationum (Symphonic Harmony of Celestial Revelations), the Latin texts dealing with the hierarchy of Heaven, from God, Father and Son to Confessors, Virgins and Innocents. Her monophonic musical language is based on a number of varied melodic formulae. Her morality play Ordo virtutum (Order of Virtues), written some 150 years after the Terentian verse plays of the nun Hrotswitha of Gandersheim, also includes music of a simpler and more syllabic kind.

☛ **Recommended Recording**
   Heavenly Revelations:
   Hymns, Sequences, Antiphons and Responds
   Naxos 8.550998

Hindemith, Paul (1895 - 1963)

Respected as one of the most distinguished viola-players of his time, Hindemith devoted the earlier part of his career to performance, first as a violinist and then as violist in the Amar-Hindemith Quartet, while developing his powers as a composer and his distinctive theories of harmony and of the place of the composer in society. His name is particularly associated with the concept of Gebrauchsmusik, and the composer as craftsman. He was prolific in composition and wrote music in a variety of forms. Attacked by the National Socialists, he left his native Germany in 1935, taking leave from the Berlin Musikhochschule, where he had served as professor of composition for some eight years. In 1940 he settled in the United States, teaching at Yale University, a position he combined after the war with a similar position at the University of Zurich. He died in his native city of Frankfurt in 1963.

Operas and Stage Works

Hindemith found himself in open conflict with the National Socialist government of Germany in 1934 with his opera Mathis der Maler, the banning of which brought about the resignation of the conductor Furtwängler from his official positions. He derived a symphony of the same title from the opera. The dance legend Nobilissima visione, based on the life of St. Francis of Assisi and first performed in London in 1938, is better known in occasional instrumental excerpts, although there is a concert suite from the work.

Orchestral Music

In addition to the Mathis der Maler Symphony, the Symphonic Metamorphoses on Themes of Carl Maria von Weber is in general repertoire. Hindemith wrote concertos for various solo instruments. Of these the concertos for his own instrument, the viola, are notable, in particular the attractive Der Schwanendreher (The Swan-Drover), based on folk-songs, and Kammermusik No. 5, also a viola concerto.

☛ **Recommended Recording**

Mathis der Maler Symphony
Nobilissima Visione
Symphonic Metamorphoses on Themes of Carl
Maria von Weber
Naxos 8.553078

Chamber Music

Among the various duo sonatas written by Hindemith, there are sonatas for violin and piano and for viola and piano that are of interest. The sonata repertoire provided for tuba, double bass, horn, harp, trumpet, viola d'amore, cor anglais and other instruments is of interest, as are the three organ sonatas.

Piano Music

Apart from his three Piano Sonatas and sonatas for two pianos and for piano duet, Ludus Tonalis is the most ambitious work for piano, a set of fugues and interludes through the keys, in the manner of J.S. Bach, preceded by an introduction that is inverted in conclusion.

☛ **Recommended Recordings**
  Piano Works (Complete) Vol. 1
  Marco Polo 8.223335

  Piano Works (Complete) Vol. 2
  Marco Polo 8.223336

  Piano Works (Complete) Vol. 3
  Marco Polo 8.223337

  Piano Works (Complete) Vol. 4
  Marco Polo 8.223338

Holmès, Augusta (1847 - 1903)

Of acknowledged Irish parentage, although rumour suggested she had been fathered by her godfather, Alfred de Vigny, Augusta Holmès was born in Paris and became a pupil of César Franck. She wrote operas, symphonic poems and dramatic symphonies and a large number of effective songs. She made a strong impression on many of her contemporaries through her intelligence and beauty and was for many years the mistress of the writer and French champion of Wagner, Catulle Mendès, husband of Judith Gautier.

Orchestral and Choral Music

The orchestral compositions of Augusta Holmès include the symphonic poems Irlande, Andromède and Pologne, the symphonic ode Ludus pro patria and the dramatic symphony Les Argonautes. Saint-Saëns, who unwisely and unsuccessfully proposed marriage to her, found some of her orchestral music noisy and over-orchestrated.

☛ **Recommended Recording**
  Andromède / Ouverture pour une comédie
  Irlande / La Nuit et l'Amour / Pologne
  Marco Polo 8.223449

Songs

Augusta Holmès left some 128 songs, a number of which continue to form part of the repertoire of French song.

Holst, Gustav (1874 - 1934)

Gustav Holst, of Scandinavian ancestry on his father's side, was born in the English spa town of Cheltenham in 1874 and studied music at the Royal College in London, using his second study, the trombone, to provide an income. He later became director of music at St. Paul's Girls' School, retaining this connection until the end of his life. His music had a variable reception in his lifetime, but he exercised a strong influence on later English composers.

Stage Works

Holst wrote a number of works for the theatre, their subjects reflecting his varied interests, from Hindu mythology to Shakespeare and the medieval world of the Wandering Scholar. From his final chamber opera The Perfect Fool, first staged in 1923, with its parodies of Verdi and Wagner, comes a better known ballet suite. The opera itself is seldom performed.

Vocal and Choral Music

As a choral conductor, Holst wrote a considerable amount of choral music, accompanied and unaccompanied, including arrangements of folk-songs, and a smaller number of solo songs.

Orchestral Music

By far the best known of all Holst's compositions is The Planets, a sequence of seven movements, reflecting the composer's interest in astrology and the generally attributed qualities of each, with Jupiter, The Bringer of Jollity, providing the melody for a popular patriotic hymn, while Mars, The Bringer of War, suggests the period of composition, between 1914 and 1916. For string orchestra he wrote the St. Paul's Suite, completed in 1913, and in 1933 the Brook Green Suite. The two

Suites for military band were written in 1911. His Suite de ballet, Opus 10, was written in 1899 and revised in 1912.

☛ **Recommended Recording**
The Planets / Suite de ballet, Op. 10
Naxos 8.550193

Honegger, Arthur (1892 - 1955)

Swiss by nationality, Arthur Honegger was born and died in France, and was for a time associated with the group of Paris composers known as Les Six, although they were not bound together by ideals such as those of the Five in 19th century Russia. Honegger was a prolific composer in many genres, writing for the theatre and concert hall, as well as for the cinema.

Orchestral Music

Honegger made some impression with his three symphonic movements, the first of a railway engine, Pacific 231, followed by Rugby, and a third with the simple title, Mouvement symphonique. Works of particular interest include the delightful Piano Concertino and the Concerto da camera for flute, cor anglais and strings and the charming Pastorale d'été, scored for chamber orchestra. The second and third of his five symphonies form part of the concert repertoire.

☞ Recommended Recordings

Crime et Châtiment / L'Idée / Farinet
Le Déserteur / Le Grand Barrage
Marco Polo 8.223466

Les Misérables (Complete Film Score)
Marco Polo 8.223181

Les Misérables / La Roue / Mermoz / Napoléon
Marco Polo 8.223134

Mayerling / Regain / Le Démon de l'Himalaya
Marco Polo 8.223467

Vocal and Choral Music

The dramatic psalm Le roi David, completed in 1921, is an impressive work, originally theatrical in intention, but transferred effectively to the concert-hall as an oratorio. Honegger's stage oratorio Jeanne d'Arc au bûcher (Joan of Arc at the Stake), completed in 1935, using a text by Paul Claudel, is an equally moving work, powerful in its use of the human voice, whether in speech or song.

Hotteterre, Jacques-Martin

(1674 - 1763)

Jacques Hotteterre is the most distinguished of a family that provided the French court with a number of players and composers in the 17th and 18th centuries. He followed the family tradition of instrument-making and performance, playing bassoon in the Grands Hautbois of the court and flute in the music of the royal chamber. He was popular as a teacher and wrote instruction manuals for the transverse flute and other wind instruments, as well as for the musette, the fashionable French bagpipe. Hotteterre was generally known as 'le Romain', suggesting a possible period spent in Rome.

Chamber Music

Hotteterre's compositions include a number of publications calling for one or two flutes, or alternative instrumentation, with other accompanying instruments. Suites in a number of movements are melodically effective and provide a useful source of information on contemporary French techniques of ornamentation.

Howells, Herbert (1892 - 1983)

Herbert Howells started his musical career as a cathedral organist. He succeeded Gustav Holst as director of music at St Paul's Girls' School in London and taught composition for many years at the Royal College of Music. A pupil of Stanford and Charles Wood at the Royal College, he wrote music within the prevailing English tradition, showing some affinity with Vaughan Williams in his choral music.

Orchestral Music

The orchestral music of Howells includes two Piano Concertos, a Pastoral Rhapsody and, in 1949, Music for a Prince. The Concerto for Strings of 1939 was followed by a Suite, also for string orchestra.

Chamber Music

Howells wrote an interesting Phantasy Quartet and a later String Quartet 'In Gloucestershire'. Among other compositions for instrumental ensemble are a Rhapsody Quintet for clarinet and string quartet, sonatas for oboe and for clarinet and piano, and three Violin Sonatas.

Organ Music

As an organist by training, Howells added significantly to the repertoire of English organ music, notably in two Organ Sonatas, four organ Rhapsodies and sets of Psalm Preludes.

☞ **Recommended Recording**
Psalm Preludes Op. 32
Naxos 8.550582

Vocal and Choral Music

Hymnus Paradisi written in 1938, a Requiem for the composer's son, was first performed at the Three Choirs Festival in the West of England in 1950, when it won considerable success. It was followed by the Missa sabrinensis and a setting of the Stabat mater. Howells also contributed to the repertoire of church music for the Church of England, with anthems and motets well suited to resonant cathedral acoustics. His songs include settings of a number of poems by his friend Walter de la Mare.

Hummel, Johann Nepomuk
(1778 - 1837)

The reputation of Hummel has been clouded by time. Born in Pressburg (the modern Bratislava) in 1778, he was a pupil of Mozart and enjoyed a successful career as a pianist and composer. He was employed by the Esterházy family at Eisenstadt as Konzertmeister, while Haydn, now in retirement in Vienna, continued as nominal Kapellmeister. He later served as Kapellmeister at Stuttgart and from 1818 at Weimar.

Orchestral Music

Recent recordings and performances have revived some interest in two of Hummel's half dozen or so piano concertos, Op. 85 and Op. 89. His Trumpet Concerto is a useful part of current repertoire.

Chamber Music

Hummel's Op. 87 Piano Quintet has particular interest in that it is scored for the same instruments as the famous Trout Quintet of Schubert, with which it is sometimes coupled in recording. Both quintets are scored for piano, violin, viola, cello and double bass.

☞ **Recommended Recording**

Flute Sonatas (Op. 2, No. 2, Op. 50 & Op. 64)
Grand Rondeau Brillant for Flute and Piano,
Op. 126 / Flute Trio, Op. 78
Naxos 8.553473

Humperdinck, Engelbert

(1854 - 1921)

Humperdinck is generally known for his fairy-tale opera Hänsel und Gretel, a Christmas favourite, first staged in Weimar in 1893. His career brought early contact with Wagner and subsequently with his family, as music tutor to Siegfried Wagner, the composer's son. He held various teaching positions of some distinction and enjoyed a fruitful collaboration in the theatre with Max Reinhardt, providing incidental music for a number of Shakespearean productions in Berlin.

Operas

If Hänsel und Gretel remains the best known of Humperdinck's operas, recent revivals abroad of Die Königskinder (The King's Children), another fairy-tale opera, suggest a renewal of its popularity.

☞ **Recommended Recordings**

Die Königskinder (Overture)
Naxos 8.550146

Moorish Rhapsody / Sleeping Beauty
The Merchant of Venice / The Canteen Woman
Marco Polo 8.223369

Ibert, Jacques (1890 - 1962)

Ibert, a winner of the Prix de Rome at the Paris Conservatoire, was for a number of years director of the French Academy in Rome. Versatile and prolific, he wrote operas, ballets and music for the theatre, cinema and radio, in addition to vocal and instrumental works, all equally beautifully crafted, with particularly idiomatic handling of wind instruments. He died in Paris in 1962.

Orchestral Music

The Flute Concerto by Ibert, written in 1934, is a useful addition to solo repertoire for an instrument whose possibilities the composer well understood, as he did the saxophone in his concertino for that instrument, composed in the following year. The orchestral music of Ibert includes suites and extracts from his theatre music, among which the scores written for A Midsummer Night's Dream and for the Orson Welles film of Macbeth should be mentioned. His Divertissement for chamber orchestra was derived from incidental music for Un chapeau de paille d' Italie (An Italian Straw Hat).

☛ Recommended Recordings

La Ballade de la Geôle de Reading
Trois Pièces de Ballet / Féerique
Chant de Folie / Suite Elisabéthaine
Marco Polo 8.223508

Macbeth / Golgotha / Don Quichotte
Marco Polo 8.223287

Petite Suite / Histoires / Les rencontres
Marco Polo 8.223409

Chamber Music

The most popular of Ibert's works for smaller groups must be the Entracte for flute or violin, with harpsichord or guitar, followed by the Interludes for flute, violin and harp, from Lifar's Le burlador, and Histoires, taken from his own piano work of that name.

d'Indy, Vincent (1851 - 1931)

Vincent d'Indy was born in Paris in 1851 and became a pupil and leading disciple of César Franck, whose music he did much to propagate. He distinguished himself as a teacher and writer on musical subjects and was an important figure in the musical life of Paris in his time, although by the time of his death a new era in music was well under way.

Orchestral Music

Vincent d'Indy wrote music in all principal genres. His Symphonie sur un chant montagnard français (Symphony on a French mountain air) for piano and orchestra, completed in 1886, is overtly patriotic, based on a French folk-song.

☛ Recommended Recordings

L'Étranger / Tableaux de Voyage
Phantaisie pour hautbois et orchestre
Prélude de "Fervaal" / "Saugefleurie" Legende
Marco Polo 8.223659

Médée / Karadec / Souvenirs
Marco Polo 8.223654

String Quartet, Op. 96 / Piano Quintet, Op. 81
Marco Polo 8.223691

String Quartets Nos. 1 and 2
Marco Polo 8.223140

Symphonie sur un chant montagnard français
Naxos 8.550754

Ippolitov-Ivanov, Mikhail Mikhaylovich (1859 - 1935)

After musical training at the Moscow Conservatory, Ippolitov-Ivanov was appointed director of the Tbilisi Conservatory in Georgia. In 1905 he returned to Moscow to teach at the Conservatory, where he worked until his death in 1935. He served as a conductor and continued the nationalist traditions established by the Five, with the firmer technical basis now provided by the Conservatory. He shared with Rimsky-Korsakov and Balakirev an interest in the relatively exotic, enhanced through his experience of musical life in Georgia.

Orchestral Music

Caucasian Sketches, written in 1894, followed by the Armenian Rhapsody and Iveriya, are evidence of Ippolitov-Ivanov's interest in the music of the various ethnic groups that formed part of the Russian Empire, of which further examples are found in his On the Steppes of Turkmenistan and Musical Pictures of Uzbekistan.

- ☞ **Recommended Recordings**
  Georgian War March from Iveria Op. 42
  Naxos 8.550230

Procession of the Sardar
from Caucasian Sketches
Naxos 8.550370
Naxos 8.550328

Symphony No. 1
Turkish Fragments and March
Marco Polo 8.220217

Spring Overture, Op. 1
Symphonic Scherzo, Op. 2
Three Musical Tableaux from Ossian, Op. 56
Jubilee March / Armenian Rhapsody, Op. 48
An Episode from the Life of Schubert, Op. 61
Marco Polo 8.223629

Ireland, John (1879 - 1962)

A pupil of Stanford at the Royal College of Music in London, John Ireland later taught composition at the Royal College, while earning his living for many years as an organist and choirmaster. His music belongs to the 20th century English musical tradition, demonstrating some lyrical affinity with Elgar, while admitting contemporary influences from abroad into a very personal idiom.

Orchestral Music

Ireland's Piano Concerto and his Concertino pastorale for strings are notable works, with his once popular A London Overture. Other orchestral music includes the prelude The Forgotten Rite and the symphonic rhapsody Mai-Dun. He provided a very competent score for the film The Overlanders.

Chamber Music

Ireland's chamber music, well crafted as always, includes two Violin Sonatas, the second particularly worthy of attention, followed by a fine Cello Sonata. He left three Piano Trios and a Fantasy Sonata for clarinet and piano.

Piano Music

Ireland wrote one Piano Sonata and a Sonatina, in addition to a large number of lyrical shorter pieces, many with characteristic titles.

Organ Music

Organ music by Ireland includes a Capriccio and a Miniature Suite, among other pieces.

Vocal and Choral Music

The coronation choral commission of 1937, These Things Shall Be, proved impressive in its time. His songs include settings of Housman, Hardy, Yeats, with nine song cycles, of which Songs of a Wayfarer and Songs Sacred and Profane are examples.

Isaac, Heinrich (c. 1450 - 1517)

It would be impossible to single out works from the enormous quantity of music written by the great Flemish composer Heinrich Isaac, a musician whose career took him to Florence, under the patronage of the Medici, and to Vienna, where he served the Emperor Maximilian, exercising a decisive influence on the music of the German part of the empire. He died in Florence in 1517. In addition to a quantity of music for the church, Isaac wrote a considerable amount of secular music, much of it vocal, including the well known Insprugk, ich muss dich lassen, a reference to the time he spent in Innsbruck in the service of the Emperor.

Ives, Charles (1874 - 1954)

The American composer Charles Ives learned a great deal from his bandmaster father, not least a love of the music of Bach. At the same time he was exposed to a variety of very American musical influences, later reflected in his own idiosyncratic compositions. Ives was educated at Yale and made a career in insurance, reserving his activities as a composer for his leisure hours. Ironically, by the time that his music had begun to arouse interest, his own inspiration and energy as a composer had waned, so that for the last thirty years of his life he wrote little, while his reputation grew.

Orchestral Music

The symphonies of Ives include music essentially American in inspiration and adventurous in structure and texture, collages of Americana, expressed in a musical idiom that makes use of complex polytonality (the use of more than one key or tonality at the same time) and rhythm. The Third Symphony, for small orchestra, reflects much of Ives's own background, carrying the explanatory title Camp Meeting and movement titles Old Folks Gatherin', Children's Day and Communion. The Fourth Symphony includes a number of hymns and Gospel songs, and his so-called First Orchestral Set, otherwise known as New England Symphony, depicts three places in New England.

Chamber Music

The first of the two string quartets of Ives has the characteristic title From the Salvation Army and is based on earlier organ compositions, while the fourth of his four violin sonatas depicts Children's Day at the Camp Meeting.

Keyboard Music

Much of the earlier organ music written by Ives from the time of his student years, when he served as organist in a number of churches, found its way into later compositions. The second of his two piano sonatas,

Concord, Mass. 1840 - 60, has the characteristic movement titles Emerson, Hawthorne, The Alcotts and Thoreau, a very American literary celebration.

Vocal and Choral Music

Ives wrote a number of psalm settings, part-songs and verse settings for unison voices and orchestra. In his many solo songs he set verses ranging from Shakespeare, Goethe and Heine to Whitman and Kipling, with a number of texts of his own creation. Relatively well known songs by Ives include Shall we gather at the river, The Cage and The Side-Show.

Janáček, Leos (1854 - 1928)

It was relatively late in life that the Moravian composer Janáček won more than local recognition. He made his early career in the capital of his native province, Brno, coupling an interest in regional folk music with a study of speech intonations, echoed in his instrumental as well as vocal writing. His opera Jenufa was first staged in Brno in 1904, but it was the performance in Prague in 1915 that brought the work of the composer a much wider public. The seven operas that followed have formed a very idiosyncratic part of current operatic repertoire, culminating in From the House of the Dead, completed in 1928, the year of Janáček's death, and based on the novel by Dostoyevsky.

Orchestral Music

The best known of Janáček's music for orchestra is the Sinfonietta, derived from an original festival piece of 1926. To this may be added the rhapsody based on the work of Gogol, Taras Bulba, and the Lachian Dances, based on folk-dances.

☞ **Recommended Recordings**

Sinfonietta / Taras Bulba / Lachian Dances
Naxos 8.550411

Piano Music Vol. 1
(Along an Overgrown Path /
Sonata 1. X. 1905 "From the street")
Naxos 8.553586

Piano Music Vol. 2
(Variations for Zdenka /
Three Moravian Dances / A recollection /
Music for Exercise Gymnastique /
In the Mist / Concertino)
Naxos 8.553587

Piano Music Vol. 3
(Sonata for Violin and Piano / Romance /
Dumka / Allegro / Capriccio)
Naxos 8.553588

Janequin, Clément (c. 1485 - 1558)

Clément Janequin enjoyed a long career in the service of the Church, of members of the nobility and finally in the service of the King of France. He was a master of the French chanson of the period.

Chansons

Janequin wrote a number of psalm settings and chansons spirituelles (Spiritual Songs) and an even greater number of secular chansons, a number of which are programmatic. Of these La bataille (The Battle) is particularly well known, with the imitative La chasse (The Hunt), Le chant des oiseaux (The Song of the Birds) and Les cris de Paris (The Street Cries of Paris).

Jenkins, John (1592 - 1678)

John Jenkins was one of the foremost English composers of consort music. He was himself distinguished as a lutenist and a player of the lyra viol. In his eight hundred or so instrumental compositions he continues the traditions of William Byrd.

☞ **Recommended Recording**

All in a Garden Green
Naxos 8.550687

Jolívet, André (1905 - 1974)

Versatile in the arts, André Jolivet was a pupil of Le Flem and later of Varèse and was, with Olivier Messiaen, Daniel Lesur and Yves Baudrier, a member of the composers grouped together as Jeune France. As director of music for the Comédie française he wrote a quantity of incidental music and elsewhere based his work on principles that stemmed from his interest in the magical and incantatory element fundamental to human music.

Orchestral Music

Jolivet wrote a number of concertos, all demanding considerable virtuosity from the soloist. These include a concerto for the ondes Martenot, an electronic instrument developed in France in the 1920s, and concertos for trumpet and piano, for flute, for piano, for harp, for bassoon and harp, for percussion, for cello and for violin.

Stage Music

In addition to his varied incidental music, whether for Molière, Claudel, Corneille or Plautus, Jolivet wrote music for the ballet and for marionette plays.

Chamber and Solo Instrumental Music

Jolivet made an early impression on Messiaen with the six piano pieces that constitute Mana. Chamber music includes music involving the flute, an instrument he particularly favoured for its primitive human associations.

Josquín, Desprez (c. 1440 - 1521)

Josquin, the descriptive part of whose name appears in various forms, occupies a leading position in the music of his generation. He represents the dominance of composers from Northern France and the Netherlands in this period, a school of music sometimes known as the Netherlands School, but influential throughout the Habsburg domains. Josquin was employed in Milan, at the papal chapel in Rome, by King Louis XII of France, at the court of the d'Estes in Ferrara and finally in his native region of Condé, where he died in 1521.

Church Music

Josquin wrote a large amount of church music. Of this eighteen Mass settings survive, including one using as a basic motif or cantus firmus the well known secular song L'homme armé; one honouring his Ferrara patron, Duke Ercole d'Este, Hercules Dux Ferrarie, its cantus firmus based on the musical transliteration of its title, and the Missa Pange lingua, which uses the Latin hymn of the same name. Josquin also wrote a large number of motets of equally faultless technique, the epitome of Renaissance musical achievement, among which may be mentioned Absalom, fili mi, Ave Maria gratia plena and his Stabat mater dolorosa.

Secular Music

Vocal music largely to French texts includes a lament for the death of the composer Ockeghem, Nymphes des bois; the chanson El grillo, with its imitation of the cricket, is a fine jeu d'esprit and the light-hearted Scaramella va alla guerra. Mille regretz is among the best known of a remarkable collection of works.

Kabalevsky, Dmitry Borisovich

(1904 - 1987)

Kabalevsky was a pupil of Myaskovsky at the Moscow Conservatory, where he himself taught from 1932, and in general did his utmost to conform with government cultural policy, occupying important positions in the Union of Soviet Composers. He wrote operas and operettas that enjoyed success in Russia, as did his patriotic vocal works and useful compositions for children.

Orchestral Music

Kabalevsky's orchestral music has won greater favour abroad than his dramatic and vocal compositions. Mention may be made of his Suite from the opera The Comedians and another from incidental music for Romeo and Juliet, with his two Cello Concertos.

☛ **Recommended Recording**

Suites: Colas Breugnon / The Comedians Romeo and Juliet Naxos 8.553411

Khachaturian, Aram Il'yich

(1903 - 1978)

Khachaturian, a Soviet composer of Armenian origin, was trained at Moscow Conservatory, where he studied composition with Myaskovsky. He later assumed important positions in the Union of Soviet Composers and continued to implement one aspect of official cultural policy in his use of regional Armenian thematic material, although his name was joined to those of Shostakovich and Prokofiev in the condemnation of formalism promulgated in 1948.

Stage Works

The 1942 ballet Gayane contains the most popular of all Khachaturian's works, the Sabre Dance. The ballet

Spartacus of 1954 contains a well known Adagio of Spartacus and Phrygia. There are concert suites from both ballets.

👉 Recommended Recordings

Gayane (Suites Nos. 1-3)
Naxos 8.550800

Spartacus (Suites Nos. 1-3)
Naxos 8.550801

Spartacus (Suite No. 4) / Masquerade (Suite)
Circus (Music from the ballet) / Dance Suite
Naxos 8.550802

The Battle of Stalingrad / Othello
Marco Polo 8.223314

Orchestral Music

Khachaturian's Violin Concerto, written in 1940, is a characteristic work and has been transcribed for solo flute by the French flautist Jean-Pierre Rampal. The composer wrote a Piano Concerto in 1936 and ten years later an effective Cello Concerto.

Kodály, Zoltán (1882 - 1967)

Kodály, a colleague of Bartók in the early collection of folk music in Hungary and neighbouring regions, made his later career in his own country, where the system of musical education he devised has had a profound effect,

as it has abroad. His own music is imbued with the spirit and musical idiom of Hungary and is in general less astringent than is sometimes the case with the music of Bartók. He was active as a composer until his death in 1967.

Stage Works

Kodály wrote relatively little for the stage. His Singspiel or musical play Háry János, more widely known in the orchestral excerpts heard frequently in the concert hall, deals with the alleged exploits of an old soldier, János, who has a vivid imagination and no regard for truth or probability. These include his single-handed defeat of Napoleon and the French armies.

Orchestral Music

In addition to the orchestral suite derived from Háry János, Kodály's Marosszék and Galanta Dances, with the Peacock Variations, make powerful use of Hungarian folk material.

👉 Recommended Recordings

Háry János Suite
Naxos 8.550142

Peacock Variations / Galanta Dances
Marosszek Dances
Naxos 8.550520

Choral Music

Kodály wrote a great deal of choral and vocal music, much of it for his choral method, an essential element in his plan for general musical education. He won his greatest early success with Psalmus hungaricus in 1923, and in 1936 celebrated the 250th anniversary of the reconquest of Buda from the Turks with a Te Deum. His Missa brevis was written during the later years of the 1939-45 war. His unaccompanied choral work Jesus and the Traders has always proved effective.

☛ Recommended Recording

Cello Works
(3 Choral Preludes /
Sonata for Solo Cello Op. 8 / Sonata Op. 4)
Naxos 8.553160

Koechlin, Charles (1867 - 1950)

A pupil of Gabriel Fauré, Koechlin occupies a position of honour among French composers, highly respected as a teacher and counting among his own pupils Poulenc and Tailleferre, while exercising a strong influence on Milhaud and the younger composers associated with Satie. His pre-eminence as a theorist has led to undue neglect of his music.

Orchestral Music

Koechlin's compositions include symphonies and symphonic poems, some of the latter inspired by Kipling's Jungle Book, as well as a symphonic poem based on Romain Rolland's Le buisson ardent, a study of composer's block.

☛ Recommended Recordings

Au loin / Sur les flots lointains
Le buisson ardent
Marco Polo 8.223704

Le Livre de la Jungle
Marco Polo 8.223484

Les Heures Persanes
Marco Polo 8.223504

Vocal Music

Koechlin made a significant addition to French song, with choral and solo settings of texts by contemporaries and earlier writers.

Chamber Music

Koechlin's works include a quantity of chamber music for various instruments, notably a flute sonata, a wind septet and a piano quintet, with a series of compositions, Les chants de nectaire, for solo flute..

Piano Music

Much of Koechlin's piano music was written before 1920. There are sets of easy pieces and exercises, five Sonatinas and sets of pieces under the title Esquisses (Sketches) and Paysages et marines (Land- and Sea-scapes).

Korngold, Erich Wolfgang
(1897 - 1957)

A composer of remarkable precocity, Erich Wolfgang Korngold was born in Brno in 1897. At the age of ten his cantata Gold won praise from Mahler and his ballet Der Schneemann (The Snowman), written when he was eleven, was staged with success at the Vienna Court Opera in 1910. His reputation as a leading composer in the romantic tradition was established when his association with Max Reinhardt took him in 1934 to Hollywood, where he remained until his death in 1957. He wrote the music for some nineteen films in America, including Robin Hood and Anthony Adverse, but his connection with Hollywood did not help his reputation as a serious composer, so that it is only now that his music can be heard again with less prejudice.

Operas

Korngold's career as a composer of opera ended with the annexation of Austria and the consequent banning of any further performances of his work there. His first opera, Der Ring der Polykrates (The Ring of Polycrates), was staged first in Munich in 1916, with his second opera, Violanta. Die tote Stadt (The Dead City) was first jointly staged in 1920 in Hamburg and Cologne and in 1975 was revived to acclaim in New York.

Orchestral Music

The best known of Korngold's orchestral works must be his Violin Concerto, written in 1945 and given its first performance by Jascha Heifetz. Other works of interest from this period of Korngold's life include his Cello Concerto, the Symphonic Serenade for strings and the Symphony. His earlier compositions in Vienna include his Piano Concerto for the left hand, the Sinfonietta and Die kleine Serenade (The Little Serenade), followed, in America, by his symphonic poem for chorus and orchestra, Tomorrow, written in 1942.

Chamber Music

Korngold's chamber music ranges from a Caprice fantastique for violin and piano, written in 1908, to a 1946 Romance Impromptu for cello and piano. Other compositions include three string quartets, a piano trio and a piano quintet.

Recommended Recordings

Piano Quintet Op. 15 / Violin Sonata Op. 6
Marco Polo 8.223385

Piano Sonatas Nos. 1 and 2 / Märchenbilder
Viel Lärmen um Nichts
Marco Polo 8.223384

Vocal Music

Korngold also wrote a number of songs, including a setting of the clown's songs from Shakespeare's Twelfth Night and a setting of Kaltneker's Sonett für Wien (Sonnet for Vienna), written in 1952.

Koussevitzky, Sergey (1874 - 1951)

Koussevitzky is principally remembered as a conductor. He started his career as a double bass virtuoso, but after the Russian revolution he established himself in the United States of America, where he followed Pierre Monteux as conductor of the Boston Symphony Orchestra in 1924, retaining his position with the orchestra until shortly before his death. He was of significant help to contemporary composers, not least through Koussevitzky Music Foundation, established in memory of his first wife.

Music for Double Bass

Koussevitzky made an important addition to a small repertoire in his Double Bass Concerto, written in 1905 with the help of Reinhold Glière. He also composed other short pieces for the instrument.

Kreisler, Fritz (1875 - 1962)

Among the most distinguished violinists of his time, Fritz Kreisler was born in Vienna and became a student at the Conservatory at the age of seven, studying with the younger Joseph Hellmesberger and later, in Paris, with Massart. His subsequent international career, interrupted briefly by diversion into medical studies and army service, consolidated his position as a leading virtuoso. As a composer he provided himself with a series of brief encore pieces, well suited to the then requirements of the recording studio. These took the form of arrangements and transcriptions as well as a more controversial series of pieces attributed to composers of the past but in fact his own composition. These too have become a standard part of violin repertoire and it seems strange, in retrospect, that anyone should have thought them anything but effective and not particularly literal pastiche. His technique in performance involved a ubiquitous vibrato, applied to fast as well as slow notes.

Violin Music

Kreisler made useful additions to violin repertoire in his many transcriptions, short compositions of acknowledged authorship and a series of pieces that he attributed to lesser known composers of the 18th century, but which were in fact his own work. Original compositions include the well known Liebesleid (Sorrow of Love) and its counterpart, Liebesfreud (Joy of Love), transcribed for piano by Rachmaninov, and the pastiche Praeludium and Allegro that he attributed to Pugnani.

☛ **Recommended Recording**
Liebesleid / Liebesfreud / Schön Rosmarin
Rondino / Caprice viennois
Naxos 8.550306

Krommer, Franz (1759 - 1831)

Born in Kamenice, Frantisek Kramár, better known by his German name as Franz Krommer, made his career in the service of various noblemen, finally settling in Vienna, where he became director of music for the Court Ballet and later entering the service of the Emperor Franz I, finally as imperial director of chamber music and court composer.

Orchestral Music

Krommer's orchestral music includes symphonies and concertos, the latter for his own instrument, the violin, and for various wind instruments, either singly or in multiple concertos. He added to the repertoire of Harmoniemusik, music for wind band, with well crafted compositions that serve their entertaining purpose admirably.

☛ **Recommended Recording**
Clarinet Concerti Opp. 35, 36 & 91
Naxos 8.553178

Chamber Music

Krommer's string quartets seemed to contemporaries to equal those of Haydn and rival those of Beethoven. He wrote a quantity of chamber music, quintets and quartets, a number of these involving wind instruments, in addition to trios and duos, all reflecting the style and taste of the period in which he lived.

Lalo, Edouard (1823 - 1892)

Born in Lille in 1823 into a family of Spanish origin that had long been settled in France, Lalo was trained as a violinist and made an early career as member of a string quartet. It was not until he was fifty that he made any great impression as a composer, particularly with a series of orchestral works, on which his international reputation chiefly depends, in spite of his other compositions, operas, chamber music and songs.

Orchestral Music

Lalo's Symphonie espagnole is in fact a violin concerto of Spanish flavour, in five movements. Written in 1874, and first performed by the Spanish violinist Pablo Sarasate, it is a popular part of current violin repertoire. His Cello Concerto in D minor, written in 1877, enjoys rather less popularity, but is perhaps of greater musical interest.

☛ **Recommended Recording**

Symphonie espagnole
Naxos 8.550494

Landowski, Marcel (1915 -)

The French composer Marcel Landowski was assisted early in his career by the support of the conductor Pierre Monteux and has had an active career in music administration, as director of the Conservatoire of Boulogne-sur-Seine, music director at the Comédie française and as music director with the Ministry for Cultural Affairs. His music retains an element of popular appeal, avoiding the experimental excess that can alienate an audience, while he is still no mere conservative.

Orchestral Music

Orchestral music by Marcel Landowski includes four symphonies, the first of them Jean de la peur (John of Fear). His concertos include works for the electronic ondes Martenot, for trumpet, for flute, for bassoon and for piano.

Vocal Music

In addition to his operas, Marcel Landowski has set a variety of texts, including a text by Rabindranath Tagore, suggesting the continuing influence of the East on his thought.

Langlais, Jean (1907 - 1991)

A pupil of Dukas and of Marcel Dupré, the French organist Jean Langlais had his earlier training at the Institution des Jeunes Aveugles (Institution for the Young Blind), where he later taught. He was appointed organist at Ste Clotilde in Paris in 1945 and had a career as a concert performer.

Organ Music

The organ music of Jean Langlais reflects his profound religious faith and makes frequent use of Gregorian chant as its basis. He wrote organ symphonies, suites, meditations on the liturgy and voluntaries, in addition to works scored for organ with other instruments.

☛ **Recommended Recording**

Suite Médiévale
5 Méditations sur l'Apocalypse
Naxos 8.553190

Vocal Music

Church music by Langlais includes settings of the Mass, notably the Mass Salve Regina and the Mass Orbis Factor.

Choral Music

The choral music of Langlais is principally religious in form, including a Messe solennelle, Missa in simplicitate, and a Solemn Mass 'Orbis Factor', as well as Psalms for four voices, chorus, organ, brass and timpani. His Canticle of the Sun, written in 1968, is scored for soprano and mezzo-soprano soloists and organ.

Larsson, Lars-Erik (1908 - 1986)

Lars-Erik Larsson occupied an important posaition in Swedish musical life, not least in his work for broadcasting, for the tehatre and cinema. His style as a composer is eclectic, ranging from the late Romantic to techniques derived from the twelve-note system outlined by Schoenberg, but original in method.

Orchestral Music

In addition to his symphonies for full orchestra, Larsson wrote a Sinfonietta for string orchestra and a popular Little Serenade for the same medium. He left a useful series of concertinos for solo instruments that include, flute, oboe, clarinet, bassoon, horn, trumpet, trombone, saxophone, violin, viola, cello, double bass and piano.

Lassus, Orlando de (1532 - 1594)

Lassus, also known by the Italian form of his name, Orlando di Lasso, belonged to the Franco-Flemish school of composers whose work was of supreme international importance in the 16th century. He was born at Mons, in Hainaut, in 1532, and as a boy entered the service of a member of the Gonzaga family, hereditary dukes of Mantua. Employment elsewhere in Italy and a stay in Antwerp was followed by a position in the musical establishment of Duke Albrecht V of Bavaria in Munich, where Lassus remained from 1556 until his death. With Palestrina and Vittoria, he is one of the most important composers of the period.

Church Music

Lassus wrote a considerable quantity of church music, including over seventy settings of the Mass, settings of the Passions from the four evangelists and a very large number of motets. From this very considerable body of work of the highest quality selection is invidious, although mention may be made of the Requiem for four voices, the Missa octavi toni and Missa Qual donna, and motets such as Tristis est anima mea and the setting of the seven penitential Psalms of David and of the Holy Week Lamentations.

☛ Recommended Recordings

Lessons I & III for Maundy Thursday
Naxos 8.550572

Lagrime di San Pietro
Naxos 8.553311

Masses for Five Voices / Infelix ego
Naxos 8.550842

Missa Bell' Amfitrit' altera
Naxos 8.550836

Secular Vocal Music

The secular vocal compositions of Lassus include madrigals, in the Italian style, some 150 French chansons and a much smaller number of German Lieder, all of great interest and forming a large body of work, including settings of Petrarch and Ariosto, Ronsard and Marot, from which selection is again invidious.

Lawes, Henry (1596 - 1662) & William (1602 - 1645)

The Lawes brothers occupy an important position in English music between Byrd and Gibbons and the generation of Matthew Locke and Henry Purcell in the later part of the 17th century. William Lawes, a loyal follower of King Charles I, was killed at the battle of Chester in 1645. Henry Lawes survived the civil war and the subsequent Commonwealth of Oliver Cromwell to be reinstated as a member of the King's Musick and the Chapel Royal on the restoration of the monarchy in 1660.

Sacred Vocal Music

Both Henry and William Lawes wrote sacred vocal music, Henry providing psalm settings and anthems and William a series of sacred songs and canons.

Secular Vocal Music

The Lawes brothers both won distinction as song composers, Henry with a vast quantity of songs and William with settings of verses by many of the leading poets and dramatists of the time.

Instrumental Music

William Lawes enjoyed the greatest success as a composer of instrumental music, with compositions for the keyboard, and, more especially, with consort music for viols, with lute and organ, including a number of dance movements.

☛ **Recommended Recording**
Consort music for Viols
Naxos 8.550601

Le Flem, Paul (1881 - 1984)

Of Breton origin, Paul Le Flem studied at the Schola Cantorum under Vincent d'Indy and Roussel, later teaching at the same establishment, where his pupils included Satie and Jolivet. His music is strongly influenced by his native Brittany, the landscape of which is reflected in his work.

Stage Music

Le Flem dramatic works include the operas Le rossignol de St-Malo (The Nightingale of St Malo) and La magicienne de la mer (The Magician of the Sea), as well as the chante-fable Aucassin et Nicolette.

Orchestral Music

In addition to his symphonies, Le Flem wrote evocative orchestral music such as En mer (At Sea) and La voix du large (The Voice of the Open Sea).

☛ **Recommended Recording**
Pour les morts / Sept pièces enfantines
Le grand jardinier de France / Symphony No. 4
Marco Polo 8.223655

Vocal Music

Le Flem set texts by Verlaine and others and arranged for chorus a number of Breton folk-songs.

Leclair, Jean-Marie (1697 - 1764)

Leclair occupies an important place in the development of violin music in France. His skill as a dancer took him from his native Lyons to Italy, where he may have received violin lessons from Somis, before returning to France to settle in Paris, where he entered the royal service in 1733, resigning four years later. Later patrons included Anne, Princess of Orange, in The Hague, and finally the Duke of Gramont, a former pupil. He was murdered, perhaps by his nephew, also a violinist, in 1764.

Instrumental Music

Although he also wrote music for the theatre, including, in 1746, an opera, Scylla et Glaucus, Leclair is chiefly known for his violin music and in particular for his first two published sets of violin sonatas. The first set of twelve, published in 1723, includes two also for flute and basso continuo, and the second dozen includes five also for flute as a possible alternative to the violin.

Lehár, Franz (1870 - 1948)

The reputation of Franz Lehár as a composer of operetta is assured. The son of a bandmaster serving principally in Hungary, he followed his father's profession, before winning, in 1902, success in the theatre in Vienna, where he succeeded in the following years in reviving the operetta, providing music of greater distinction, with tenor arias written specifically for Richard Tauber.

Operettas

Lehár wrote nearly forty operettas. Of these by the far the best known is Die lustige Witwe (The Merry Widow), first staged in Vienna in 1905, the favourite operetta of Adolf Hitler.

☛ Recommended Recording

Freunde, das Leben ist lebenswert! from Giuditta
Meine Lippen, sie küssen so heiß from Giuditta
O Mädchen, mein Mädchen from Friederike
Dein ist mein ganzes Herz from The Land of Smiles
Wer hat die Liebe uns ins Herz gesenkt from The Land of Smiles
Immer nur lächeln from The Land of Smiles
Von Apfelblütten einen Kranz from The Land of Smiles
Lippen schweigen from The Merry Widow
Naxos 8.550941

O Vaterland from The Merry Widow
Vilja-Lied from The Merry Widow
Gern hab' ich die Frau'n geküßt from Paganini
Niemand liebt dich so wie ich from Paganini
Einer wird kommen from The Czarevich
Wolgalied from The Czarevich
Hör'ich Cymbalklänge from Gipsy Love
Mein Ahnherr war der Luxemburg from The Count of Luxembourg
Naxos 8.550942

Liebe, du Himmel auf Erden from Paganini
Naxos 8.550943

Orchestral Music

Lehár also made a significant contribution to Viennese light music with some 65 waltzes and 50 or more marches.

Lekeu, Guillaume (1870 - 1894)

Belgian in origin, Guillaume Lekeu studied in Paris with his compatriot César Franck and with Vincent d'Indy. He died of typhoid fever at the age of 24.

Chamber Music

Lekeu is best remembered for his G major Violin Sonata, an intensely lyrical work, and his sonata for piano, with a sonata for cello and piano that was completed after the composer's death by d'Indy, who also completed Lekeu's unfinished Piano Quartet. He also left a completed piano trio.

Vocal Music

Vocal music by Lekeu includes settings of words of his own, notably the Trois poèmes (Three Poems).

Leoncavallo, Ruggiero (1857 - 1919)

Neapolitan by birth, Leoncavallo studied music in Naples and literature at Bologna, and seemed about to make a career as a librettist. His operatic ambitions found their only really successful result in Pagliacci, for which he wrote both words and music.

Operas

Pagliacci, a story of love and jealousy in a troupe of commedia dell'arte actors, has achieved a permanent place in operatic repertoire, often, in view of its relative brevity, coupled with Mascagni's Cavalleria rusticana. Leoncavallo's first opera, Chatterton, won no favour, while his version of La bohème was soon eclipsed by that of Puccini.

☛ Recommended Recording

Pagliacci (Complete Opera)
Naxos 8.660021

Liadov, Anatol Konstantinovich (1855 - 1914)

The son of a conductor at the Mariinsky Theatre in St Petersburg, Anatol Liadov was trained at the Conservatory, where he was briefly a pupil of Rimsky-Korsakov and later a member of the teaching staff. He was associated with Balakirev and subsequently became a member of Belyayev's circle, helping, in particular, in the establishment of the publishing-house that Belyayev established for Russian composers. He was a thoroughly competent musician, conductor and composer, but did not apply himself consistently to work. His failure to supply music for the Dyagilev ballet in Paris in 1910 allowed Stravinsky his first chance with the Ballets russes. His compositions are characteristic of the period in Russian nationalism, when nationalism was joined with technical competence inculcated at the Conservatories.

Orchestral Music

The best known orchestral compositions by Liadov are the descriptive Russian fairy-tale pieces Kikimora, Baba-Yaga and Volshebnoye ozero (The Enchanted Lake). His last orchestral work was the symphonic poem Skorbnaya pesn (Nénie). All are very much in the nationalist tradition exemplified by Rimsky-Korsakov.

☛ **Recommended Recording**
   Kikimora / Baba Yaga / Apocalypse
   Enchanted Lake / Polonaises / Nénie
   Mazurka / Ballade / Intermezzo
   Marco Polo 8.220348

Piano Music

Liadov wrote a number of shorter piano pieces, including Fugues and a set of Canons, testimony to his contrapuntal ability. Other pieces have characteristic titles, examples of pleasing and well crafted compositions for which there was a ready market.

☛ **Recommended Recording**
   Piano Miniatures
   (Biryulki / Mazurkas / Preludes / Kukolki
   Arabesque
   Variations on a Popular Polish Song)
   Marco Polo 8.220416

Vocal and Choral Music

Liadov wrote a setting of the final scene of Schiller's Die Braut von Messina (The Bride from Messina) for his Conservatory graduation. Of some 26 songs, eighteen are Children's Songs.

Ligeti, György (b. 1923)

Of Hungarian-Jewish origin, Ligeti made his career in Hungary until 1956, when he moved to Vienna, now to be influenced by contact with more experimental Western techniques of composition, notably with work at the electronic studios in Cologne. His music now achieved a wider international reputation, incorporating contemporary techniques and experiment in a musical idiom that has proved both influential and palatable.

Orchestral Music

It was with compositions such as Atmosphères in 1961 that Ligeti began to win a wider reputation. Other orchestral works that have aroused interest include a

Chamber Concerto for thirteen instruments, the Cello Concerto and the Concerto for flute, oboe and strings. Lontano, written in 1967, has a place in contemporary repertoire, with Ramifications, for twelve strings and San Francisco Polyphony.

Chamber Music

In the second of his string quartets, Ligeti made a strong impression, while his Ten Pieces for wind quintet allow a degree of individual virtuosity to the players.

Vocal Music

Ligeti's Requiem, completed in 1965, makes considerable use of counterpoint and is a moving and colourful work. It was followed by Lux aeterna, a setting of the last part of the Requiem Mass, for sixteen solo voices, in which he again makes considerable use of the technique of canon.

Liszt, Franz (1811 - 1886)

Liszt was the son of a steward in the service of the Esterházy family, patrons of Haydn. He was born in 1811 at Raiding in Hungary and moved as a child to Vienna, where he took piano lessons from Czerny and composition lessons from Salieri. Two years later, in 1823, he moved with his family to Paris, from where he toured widely as a pianist. Influenced by the

phenomenal violinist Paganini, he turned his attention to the development of a similar technique as a pianist and in 1835 left Paris with his mistress, the Comtesse d'Agoult, with whom he travelled widely during the following years, as his reputation as a pianist of astonishing powers grew. In 1844 he separated from his mistress, the mother of his three children, and in 1848 settled in Weimar as Director of Music Extraordinary, accompanied by Princess Sayn-Wittgenstein and turning his attention now to composition and in particular to the creation of a new form, the symphonic poem. In 1861 Liszt moved to Rome, where he found expression for his long-held religious leanings. From 1869 he returned regularly to Weimar, where he had many pupils, and later he accepted similar obligations in Budapest, where he was regarded as a national hero. He died in Bayreuth in 1886, four years after the death of his son-in-law Wagner. As a pianist, he had no equal, and as a composer he suggested to a younger generation of musicians the new course that music was to take.

Orchestral Music

Liszt's symphonic poems met strong criticism from champions of pure music, who took exception to his attempts to translate into musical terms the greatest works of literature. The best known of the symphonic poems are Ce qu'on entend sur la montagne, based on

Victor Hugo, Les préludes, based on Lamartine, works based on Byron's Tasso and Mazeppa, and Prometheus, with the so-called Faust Symphony in Three Character-Sketches after Goethe and the Symphony on Dante's Divina commedia. Other orchestral works include two episodes from Lenau's Faust, the second the First Mephisto Waltz, to which a second was added twenty years later, in 1881. Liszt wrote two piano concertos, and, among other works for piano and orchestra, a Totentanz or Dance of Death and a Fantasy on Hungarian Folk-Melodies. Liszt's Hungarian Rhapsodies, written for piano, have been effectively arranged for orchestra.

☛ Recommended Recordings

A Faust Symphony
Naxos 8.553304

Symphonic Poems
(From the Cradle to the Grave / Hamlet / Orpheus / The Ideals)
Naxos 8.553355

Symphonic Poems
Tasso, Les Préludes, Mazeppa, Prometheus
Naxos 8.550487

Piano Concertos Nos. 1 & 2 / Totentanz
Naxos 8.550187

Hungarian Rhapsodies Nos. 1, 2 & 6
Naxos 8.550142

Piano Music

Liszt wrote a great deal of music for the piano, some of which was later revised, and consequently exists in a number of versions. In addition to original piano music, he also made many transcriptions of the work of other composers and wrote works based on national themes. The violinist Paganini was the immediate inspiration for the Etudes d'exécution transcendante d'après Paganini, dedicated to Clara Schumann, wife of the composer Robert Schumann, and based on five of the 24 Caprices for solo violin by Paganini and on the latter's La campanella. The Transcendental Studies, revised in 1851, Etudes d'exécution transcendante, form a set of twelve pieces, including Wilde Jagd (a Wild Hunt), Harmonies du soir (Evening Harmony), and Chasse-Neige. The three collections, later given the title Années de pèlerinage (Years of Pilgrimage), wander from Switzerland, in the first book, to Italy in the second two, a series of evocative poetic pictures, inspired by landscape, poems and works of art. The earlier volumes stem from the years of wandering with Marie d'Agoult, and the last from the final period of Liszt's life, based in Rome. The Harmonies poétiques et religieuses, written between 1845 and 1852, represent, in the ten pieces included, something of the composer's lasting religious feelings, evident also in the Légendes of 1863, the first of the two representing St. Francis of Assisi preaching to the birds and the second St. Francis de Paul walking on the water. The remarkable Weinen, Klagen, Sorgen, Zagen, based on a theme from a Bach cantata, mourns the death of his elder daughter Blandine. His Fantasia and Fugue on the letters of the name of Bach - B flat - A - C & H(which is B natural in English notation) - was originally written for organ. Liszt wrote one sonata, novel in its form.

The Hungarian Rhapsodies, eventually appearing as a set of nineteen pieces, are based on a form of art music familiar in Hungary and fostered by gypsy musicians, although these works are not, as Liszt thought, a re-creation of true Hungarian folk- music. The Rhapsodie espagnole makes use of the well known La folia theme, used by Corelli and many other Baroque composers, and the jota aragonesa. Transcriptions of his own orchestral and choral compositions include a version of the second of his three Mephisto Waltzes, works that supported legends that had once dogged Paganini of diabolical assistance in performance. Of the many other transcriptions for piano those of the Beethoven Symphonies are among the most remarkable. There are a number of operatic transcriptions and fantasies, including Reminiscences de Don Juan, based on Mozart's Don Giovanni, one of a number of bravura piano works using themes from opera, that include a dozen or so based on the work of his friend and son-in-law Wagner.

➡ **Recommended Recordings**

Fantasia & Fugue on B.A.C.H.
Variations on Weinen, Klagen, Sorgen, Zagen
Naxos 8.550408

Années de pèlerinage I: Suisse
Naxos 8.550548

Années de pèlerinage II: Italie
Naxos 8.550549

Années de pèlerinage III
Naxos 8.550550

Piano Sonata / Les jeux d'eau à la Villa d'Este
Vallée d'Obermann / La campanella
Naxos 8.550510

Symphonie fantastique
(Piano Transcription of Berlioz Symphony)
Naxos 8.550725

Locatelli, Pietro Antonio

(1695 - 1764)

The Italian composer and violinist Pietro Antonio Locatelli was born in Bergamo, later moving to Rome, where he might have studied with Corelli, but more probably was a pupil of Valentini. He won a reputation as a virtuoso, performing in Italy, in Bavaria and in Berlin. In 1729 he settled in Amsterdam, where he taught and conducted an amateur orchestra and was able to pursue his wider cultural interests.

Orchestral Music

Locatelli wrote a number of concerti grossi, following the example of Corelli. The first set, published in Amsterdam in 1720, include twelve fugues. L'arte del violino (The Art of the Violin), published in 1733, contains twelve violin concertos and 24 Caprices, precursors of Paganini's famous set for unaccompanied violin. A further set of six concertos was published two years later and a set of six, published in 1744, is scored for four violins, two violas and basso continuo. Locatelli combines the Roman style of Corelli with, in his solo concertos, the virtuosity of Vivaldi in Venice.

Instrumental Music

In his Concerti grossi, works for string orchestra with a smaller group of soloists, Locatelli at first follows the pattern of Corelli, with one or two violas added to Corelli's solo group of two violins, cello and harpsichord. There is also a Concerto grosso that includes a group of solo wind instruments, in addition to solo violin concertos. Some of these works have programmatic titles. His L'arte del violino (The Art of the Violin) includes 24 Caprices for unaccompanied violin, challenging works that have been regarded by some as foreshadowing the Caprices of Paganini in the following century.

Locatelli also published sets of trio sonatas and solo sonatas, including a set of the latter for flute and basso continuo.

☛ **Recommended Recordings**

Concerto Grossi, Op. 1 Nos. 1-6
Naxos 8.553445

Concerto Grossi, Op. 1 Nos. 7-12
Naxos 8.553446

Locke, Matthew (1621-2 - 1677)

The English composer Matthew Locke lived through the turbulence of the Civil War. He was trained as a chorister at Exeter Cathedral under a brother of Orlando Gibbons and seems to have followed the king's son, Prince Charles, into exile, although he was back in England by 1651. With the restoration of the monarchy in 1660, he entered the royal service, holding various positions, and in particular, as a Catholic convert, that of organist to Catherine of Braganza, the Queen. On his death in 1677 he was succeeded as composer-in-ordinary for the King's Violins by his friend Henry Purcell.

Instrumental Music

Locke wrote church music to English and to Latin texts, with settings of the morning and evening service of the Church of England. His secular works include songs and incidental music for the theatre, but it is as a composer of instrumental music that he is chiefly remembered, in particular for a number of suites, such as The Broken Consort, a set of 24 pieces in six suites, with a second part containing twenty dances, the Little Consort, consisting of forty dances in ten suites, and a number of similar works.

Lortzing, Albert (1801 - 1851)

Lortzing, born in Berlin in 1801, had early stage experience as an actor and singer, with his parents, who had turned their amateur theatrical experience to good use when the family leather business declined. He enjoyed success as a composer of opera, but was less effective as a conductor, and suffered considerable financial hardship, partially alleviated by final appointment, in 1850, to a minor Berlin theatre specialising in farces and plays for which he provided the music.

Operas

Lortzing's opera Zar und Zimmermann (Tsar and Carpenter), based on an episode in the life of Peter the Great of Russia and written in 1837, retains a place in general international repertoire. Others include Undine, a magic opera based on the well known story of the water-sprite and her love for a mortal, Der Wildschütz and Der Waffenschmied.

☛ Recommended Recordings

Waffenschmied / Wildschütz (Overtures)
Naxos 8.550146

Overtures
(Regina / Hans Sachs / Undine / Wildschütz
Pole und sein Kind / Waffenschmied
Zar und Zimmermann)
Marco Polo 8.220310

Lully, Jean-Baptiste (1632 - 1687)

Italian by birth, Lully made his career in France, where he rose from the position of a page to Mlle de Montpensier to that of Composer of the King's Music, Master of Music to the Royal Family and to a position of complete control of all musical performances that involved singing throughout. He collaborated with Molière and with Corneille and, more particularly, with the poet Quinault, creating a specifically French form of opera in various genres, comédies-ballets and tragédies lyriques, in both of which there was an element of dance, a French royal preoccupation. He was the most important French composer of his period, influential in his development of the so-called French Overture, with its introductory slow dotted rhythms and following fugal section and his insistence on orchestral discipline, particularly in the matter of string bowing.

Stage Music

The tragédies lyriques of Lully exercised a strong influence over French opera in his life-time and in the years that followed his death in 1687. These works are usually treatments of subjects drawn from classical mythology. With changes of fashion, they are rarely heard nowadays in the theatre, although overtures and dances from the operas may appear in instrumental programmes. The comédies-ballets in the creation of which Molière was a junior partner are now generally performed without the music and ballet that was an essential element in the original work, although the music for Le bourgeois gentilhomme may be better remembered.

Church Music

Lully was also influential in the choice of music and musicians for the royal chapel. His compositions for the church include a number of motets, some six Grands motets and 14 Petits motets. An example of the first is the fine setting of the Dies irae from the Requiem Mass, for double choir, of the Te Deum, and the Miserere, the last a favourite of the king. Examples of the second are his settings of the Vespers Psalm Dixit Dominus, the Anima Christi and the Regina coeli.

Instrumental Music

Instrumental works by Lully include various sets of dances from his stage works and eighteen Trios pour le coucher du Roi.

Lumbye, Hans Christian
(1810 - 1874)

Hans Christian Lumbye started concerts in the manner of Strauss in his native Copenhagen, after hearing the bands of Lanner and the older Johann Strauss. Leading his orchestra from the violin, he provided entertainment at the Tivoli Gardens, toured abroad, and collaborated with the famous choreographer August Bournonville, with ballet music that includes the final Galop from Napoli.

Dance Music

Lumbye wrote a very large quantity of attractive dance music in the manner that Lanner and Strauss had made popular, waltzes, polkas galops and marches.

Lutosławski, Witold (1913 - 1994)

Witold Lutosławski was born and studied in Warsaw, winning a distinguished international reputation particularly from the 1950s onwards, a leading composer among a group of creative artists of outstanding ability, remarkable in his handling of forms and textures of great originality.

Orchestral Music

The genius of Lutosławski was early evident in his 1938 Symphonic Variations. The years after the war brought a return to more conventional national modes of composition, heard in his Little Suite and Concerto for Orchestra. Later works have allowed a more experimental approach on a broader palette, to be heard in his Funeral Music of 1958, his Second Symphony and the Prelude and Fugue for thirteen string instruments.

☞ **Recommended Recordings**

Symphonic Variations / Little Suite
Symphony No. 2 / Piano Concerto
Naxos 8.553169

Symphony No. 4 / Chain II / Interlude
Partita / Funeral Music
Naxos 8.553202

Vocal and Choral Music

Characteristic works for voice and orchestra include Paroles tissés for tenor and chamber orchestra, and Three Poems by Henri Michaux for twenty voices and orchestra.

MacDowell, Edward (1860 - 1908)

The American pianist and composer Edward MacDowell was one of the first American composers to achieve any degree of international fame. He studied in Paris, eventually at the Conservatoire, before moving to study the piano with Carl Heymann at the Hoch Conservatory in Frankfurt, where he had composition lessons with Joachim Raff. There was encouragement from Liszt and further years spent in Europe until his return to the United States in 1888. There he succeeded in establishing himself as a teacher, pianist and composer, with appointment as the first Professor of Music at Columbia, a position he held until 1904. His last years were clouded by mental illness.

Orchestral Music

MacDowell's two piano concertos were a useful vehicle for his own performance. These and other compositions are in the style that he had studied in Europe.

Piano Music

Piano music by MacDowell is effective if not innovative. It includes four sonatas, the Tragica, Eroica, Norse and Keltic, studies and a quantity of genre pieces.

☛ Recommended Recording

Piano Music Volume 1
Woodland Sketches / Sea Pieces
Fireside Tales / New England Idylls
Marco Polo 8.223631

Piano Music Volume 2
First Modern Suite / Amourette
In Lilting Rhythm / Six Idylls / Sonata No. 3
Marco Polo 8.223632

Piano Music Volume 3
Sonata No. 4 ("Keltic"), Op. 59
Forgotten Fairy Tales, Op. 4
Six Poems after Heine, Op. 31
Twelve Virtuoso Studies, Op. 46
Marco Polo 8.223633

Vocal Music

Songs by MacDowell include settings of poems by Heine, Goethe and other German poets, with solo songs and works for male voices with English texts, the latter written for his New York Mendelssohn Glee Club.

Machaut, Guillaume de

(c. 1300 - 1377)

Guillaume de Machaut, a leading French composer and poet of the 14th century, was born in Rheims, were he spent the greater part of his life, after earlier employment in the service of John of Luxemburg, King of Bohemia. He was employed subsequently by various members of the nobility, including the future Charles V of France. He held various church benefices and as a musician was pre-eminent in the period in the history of music known as the Ars nova, when composers created music of increased rhythmic complexity.

Church Music

Machaut's best known composition is his Messe de Notre Dame, Mass of Our Lady, an early example of a cyclic setting of the liturgical text, in which the sections are musically related. His Hoquetus David makes similar use of the technique of isorhythm, in which a given basic sequence of notes, derived normally from plainchant, is divided into a repeated rhythmic pattern. The hocket referred to in the title is a musical hiccough, a popular technical device of the time, in which the musical line is interrupted by sudden rests.

Secular Music

Machaut was a prolific composer of secular vocal music, in the contemporary metrical and musical forms of lais, virelais, ballades and rondeaux.

Magnard, Albéric (1865 - 1914)

The son of a well known Paris journalist, Albéric Magnard studied law, before entering the Paris Conservatoire, where his teachers included Dubois and Massenet. He later took lessons with Vincent d'Indy. He taught counterpoint at the Schola Cantorum and was killed at the beginning of the war of 1914 when he attempted to resist German attack on his house.

Operas

The second of Magnards's operas, Gercoeur, a tragedy in music, was destroyed during the German attack on his house at Baron but later reconstructed by Ropartz. His other two operas are Yolande and Bérénice, based on the tragedy of Racine.

Orchestral Music

Magnard left four symphonies, in which he followed the principles of César Franck, with very full orchestration.

Chamber Music

Of Magnard's chamber music, his Piano Trio in F minor, Quintet for piano and wind, a string quartet, a violin sonata and a cello sonata deserve mention.

Mahler, Gustav (1860 - 1911)

Born at Kaliste in Bohemia, the son of a Jewish pedlar, Gustav Mahler later described himself as three times homeless, a Bohemian in Austria, an Austrian among Germans and a Jew throughout the world, everywhere an intruder, never welcomed. His principal musical training was at the Vienna Conservatory, after which he embarked on a career as a conductor which took him to important positions in Budapest, Hamburg and finally at the Vienna State Opera, where he made a number of major reforms. Hostility fomented by sections of the press forced his resignation in 1907, after which he briefly continued a distinguished international career as a conductor, notably in New York, until his death in 1911. As a composer Mahler wrote symphonies that absorbed into their texture and form the tradition of

German song in music that reflected in many ways the spirit of the time in which he lived, in all its variety.

Orchestral Music

Mahler completed nine symphonies, leaving a tenth unfinished, in addition to Das Lied von der Erde (The Song of the Earth), a symphony in all but name, settings of a series of poems derived from the Chinese. The first of the symphonies, sometimes known as "Titan", includes a remarkable ironic funeral march that transforms a nursery tune. Symphonies Nos. 2, 3, 4 and 8 make use of voices, the last of these on a massive scale. The symphonies, in their variety of mood, offer a reflection of the world, with music that may occasionally be garish and yet often reaches unsurpassable heights.

☛ **Recommended Recordings**

Das Lied von der Erde
Naxos 8.550933

Symphony No. 1 "Titan"
Naxos 8.550120

Symphony No. 2 "Resurrection" (2 CD's)
Naxos 8.550523-4

Symphonies Nos. 3 and 10 (Adagio) (2 CD's)
Naxos 8.550525-6

Symphony No. 4
Naxos 8.550527

Symphony No. 5
Naxos 8.550528

Symphony No. 6 (2 CD's)
Naxos 8.550529-30

Symphony No. 7
Naxos 8.550531

Symphony No. 9 (2 CD's)
Naxos 8.550535-6

Vocal Music

In addition to the vocal element in his symphonies, Mahler wrote a number of songs of singular beauty, some of which were re-used in orchestral settings. The songs include settings of poems from the Romantic anthology Des Knaben Wunderhorn (The Boy's Magic Horn), Lieder eines fahrenden Gesellen (Songs of a Wayfarer) and Rückert's Kindertotenlieder (Songs of the Death of Children).

Marais, Marin (1656 - 1728)

Marin Marais, player of the viola da gamba and pupil of Sainte-Colombe, has won much wider recent fame through the cinema. In his own time he was accounted the principal virtuoso of his time on the instrument, for which he wrote a number of compositions.

He studied composition with Lully and as a member of the French royal musical establishment performed with him.

Instrumental Music
The instrumental music of Marais consists chiefly of his various collections of pieces for one or more viols, which include the now well known Variations on Les folies d'Espagne (La Follia).

Operas
The four operas of Marais were written under the influence of Lully and enjoyed contemporary success.

☛ **Recommended Recordings**

Masterworks for Viols
Naxos 8.550750

Sonate à la Maresienne
Suite in D Major / Les Voix humaines
Suite for two trebles and basso continuo
Tombeau de M. Meliton / Couplets de felves
Naxos 8.553081

Marcello, Alessandro (1684 - 1750)
A Venetian nobleman and younger contemporary of Vivaldi, Alessandro Marcello was a dilettante with diverse interests in the arts. As a member of the Arcadian Academy, a society of those interested in the arts, and under the Arcadian pseudonym Eterio Stinfalico, he published several sets of instrumental concerti.

Instrumental Music
The best known concerto of Alessandro Marcello is for oboe, strings and continuo, transcribed by Johann Sebastian Bach among a set of concerto transcriptions for solo harpsichord.

☛ **Recommended Recordings**

Oboe Concerto in C Minor
Naxos 8.550014

Oboe Concerto in D Minor
Naxos 8.550556

Marcello, Benedetto (1686 - 1739)
The younger brother of Alessandro Marcello, Benedetto Marcello was a more prolific composer, writing stage works, church music, secular vocal and instrumental music. In his book Il teatro alla moda, published about 1720, Marcello gives a satirical account of contemporary operatic practice.

Instrumental Music

Benedetto Marcello's compositions include a set of twelve concerti for strings, as well as sets of sonatas for one and two cellos.

Marenzio, Luca (1553 or 1554 - 1599)

Marenzio spent much of his later career in the service of influential ecclesiastical patrons in Rome, in particular Cardinal Luigi d'Este, a member of the ruling family of Ferrara, important patrons of the arts. After the cardinal's death he was for a time in Florence in the service of Ferdinando de' Medici, Grand Duke of Tuscany. He was a prolific composer of vocal music and is best known today for his madrigals, although he wrote a considerable quantity of sacred music.

Secular Vocal Music

Characteristic madrigals by Marenzio, on the usual pastoral subjects, include Cruda Amarilli, Care mie selve, settings of Guarini. Marenzio published a number of collections of madrigals for four, five or six voices and is of historical importance in the development of the Italian madrigal, imitated towards the end of the 16th century in England. These compositions, over four hundred in number, include settings of verses by Dante, Petrarch, Ariosto, Guarini and Tasso.

Marschner, Heinrich (1795 - 1861)

Marschner occupies an important position in the history of German Romantic opera after the death of Weber. He began his musical career in Pressburg (the modern Bratislava), teaching in a noble family and serving as director of music in another, before moving to Dresden, where his first opera was staged, working subsequently in Leipzig and finally in Hanover, where he died in 1861.

Operas

The best known of Marschner's thirteen operas is Hans Heiling, based on the story of a marriage between an Earth Spirit and a mortal woman and first performed in Berlin in 1833. The opera brought the composer a considerable reputation, although this did not materially affect his position in Hanover, where he was music director of the Court Theatre.

☛ Recommended Recordings

Hans Heiling (Overture)
Naxos 8.550146

Hans Heiling (Complete Opera) (2 CD's)
Marco Polo 8.223306-7

Overtures
(Kaiser Adolph / Des Falkners Braut
Prinz Friedrich / Lukretia / Der Bäbu
Der Goldschmied / Der Templer und die Jüdin
Grande Ouverture solenne)
Marco Polo 8.223342

Martín, Frank (1890 - 1974)

Swiss and of remoter French ancestry, Frank Martin later settled in Holland, while teaching composition in Cologne. He had earlier been associated with the Dalcroze Institute, while enjoying a career also as a keyboard-player and teacher. His music combines a German element with French in a musical idiom that is his own, tonal, once the principles of Schoenberg's serialism had been absorbed and adapted to his own particular use.

Stage Music

Martin wrote two operas, a version of Shakespeare's The Tempest (Der Sturm) and of Molière's Monsieur de Pourceaugnac. Ballets include Das Märchen vom Aschenbrödel (The Story of Cinderella) and there is what is described as an oratorio/spectacle in Le mystère de la Nativité (The Mystery of the Nativity). He provided incidental music for plays from the Oedipus trilogy of Sophocles, to Racine's Athalie and Shakespeare's Romeo and Juliet.

Orchestral Music

Frank Martin's Petite symphonie concertante, for harpsichord, harp, piano and two string orchestras is probably the best known of his compositions. His concertos include a somewhat astringent First Piano Concerto, a Concerto for wind instruments, percussion and strings, a Violin Concerto, a Harpsichord Concerto, a Second Piano Concerto and a Cello Concerto. His five Ballades are also scored for solo instruments, with a small orchestra, featuring respectively, saxophone, flute, trombone or tenor saxophone and cello, with a final Ballade for viola, wind, harpsichord and harp.

Chamber Music

Chamber music by Frank Martin includes a variety of music, including three of the Ballades later orchestrated, a Sonata da chiesa for viola d'amore and organ, two Violin Sonatas and a String Quartet.

Keyboard Music

Martin's piano music ranges from an Ouverture et foxtrot for two pianos to a final Fantaisie sur des rythmes flamenco (Fantasy on Flamenco Rhythms). He wrote a Passacaglia for organ.

Vocal and Choral Music

Choral music includes the oratorios Golgotha and In terra pax and a cantata, Pilate, as well as a setting of the Mass and a Requiem. His song settings range from Ronsard to Rilke.

Martinů, Bohuslav (1890 - 1959)

Born in a church tower in the Bohemian village of Policka, Bohuslav Martinů was a prolific enough composer as a child, before he entered Prague Conservatory as a violin student in 1906. His interest, however, lay in composition. Failing to complete his course at the Conservatory or at the Prague Organ School, to which he had been transferred, he worked as an orchestral player before moving, in 1923, to Paris. The approach of the German armies in 1940 forced him to make his way, as best he could, to the United States, where he was encouraged by commissions from Koussevitzky. Political events in Czechoslovakia prevented his intended return after the war, and he spent his final years abroad, dying in Switzerland in 1959.

Stage Music

Martinů was an immensely prolific and varied composer. His sixteen operas include The Greek Passion, after Kazantzakis, Ariadne, after Neveu, and the radio opera Comedy on the Bridge. Ballet scores include Spalicek, based on fairy-tales and nursery rhymes.

Orchestral Music

An impressive list of orchestral compositions includes six symphonies, the first of them written for Koussevitzky, who commissioned one a year. There are concertos for a variety of instruments, including five for piano and a useful Rhapsody-Concerto for viola and orchestra. The variety of his terms of reference may be seen in his Frescos of Piero della Francesca, The Parables and his earlier Villa by the Sea, based on the evocative painting of Böcklin. His Czech origins are generally identifiable in his music, which nevertheless reflects the influence also of France, while returning at times to earlier musical traditions.

Choral Music

Major choral works by Martinu must include his oratorio on the Babylonian epic of Gilgamesh and the Biblical The Prophecy of Isaiah.

Chamber Music

There is a bewilderingly large amount of chamber music by Martinů, duos, trios, quartets, quintets, sextets, septets, octets and nonets. Among these the seven string quartets deserve particular mention, in addition to the works for violin and piano and three cello sonatas.

☛ **Recommended Recordings**

Flute Trios / Madrigal Sonata
Promenades for Flute, Violin and Piano
Naxos 8.553459

Quartet for Oboe, Violin, Cello & Piano
String Quintet / Viola Sonata No. 1
Piano Quartet No. 1
Naxos 8.553916

Operas

The operas of Martinů include works expressly designed for broadcasting, television or the cinema. His last opera, staged after his death, was The Greek Passion, based on Kazantzakis.

Ballets

Various ballet scores, many unperformed, form part of an interesting if neglected repertoire.

Orchestral Music

Martinů left six symphonies, the last with the title Fantaisies symphoniques. There are symphonic poems and descriptive pieces and a number of concertos. These last include five piano concertos, the last, written in 1957, with the title Fantasia concertante, a Violin Concerto, a Double Violin Concerto and two Cello Concertos.

Keyboard Music

In addition to a large number of shorter piano pieces of all kinds, Martinů wrote a Fantaisie and other pieces for two pianos, as well as music for harpsichord, leaving his organ Vigilia unfinished at the time of his death in 1959.

Vocal and Choral Music

Choral works by Martinů include the remarkable oratorio Gilgamesh, based on the ancient Babylonian epic of that name. There are choral works of biblical derivation and a number of choral arrangements of traditional Czech, Slovak and Moravian material. His songs include Magic Nights, settings of poems translated from the Chinese.

☛ **Recommended Recording**
Gilgamesh
Marco Polo 8.223316

Mascagni, Pietro (1863 - 1945)

An Italian composer and conductor, Pietro Mascagni is chiefly remembered in the first capacity as the composer of the one-act opera Cavalleria rusticana. As a conductor he worked at La Scala in Milan, increasingly associated with the régime of Mussolini. He died in Rome in 1945.

Operas

Mascagni won his first success with Cavalleria rusticana (Rustic Chivalry), first staged in Rome in 1890. This is an example of verismo, operatic realism, that exercised considerable influence. The opera deals with a tale of love and jealousy in a Sicilian village, the drama ending in the death of Turiddu, the young Santuzza's faithless lover, whom she betrays to a man whom he has deceived.

Of Mascagni's later operas L'amico Fritz and Iris, the latter set in Japan, won some success. Both have provided popular tenor arias.

☞ **Recommended Recording**

Cavalleria Rusticana (Complete Opera)
Naxos 8.660022

Massenet, Jules (1842 - 1912)

The leading operatic composer of his generation in France, Jules Massenet studied at the Paris Conservatoire, winning the Prix de Rome in 1863. In Paris once more, after his obligatory three years stay at the Villa Medici in Rome, he achieved initial success with his operas Don César de Bazan and Marie-Madeleine, the latter heroine, a repentant female sinner, exercising a particular interest and influence on Massenet's future work. He maintained a dominant position in French opera at least until the appearance of Debussy's Pelléas et Mélisande, an innovative work that nevertheless shows something of the influence of Massenet.

Operas

Of some three dozen stage works, Massenet's opera Manon is perhaps the best known, a version of the novel by the Abbé Prévost also used by Puccini. The opera Werther is based on Goethe's Sorrows of the Young Werther, while Thaïs is known by name to many because of the famous violin solo, Méditation. The opera Le Cid, based on the play by Corneille on the subject of the historical Spanish hero and first staged in Paris in 1885, has a spectacular second act ballet-fiesta, which forms part of a subsequent orchestral suite.

☞ **Recommended Recordings**

Werther: Pourquoi me réveiller
Naxos 8.550343

Thaïs: Méditation (For violin and piano)
Naxos 8.550306

Le Cid (Ballet Music)
Naxos 8.550086

Suites (Esclarmonde / Cendrillon)
Suite No. 1, Op. 13
Marco Polo 8.223354

Suites Nos. 1-3 / Hérodiade (Ballet Suite)
Naxos 8.553124

Suites Nos. 4-7
Naxos 8.553125

Mendelssohn-Bartholdy, Felix (1809 - 1847)

Felix Mendelssohn, grandson of the distinguished Jewish thinker Moses Mendelssohn, the additional surname Bartholdy adopted on his conversion to Christianity, was

born in Hamburg, the son of a banker. The family moved to Berlin, where Mendelssohn was brought up, able to associate with a cultured circle of family friends. He was associated with the revival of public interest in the music of Johann Sebastian Bach and in the early 1830s travelled abroad for his education, spending time in Italy and also visiting England, Wales and Scotland. He was later conductor of the Gewandhaus Orchestra in Leipzig, where he also established a Conservatory, his stay there interrupted briefly by a return to Berlin. He died in Leipzig in 1847. Prolific and precocious, Mendelssohn had many gifts, musically as composer, conductor and pianist. His style of composition combined something of the economy of means of the classical period with the romanticism of a later age.

Orchestral Music

(a) Symphonies

Mendelssohn wrote five symphonies, in addition to an attractive series of twelve early symphonies for strings, completed at the age of fourteen. Of the mature symphonies the Italian Symphony, Symphony No. 4, completed in 1833 and reflecting the composer's experiences in Italy during his Grand Tour, is the most popular, closely followed by Symphony No. 3, the Scottish, with its echoes of the Palace of Holyrood in the days of Mary Queen of Scots. Symphony No. 5, the

Reformation, written in 1832 to celebrate the third centenary of the Augsburg Confession, is less often heard, as is Symphony No. 2, the choral Lobgesang, written to mark the fourth centenary of the invention of printing in 1840.

(b) Overtures

The concert overtures of Mendelssohn include the 1826 Overture, A Midsummer Night's Dream, a work in many ways typical of the composer's deftness of touch in its evocation of the fairy world of the play for which he later wrote incidental music. The Hebrides, otherwise known as Fingal's Cave, evokes a visit to Scotland and the sight of the sea surging over the Giant's Causeway. Meeresstille und glückliche Fahrt (Calm Sea and Prosperous Voyage) is based on a poem by Goethe, a writer who had received the young Mendelssohn at Weimar and prophesied for him a successful career. The Overture Ruy Blas, completed in 1839, is based on the play by Victor Hugo.

(c) Concertos

The best known of Mendelssohn's concertos must be the Violin Concerto in E minor, the third to make use of the solo violin. The E minor Concerto was written in 1844 and first performed in Leipzig the following year. Two piano concertos, the first written in 1831 and the second in 1837, are heard less frequently.

☞ **Recommended Recordings**

Piano Concertos Nos. 1 & 2
Capriccio brillante Op. 22
Rondo brillante Op. 29
Naxos 8.550681

Concertos for Two Pianos
Naxos 8.553416

Symphonies Nos. 1 and 5 "Reformation"
Naxos 8.550957

Symphony No. 3 "Scottish" / Ruy Blas
Hebrides / Calm Sea and Prosperous Voyage
Naxos 8.550222

Symphony No. 4 "Italian"
Naxos 8.550055

Violin Concerto in E minor
Naxos 8.550153

String Symphonies Nos. 1-6
Naxos 8.553161

String Symphonies Nos. 7-9
Naxos 8.553162

Chamber Music

Mendelssohn wrote his first chamber music at the age of ten. One of the most delightful works is the Octet, for double string quartet, written to celebrate the 23rd birthday of a violinist friend in 1825. Evidence of earlier precocity is heard in the equally fine Sextet for violin, two violas, cello, double bass and piano, written in 1824. The two string quintets and six string quartets may enjoy less general popularity, although they contain many felicities, String Quartet No. 4 in E minor offering a characteristic view of the composer's command of technique and mood, ranging from the fairy world of the Scherzo to the passion of the Finale. The two late piano trios, the Piano Trio in D minor and the Piano Trio in C minor represent the composer at his very best.

Mendelssohn was himself both pianist and violinist. Of his duo sonatas, however, the two Cello Sonatas and the Variations concertantes for cello and piano, with a late Song without Words for cello and piano, make an important part of 19th century cello repertoire.

☞ **Recommended Recordings**

Cello Sonatas Nos. 1 and 2
Variations concertantes / Lied ohne Worte
Naxos 8.550655

Piano Quartet No. 1 / Sextet Op. 110
Naxos 8.550966

Piano Quartets Nos. 2 & 3
Naxos 8.550967

String Quartets Op. 44, No. 1 & Op. 89
Capriccio Op. 81, No. 3 / Fugue Op. 81, No. 4
Naxos 8.550861

String Quartets Op. 12 & 44, No. 2
String Quartet in E Flat Major
Naxos 8.550862

String Quartets Op. 13 & 44, No. 3
Tema con variazioni Op. 81, No. 1
Scherzo Op. 81, No. 2
Naxos 8.550863

Piano Music

The 19th century was the age of the piano, a period in which the instrument, newly developed, became an essential item of household furniture and the centre of domestic music-making. Short piano pieces always found a ready market, none more than Mendelssohn's eight albums of Lieder ohne Worte (Songs without Words), a novel title that admirably describes the length, quality and intention of these short pieces.

☛ Recommended Recordings

Songs without Words Vol. 1
Naxos 8.550316

Songs without Words Vol. 2
Naxos 8.550453

Six Preludes and Fugues, Op. 35
Three Caprices, Op. 33
Perpetuum mobile, Op. 119
Naxos 8.550939

Three Preludes, Op. 104a
Three Etudes, Op. 104b
Variations serieuses, Op. 54
Christmas Pieces, Op. 72 / Barcarole
Scherzo in B Minor / Sonata, Op. 6
Naxos 8.550940

Stage Music

Mendelssohn's music for the theatre includes full incidental music for Shakespeare's A Midsummer Night's Dream, written for the new King of Prussia and first used at Potsdam in 1843, preceded by the Overture written in 1826. The music typically captures the enchanted fairy world of the play. In connection with the King's attempts to revive Greek tragedy Mendelssohn also wrote incidental music for the Antigone and Oedipus at Colonus of Sophocles, as well as for Racine's Athalie. His attempts at opera have not survived in modern repertoire.

☛ Recommended Recording

A Midsummer Night's Dream
Naxos 8.550055

Vocal and Choral Music

Mendelssohn wrote a number of works for possible church use, both Protestant and Catholic. Of these the best known must be Hear my prayer, a favourite with boy trebles. The carol Hark the herald angels sing was adapted by W.H. Cummings from a chorus in a secular cantata. His oratorios Elijah and St. Paul remain traditionally popular with choral societies. In addition to settings of psalms,which include a setting of Psalm 100, Jauchzet den Herrn (Praise the Lord) and sacred and secular cantatas, Mendelssohn wrote a number of choral songs and a larger quantity of solo songs, a pleasing addition to the repertoire of German song, intended for intimate social gatherings rather than the concert hall. Among the most exciting of songs is Hexenlied (Witches' Song), a setting of verse by Hölty, one of an early set of twelve songs written in 1828. A second dozen, published two years later, includes the contrasting Im Frühling (In the Spring) and Im Herbst (In the Autumn). Mendelssohn wrote his last songs in the year of his death, 1847.

Mercadante, Saverio (1795 - 1870)

The Italian opera composer Saverio Mercadante studied music in Naples and at first showed an interest in instrumental composition. The encouragement of Rossini led him to compose for the opera, where he won considerable success with his seventh such work, in 1821. He worked for a time in Vienna, in Madrid and in Lisbon, but re-established himself in Italy in 1831. In the early 1840s he seemed the most important composer of Italian opera, now influenced by Meyerbeer in Paris and introducing new elements of drama into the form. In later life he seems to have been jealous of the success of Verdi, who came to dominate Italian opera in the second half of the century.

Operas

Mercadante wrote some sixty operas. Of these Il giuramento (The Oath) is possibly the most significant, the first to show those new dramatic elements, responding to the text which, like Ponchielli's Gioconda, was based on Victor Hugo's Angelo.

Orchestral Music

Mercadante was able to return to orchestral composition after his appointment in 1840 as director of the Naples Conservatory. His early works include six flute concertos, with subsequent tributes, as occasion arose, to Bellini, Donizetti and finally Rossini.

Merulo, Claudio (1533 - 1604)

One of the most famous organists of his time, Claudio Merulo held appointment as organist at St Mark's in Venice from 1557 until 1584, subsequently entering the service of the Duke of Mantua and then of the Duke of Parma.

Organ Music

Merulo has been much admired for his Toccatas. He left organ music in other forms of the time, Ricercari, Canzone, motet transcriptions and organ Masses, these last published in 1568 in his Messe d'intavolatura d'organo.

Church Music

Church music by Merulo includes Masses, two Magnificats and a number of motets in the Venetian style of the time.

Madrigals

Merulo was also a prolific composer of madrigals, leaving a considerable body of work in this form, with collections for three, four and five voices.

☛ Recommended Recordings

Missa in dominicis diebus / Toccata / Magnificat
Naxos 8.553334

Missa apostolorum / Toccata / Magnificat
(2 CD's)
Naxos 8.553420-1

Missa Virginis Mariae / Toccata
Magnificat (2 CD's)
Naxos 8.553335-6

Messiaen, Olivier (1908 - 1992)

Olivier Messiaen has exercised a remarkable influence over composers both in his native France and elsewhere, although his own work is unique in its individuality. Educated at the Paris Conservatoire, where his teachers included the great French organist Marcel Dupré, he became principal organist of La Trinité in Paris after graduation in 1930, a position he retained for many years. Messiaen's musical language is derived from a number of varied sources, including Greek metrical rhythms, Hindu tradition, the serialism of Schoenberg, Debussy and bird-song, with his whole work and life deeply influenced by the spirit of Catholicism.

Orchestral Music

Of orchestral works by Messiaen particular mention may be made of the Turangalila Symphony, with its Hindu inspiration, and the mystical L'Ascension, later arranged also for organ.

Piano Music

Two extended compositions for piano by Messiaen suggest two of the sources of his inspiration. Vingt regards sur l'enfant Jésus, a title defying elegant translation, takes twenty different views of the Child Jesus, from the Father, the star and the Virgin to that of the Church of Love. The work was first performed in

Paris in 1945 by the composer's wife, the pianist Yvonne Loriod. The Catalogue d'oiseaux of 1959 is derived from bird-song, from Le chocard des alpes and Le loriot to Le courlis cendré.

☞ **Recommended Recording**

Vingt regards sur l'enfant Jésus (2 CD's)
Naxos 8.550829-30

Organ Music

Messiaen made a significant addition to organ repertoire, his compostions for the instrument including La nativité du Seigneur (The Birth of the Lord), L'Ascension and Les corps glorieux (Bodies in Glory), the last described as seven brief visions of the life of the resurrected.

Chamber Music

Among the best known of Messiaen's varied works for smaller groups of instruments is the Quatuor pour la fin du temps (Quartet for the End of Time), written in 1941 during a period of war-time imprisonment in Silesia. This apocalyptic work was composed for the instruments available, clarinet, piano, violin and cello and was first performed in the prison camp.

Meyerbeer, Giacomo (1791 - 1864)

Born near Berlin in the year of Mozart's death into a family of cultured interests, Meyerbeer was a pupil of Abt Vogler and near contemporary of his fellow-pupil, Weber. He made his career in Paris, where he became the most important composer of French grand opera, although retaining wide cosmopolitan connections, in particular as Generalmusikdirektor from 1842 under King Friedrich Wilhelm IV of Prussia, in whose service he continued after his resignation from his original position in 1848. Meyerbeer was a man of independent means, a fact that enabled him to exercise considerable care over the composition of operas and the choice of appropriate singers and to exercise some control over the press.

Operas

Meyerbeer won his first great success at the Paris Opéra in 1831 with Robert le diable (Robert the Devil). This was followed by Les Huguenots, Le Prophète and finally by L'Africaine, all three with texts by the famous librettist Eugène Scribe. The last of these grand operas was staged in Paris in 1865, the year after the composer's death. Constant Lambert's 1937 ballet score Les patineurs (The Skaters) was arranged from two of Meyerbeer's operas, Le Prophète and the earlier L'Étoile du Nord (The North Star).

Milhaud, Darius (1892 - 1974)

Born into a Jewish family in the southern French city of Aix-en-Provence, Darius Milhaud was trained at the Paris Conservatoire, originally as a violinist, before turning to composition. He enjoyed a close association with the diplomat-poet Paul Claudel, whom he accompanied to Brazil as secretary, after Claudel's appointment as Minister at the French delegation in Rio de Janeiro. On his return to Paris in 1918, after two years abroad, Milhaud was for a time in the circle of Jean Cocteau and a member of the diverse group of French composers known as Les Six. Extremely prolific as a composer in many genres, Milhaud spent the years of the 1939 war in the United States, where he taught, combining this position with a similar post at the Paris Conservatoire after 1947.

Stage Works

Darius Milhaud wrote a considerable amount of music for the theatre, operas, ballets and incidental music, as well as film and radio scores. Collaboration with Claudel brought the opera Christophe Colombe and a number of compositions of incidental music for plays ranging from those of Shakespeare to the work of contemporaries such as Brecht, Supervielle, Giraudoux and Anouilh. With Cocteau he wrote the ballets Le Boeuf sur le Toit (The Ox on the Roof) and the jazz La Création du Monde, for the Ballets nègres. These represent only a small fraction of his dramatic work.

Orchestral Music

Milhaud was equally prolific as a composer of orchestral music of all kinds, including twelve symphonies and a variety of concertos, some of which reflect the influence of his native Provence.

Vocal and Choral Music

Milhaud contributed widely also to the repertoire of French song both in choral settings and in songs for solo voice and piano, with texts chosen from a great variety of sources from Rabindranath Tagore and André Gide to the words of Pope John XXIII, the last in a choral symphony Pacem in terris.

Chamber Music

In addition to eighteen string quartets and useful additions to duo sonata repertoire, not least for viola, an instrument used for the Quatre Visages of 1943, representations in music of four different kinds of girls, Milhaud provided for wind quintet the charming suite La Cheminée du Roi René and the attractive Pastorale of 1935 for oboe, clarinet and bassoon. He shows here, as elsewhere, a characteristically French adroitness in writing for woodwind instruments.

Piano Music

Two works in particular have proved attractive additions to repertoire. The first, Saudades do Brasil, a suite for piano, is based on music heard in Brazil during the composer's stay there between 1916 and 1918. Scaramouche, arranged for two pianos from incidental music for Molière's Le Médecin Volant, is a lively jeu d'esprit, in the spirit of the commedia dell'arte character of the title.

☞ Recommended Recording

Saudades do Brazil / La Muse ménagère
L'album de Madame Bovary
Naxos 8.553443

Moeran, E.J. (1894 - 1950)

Anglo-Irish in origin, E.J.Moeran was born in Norfolk and became a pupil of John Ireland after service in the 1914-18 war, in which he was wounded. East Anglia continued to influence his music, coupled with the influence of Ireland. He enjoyed a respected if minor position in the English music of his time.

Orchestral Music

Moeran's Violin Concerto and the cello concerto he wrote for his future wife, the cellist Peers Coetmore, make interesting and characteristic additions to the solo repertoire of the instruments. Other orchestral works include the symphonic impression In the Mountain Country, Lonely Waters for small orchestra, a sinfonietta, the Symphony in G minor and two rhapsodies.

Chamber Music

Moeran's Cello Sonata, his last major work, is particularly effective, with his Violin Sonata of 1923 and Fantasy Quartet for oboe and strings.

☞ Recommended Recording

Cello Sonata
Marco Polo 8.223718

Vocal Music

Moeran wrote part-songs, with solo songs that include Ludlow Town, Six Norfolk Folk-Songs and settings of Shakespeare songs.

Mompou, Federico (1893 - 1987)

Catalan by birth, Federico Mompou studied in his native Barcelona, before moving to Paris, where, before and after the war, he spent over twenty years. His music, much of it for piano, is economical in means, with something of the sparse texture familiar from Satie, another perceptible influence.

Piano Music

Mompou's piano music, including delicately conceived miniatures, is intimately expressive, generally avoiding ostentatious gestures. His early Impresiones intimas (Intimate Impressions) and Scènes d'enfants (Children's Scenes) lead to the later Música callada, four collections written between 1959 and 1967.

Vocal Music

Songs by Mompou, which in general avoid the extremes of nationalism, although perceptibly Catalan in inspiration, range from L'hora gris (Grey Hour) of 1915 to the later settings of St John of the Cross.

Monteverdi, Claudio (1567 - 1643)

Born in Cremona in 1567, Claudio Monteverdi served at the court of the Dukes of Mantua from the early 1590s until 1612, when he moved to Venice as maestro di cappella at the basilica of St. Mark, a position he retained until his death in 1643. His importance as a proponent of the so-called seconda prattica, the new concerted music characteristic of the early Baroque, is unquestioned, as is his pre-eminence in the development of the new form of opera that sprang from the combination of music and rhetoric in the art of Italian monody.

Stage Works

The earliest opera to retain a place in modern repertoire is Monteverdi's L'Orfeo, a dramatic version of the story of the legendary Orpheus, the musician who sought to bring his beloved Eurydice back from the Underworld by the power of music. This was written for the court of the Duke of Mantua in 1607, with a libretto by Alessandro Striggio. A second opera of the period, L'Arianna, dealing with the fate of the Cretan princess Ariadne, deserted on the island of Naxos by the Athenian prince she had rescued, Theseus, is lost, although the famous Lament of Arianna survives both as a solo song and in the form of a madrigal. The words are by the Florentine nobleman Ottavio Rinuccini, who provided the text for the ballet Il Ballo dell'ingrate. Il Combattimento di Tancredi e Clorinda (The Combat of Tancredi and Clorinda), a setting of an episode in Tasso's Gerusalemme liberata, allows Monteverdi to exhibit his newly developed stile concitato (agitated style), in an interpretation of ancient Greek philosophical principles expressed by Plato. To stile concitato is added stile molle (soft style) for humility, and stile temperato (moderate style) to represent that human emotional state. Monteverdi's last two surviving operas are Il Ritorno d'Ulisse in patria (The Return of Ulysses to his Native Country), staged in Venice in 1640, and the final L'incoronazione di Poppea (The Coronation of Poppaea)

of 1642, set in imperial Rome in the time of Nero, whose love for the courtesan Poppaea is the subject of the opera.

Secular Vocal Music

Monteverdi published a number of collections of songs and madrigals. Of these the Lament of Arianna has been mentioned, while the Combattimento di Tancredi e Clorinda was also published in a set of Madrigali guerrieri et amorosi (Madrigals of War and of Love), designed for singing without dramatic action. This particularly rich repertoire of vocal music includes the duet, also in the form of a five-part madrigal, Zefiro torna (Zephyr, turn), from the poet Petrarch and Ecco mormorar l'onde (Lo the murmur of the waves), a setting of Tasso. These and other songs and madrigals by Monteverdi were brought to modern attention by the French composer, teacher and musicologist Nadia Boulanger in memorable realisations and recordings in the 1940s.

☞ **Recommended Recordings**
Lament
Naxso 8.553317

Canzonette
Naxos 8.553316

Ballo delle ingrate
Combattimento di Tancredi e Clorinda
Naxos 8.553322

Church Music

Possibly as an advertisement of his varied abilities as a composer, Monteverdi wrote in 1610 a setting of the service of Vespers for the Blessed Virgin Mary in the modern style that would appeal to the officials of St. Mark's in Venice. At the same time, perhaps with a view to possible employment in the more conservative papal service in Rome, he wrote a six voice Mass setting in the old style. The Vespers offer a dramatic and colourful exploitation of the possibilities of the new style in a work of great variety and interest well suited to the spacial effects available to performers in the great basilica of St. Mark, with its galleries and traditions of writing for contrasted groups of performers spacially separated.

☞ **Recommended Recording**
Vespers (1610) (2 CDs)
Naxos 8.550662-3

Morley, Thomas (1557 or 1558 - 1602)

Morley contributed significantly to the development of the English madrigal, imitated from Italian models. He was probably a pupil of William Byrd, to whom he dedicated his popular book A Plaine and Easie Introduction to Practicall Musicke, published in 1597. Morley was employed at St. Paul's in London and became a Gentleman of the Chapel Royal in 1592, publishing his first set of part-songs in 1593. He was later concerned in printing and publishing music, for which he was granted a share in the monopoly in 1598.

Church Music

Morley wrote music for the liturgy of the Church of England, service settings, psalm settings and a number of Latin motets, under the influence of Byrd and a possible indication of his own religious sympathies at the time. Of particular interest is the setting of the De profundis, Out of the deep, in a second setting as a verse anthem, a peculiarly English form derived from the consort song of the period, involving the contrast of solo voices with the choir, with instrumental accompaniment from the organ or other groups of instruments.

Madrigals

It is as a composer of madrigals that Morley is widely known. The Canzonets or Little Short Songs to Three Voyces, published in 1593 were followed by a collection of four-part Madrigals in 1594 and a series of other publications during the decade, some of them adaptations and arrangements of Italian madrigals. In 1601 Morley published the collaborative Triumphs of Oriana, a tribute to Queen Elizabeth for which he collected madrigals by 23 composers as an offering to the aging Arcadian Queen of the Shepherds. Well known madrigals by Morley include Aprill is in my mistris face, My bonny lasse shee smyleth, Now is the month of maying, O sleep, fond fancy, Sing wee and chaunt it, Sweet nymphe, come to thy lover and Though Philomela lost hir love. Solo songs by Morley include It was a lover and his lasse, a song that appears in Shakespeare's pastoral comedy As You Like It.

Keyboard Music

Morley added to the contemporary repertoire for virginals, the general term for the harpsichord of the period. Keyboard music of this kind includes paired pavans and galliards, song variations, including a set of variations on the popualr song Go from my window, and a Passymeasures pavan, a title that recalls the words of Sir Toby Belch in Shakespeare's comedy Twelfth Night.

Instrumental Music

Following the custom of the time Morley also wrote for lute and for various groups of instruments, including arrangements of music by other composers.

Moszkowsky, Moritz (1854 - 1925)

A pianist and composer, Moritz Moszkowsky was born in Breslau and made his early career in Berlin, before moving to Paris in 1897. He enjoyed a reputation as a pianist, conductor and a composer, in general, of lighter music.

Piano Music

Moszkowsky's two books of Spanish Dances, originally for piano duet and then arranged for solo piano, had considerable contemporary appeal and were echoed in the ballet music of his less successful Spanish opera Boabdil, der letzte Maurenkönig (Boabdil, the Last King of the Moors). Other piano music includes a set of Concert Studies, a set of Miniatures, a Suite, the Caprice espagnole, again in Spanish vein, Etincelles and Serenata.

☛ Recommended Recordings

> Etincelles, Op. 36
> Naxos 8.550107
>
> Serenata, Op. 15
> Naxos 8.550141
>
> Caprice espagnole, Op. 37
> Naxos 8.550218

Orchestral Music

Moszkowsky attempted the exotic in his suite Aus aller Herren Länder. His compositions for orchestra include a Piano Concerto and a Violin Concerto.

Mozart, Leopold (1719 - 1787)

The father of Wolfgang Amadeus Mozart, Leopold Mozart, distinguished as a violin teacher, sacrificed his own career as a composer to foster that of his son. He was a man of wide interests, the son of an Augsburg bookseller, and left university to join the musical establishment of the Archbishop of Salzburg, a prelate in whose service he rose to become court composer and deputy Kapellmeister, a position he maintained, without further advancement, until his death in 1787.

Orchestral Music

Leopold Mozart gave much less care to the preservation of his own work than he did to that of his son. A variety of surviving compositions include the Divertimento, Die musikalische Schlittenfahrt (The Musical Sleigh-Ride), Die Bauernhochzeit (The Peasants' Wedding) and a Burlesque Symphony, but these are by no means typical of a body of work that deserves further exploration.

☛ Recommended Recording

> Sinfonia di caccia / Sinfonia Pastorale
> Sinfonias in B flat & G / Kleine Sinfonie für Musikfreunde
> Naxos 8.553347

Mozart, Wolfgang Amadeus

(1756 - 1791)

The youngest child and only surviving son of Leopold Mozart, Wolfgang Amadeus was born in Salzburg in 1756, the year of publication of his father's influential treatise on violin-playing. He showed early precocity both as a keyboard-player and violinist, and soon turned his hand to composition. His obvious gifts were developed under his father's tutelage, with those of his elder sister, and the family, through the indulgence of their then patron, the Archbishop of Salzburg, was able to travel abroad, specifically, between 1763 and 1766, to Paris and to London. A series of other journeys followed, with important operatic commissions in Italy between 1771 and 1773. The following period proved disappointing to both father and son, as the young Mozart grew to manhood, irked by the lack of opportunity and lack of appreciation of his gifts in Salzburg, where a new Archbishop proved less sympathetic. A visit to Munich, Mannheim and Paris in 1777 and 1778 brought no substantial offer of other employment and by early 1779 Mozart was reinstated in Salzburg, now as court organist. Early in 1781 he had a commissioned opera, Idomeneo, staged in Munich for the Elector of Bavaria and dissatisfaction after being summoned to attend his patron the Archbishop in Vienna led to his dismissal. Mozart spent the last ten years of his life in precarious independence in Vienna, his material situation not improved by a marriage imprudent for one in his circumstances. Initial success with German and then Italian opera and series of subscription concerts were followed by financial difficulties. In 1791 things seemed to have taken a turn for the better, in spite of the lack of interest of the successor to the Emperor Joseph II, who had died in 1790. In late November, however, Mozart became seriously ill and died in the small hours of 5th December. Mozart's compositions were catalogued in the 19th century by Köchel, and they are generally now distinguished by K. numbering from this catalogue.

Operas

Mozart was essentially an operatic composer, although Salzburg offered him no real opportunity to exercise his talents in this direction. The greater stage works belong to the last decade of his life, starting with Idomeneo in Munich in January 1781. In Vienna, where he then settled, his first success came with the German opera or singspiel Die Entführung aus dem Serail (The Abduction from the Seraglio), a work on a Turkish theme, staged at the Burgtheater in 1782. Le nozze di Figaro (The Marriage of Figaro), an Italian comic opera with a libretto by Lorenzo da Ponte based on the controversial play by Beaumarchais, was staged at the same theatre in 1786 and Don Giovanni, with a libretto again by da

Ponte, in Prague in 1787. Così fan tutte (All Women Behave Alike) was staged briefly in Vienna in 1790, its run curtailed by the death of the Emperor. La clemenza di Tito (The Clemency of Titus) was written for the coronation of the new Emperor in Prague in 1791, no such commission having been granted Mozart in Vienna. His last stage work, a Singspiel, was Die Zauberflöte (The Magic Flute), mounted at the end of September at the Theater auf der Wieden, a magic opera that was running with success at the time of the composer's death.

☞ **Recommended Recordings**

Ascanio in Alba (2 CD's)
Naxos 8.660040-1

Così Fan Tutte (3 CD's)
Naxos 8.660008-10

Così Fan Tutte (Highlights)
Naxos 8.553172

Overtures (complete)
Naxos 8.550185

Tenor Arias (from Die Zauberflöte, Die Entführung aus dem Serail, Don Giovanni, Così fan tutte and La clemenza di Tito)
Naxos 8.550383

The Magic Flute (2 CD's)
Naxos 8.660030-1

Church Music

As he lay dying Mozart was joined by his friends to sing through parts of a work that he left unfinished. This was his setting of the Requiem Mass, commissioned by an anonymous nobleman, who had intended to pass the work off as his own. The Requiem was later completed by Mozart's pupil Süssmayer, to whom it was eventually entrusted. Mozart composed other church music, primarily for use in Salzburg. Settings of the Mass include the Coronation Mass of 1779, one of a number of liturgical settings of this kind. In addition to settings of litanies and Vespers, Mozart wrote a number of shorter works for church use. These include the well known Exsultate, jubilate, written for the castrato Rauzzini in Milan in 1773 and the simple four-part setting of the Ave verum, written to oblige a priest in Baden in June 1791. Mozart's Church or Epistle Sonatas were written to bridge the liturgical gap between the singing of the Epistle and the singing of the Gospel at Mass. Composed in Salzburg during a period from 1772 until 1780, the sonatas are generally scored for two violins, bass instrument and organ, although three of them, intended for days of greater ceremony, involve a slightly larger ensemble.

Recommended Recordings

Coronation Mass / Laudate Dominum
Ave verum / Exsultate, jubilate
Naxos 8.550495

Requiem
Naxos 8.550235

Church Sonatas
Naxos 8.550512

Vocal and Choral Music

In addition to a smaller number of works for vocal ensemble, Mozart wrote concert arias and scenes, some of them for insertion into operas by others. Songs, with piano accompaniment, include a setting of Goethe's Das Veilchen (The Violet).

Orchestral Music

(a) Symphonies

Mozart wrote his first symphony in London in 1764-5 and his last in Vienna in August 1788. The last three symphonies, Nos. 39, 40 and 41, were all written during the summer of 1788, each of them with its own highly individual character. No. 39, in E flat major, using clarinets instead of the usual pair of oboes, has a timbre all its own, while No. 40 in G minor, with its ominous and dramatic opening, is now very familiar. The last symphony, nicknamed in later years the Jupiter symphony, has a fugal last movement, a contrapuntal development of what was becoming standard symphonic practice. All the symphonies, of course, repay listening. Of particular beauty is Symphony No. 29, scored for the then usual pairs of oboes and French horns and strings, written in 1774, the more grandiose Paris Symphony, No. 31, written in 1778 with a French audience in mind, the Haffner, the Linz and the Prague, Nos. 35, 36 and 38. The so-called Salzburg Symphonies, in three movements, on the Italian model, and scored only for strings, were probably intended for occasional use during one of Mozart's Italian journeys. They are more generally known in English as Divertimenti, K. 136, 137 and 138. The symphonies are not numbered absolutely in chronological order of composition, but Nos. 35 to 41 were written in Vienna in the 1780s and Nos. 14 to 30 in Salzburg in the 1770s.

Recommended Recordings

Symphonies Nos. 1-5
Naxos 8.550871

Symphonies Nos. 6-10
Naxos 8.550872

Symphonies Nos. 11-14
Naxos 8.550873

Symphonies Nos. 15-18
Naxos 8.550874

Symphonies Nos. 19, 20 and 37
Naxos 8.550875

(b) Cassations, Divertimenti and Serenades

The best known Serenade of all is Eine kleine Nachtmusik (A Little Night-Music), a charming piece of which four of the five original movements survive. It is scored for solo strings and was written in the summer of 1787, the year of the opera Don Giovanni and of the death of the composer's father. The Serenata notturna, written in 1776 in Salzburg uses solo and orchestral strings and timpani, while the Divertimento K. 247, the Lodron Night-Music, dating from the same year, also served a social purpose during evening entertainments in Salzburg. Cassations, the word more or less synonymous with Divertimento or Serenade, again had occasional

use, sometimes as a street serenade, as in the case of Mozart's three surviving works of this title, designed to mark end of year university celebrations. Generally music of this kind consisted of several short movements. Other examples of the form by Mozart include the so-called Posthorn Serenade, K. 320, which uses the posthorn itself during its course and the Haffner Serenade, designed to celebrate an event in the Haffner family in Salzburg. The Serenade K. 361, known as the Gran Partita, was written during the composer's first years of independence in Vienna and scored for a dozen wind instruments and a double bass.

☛ Recommended Recordings

Serenade K. 320 "Posthorn" / Notturno
Naxos 8.550092

Serenade K. 361 "Gran Partita"
Naxos 8.550060

(c) Dance Music

Mozart wrote a great deal of dance music both in Salzburg and in Vienna. His only court appointment under the Emperor Joseph II was as a composer of court dance music, a position that, in his words, paid him too much for what he did and not enough for what he could have done. The dance music includes German dances, Ländler, and Contredanses, popular forms of the time.

☞ **Recommended Recording**

German Dances K. 586, 600, 605
Naxos 8.550412

(d) Concertos

Mozart wrote some 30 keyboard concertos. The earliest of these are four arrangements of movements by various composer, made in 1767, in the form of keyboard concertos. In 1772 Mozart arranged three sonatas by the youngest son of J.S. Bach, Johann Christian, to form keyboard concertos. These last three concertos are not generally included in the numbering of the concertos. Apart from these arrangements Mozart wrote six keyboard concertos during his years in Salzburg. The more important compositions in this form, designed clearly for the fortepiano, an instrument smaller than the modern pianoforte and with a more delicately incisive tone, were written in Vienna between 1782 and 1791, principally for the composer's use in subscription concerts with which he at first won success in the imperial capital. Of the 27 numbered concertos particular mention may be made of the Concertos in C minor and D minor, Nos. 24 and 20, K. 491 and 466. Mozart completed his last piano concerto No. 27, K. 595 in B flat major, in January 1791.

Mozart wrote a series of five concertos for solo violin one in 1773 and four in 1775 in 1775 at a time when he was concertmaster of the court orchestra in Salzburg. Of these the last three, K. 216 in G major, K. 218 in D major and K. 219 in A major are the best known, together with the splendid Sinfonia concertante of 1779, for solo violin and solo viola. The Concertone for two solo violins, written in 1774, is less frequently heard.

Mozart's concertos for solo wind instruments include a concerto for bassoon, two concertos for solo flute and a concerto for solo oboe, with a final concerto for clarinet written in October 1791. Mozart wrote four concertos for French horn, principally for the use of his friend, the horn-player Ignaz Leutgeb and a Sinfonia concertante for solo wind instruments, designed for performance by

Mannheim friends in Paris. During his stay in France in 1778 he also wrote a fine concerto for flute and harp, intended for unappreciative aristocratic patrons there.

☞ **Recommended Recordings**

Piano Concertos Nos. 1-4
Naxos 8.550212

Piano Concertos Nos. 5 & 26 / Rondo
Naxos 8.550209

Piano Concertos Nos. 6, 8 & 19
Naxos 8.550208

Piano Concertos Nos. 7, 10 & 15
Naxos 8.550210

Piano Concertos Nos. 9 & 27
Naxos 8.550203

Piano Concertos Nos. 11 & 22
Naxos 8.550206

Piano Concertos Nos. 12, 14 & 21
Naxos 8.550202

Piano Concertos Nos. 13 & 20
Naxos 8.550201

Piano Concertos Nos. 16 & 25 / Concert Rondo
Naxos 8.550207

Piano Concertos Nos. 17 & 18
Naxos 8.550205

Piano Concertos Nos. 20 & 21
Naxos 8.550434

Piano Concertos Nos. 23 & 24
Naxos 8.550204

Violin Concertos Nos. 1 & 2 / Rondo / Andante
Naxos 8.550414

Violin Concertos Nos. 3 & 5 / Rondo / Adagio
Naxos 8.550418

Violin Concerto No. 4
Sinfonia concertante K. 364
Naxos 8.550332

Flute Concertos Nos. 1 & 2 / Andante K. 315
Naxos 8.550074

Flute & Harp Concerto K. 299
Sinfonia concertante K. 297b
Naxos 8.550159

Oboe Concerto / Bassoon Concerto
Clarinet Concerto
Naxos 8.550345

Chamber Music

It was inevitable that Mozart should also show his mastery in music for smaller groups of instruments. With some reluctance he accepted a commission in Mannheim for a series of quartets for flute and string trio, two of which he completed during his stay there in 1777/8. A third flute quartet was completed in Vienna in 1787, preceded by an oboe quartet in Munich in 1781, a quintet the following year for French horn, violin, two violas and cello and finally, in 1789, a clarinet quintet, the wind part for his friend Anton Stadler, a virtuoso performer on the newly developed clarinet and on the basset-clarinet, an instrument of extended range of his own invention.

Mozart's work for string instruments includes a group of string quintets, written in Vienna in 1787 and, over the course of around twenty years, some 23 string quartets. Particularly interesting are the later quartets, a group of six dedicated to and influenced by Joseph Haydn and three final quartets, the so-called Prussian Quartets, intended for the cello-playing King of Prussia, Friedrich Wilhelm II. To the body of music of more serious intention may be added Ein musikalische Spass, K. 522 (A Musical Joke) for two horns and solo strings, written in 1787. The music is a re-creation of a work played for and presumably composed by village musicians, including formal solecisms and other deliberate mistakes of structure and harmony.

There are other chamber music compositions, principally written during the last ten years of Mozart's life in Vienna, involving the use of the piano, an instrument on which Mozart excelled. These later compositions include six completed piano trios, two piano quartets, and a work that Mozart claimed to consider his best, a quintet for piano, oboe, clarinet, bassoon and French horn, K. 452.

Mozart added considerably to the violin and piano sonata repertoire, writing his first sonatas for these instruments between the ages of six and eight and his last in 1788, making up a total of some thirty compositions. On the whole the later sonatas intended for professional players of a high order have more to offer than the sonatas written for pupils or amateurs, although there is fine music, for example, in the set of six sonatas written during the composer's journey to Mannheim and Paris in 1777 and 1778.

☛ Recommended Recordings

Clarinet Trio "Kegelstatt"
Clarinet Quartets K. 317d & K. 496
Naxos 8.550439

Flute Quartets (complete)
Naxos 8.550438

Oboe Quartet K. 370 / Horn Quintet K. 407
Musical Joke K. 522
Naxos 8.550437

String Quartets K. 464 & K. 428
Naxos 8.550540

String Quartets, K. 80, K. 115, K. 157 & K. 387
Naxos 8.550541

String Quartets K. 458, K. 158, K. 159 & K. 156
Naxos 8.550542

String Quartets K. 136, K. 137, K. 138 & K. 465
Naxos 8.550543

String Quartets K. 160, K. 168, K. 169
& K. 589
Naxos 8.550544

String Quartets K. 170, K. 171 & K. 421
Naxos 8.550546

String Quartets K. 172, K. 173
& K. 575 "Prussian No. 1"
Naxos 8.550545

Violin Sonatas Vol. 1
K. 304, K. 305, K. 306 and K. 377
Naxos 8.553110
Violin Sonatas Vol. 2
K. 296, K. 301, K. 302 and K. 303
Naxos 8.553111

Piano Music

Mozart's sonatas for the fortepiano cover a period from
1766 to 1791, with a significant number of mature
sonatas written during the years in Vienna. The sonatas
inculde much fine music, ranging from the slighter C
major Sonata for beginners K. 545 to the superb B flat
Sonata, K. 570. In addition to his sonatas he wrote a
number of sets of variations, while his ephemeral
improvisations in similar form are inevitably lost to us.
The published works include operatic variations as well
as a set of variations on the theme Ah, vous dirai-je,
maman, known in English as Twinkle, twinkle, little star.

☛ **Recommended Recordings**

Piano Sonatas K. 310, K. 333 & K. 533
Naxos 8.550445

Piano Sonatas K. 311, K. 332,
K. 545 & K. 570
Naxos 8.550446

Piano Sonatas K. 279, K. 282,
K. 283 & K. 284
Naxos 8.550447

Piano Sonatas K. 281, K. 309,
K. 331 & K. 576
Naxos 8.550448

Piano Sonatas K. 280, K. 333,
K. 457 & K. 475
Naxos 8.550449

Piano Sonatas K. 457 & K. 351 /
Fantaisie K. 475 / Variations K. 265
Naxos 8.550258

Piano Variations K. 24, 25, 54, 179,
180 & 354
Naxos 8.550611

Piano Variations K. 264, 265, 352, 353 & 398
Naxos 8.550612

Piano Variations K. 455, 460, 500, 573 & 613
Naxos 8.550613

Organ Music

There is very little organ music by Mozart or, indeed, by
other great composers of the period, although organ
improvisation was an art generally practised, then as

now. Mozart's organ music includes a few compositions for mechanical organ, one improvisation, transcribed from memory by a priest who heard most of it, and a number of smaller compositions perhaps intended for organ, written in childhood. Mozart's last appointment in Salzburg was as court organist, and there are significant organ parts in some of the church sonatas he wrote during that brief period, in 1779 and 1780.

☛ **Recommended Recording**
Organ Works
Naxos 8.550514

Mundy, John (c. 1555 - 1630)

John Mundy, son of the composer William Mundy, spent much of his life as organist at St George's Chapel, Windsor. It is not always possible to distinguish between his work and his father's, when the ascription is only given as to Mundy.

Church Music

John Mundy wrote English and Latin church music, the former including verse anthems and full anthems. Notable among his Latin church music is his setting of the Lamentations and his In te Domine speravi.

Instrumental Music

Instrumental music by John Mundy includes a few virginal pieces included in the Fitzwilliam Virginal Book, the collection compiled by Francis Tregian during his ten years of imprisonment in the London Fleet prison, condemned as a Catholic recusant.

Mundy, William (c. 1529 - 1591?)

Father of John Mundy, William Mundy was a vicar-choral at St Paul's Cathedral in London and in 1564 became a Gentleman of the Chapel Royal, a position in which he was succeeded in 1591 by Anthony Anderson. Problems of distinguishing between the music of father and son are mentioned above.

Church Music

William Mundy left settings of the Church of England Services, full anthems, verse anthems and Latin liturgical settings, in a generally conservative musical style.

☛ **Recommended Recording**
Kyrie / Magnificat
Naxos 8.550937

Mussorgsky, Modest Petrovich

(1839 - 1881)

Mussorgsky was one of the five Russian nationalist composers, roughly grouped under the influence of the unreliable Balakirev. Initially an army officer and later, intermittently, a civil servant, Mussorgsky left much unfinished at his death in 1881, nevertheless his influence on composers such as Janáček was considerable, not least in the association he found between speech intonations and rhythms and melody. Rimsky-Korsakov, a musician who had acquired a more conventional technique of orchestration and composition, revised and completed a number of Mussorgsky's works, versions which now may seem inferior to the innovative original compositions as Mussorgsky conceived them.

Operas

The greatest of Mussorgsky's creations was the opera Boris Godunov, based on Pushkin and Karamazin, with a thoroughly Russian historical subject. He completed the first version in 1869 and a second version in the 1870s, but it was Rimsky-Korsakov's version that was first performed outside Russia. The opera provides an important part for a bass in the rôle of Boris. Other operas by Mussorgsky include Khovanshchina, completed and orchestrated by Rimsky-Korsakov. A later version by

Shostakovich restores more of the original text. The opera Sorochintsy Fair, after Gogol, completed by Lyadov and others, includes the orchestral favourite Night on the Bare Mountain, an orchestral witches' sabbath.

☛ **Recommended Recording**

Night on the Bare Mountain
Naxos 8.550051

Piano Music

Mussorgsky's 1874 suite Pictures at an Exhibition, a tribute to the versatile artist Hartman, has proved the most popular of all the composer's works, both in its original version for piano and in colourful orchestral versions, of which that by Maurice Ravel has proved the most generally acceptable. Linked by Promenades for the visitor to the exhibition, Mussorgsky represents in music a varied collection, from the Market of Limoges and the Catacombs to the final Great Gate of Kiev, a monumental translation into music of an architectural design for a triumphal gateway.

☛ **Recommended Recordings**

Pictures at an Exhibition
Naxos 8.550044

Pictures at an Exhibition (orch. Ravel)
Naxos 8.550051

Vocal Music

Mussorgsky wrote a number of choral works and songs, many of the latter of considerable interest, including the group The Nursery. The Song of the Flea, based on Goethe's Mephistophelean song in Faust, is a bass favourite.

Myaskovsky, Nikolay Yakovlevich (1881 - 1950)

Trained originally at the Russian Academy of Military Engineering, Myaskovsky left the army in order to study at St Petersburg Conservatory, where he befriended the young Prokofiev. His own teachers were Rimsky-Korsakov and Liadov. He became professor of composition at Moscow Conservatory in 1921, retaining the position until his death in 1950, respected by his friend Prokofiev and by pupils such as Kabalevsky and Khachaturian. With Shostakovich, Prokofiev and other composers, he suffered official criticism in 1948, when he was accused of formalism, a popular current charge.

Orchestral Music

Myaskovsky completed 27 symphonies, the last in the years after his condemnation. Some of the symphonies were intended to suit the purposes of Soviet aesthetic policy, celebrating Revolution or, in Symphony No. 12, the triumphs of collective farming. Other orchestral works include a Violin Concerto and a Cello Concerto, all in an approachable diatonic style.

☞ Recommended Recordings

Symphonies Nos. 5 and 9
Marco Polo 8.223499

Symphony No. 6
Marco Polo 8.223301

Symphonies Nos. 7 and 10
Marco Polo 8.223113

Symphony No. 8
Marco Polo 8.223297

Symphony No. 12 / Silence
Marco Polo 8.223302

Chamber Music

Myaskovsky wrote thirteen string quartets and sonatas for violin, viola and cello, with piano.

Piano Music

The Piano Sonatas of Myaskovsky, nine in number, are written in a generally similar idiom. There are also a number of shorter piano pieces, including three sets of Children's Pieces.

☞ Recommended Recordings

Piano Sonatas Nos. 1 and 4
Marco Polo 8.223469

Piano Sonatas Nos. 2, 3 and 5
Marco Polo 8.223156

Piano Sonatas Nos. 6-9
Marco Polo 8.223178

Vocal and Choral Music

In his choral works Myaskovsky responded to contemporary Soviet demands, while his solo songs include settings of translations of poems by Robert Burns.

Nicolai, Otto (1810 - 1849)

A native of Königsberg, Otto Nicolai was educated largely in Berlin, through the intervention of a sympathetic patron, and made a name for himself there, without great material success. A period in Rome as organist at the Prussian Embassy aroused his interest in opera, an enthusiasm he was able to pursue at the Court Opera in Vienna, finally, in the year before his death, achieving the position of director of the Berlin Cathedral choir and Kapellmeister of the Berlin Opera.

Operas

Nicolai is best known for his opera based on Shakespeare's comedy The Merry Wives of Windsor, Die lustigen Weiber von Windsor, rejected by the opera in Vienna, but first performed in Berlin in March 1849, two

months before Nicolai's early death. The opera occupies an important position in German Romantic operatic repertoire.

Nielsen, Carl (1865 - 1931)

The principal post-Romantic Danish composer, Carl Nielsen, was born in 1865, the son of a painter and village musician. Childhood experience as an amateur performer led to subsidised study at the Copenhagen Conservatory and a long career during which he developed his own personal style of composition, in particular in a series of important symphonies.

Orchestral Music

Nielsen wrote six symphonies, distinguished by the titles given them as well as in numbering. Of these the best known are Symphony No. 2, The Four Temperaments, and Symphony No. 4, The Inextinguishable. Symphony No. 5, written after the 1914-18 war, represents, in its two movements, the composer's struggle to develop new and stronger rhythms and more advanced harmony. His concertos for clarinet, for flute and for violin have also found a place, as has the overture taken from the opera Maskarade.

Symphonies Nos. 1 & 6 "Sinfonia semplice"
Naxos 8.550826

Symphonies Nos. 2 "The Four Temperaments"
& 3
Naxos 8.550825

Symphonies Nos. 4 "Inextinguishable" & 5
Naxos 8.550743

Chamber Music

Nielsen's 1922 Wind Quintet is a particularly pleasing element in wind chamber music repertoire, of greater interest than the composer's earlier string quartets.

☞ **Recommended Recording**

Wind Quintet, Op. 43
Naxos 8.553050

Obrecht, Jacob (c. 1450 - 1505)

Jacob Obrecht was a leading composer of the dominant Netherlands school in the later 15th century, with a career that took him from Bergen op Zoom as far as Ferrara, where he died in 1505.

Church Music

Obrecht wrote some thirty settings of the ordinary of the Mass, using various contemporary forms. In common with many other composers of the time he wrote a setting using the well known popular song L'homme armé. A similar number of motets include a number of Marian antiphons. Relatively little of Obrecht's secular vocal music has survived.

Ockeghem, Johannes (c. 1410 - 1497)

Ockeghem belongs to the dominant Franco-Flemish school of composers whose influence pervaded the rest of Europe in the second half of the 15th century. He was in the service of the Dukes of Burgundy and from 1452 came to occupy a position of importance at the French court, holding various church benefices and serving as a diplomat.

Church Music

Only thirteen Mass settings by Ockeghem survive, including the Missa Quinti Toni, a Mass on L'homme armé and the remarkable Missa prolationum, with its command of technical contrapuntal resources. A smaller number of motets survive.

Secular Vocal Music

Ockeghem left a series of chansons, generally for three voices, on poetic texts typical of the time.

Offenbach, Jacques (1819 - 1880)

The son of a Cologne synagogue cantor, Offenbach and his violinist brother Julius were trained at the Paris Conservatoire, and Jacques Offenbach thereafter found employment initially as a cellist at the Opéra-Comique followed by a successful early career as a virtuoso on the instrument, for which he wrote a number of works, including a Concerto militaire and a Concertino. He was for five years conductor at the Théatre Français, but in 1855 rented his own theatre, where his early light-hearted stage-works were performed. He continued a successful career devoted largely to operetta and opéras comiques until his death in 1880.

Stage Works

Of nearly a hundred lighter pieces for the stage, Orphée aux enfers (Orpheus in the Underworld) is best known, in particular for its famous can-can. Other operettas include La belle Hélène (Fair Helen) and La vie parisienne. Of a weightier cast is Offenbach's final opera, Les contes d'Hoffmann (The Tales of Hoffmann), completed after the composer's death by Bizet's friend Guiraud and based, as the title suggests, on stories by E.T.A. Hoffmann, including the tale of Dr. Coppelius and his life-like creation, the doll Coppélia.

☞ **Recommended Recordings**

Overtures (La vie parisienne / La belle Hélène)
Naxos 8.550473

Overtures
(La belle Hélène / Orphée aux enfers)
Naxos 8.550468

Orff, Carl (1895 - 1982)

The German composer Carl Orff is widely known for his work in music education, particularly in exploration of the connections between music and movement. In his compositions he found a similar connection between the dramatic and the musical, couched in his very personal style of writing, with its insistent, repeated patterns of notes and compelling rhythms.

Stage Works

The best known of all Orff's works is the Carmina Burana, a large scale work making use of the medieval Latin and Old German lyrics found at the monastery of Benediktbeuern. The work has become even more familiar to unmusical audiences by use of elements from it in advertising and in films. Carmina burana is generally performed only as a form of secular oratorio, in the concert- hall, rather than on the stage, as is Catulli carmina (Songs of Catullus), again intended for theatrical use.

Pachelbel, Johann (1653 - 1706)

An important German composer of Protestant church music, Johann Pachelbel brought to his art an element acquired from acquaintance with Catholic forms of music in Vienna and Italy. He was employed as an organist at Erfurt, then at court in Stuttgart, as organist at Gotha and finally from 1695 in his native city of Nuremberg, where he died in 1706.

Chamber Music

Although chamber music represents only a small part of Pachelbel's achievement as a composer, his Canon and Gigue have in recent years won enormous popularity.

Organ Music

As a leading performer on the instrument, Pachelbel wrote a considerable amount of organ music, including a series of organ chorales, based on well known Lutheran hymn-tunes. Other organ music includes works in forms later used by Bach, fugues, toccatas, fantasias and a set of six chaconnes.

Church Music

Pachelbel composed a number of sacred concertos, works for voices and a small group of instruments on sacred texts as well as a number of Magnificat and other settings for the evening service of Vespers.

Paderewski, Ignacy Jan

(1860 - 1941)

Paderewski, trained in Warsaw, later became a pupil of Leschetizky in Vienna, embarking then on a distinguished international career as a virtuoso pianist. He abandoned his career as a musician for three years, from 1918 to 1921, when he held the positions of Prime Minister and Foreign Minister of Poland, in continuation of his fight for Polish independence. This struggle he had resumed at the time of his death in 1940, during the course of a visit to the United States of America to arouse support for his cause.

Piano Music

Paderewski wrote a number of attractive short pieces for piano in the early years of his career. These include the very well known Mélodie in G flat major, and the Menuet célèbre.

Orchestral Music

Paderewski left a Piano Concerto, written in 1888, and a Fantaisie polonaise sure des thèmes originaux (Polish Fantasy on Original Themes) for piano and orchestra. His only Symphony was completed in 1909.

Paganíní, Nícolò (1782 - 1840)

Paganini was the greatest violinist of his age, exercising a strong influence on the developing technique of violin-playing and, through his virtuosity on the instrument, on the ambitions of performers on other instruments. Born in Genoa in 1782, he studied there, at first with his father. He spent eight years, from 1801, at Lucca, later as solo violinist to the court of Napoleon's sister, installed there as ruler by her brother. From 1810 he travelled as a virtuoso, at first in Italy and then, from 1828, abroad, causing a sensation wherever he went, his phenomenal technique giving rise to rumours of diabolical assistance. His career went into partial decline from 1834, followed by a significant deterioration in health. He died in Nice in 1840.

Music for Violin & Orchestra

Paganini wrote a number of works for violin and orchestra for his own concert use. These include five numbered concertos, the second of which, the Concerto in B minor, contains the movement La campanella, borrowed later by Liszt. Sets of variations for violin and orchestra include I Palpiti, based on an operatic aria by Rossini, and Le Streghe, based on a theme from an opera by Mozart's pupil Süssmayr.

Recommanded Recording

Violin Concertos Nos. 1 & 2
Naxos 8.550649

Chamber Music

Music of another kind is provided in the works for violin and guitar written by Paganini, who also had a considerable interest in the second instrument. These compositions include groups of sonatas and a set of quartets for guitar and string trio.

☞ **Recommended Recordings**

Centone di Sonate Vol. 1
Naxos 8.553141

Centone di Sonate Vol. 2
Naxos 8.553142

Centone di Sonate Vol. 3
Naxos 8.553143

Six Sonatas, Op. 2 / Duetto amoroso
Cantabile and Valse / Variazioni di bravura
Naxos 8.550759

Music for Violin and Guitar
Naxos 8.550690

Violin Solo

Paganini's Twenty-Four Caprices for unaccompanied violin provide a compendium of violin technique and vehicles for dazzling virtuoso display. The last of the Caprices was used by Brahms for two books of piano variations on the theme and by Rachmaninov in his Rhapsody on a Theme of Paganini for piano and orchestra.

☞ **Recommended Recording**

24 Caprices
Naxos 8.550717

Paisiello, Giovanni (1740 - 1816)

Among the most important composers of Italian opera in the later 18th century, Paisiello was trained principally in Naples, where he first established his reputation as a composer. In 1776 he was invited to move to St Petersburg, where he worked as a composer of opera and director of the court orchestra, winning the favour of the Empress Catherine II. In 1784 he was able to accept an invitation to return to Naples, where he enjoyed royal favour, only temporarily withdrawn after his acquiescence in the republican régime of 1799. He spent two years in Paris, from 1802 to 1804, as director of music for Napoleon. His employment in Naples continued under Ferdinand IV and then under the usurper Joseph Buonaparte and his successor Joachim Murat. The final defeat of Napoleon in 1815 and the return of King Ferdinand removed Paisiello from his official positions.

Operas

Paisiello's chief fame was as a composer of operas, of which he wrote some eighty. L'idolo cinese (The Chinese Idol) was a favourite of Lady Hamilton, later the mistress of Nelson. His Il barbiere di Siviglia (The Barber of Seville), first performed in St Petersburg in 1782, proved a dangerous rival to Rossini's later opera on the same subject. He set a number of libretti by the Vienna court poet Metastasio and turned to Cervantes in his Don Chisciotte della Mancia (Don Quixote de la Mancha). His style, which seems to have had some influence on Mozart, who heard his Il re Teodoro in Venezia (King Teodoro in Venice) in Vienna in 1784, is concise and melodious, with the necessary sparkle in his comedies, although his heroic and tragic operas seem sometimes to be matched with music that is too light-hearted.

Vocal and Choral Music

Paisiello composed a number of cantatas, designed for entertainment or in formal celebration of some royal occasion. Sacred works include oratorios on the subject of Susanna and of The Conception of the Virgin Mary, with a setting of Metastasio's La passione di Gesù Cristo (The Passion of Jesus Christ). He made a number of settings of the Mass, including, in 1814, a Mass for the chapel of Louis XVIII, which followed earlier Masses for Napoleon. There are other liturgical compositions, some again designed for official occasions of celebration.

Instrumental Music

Paisiello's instrumental music includes divertimenti, keyboard concertos, string and flute quartets and sonatas for harpsichord and violin.

Palestrina, Giovanni Pierluigi da (1525/6 - 1594)

Palestrina, his name derived from his probable place of birth, was one of the principal composers of the late 16th century, his style taken as a model by later generations. His musical language represents the climax of musical achievement of the period, above all in his mastery of earlier Franco-Flemish polyphonic techniques, now used with complete assurance, particularly in the provision of music for the Catholic liturgy both before and after the reforming Council of Trent. Palestrina's career was largely spent in Rome, at the basilica of Santa Maria Maggiore, the Cappella Giulia at St. Peter's and at St. John Lateran.

Church Music

Palestrina wrote a large number of settings of the ordinary of the Mass. Of these the Missa Papae Marcelli, popularly supposed to have been written to convince the authorities at the Council of Trent that there was still a place for polyphony in the musical performance of the Catholic liturgy, is among the best known. Missa Aeterna Christi munera, a Mass that makes use of the plainchant of the title as its basis, is a fine example of Palestrina's technical command, but a similar claim might be made for almost any other of the 100 or so surviving Mass settings. The very large number of surviving motets offers a similar embarrassment of choice. Palestrina's liturgical music also includes settings of the Lamentations for Holy Week, taken from the Book of Jeremiah, litanies, settings of the Magnificat and offertories. In addition to generally conservative Italian madrigals, he also wrote a number of five-voice Italian sacred madrigals.

Missa Hodie Christus natus est / Stabat mater
Naxos 8.550836

Missa Papae Marcelli
Missa Aeterna Christi munera
Naxos 8.550573

Missa de beata Virgine
Naxos 8.553313

Parry, Hubert (1848 - 1918)

An English composer and teacher of relative insignificance in the former capacity, Hubert Parry exercised a strong influence over the music of his time in England, occupying positions both at Oxford and at the newly established Royal College of Music. Some of his compositions have remained popular in England, although much of what he wrote is now generally neglected.

Church Music

Anthems and service-settings by Parry for the Anglican liturgy remain a part of cathedral repertoire, as do a number of well known hymn-tunes,

Choral and Vocal Music

Parry's setting of Milton's Blest Pair of Sirens remains a staple item in amateur choral repertoire in England, while part-songs and solo songs also retain an occasional and deserved place in vocal repertoire.

Orchestral Music

Parry's five symphonies are seldom heard, but the English Suite and Lady Radnor's Suite, both for string orchestra, make a useful addition to English string orchestra repertoire.

■ **Recommended Recordings**

An English Suite / Lady Radnor's Suite
Naxos 8.550331

Symphony No. 2 "Cambridge"
Overture to an Unwritten Tragedy
Symphonic Variations
Naxos 8.553469

Pärt, Arvo (1935 -)

A native of Estonia, Arvo Pärt at first wrote in a style perceptibly influenced by Russian composers, later developing a language of his own through the exploration of the twelve-note system and a certain eclecticism that has led to an interest in early musical traditions, tempered by deep religious feeling.

Orchestral Music

In 1976 Pärt wrote a moving tribute to Benjamin Britten, Cantus in Memory of Benjamin Britten, for string orchestra and bell. His Cello Concerto (Pro et Contra) and three symphonies reflect the course his music has taken.

☛ Recommended Recording

Fratres / Festina / Summa
Cantus in memory of Benjamin Britten
Naxos 8.553750

Chamber Music

A wind Quintetino of 1965 has been followed by the interesting work Fratres, fro violin and piano, and Spiegel im Spiegel (Mirror in the Mirror) for cello and piano.

Vocal and Choral Music

Pärt has made a particularly strong impression with works such as his Passio Domini Nostri Jesu Christi secundum Johannem (St John Passion), his Stabat mater, for three solo voices and string trio, his Miserere of 1989 and the Biblical Sarah was ninety-years old.

Instrumental Music

Music for smaller ensembles and solo instruments by Pärt includes his 1977 Fratres for violin and piano and Spirgel im Spiegel for cello and piano, together with his organ Pari intervalli.

☛ Recommended Recording

Fratres / Festina / Summa
Cantus in memory of Benjamin Britten
Naxos 8.553750

Penderecki, Krzysztof (1933 -)

Penderecki occupies an important position in the music of his native Poland, while establishing an international reputation with music that had a wide effect. His earlier more experimental musical language was later subtly modified by his return to earlier traditions as a source of inspiration.

Vocal and Choral Music

The best known composition by Penderecki is his St. Luke Passion, the Passio et mors domini nostri Jesu Christi secundum Lucam, completed in 1965. This was followed in 1971 by Utrenia, a choral work that deals with the events following the Crucifixion, drawing inspiration from the Orthodox liturgy.

Pergolesi, Giovanni Battista

(1710 - 1736)

Pergolesi was a composer of considerable importance in the development of Italian comic opera in the early 18th century, making a singular contribution during a remarkably brief career. Born in 1710, he studied in Naples and became maestro di cappella there to a member of the viceregal court in 1732, later entering the service of another nobleman, after the Bourbon restoration. He died in 1736.

Operas

Pergolesi's opera La Serva Padrona, an intermezzo performed together with another opera, was first staged in Naples in 1733. The work later won international fame, particularly in Paris, when a production in 1752 gave rise to the so-called Guerre des bouffons between the rival French and Italian opera companies.

Orchestral & Chamber Music

Pergolesi's early death left much of his music unpublished, and his subsequent fame led to the wrong attribution of a number of works, as composers or promoters sought to make use of his posthumous reputation. Stravinsky's delightful ballet score for Dyagilev's Pulcinella made use of music that was entirely, if erroneously attributed to Pergolesi.

Church Music

Pergolesi left a number of settings of liturgical texts, a body of music considerably augmented by later false attributions. The well known setting of the Stabat mater, for soprano, alto, strings and organ, was written at Pozzuoli in 1736, during his final months of retirement in a Franciscan monastery there in anticipation of his death.

☛ **Recommended Recording**

Stabat Mater / Orfeo (Cantata)
Naxos 8.550766

Pérotin (c. 1200)

Pérotin was a successor of the composer Léonin in later 12th century Paris, active in his revision of the latter's Magnus Liber and in the composition of organum, discant and conductus, as polyphonic practices in Western music developed.

Church Music

Examples of four-voice and three-voice organa by Pérotin survive, representing a significant advance in polyphonic technique. Organum, in its simplest form, consisted of the addition at first of a parallel part, at the distance of a fourth or fifth, to an original plainchant melody. By the 12th century the additional melodic lines were no mere parallel additions to the original but of greater rhythmic and melodic variety, based, as before, on the underlying original plainchant of the traditional Catholic liturgy.

Pfitzner, Hans (1869 - 1949)

The German composer and conductor Hans Pfitzner was an important figure in his own generation, a friend of the writer Thomas Mann and conductor Bruno Walter, and a romantic in the tradition of Schumann and Brahms. He was for some years director of the conservatory, conductor of the symphony orchestra and director of the opera at Strasbourg, where his best known opera Palestrina was first performed. He lost his position as a life member of the Munich Academy of Music in 1934 and most of his possessions during the war, when his house was destroyed by bombing.

Operas

The best known of Pfitzner's stage works is his much admired opera Palestrina, treating the story of the 16th century composer Palestrina's alleged rescue of polyphony, when its use in Catholic church music was threatened by some of the reforming bishops at the Council of Trent. Pfitzner wrote the libretto himself, after a period of considerable research.

☛ Recommended Recording

Das Herz (Complete Opera) (2 CD's)
Marco Polo 8.223627-8

Choral and Vocal Music

Pfitzner's literary interests are reflected in his choral fantasy Das dunkle Reich (The Dark Kingdom), using texts by Michelangelo, Goethe and others, and in the cantata Von deutscher Seele, with its text by Eichendorff, a poet whom he greatly admired and whose poems he set in a number of songs.

☛ Recommended Recording

Piano Concerto Op. 31
Das Herz (Liebesmelodie)
Das Christ-Elflein (Overture)
Marco Polo 8.223162

Pierné, Gabriel (1863 - 1937)

A pupil of César Franck and Massenet and successor of the former as organist at Ste Clotilde in Paris, Gabriel Pierné won distinction as a composer and as a conductor, in the second capacity directing the Concerts Colonne from 1903, at first as a deputy to Eduard Colonne and then as his successor from 1910 until 1934. As a composer he was versatile, whether in more serious music or in a lighter-hearted but always technically assured idiom.

Stage Music

Pierné's music for the theatre includes several operas, from La coupe enchantée (The Magic Cup), based on La Fontaine, to the mystery play Les enfants à Bethléem (The Children at Bethlehem) and the incidental music for Pierre Loti's Ramuntcho, with the ballet Cydalise et le chèvre-pied (Cydalise and the Goat-Foot).

Orchestral Music

Orchestral music by Pierné includes a piano concerto, a concert-piece for harp and orchestra and the symphonic poems Paysages franciscains (Franciscan Landscapes).

Chamber Music

Pierné's sonatas for flute and piano, for violin, for cello and his Sonata da camera for flute cello and piano are interesting elements of chamber music repertoire, with the Canzonetta for clarinet and piano, Voyage au pays (Journey to the Country) for flute, harp and string trio a piano quintet and a Solo de concert for bassoon and piano.

☞ **Recommended Recordings**

*Fifteen Pieces / Sérénade à Colombine
Sérénade à Izeyl / Scherzando de Concert
Etude de Concert
Marco Polo 8.223115*

*Flute Sonata Op. 36 / Piano Trio Op. 45
Marco Polo 8.223189*

Choral and Vocal Music

Choral music includes the oratorio La croisade des enfants (The Children's Crusade) and a number of songs, ranging in mood from the relatively superficial to works of much greater depth.

Pizzetti, Ildebrando (1880 - 1968)

Among the most respected Italian composers of his generation, Pizzetti has in recent years suffered some neglect, in due, in part, to his natural conservatism in an age of experiment. He was, however, versatile and prolific, ambitious in opera, with interesting additions to choral and vocal repertoire, as to chamber music.

Operas

Pizzetti wrote over twenty operas, collaborating in earlier years with D'Annunzio, with whom he wrote the opera Fedra (Phaedra). His Assassinio nella catedrale (Murder in the Cathedral) treats a translation T.S.Eliot's play, while his last opera, Clitennestra (Clytemnestra), with a libretto by the composer, was staged at La Scala, Milan, in 1965.

Choral and Vocal Music

Pizzetti's choral music, much of which again draws its literary source from ancient Greece and Rome, includes a Requiem and a cantata Vanitas vanitatum (Vanity of Vanities) with a text from Ecclesiastes.

Chamber Music

In addition to various works for piano, Pizzetti left two string quartets, as well as interesting duo sonatas for violin and for cello and piano.

☛ **Recommended Recordings**

String Quartets in A Major and D
Marco Polo 8.223722

Trio in A for Violin, Cello and Piano
Sonata in A for Violin and Piano
Tre Canti for Violin and Piano
Marco Polo 8.223812

Ponchielli, Amilcare (1834 - 1886)

Ponchielli was among the most important Italian opera composers of the 19th century, second only to Verdi in the third quarter of the century.

Operas

The best known of the eleven operas written by Ponchielli is La Gioconda, with the famous Dance of the Hours from the opera a popular favourite.

☛ **Recommended Recordings**

La Gioconda: Dance of the Hours
Naxos 8.550081

La Gioconda: Cielo e mar
Naxos 8.550497

Poulenc, Francis (1899 - 1963)

The French composer Francis Poulenc only undertook formal musical training with Charles Koechlin in 1921, by which time he had already become identified with Les Six, the six French composers of the circle of Jean Cocteau, including Honegger, Auric and Milhaud. Initially apparently light-weight in style, the death of a close friend in 1935 brought a new depth to his work, at the same time as the start of a long collaboration with the singer Pierre Bernac.

Stage Works

Poulenc won considerable success with his comic opera Les Mamelles de Tirésias, with a text by Apollinaire, written during the later days of the war and staged in Paris in 1947. The tragic opera Dialogue des Carmélites, with a libretto by Georges Bernanos dealing with the execution of Carmelite nuns during the French Revolution and based on Gertrud von le Fort's novel Die Letzte am Schafott (The Last on the Scaffold), has entered international repertoire. Other stage works, in addition to a number of scores of incidental music and film music, include the ballet Les Biches, first staged in Monte Carlo in 1924.

Orchestral Music

Poulenc's orchestral music includes a suite from Les biches, a charming Concert champêtre for harpsichord and small orchestra, as well as concertos for organ, for piano and for two pianos.

Choral and Vocal Music

Poulenc made a significant and idiomatic contribution to the art of French solo song, in addition to a number of choral works. His solo songs range from settings of Apollinaire and Cocteau to settings of Ronsard. His melodrama L'Histoire de Babar, for reciter and piano, tells the story of Babar the Elephant, the creation of Jean de Brunhoff, a simple tale for children. His church music, after his inner conversion to the Catholic religion of his childhood in 1935, is marked by a Mass setting of 1937, and, more notably, the moving Stabat mater of 1950. In 1959 came the Gloria, for solo soprano, chorus

and orchestra, with a final more sombre Sept répons des ténèbres in 1961.

☞ **Recommended Recording**
   Stabat Mater / Gloria / Litanies à la vierge noire
   Naxos 8.553176

Chamber Music

French composers of the present century have shown a particular deftness in the handling of woodwind instruments. This ability is exemplified in Poulenc's sonatas for flute, for clarinet and for oboe and piano, in addition to an attractive Trio for oboe, bassoon and piano.

☞ **Recommended Recording**
   Violin Sonata
   Naxos 8.550276

Piano Music

The best known of all Poulenc's music was at one time the three Mouvements perpétuels of 1918. There is a piano duet sonata of the same year and a number of attractive short pieces, including a neo-classical Suite after Claude Gervaise and the elegant Promenades.

Praetorius, Michael (c.1571 - 1621)

In the 1590s Michael Praetorius settled in Wolfenbüttel as organist to Duke Heinrich Julius of Brunswick-Wolfenbüttel and was later appointed court Kapellmeister. In 1613 he moved temporarily to Dresden, at the request of the Elector of Saxony, returning to Wolfenbüttel in 1616, although continuing to undertake other work, not least in the re-organization of musical establishments. His writings on music include the important Syntagma musicum, the second volume of which gives useful information on the musical instruments of his time.

Church Music

Descended from a family of strict Lutheran persuasion, Praetorius based a great deal of his music on Lutheran hymns and on the Latin Lutheran liturgy of the time. His Musae Sioniae, in nine parts, contains a variety of Lutheran church music, polyphonic and homophonic, with a number of works which have become a well enough known part of present choral and hymn repertoire, in particular the familiar carol Es ist ein Ros entsprungen (A Rose has grown), In dulci jubilo and Puer natus in Bethlehem (A Boy is born in Bethlehem).

Instrumental Music

Instrumental music by Michael Praetorius is confined to his collection of dances, Terpsichore. A set of organ chorales is included in the seventh book of Musae Sioniae.

Prokofiev, Sergey (1891 - 1953)

Sergey Prokofiev, precocious as a child, entered the St. Petersburg Conservatory in 1904, by which time he had already written a great deal of music. At the Conservatory he shocked the more conservative director, Glazunov, but learned much from an older fellow-student, the composer Myaskovsky. After the Revolution he was given permission to travel abroad and he remained intermittently out of Russia, in America and then in Paris, until his final return to Russia in 1936. At home, though in touch again with the root of his inspiration, he found himself out of favour with the authorities and in 1948 the subject of particular and direct censure. His death in 1953, on the same day as Stalin, deprived him of the enjoyment of the subsequent relaxation in musical censorship that then took place. In style Prokofiev is ironic, writing in a musical language that is often acerbic.

Stage Works

Prokofiev first attempted to write an opera at the age of nine. Maturer operas include The Love for Three Oranges, written in 1919 for Chicago, The Fiery Angel and War and Peace, the last based on Tolstoy's novel. An early ballet score for Dyagilev proved unacceptable, but later ballets, once rejected as undanceable, include Romeo and Juliet, and in 1944 Cinderella. Both ballets as well as the first mentioned opera are known to concert audiences from orchestral suites based on them by the composer. Film scores by Prokofiev include Alexander Nevsky, written for Eisenstein's film of that name, and music for the same director's Ivan the Terrible. Music for the film Lieutenant Kijé, a fictional character, created by a clerical error and maintained in existence to the end, was written in 1933.

☛ Recommended Recordings

Cinderella Suites Nos. 1-3 / Scythian Suite
On the Dneiper, Symphonic Suite, Op. 51bis
(2 CD's)
Naxos 8.550968-9

Suites: Cinderella / Lieutenant Kijé
The Love for Three Oranges
Naxos 8.550381

Romeo and Juliet (2 CD's)
Naxos 8.553184-5

Romeo and Juliet (Highlights)
Naxos 8.550380

Orchestral Music

(a) Symphonies

Prokofiev wrote seven symphonies. Of these the Classical Symphony, a work written in 1916-17 with the work of Haydn in mind, is the best known. The Fifth Symphony of 1944 is a work on a much larger scale.

☛ Recommended Recordings

Symphonies No. 1 "Classical" & No. 5
Naxos 8.550237

Symphonies Nos. 3 & 7
Naxos 8.553054

Symphony No. 5 / The Year 1941
Naxos 8.553056

Symphony No. 6, Op. 111 / Waltzes, Op. 110
Naxos 8.553069

(b) Concertos

Of Prokofiev's five piano concertos the third is best known, written in the composer's instantly recognisable musical language, from the incisive opening to the motor rhythms that follow, in a mixture of lyricism and acerbic wit.

More overtly romantic in feeling are the two fine violin concertos. His early Cello Concerto was followed in 1952, fourteen years later, by a Cello Concertino, completed by the cellist Rostropovich and the composer Kabalevsky after Prokofiev's death.

☞ Recommended Recordings
Piano Concertos Nos. 1, 3 and 4
Naxos 8.550566

Piano Concertos Nos. 2 and 5
Naxos 8.550565

Choral and Vocal Music
In addition to a wide variety of choral and vocal music, which includes a concert version of the film score for Alexander Nevsky, Prokofiev wrote a number of less memorable works for various occasions of political importance.

Chamber Music
Chamber music by Prokofiev includes two sonatas for violin and piano, the second originally for flute and piano and revised by the composer, with the help of the violinist David Oistrakh. He completed his C major Cello Sonata in 1949 but a second sonata for the instrument was left unfinished at the time of his death. The Five Melodies for violin and piano, based on earlier songs, are also in general repertoire.

☞ Recommended Recordings
String Quartets Nos. 1 & 2
Cello Sonata, Op. 119
Naxos 8.553136

Piano Music
Prokofiev, himself a formidable pianist, completed nine piano sonatas out of a projected eleven. His music for piano also includes piano versions of music from the ballets Romeo and Juliet and Cinderella.

☞ Recommended Recordings
Piano Sonatas Nos. 2, 7 & 8
Naxos 8.553021

Music for Children
One of the most widely known of all Prokofiev's compositions is his tale for children Peter and the Wolf, for narrator and orchestra, a simple pedagogical work to introduce to children the instruments of the orchestra, with instruments or groups of instruments representing characters in the story.

☞ Recommended Recording
Peter and the Wolf
Naxos 8.550499

Puccini, Giacomo (1858 - 1924)

Descended from a family of musicians, Puccini was the most important Italian opera composer in the generation after Verdi. He was born and educated in Lucca, later studying under Ponchielli at the Milan Conservatory. He began his career as a composer of opera with Le Villi, on the story familiar from Adam's ballet Giselle, but first won significant success in 1893 with Manon Lescaut. A musical dramatist of considerable power, if sometimes lacking in depth, he wrote in all twelve operas, the last, Turandot, still unfinished at the time of his death in 1924.

Operas

The opera Manon Lescaut, using the full name of the heroine of the 18th century Abbé Prévost's novel to distinguish the work from Massenet's treatment of the same subject, won great success. Manon seduced by the old Géronte returns to her former lover, Des Grieux, but is betrayed to the authorities and transported to America, where she dies in the arms of her lover, who has followed her. La Bohème, first staged in 1896, centres on the love of Mimì and the poet Rodolfo in the Latin Quarter of Paris, a story of innocent love, betrayal and the final death of the heroine. Tosca, staged first in Rome in 1900, deals with the love of the singer Tosca for the painter Cavaradossi, their implication in revolutionary activities and death through the machinations of the wicked police-chief Scarpia, himself murdered by Tosca. Madama Butterfly is a story of love betrayed, the innocent Japanese heroine of the title deserted by her faithless American husband and finally compelled to suicide. La Fanciulla del West (The Girl of the Golden West) is set in a slightly improbable Wild West, while the triptych, Il Trittico, three short operas, attempts a change of mood. The last opera, Turandot, based on a Chinese story by the 18th century dramatist Gozzi, makes inappropriate use of Chinese melodies, but is a moving study of the love of the suitor Prince Calaf for the icy-hearted and cruel Princess Turandot. All ends happily, but not before moments of suspense, marked by the famous tenor aria Nessun dorma (Let no-one sleep).

☛ Recommended Recordings

La Bohème (2 CD's)
Naxos 8.660003-4

La Bohème (Highlights)
Naxos 8.553151

Madama Butterfly (2 CD's)
Naxos 8.660015-16

Madama Butterfly (Highlights)
Naxos 8.553152

Manon Lescaut (2 CD's)
Naxos 8.660019-20

Tosca (2 CD's)
Naxos 8.660001-2
Tosca (Highlights)
Naxos 8.553153

Chamber Music

Some of the musical material of a particularly poignant moment in Manon Lescaut appears in a set of pieces for string quartet by Puccini, Crisantemi (Chrysanthemums), part of a very small output of instrumental music, little of which was published by the composer.

Purcell, Henry (1659 - 1695)

Henry Purcell was one of the greatest English composers, flourishing in the period that followed the Restoration of the monarchy after the Puritan Commonwealth period. Purcell spent much of his short life in the service of the Chapel Royal as a composer, organist and singer. With considerable gifts as a composer, he wrote extensively for the stage, particularly in a hybrid musico-dramatic form of the time, for the church and for popular entertainment, a master of English word-setting and of contemporary compositional techniques for instruments and voices. He died in 1695, a year after composing funeral music for Queen Mary.

Stage Works

Purcell wrote only one full opera, a short work supposedly designed for a girls' school. The tragic story of Dido and Aeneas, with a libretto by Nahum Tate, has a perfection of its own. Dido's final lament, before she kills herself, follows the model for such compositions established by Monteverdi eighty years before. Other stage works by Purcell are in the hybrid form now known as semi-opera, combining spoken drama and a musical element that in the concert-hall may be performed apart from its wider dramatic context. These semi-operas include King Arthur, with a text by the poet John Dryden, a work that includes fascinating music for a chorus of cold people, frozen by the Cold Genius but thawed by the power of Love. The Fairy Queen, based on Shakespeare's A Midsummer Night's Dream, includes an interesting if apparently inappropriate Chinese masque, while The Tempest, again based on Shakespeare, includes songs and dance music of great interest.

Purcell provided incidental music, dances and songs, for a great many plays. Incidental music of this kind includes the music for Aphra Behn's Abdelazar or The Moor's Revenge, a rondeau from which provides the theme for Benjamin Britten's Young Person's Guide to the Orchestra.

The Fairy Queen (2 CDs)
Naxos 8.550660-1

Church Music

Purcell provided a number of verse anthems and full anthems for the liturgy of the Church of England, as well as settings of the Morning and Evening Service, the Magnificat and Nunc dimittis, Te Deum and Jubilate. The anthems offer considerable musical interest, exemplified in the verse anthems Rejoice in the Lord alway and My heart is inditing. Other sacred vocal music includes the Latin psalm setting Jehovah, quam multi sunt as well as settings of sacred poems by contemporary writers.

● **Recommended Recordings**

Music on the Death of Queen Mary
Full Anthems & Organ Music
Naxos 8.553129

Ode for St. Cecilia's Day / Te Deum
Raise, Raise the Voice
The Noise of Foreign Wars / Trumpet Sonata
Jubilate Deo
Naxos 8.553444

Secular Vocal Music

Purcell's secular vocal music includes a number of Odes for the feast of St. Cecilia, patron saint of music and a number of Welcome Songs and other celebrations of royal occasions. He wrote a considerable quantity of solo songs, in addition to the songs included in his work for the theatre. These solo songs and the songs for two or more voices offer a particularly rich repertoire, exemplified by the song Music for a while, from the play Oedipus and Man is for a woman made, from The Mock Marriage. Other vocal works include a number of catches, rounds for popular entertainment.

Instrumental Music

Instrumental music by Purcell, in addition to the theatre music, includes sets of fantasias for viols and two sets of trio sonatas.

Keyboard Music

Although Purcell was employed for over half his life as an organist of the Chapel Royal and at Westminster Abbey, he wrote relatively little for the instrument. His harpsichord music includes a number of suites, some of which include transcriptions of his own theatre music.

Rabaud, Henri (1873 - 1949)

Henri Rabaud, desceded from a family with distinguished musical traditions, was a pupil of Gédalge and Massenet at the Paris Conservatoire, of which he became director after Fauré's retirement. He was conservative as a composer and active as a conductor.

Dramatic Music

Rabaud's opera Mâruf, savetier du Caire (Mâruf, Cobbler of Cairo) combines the Wagnerian and the exotic and he wrote other operas, incidental music and film scores, the latter including the 1925 score for Joueur d'échecs (Chess-Player).

Orchestral Music

Orchestral music by Rabaud includes a Divertissement on Russian songs and Eglogue, a Virgilian poem for orchestra, as well as the symphonic poem Procession nocturne.

☛ **Recommended Recording**

Dances from "Mâruf" / Procession Nocturne
Suites Anglaises Nos. 2 and 3 / Églogue
Divertissement
Marco Polo 8.223503

Rachmaninov, Sergey (1873 - 1943)

After study at the St. Petersburg and Moscow Conservatories, Sergey Rachmaninov embarked on a career in Russia as a composer, pianist and conductor. Exile from his own country after the Communist Revolution of 1917 forced an increased concentration on performance, as one of the most distinguished pianists of the day, activity that enabled him to support his family but left less time for his work as a composer. For practical reasons he eventually based himself in the United States, while keeping a villa in Switzerland. He died in Beverly Hills in 1943.

Orchestral Music

The second of Rachmaninov's four piano concertos holds an unchallenged position among romantic works in this form, its popularity closely rivalled by the Rhapsody on a Theme of Paganini, for piano and orchestra. While the Symphonic Dances of 1940 enjoy some popularity, as well as the symphonic poem The Rock and the dark-hued Isle of the Dead, with its recurrent motif from the Latin Requiem Mass, the second of his three numbered symphonies is still more familiar.

☛ **Recommended Recordings**

Piano Concerto No. 2
Rhapsody on a Theme of Paganini
Naxos 8.550117

Piano Concerto No. 3
Prince Rostislav Overture
Naxos 8.550666

Symphonic Dances / Isle of the Dead
Naxos 8.550583

Symphony No. 2 / The Rock
Naxos 8.550272

Piano Music

Rachmaninov's Prelude in C sharp minor won early popularity that largely outweighed its merits. Other piano works include the Etudes-tableaux of 1911 and 1916-17, two sonatas, sets of Preludes and Moments musicaux, transcriptions, including the two Kreisler pieces Liebeslied and Liebesfreud, and the impressive Variations on a Theme of Corelli, his last original composition for solo piano, composed in 1931 and based on the popular Baroque dance theme of La Follia, also used by Corelli in a violin sonata.

☞ Recommended Recordings

Etudes-tableaux Opp. 33 & 39
Naxos 8.550347

Preludes Op. 23
Cinq morceaux de fantaisie, Op. 3
Naxos 8.550348

Preludes, Op. 32 / Liebeslied & Liebesfreud
Naxos 8.550466

Sonata No. 2, Op. 36
Variations on a Theme of Corelli
Moments musicaux, Op. 16
Naxos 8.550349

Raff, Joachim (1822 - 1882)

Joachim Raff enjoyed the highest reputation in his lifetime, later to be remembered only for his famous Cavatina, an attractive short piece that appeared in many arrangements. Encouraged by Mendelssohn and then by Liszt, he served the latter as an assistant at Weimar, orchestrating Liszt's earlier symphonic poems. His own work as a composer started in earnest when he left Weimar in 1856, to settle in Wiesbaden and then, from 1877, in Frankfurt as director of the Hoch Conservatory, a position he retained until his death in 1882.

Orchestral Music

Recent attempts have been made to re-assess Raff's music. His eleven symphonies go some way towards a synthesis of pure music and the programmatic element of the Neo-German school exemplified in the symphonic poems of Liszt. Most of the symphonies have titles of one sort or another, the last four representing aspects of the four seasons. He wrote concertos for piano, for violin and for cello, and other works for solo instrument and orchestra, as well as a series of suites and overtures.

Chamber Music

Raff contributed to the repertoire of German chamber music with works ranging from piano quintets to duo sonatas, the last including five sonatas for violin and piano.

Piano Music

Equally prolific in his work for the piano, Raff wrote a large number of shorter pieces, as well as transcriptions and fantasies derived from the current operatic repertoire.

Vocal and Choral Music

In addition to works for choir, including several psalm settings, Raff published four volumes of part-songs, three of them for male voices.

Opera

Raff enjoyed some success with his first opera, König Alfred, first staged in Weimar in 1853. One other of his six operas, Dame Kobold, received some contemporary attention.

☛ **Recommended Recordings**

Aus Thüringen / Italian Suite
Marco Polo 8.223194

Symphony No. 1 "An das Vaterland"
Marco Polo 8.223165

Symphony No. 2
Overtures (Romeo and Juliet / Macbeth)
Marco Polo 8.223630

Symphonies Nos. 3 & 10
Marco Polo 8.223321

Symphonies Nos. 4 & 11 "Der Winter"
Marco Polo 8.223529

Symphony No. 5 "Lenore"
Ein feste Burg ist unser Gott (Overture)
Marco Polo 8.223455

Symphony No. 6
Marco Polo 8.223638

Symphony No. 7 "In den Alpen"
Concert Overture Op. 123
Marco Polo 8.223506

Symphonies Nos. 8 & 9
Marco Polo 8.223362

Rameau, Jean-Philippe

(1683 - 1764)

Rameau was the leading French composer of his time, in particular after the death of Couperin in 1733. He made a significant and lasting contribution to musical theory. Born in Dijon, two years before the year of birth of Handel, Bach and Domenico Scarlatti, Rameau spent the earlier part of his career principally as organist at Clermont Cathedral. In 1722 or 1723, however, he settled in Paris, publishing further collections of harpsichord pieces and his important Treatise on Harmony, written before his removal to Paris. From

1733 he devoted himself largely to the composition of opera and to his work as a theorist, the first under the patronage of a rich amateur, in whose house he had an apartment.

Keyboard Music

Sixty of Rameau's 65 harpsichord pieces were written by 1728, with a final group appearing in 1741. Published in 1706, 1724 and around the year 1728, these collections, with the final collection of 1741, consist of genre pieces and dances, in the established tradition of French composers for the keyboard.

☛ Recommended Recordings

Suite in A Minor • Suite in E Minor / Major • Suite in D Minor / Major
Naxos 8.553047

Suite in A Minor • Suite in G Major / Minor Pièces de Clavecin en Concerts • La Dauphine
Naxos 8.553048

Chamber Music

In the later part of his career Rameau also wrote a series of suites, the Pièces de clavecin en concerts, for harpsichord, flute or violin and second violin or tenor viol.

☛ Recommended Recording

Pièces de clavecin en concerts
Naxos 8.550464

Ravel, Maurice (1875 - 1937)

French, of paternal Swiss and maternal Basque descent, Ravel combined skill in orchestration with meticulous technical command of harmonic resources, writing in an attractive musical idiom that was entirely his own, in spite of contemporary comparisons with Debussy, a composer his senior by some twenty years.

Stage Works

(a) Operas

Ravel wrote two operas, the first, described as a comédie-musicale, L'heure espagnole (The Spanish Clock) and the second, with a libretto by Colette, the imaginative L'enfant et les sortilèges (The Child and the Enchantments), in which the naughty child is punished when furniture and animals assume personalities of their own.

(b) Ballets

Ravel wrote his ballet Daphnis et Chloé in response to a commission from the Russian impresario Dyagilev. The work, described as a symphonie choréographique is based on the Hellenistic pastoral novel of Longus. Ma mère l'oye (Mother Goose), originally for piano duet, was orchestrated and used for a ballet, as were the Valses nobles et sentimentales and the choreographic poem La valse. Ravel's last ballet score was the famous Boléro, a work he himself described as an orchestrated crescendo.

☞ Recommended Recordings

Boléro / Daphnis et Chloé Suite No. 1
Ma mère l'oye / Valses nobles et sentimentales
Naxos 8.550173

La Valse / Daphnis et Chloé Suite No. 2
Naxos 8.550424

Orchestral Music

In addition to the scores for ballet and arrangements of piano works for the same purpose, Ravel wrote an evocative Rapsodie espagnole (Spanish Rhapsody). Other orchestrations of original piano compositions include a version of the very well known Pavane pour une infante défunte (Pavane for a Dead Infanta), the Menuet antique, Alborada del gracioso from Miroirs and pieces from Le tombeau de Couperin. Ravel wrote two piano concertos, the first, completed in 1930, for the left hand only, commissioned by the pianist Paul Wittgenstein, who had lost his right arm in the war, and the second, completed in 1931, for two hands.

☞ Recommended Recordings

Rapsodie espagnole
Pavane pour une infante défunte
Naxos 8.550424

Piano Concerto for the Left Hand
Piano Concerto in G Major
Naxos 8.550753

Vocal Music

Songs by Ravel include the remarkable Shéhérazade, settings of a text by Tristan Klingsor for mezzo-soprano and orchestra, and the Don Quichotte à Dulcinée (Don Quixote to Dulcinea) songs, originally written for a film of Don Quixote in which the famous Russian bass Chaliapin was to star. Songs with piano include settings of the Jules Renard Histoires naturelles, with its instinctive sympathy with the birds and the cricket portrayed.

Chamber Music

Ravel's chamber music includes the evocative nostalgia of the Introduction and Allegro for harp, flute, clarinet and string quartet, a violin sonata with a jazz-style blues movement, a piano trio and a string quartet. Tzigane, written for the Hungarian violinist Jelly d'Arányi, is a remarkable excursion into extravagant gypsy style.

☛ **Recommended Recordings**

String Quartet / Introduction and Allegro
Naxos 8.550249

Violin Sonata
Naxos 8.550276

Tzigane (orch.Ravel)
Naxos 8.550494

Piano Trio
Naxos 8.550934

Piano Music

Ravel was himself a good pianist. His music for the piano includes compositions in his own nostalgic archaic style, such as the Pavane and the Menuet antique, as well as the more complex textures of pieces such as Jeux d'eau (Fountains), Miroirs and Gaspard de la nuit, with its sinister connotations. The Sonatina is in Ravel's neo-classical style and Le tombeau de Couperin is in the form of a Baroque dance suite.

☛ **Recommended Recordings**

Piano Music Vol. 1
Pavane / Jeux d'eau / Miroirs / Sonatine
Naxos 8.550683

Piano Music Vol. 2
Valses nobles et sentimentales
Gaspard de la nuit / Le tombeau de Couperin
La valse
Naxos 8.553008

Reger, Max (1873 - 1916)

Reger enjoys a particularly high reputation among organists, to whose repertoire he made important additions. Born in Bavaria in 1873, he was a pupil of the important theorist Hugo Riemann and taught at the University of Leipzig, before his appointment as conductor of the Meiningen Court Orchestra in 1911. In addition to his activities as a teacher, conductor and composer, he was also a pianist and organist.

Orchestral Music

Among a variety of orchestral works, including a piano concerto and a violin concerto, Reger's Variations and Fugue on a Theme of Mozart, an arrangement of his work of the same title for two pianos, is typical of his resourceful and sometimes complex use of the theme on which it is based.

☛ **Recommended Recording**

Variations and Fugue on a theme by Mozart,
Op. 132
Variations and Fugue on a theme by Hiller,
Op. 100
Naxos 8.553079

Chamber Music

Reger wrote a considerable amount of chamber music of all kinds, with a number of violin sonatas and other duo sonatas, as well as string quartets and works for other groups of players. While of interest, nothing of this has become a part of popular repertoire, either for players or audiences.

Vocal and Choral Music

Among choral compositions by Reger the eight Geistliche Gesänge (Spiritual Songs), Op. 138, have proved particularly moving. Once again his choral works and songs have failed to achieve any significant position in performing repertoire.

Piano Music

Reger wrote a number of short piano pieces. His Variations and Fugue on a Theme of Mozart, Op. 132a, for two pianos, is probably the best known of his compositions for piano. Other sets of variations include Variations and Fugue on a Theme of Beethoven, Op. 86, for two pianos, Variations and Fugue on a Theme of J.S. Bach, Op. 81 and Variations and Fugue on a Theme of Telemann, Op. 134, for one piano.

☞ Recommended Recordings

Six Pieces Op. 24 / Silhouetten Op. 53
Blätter und Blüten Op. 58
Naxos 8.550932

Variations and Fugue on a Theme of
J.S. Bach, Op. 81
Naxos 8.550469

Organ Music

Reger's organ music offers a considerable challenge to performers and some works are said to have been composed as just such a challenge to his friend, the organist Karl Straube. Notable organ works include Chorale Fantasias on Ein' feste Burg ist unser Gott, Op. 27, and other Lutheran chorale tunes. His compositions for organ include a Fantasia and Fugue on the name of Bach.

☞ Recommended Recording

Toccata Op. 59, No. 5 / Fugue Op. 59, No. 6
Benedictus Op. 59, No. 9
Naxos 8.550955

Reich, Steve (1936 -)

The experimental American composer Steve Reich studied the work of the philsopher Wittgenstein at Cornell University, subsequently studying composition with Milhaud and with Berio. He showed an early interest in electro-acoustic music, then in the music of Africa. His music has experimented particularly with the multiple use of the same instrument and forms of exact but not simultaneous repetition.

Instrumental Music

Steve Reich's instrumental music includes Variations for wind, strings and keyboard, Music for 18 Musicians and a number of works that make use of unusual combinations of instruments, often a variety of percussion instruments, with recorded tape.

Reicha, Antoine (1770 - 1836)

Antoine Reicha, born Antonín Rejcha in Prague, moved in adolescence with his family to Bonn, playing violin and flute under his uncle in the court orchestra in which Beethoven also served. In 1794 he moved to Hamburg, extending further his interests, teaching and composing. In 1799 he tried for operatic success in Paris, but when this failed he moved to Vienna, renewing acquaintance with Beethoven and Haydn. Here he won considerable success, returning to Paris once more in 1808, where he enjoyed esteem as a composer and, above all, as a teacher at the Conservatoire, including among his pupils Berlioz and Liszt, and, for a short time, César Franck. He was the author of a number of important theoretical treatises.

Stage Music

Reicha wrote operas and Singspiel. These are seldom if ever performed.

Orchestral Music

Reicha was as prolific in the composition of orchestral music as in other genres, with a series of symphonies, overtures and concertos.

Chamber Music

It is for his chamber music that Reicha is particularly remembered and performed, notably for his two dozen or so wind quintets. He wrote for varied combinations of instruments, including a series of quartets and quintets for a wind instrument with string quartet.

☛ **Recommended Recording**
   Wind Quintets, Opp. 88, No. 2 & 100, No. 5
   Naxos 8.550432

Piano Music

Much of Reicha's piano music is primarily of pedagogical interest, as, for example, L'art de varier (The Art of Variation), written in Vienna for Prince Louis Ferdinand, whom he served as teacher and Kapellmeister.

Operas

Reicha's operas can be of only historical interest, with three of them providing examples for his Art du compositeur dramatique (Art of the Dramatic Composer) a guide to the contemporary technique of operatic composition.

Vocal and Choral Music
Among many choral and vocal works by Reicha are settings of the Requiem and other liturgical and sacred texts. Secular works include a setting of Bürger's romantic ballad Lenore.

Respighi, Ottorino (1879 - 1936)
The Italian composer Ottorino Respighi studied music in his native Bologna and later, briefly, with Rimsky-Korsakov in St. Petersburg. A viola-player and pianist, as well as a composer, he settled in Rome in 1913, earning a reputation also for his interest in early music and for his work as a teacher.

Orchestral Music
Respighi is chiefly known for his vivid symphonic poems, in particular Fontane di Roma (Fountains of Rome), Pini di Roma (Pines of Rome), and Feste romane (Roman Festivals), the last even more a celebration of the revived spirit of nationalism in the Italy of his time. Concertos for violin and for piano occupy a lesser position in general repertoire. Other orchestral

compositions include Trittico botticelliano (Triptych after Botticelli) and music from his opera Belfagor.

☛ Recommended Recordings
Cantatas (Aretusa / La Sensitiva / Il Tramonto)
Quattro Liriche
Marco Polo 8.223347

La bella dormente nel bosco
Marco Polo 8.223742

La Pentola Magica / Sèvres
Scherzo Veneziano
Marco Polo 8.223346

La Primavera
Quattro liriche su poesie popolari armene
Marco Polo 8.223595

Lucrezia
Marco Polo 8.223717

Piano Concerto in A Minor / Toccata
Fantasia Slava
Naxos 8.553207

Pini di Roma (Pines of Rome)
Fontane di Roma (Fountains of Rome)
Feste romane (Roman Festivals)
Naxos 8.550539

Preludio, Corale e Fuga / Variazioni Sinfoniche
Suite in E Major / Ouverture Carnevalesca
Burlesca
Marco Polo 8.223348

Sinfonia Drammatica
Naxos 8.550951

Arrangements

Respighi's La boutique fantasque, based on Rossini, is well known to ballet audiences. Other orchestral arrangements include three sets of orchestrated Antiche arie e danze per liuto (Ancient Airs and Dance for Lute) and Gli uccelli (The Birds), based on compositions by Rameau, Pasquini and others.

Rheinberger, Joseph (1839 - 1901)

Much respected in his life-time, the German composer and organist Joseph Rheinberger is chiefly remembered for his organ music. He showed phenomenal early ability and was trained at the Munich Conservatory, where he was later employed as a professor, until his death in 1901. His pupils in Munich included Humperdinck, Wolf-Ferrari and the great conductor Furtwängler.

Organ Music

Although Rheinberger contributed to other forms of music, dramatic and orchestral, sacred and secular, he is now remembered for his twenty organ sonatas and other shorter compositions for the instrument.

Chamber Music

Chamber music by Rheinberger includes suites for organ and violin and organ with violin and cello, in addition to music for the usual chamber ensembles.

Orchestral Music

In addition to two organ concertos, Rheinberger wrote relatively little, with one surviving symphony, a symphonic poem and a small number of concert overtures.

Vocal and Choral Music

Although Rheinberger wrote music for the theatre and a number of secular songs, he is principally remembered for his contribution to church music, witnessed in a number of Mass settings, three settings of the Requiem and two of the Stabat mater.

Rimsky-Korsakov, Nikolay Andreyevich (1844 - 1908)

One of the Five, the leading group of 19th century Russian nationalist composers, Rimsky-Korsakov embarked at first on a career as a naval officer, following the traditions of his family, later resigning from the service to devote himself entirely to music. He was proficient as an orchestrator and set himself to smoothing out some of the apparent crudities in the work of some of his fellow-composers, completing and revising works such as Borodin's opera Prince Igor and much of the seemingly uneven writing of Mussorgsky. He was respected as a teacher, his pupils including the young Stravinsky. Most generally known for his orchestral compositions, Rimsky-Korsakov wrote songs and choral music, chamber music and works for piano. His textbook on orchestration has been widely if not always wisely used.

Operas

Of the fifteen operas completed by Rimsky-Korsakov, mention may be made of The Snow Maiden, The Maid of Pskov, The Tale of Tsar Saltan, Mlada, Sadko, The Legend of the Invisible City of Kitezh and the satirical and once banned Le coq d'or (The Golden Cockerel). Orchestral and instrumental excerpts from some of these may be very familiar, including the famous Flight of the Bumble Bee, from The Tale of Tsar Saltan, a prince who turns himself into a bee and stings his wicked aunts.

☛ Recommended Recordings

Tsar Saltan (Suite)
Naxos 8.550726

Suites: Mlada / The Snow Maiden
Le coq d'or (The Golden Cockerel)
Naxos 8.550486

Orchestral Music

Of the various orchestral works of Rimsky-Korsakov Capriccio espagnol (Spanish Caprice) and the Arabian Nights Sheherazade are by far the best known, followed by the Russian Easter Festival Overture. The title of the Capriccio espagnol is self-explanatory, while Sheherazade, with no detailed and specific programme, is based on the tales told by the princess Sheherazade, represented by a solo violin, in her effort to postpone the sentence of death declared on her by her master, the Caliph.

☛ Recommended Recordings

Sheherazade
Naxos 8.550726

Symphonies Nos. 1 & 2
Naxos 8.550811

Symphony No. 3 / Sinfonietta Op. 31
Naxos 8.550812

Rodrigo, Joaquín (1901 -)

The Spanish composer Joaquin Rodrigo, blind from the age of three, has enriched Spanish music in particular through his concertos for guitar, compositions for which he is best known abroad. Rodrigo studied for a time in Paris, where he spent the turbulent years of the Spanish civil war, his subsequent career largely centred on Madrid.

Orchestral Music

The best known work of Rodrigo is the Concierto de Aranjuez, for guitar and orchestra, written in 1939, closely followed in popularity by his Fantasia para un gentilhombre. Other guitar concertos include a Concierto madrigal for two guitars and a Concierto andaluz for four guitars. He has written concertos for other solo instruments, including the violin, the cello and the piano and a Concierto serenata for solo harp and orchestra, all in a style that has remained consistent throughout his career, both here and in his stage and vocal compositions.

☛ **Recommended Recording**
Concierto de Aranjuez
Naxos 8.550729

Roger-Ducasse, Jean (1873 - 1954)

A pupil of Gabriel Fauré at the Paris Conservatoire, Jean Roger-Ducasse succeeded Dukas as professor of composition at the same institution. As a composer he developed a personal style, firmly rooted in tradition.

Stage Works

The lyric comedy Cantegril was staged at the Paris Opéra-Comique in 1931, five years after the mounting of his lyric mimodrama Orphée at the Opéra.

Orchestral Music

Roger-Ducasse showed his mastery of orchestration in his Suite française of 1907. Other orchestral compositions include the Marche française of 1914, a Petite Suite and a set of Variations plaisantes (Pleasant Variations) on a serious theme for harp and orchestra. His music for chorus and orchestra includes a triptych Ulysse et les sirènes (Odysseus and the Sirens) and his earlier work based on Faust, Au jardin de Marguerite (In the Garden of Marguerite).

☛ **Recommended Recordings**
Marche française / Nocturne de printemps
Petite Suite / Le joli jeu de furet / Orphée
Marco Polo 8.223501

Prélude d'un ballet / Suite française
Au jardin de Marguerite / Epithalame
Marco Polo 8.223641

Chamber Music

Chamber music of interest by Roger-Ducasse includes a string quartet and a piano quartet.

Roman, Johan Helmich

(1694 - 1758)

Master of the Swedish royal chapel and a leading composer in Sweden in the first half of the 18th century, Johan Helmich Roman studied in England with Pepusch, compiler of the music of The Beggar's Opera. His music shows distinct traces of his experience in England, where he also met composers such as Handel and Geminiani. He was a prolific composer in various genres.

Orchestral Music

The best known composition by Roman is his Drottningsholm Music for the royal wedding of the Crown Prince and his Prussian bride in 1744. Other surviving music includes sinfonias, concertos, suites and overtures.

Chamber Music

Roman's chamber music includes flute sonatas and trio sonatas, characteristic of the transitional style current in the middle of the eighteenth century.

Ropartz, Joseph Guy (1864 - 1955)

At first trained in law, the French composer and conductor Joseph Guy Ropartz studied composition with Massenet and then with César Franck. He spent much of his career in Nancy and then in Strasbourg, before retiring to his native Brittany, this last a continuing influence on his music.

Orchestral Music

Ropartz wrote five symphonies. His La chasse du Prince Arthur (The Hunt of Prince Arthur) turns for inspiration to Celtic legend.

☛ **Recommended Recording**

Psalm 136 / Dimanche / Nocturnes
Les Vêpres sonnent
Le Miracle de Saint Nicolas
Marco Polo 8.223774

Chamber Music

Six string quartets and three violin sonatas bear witness to the skill of Ropartz in handling chamber music forms, as well as two sonatas for cello and piano.

Vocal and Choral Music

Ropartz made some contribution to sacred music, notably in his Requiem of 1938.

Rore, Cipriano de (1515 or 1516 - 1565)

The Flemish composer Cipriano de Rore, active, like many of his compatriots, in Italy, is of importance in the contemporary synthesis of Flemish counterpoint and Italian gifts of melody. Associated with composers such as Willaert in Venice, he was by 1547 master of the chapel at Ferrara, later taking service with Margaret of Parma, at first in the Netherlands and then in Parma itself, where he died in 1565.

Secular Vocal Music

Cipriano de Rore is principally known for his Italian madrigals, published in several collections during his life-time and immediately after his death. He also wrote a small number of French chansons and a number of secular Latin motets.

Sacred Vocal Music

Cipriano de Rore wrote a similar amount of sacred vocal music, settings of the Mass and the Magnificat and motets. These compositions typify the style of polyphonic composition current in the generation after Josquin, leading to the changes of the later part of the 16th century.

Rossini, Gioacchino (1792 - 1868)

Rossini occupied an unrivalled position in the Italian musical world of his time, winning considerable success relatively early in his career. The son of a horn-player and a mother who made a career for herself in opera, as a boy he had direct experience of operatic performance, both in the orchestra pit and on stage. His operas from his first relative success in 1810 until 1823 were first performed in Italy. There followed a period of success in Paris, leading to his final opera, Guillaume Tell, staged in Paris in 1829. The revolution of 1830 prevented the fulfilment of French royal commissions for the theatre, but in his later life he continued to enjoy considerable esteem, both in Paris, where he spent much of his last years, and in his native Italy. There he spent the years from 1837 until 1855, before returning finally to France, where he died in 1868.

Operas

Of Rossini's three dozen or so operas, Il Barbiere di Siviglia (The Barber of Seville) is probably the best known, a treatment of the first play of the Figaro trilogy by Beaumarchais on which Mozart had drawn thirty years before in Vienna. Other well known comic operas by Rossini include La Scala di Seta (The Silken Ladder), Il Signor Bruschino, L'Italiana in Algeri (The Italian Girl in Algiers), Il Turco in Italia (The Turk in Italy), La Cenerentola (Cinderella) and La Gazza ladra (The Thieving Magpie). More serious subjects were tackled in Otello, Semiramide, Mose in Egitto (Moses in Egypt) and the French Guillaume Tell (William Tell), based on the

play by Schiller. The Overtures to many of these operas are a recurrent element in the repertoire of the concert-hall.

☞ **Recommended Recordings**

Il Barbiere di Siviglia (Complete Opera)
(The Barber of Seville) (3 CDs)
Naxos 8.660027-29

Overtures: Il Barbiere di Siviglia
(The Barber of Seville)
La Cenerentola (Cinderella) / Semiramide
Guillaume Tell (William Tell)
La Gazza ladra (The Thieving Magpie)
La Scala di Seta (The Silken Ladder)
L'Italiana in Algeri (The Italian Girl in Algiers)
Il Signor Bruschino
Naxos 8.550236

Tancredi (2 CD's)
Naxos 8.660037-8

Arias for Mezzo-soprano
Naxos 8.553543

Church Music

Church music by Rossini includes the Petite Messe solennelle, originally for twelve solo voices, two pianos and harmonium, but rescored four years later, in 1867, with orchestral accompaniment. Rossini's Stabat mater was written in 1841 in its final version.

Chamber Music

Instrumental compositions by Rossini include his early String Sonatas, designed for two violins, cello and double bass and thought to have been written when the composer was twelve. The String Sonatas show a precocious command of Italian operatic style, here translated into instrumental terms.

The so-called Péchés de vieillesse (Sins of Old Age) consist of thirteen volumes of varied music, some vocal, some instrumental, five of the collections designed for the piano, pieces that demonstrate both the well known wit of the composer as well as his continuing technical command of musical resources.

☞ **Recommended Recordings**

String Sonatas Nos. 1-3
Naxos 8.550621

String Sonatas Nos. 4-6
Naxos 8.550622

Roussel, Albert (1869 - 1937)

By training a naval officer, the French composer Albert Roussel devoted himself fully to music from 1894, studying and teaching at the Schola Cantorum established by César Franck's disciple Vincent d'Indy. He remained apart from the principal fashionable trends in the music of his time, while continuing to enjoy considerable respect as a composer.

Stage Works

Two ballet scores by Roussel have won some place in orchestral repertoire. These are Le festin d'araignée (The Spider's Banquet) and Bacchus et Ariane.

Rubinstein, Anton (1829-1894)

Not to be confused with the great pianist Artur Rubinstein, born in 1887, Anton Rubinstein, an even greater performer in his time and a clear rival to Liszt and other great pianists of the 19th century, had a marked effect on the development of music in Russia, establishing the first system of professional musical training at a new Conservatory in St. Petersburg in 1862. His brother Nikolay set up a similar institution in Moscow. The Conservatories were not welcomed by the nationalist composers, who regarded them as a German intrusion, although the Rubinsteins were Russian, if of German-Jewish extraction. As a composer Anton Rubinstein was prolific, writing, as his brother suggested, enough music for both of them. His very technical facility told against him so that by the time of his death his work was not properly valued by supporters of Russian musical nationalism.

Operas

Rubinstein wrote seventeen operas. These are no longer part of general repertoire, but excerpts from the fantastic opera The Demon and the opera Feramors may be heard occasionally in concert extracts.

☞ Recommended Recording

The Demon (Complete Opera) (2 CD's)
Marco Polo 8.223781-2

Orchestral Music

Rubinstein's orchestral compositions include six symphonies, of which the second, "Ocean", is the best known. He wrote five piano concertos and other works for piano and orchestra and concertos for both violin and cello.

☞ Recommended Recordings

Ballet Music (Demon / Feramors / Nero)
Marco Polo 8.220451

Fantasy Op. 84 / Concert Piece Op. 113
Marco Polo 8.223190

Piano Concertos Nos. 1 and 2
Marco Polo 8.223456

Piano Concertos Nos. 3 and 4
Marco Polo 8.223382

Piano Concerto No. 5 / Caprice Russe
Marco Polo 8.223489

Symphony No. 1 / Ivan the Terrible
Marco Polo 8.223277

Symphony No. 2 "Ocean"
Marco Polo 8.220449

Symphony No. 3 / "Eroica" Fantasia, Op. 110
Marco Polo 8.223576

Symphony No. 4 "Dramatic"
Marco Polo 8.223319

Symphony No. 5 / Faust / Dmitry Donskoy
Marco Polo 8.223320

Symphony No. 6
Marco Polo 8.220489

Violin Concerto / Don Quixote
Marco Polo 8.220359

Chamber Music

As prolific here as in other forms of music, Rubinstein wrote a number of string quartets, three violin sonatas and two cello sonatas, in additon to other chamber works, none often heard, except possibly the sonata for viola and piano, a useful addition to an otherwise exiguous repertoire for the viola.

Piano Music

Rubinstein, as a leading virtuoso of the instrument, wrote a quantity of music for the piano. Of all the sonatas, suites, serenades and other pieces, the Melody in F remains notorious in its popularity.

☞ **Recommended Recordings**

Piano Music Volume 1
Album de Peterhof, Op. 75
Marco Polo 8.223176

Piano Music Volume 2
Soirées musicales, Op. 109
Marco Polo 8.223177

Saint-Saëns, Camille (1835 - 1921)

Once described as the French Mendelssohn, Saint-Saëns was a talented and precocious child, with interests by no means confined to music. He made an early impression as a pianist. Following established French tradition, he was for nearly twenty years organist at the Madeleine in Paris and taught at the Ecole Niedermeyer, where he befriended his pupil Gabriel Fauré. Prolific and versatile as a composer, by the time of his death in 1921 his popularity in France had diminished very considerably, as fashions in music changed.

Operas

The best known of the thirteen operas completed by Saint-Saëns is Samson et Dalila, a romantic treatment of the biblical story

Vocal and Choral Music

Saint-Saëns wrote a number of sacred and secular choral works and made a considerable contribution to the body of French solo song.

Orchestral Music

(a) Symphonies etc.

The third of the three numbered symphonies of Saint-Saëns, the so-called "Organ" Symphony, so named from the use of the instrument in the work, is the best known. Other popular orchestral works include Le Rouet d'Omphale (Omphale's Wheel) and Danse macabre.

☞ Recommended Recording

Symphony No. 3 "Organ"
Le Rouet d'Omphale
Bacchanale from Samson et Dalila
Naxos 8.550138

(b) Concertos etc.

Saint-Saëns, a fine pianist himself, wrote five piano concertos, three violin concertos and two cello concertos. Both the Introduction and Rondo capriccioso and Havañaise are familiar in the repertoire for violin and orchestra.

☞ Recommended Recordings

Piano Concertos Nos. 2 & 4
Naxos 8.550334

Havanaise
Naxos 8.550494

Violin Concerto No. 3
Introduction and Rondo Capriccioso
Romance in C / Caprice andalous
Morceau de concert
Naxos 8.550752

Chamber Music

Saint-Saëns was equally prolific in his provision of chamber music, with a series of duo sonatas, including two violin sonatas, two cello sonatas and a variety of other pieces. His Carnival of the Animals, often heard in more expanded form, was in origin a private joke for the enjoyment of the composer's friends.

☞ Recommended Recordings

Le carnaval des animaux
(The Carnival of the Animals)
Naxos 8.550335

Violin Sonata No. 1
Naxos 8.550276

Piano Trios Nos. 1 & 2
Naxos 8.550935

Salieri, Antonio (1750 - 1825)

Thanks to Pushkin and Rimsky-Korsakov, as well as Shaffer and the film Amadeus, Salieri has been cast as the villain in the tragedy of Mozart's early death. Antonio Salieri occupied a position of great importance in the music of Vienna. From 1774 he was court composer and conductor of the Italian opera, serving as court Kapellmeister from 1788 until 1824. Born in Legnago, he was brought as a boy to Vienna by Florian Gassmann, his predecessor as court Kapellmeister who supervised his musical training and education. He owed much to the influence and patronage of Gluck, to whom he seemed a natural successor in the field of opera. He won similar success to the latter also in Paris with his operas for the French stage. His pupils included Beethoven and Schubert, Czerny, Hummel, Moscheles and one of Mozart's sons. He was a prolific composer, principally in vocal music of all kinds.

Operas

Salieri wrote some 45 operas, ranging from Tarare, with a libretto by Beaumarchais, for Paris and settings of libretti by Lorenzo da Ponte for Vienna to the Shakespearean comedy Falstaff and the operetta Prima la musica poi le parole (First the Music then the Words), staged at the imperial palace of Schönbrunn in 1786 on the same evening as Mozart's German Singspiel Der Schauspieldirektor (The Impresario).

☞ **Recommended Recording**

Overtures
Il Talismano / Axur / Les Danaïdes
Il Moro / Armide / L'Angiolina / Don Chisciotte
Eraclito e Democrito
Marco Polo 8.223381

Vocal and Choral Music

Salieri wrote a quantity of church music, as well as oratorios. He left still more secular vocal music, ranging from cantatas and choruses to duets and solo arias.

Instrumental Music

Rather less instrumental music by Salieri survives. This includes music for the ballet, sinfonias, concertos and music for various smaller ensembles.

Orchestral Music

As well as a significant quantity of ballet music, Salieri wrote concertos, including an organ concerto and a piano concerto, a Birthday Symphony and a set of variations on La folia di Spagna, (The Folly of Spain) the dance tune used by Corelli and many other Baroque composers.

Chamber Music

Salieri's chamber music consists principally of serenades, cassations and marches.

Sammartini, Giovanni Battista

(1700 or 1701 - 1775)

The son of a French oboist who had settled in Italy, Sammartini was born in Milan, where he won an early reputation, serving as maestro di cappella to the Congregation of the Ss Entierro from 1728 for many years. He occupies an important place in the genesis of the symphony and won a considerable reputation abroad, with works published in London and Paris. In Milan he was highly respected and led an active career to the very end as a composer and conductor.

Orchestral Music

Of Sammartini's orchestral music 68 symphonies survive, with six violin concertos, one double violin concerto, two flute concertos, in addition to sets of concerti grossi and overtures. These vary in style from an early mixture of Baroque and classical to an intermediate style and a final style that is in general classical.

☛ Recommended Recording

Sinfonia in A Major
Naxos 8.550877

Chamber Music

Chamber music by Sammartini consists of quintets, quartets and trio sonatas, of the last some two hundred. There are thirty or so keyboard sonatas, for harpsichord or organ, with eleven violin sonatas and six sonatas for harpsichord with violin.

Vocal and Choral Music

Sammartini wrote sacred choral music, cantatas and liturgical settings, as well as secular arias and cantatas. Much of this body of work has been lost.

Satie, Erik (1866 - 1925)

A French composer as eccentric in his way of life as in his music, Satie exercised considerable influence over some of his more distinguished contemporaries, including Debussy, Ravel and Poulenc, particularly through his tendency to extreme simplicity. A number of his compositions have become very familiar to many, largely through their use in other contexts.

Stage Works

Best known among the various stage works of Satie is his collaboration with Jean Cocteau, Parade, described as a ballet réaliste, first performed in Paris in 1917.

Piano Music

It is principally the piano pieces by Satie that have won some popularity. Among these, many with characteristically eccentric titles, are the Gymnopédies, the three Gnossiennes and the three Sarabandes.

☞ Recommended Recordings

Piano Music Vol. 1
Naxos 8.550696

Piano Music Vol. 2
Naxos 8.550697

Piano Music Vol. 3
Naxos 8.550698

Piano Music Vol. 4
Naxos 8.550699

Sauguet, Henri (1901 - 1989)

Encouraged by Milhaud to move from his native Bordeaux to Paris to study with Koechlin, Henri Sauguet was influenced by his meeting with Satie and with other young musicians established the so-called Ecole d'Arcueil, its name drawn from the suburb where Satie had chosen to live. He won a reputation in particular for his ballet music, which has all the clarity and elegance associated with a certain kind of French music.

Stage Music

Sauguet's first opera Le plumet du colonel (The Colonel's Helmet) won some success in 1924 but it was his version of Stendhal's La chartreuse de Parme, completed in 1936 and revised in 1968, was a work of much greater interest. His contributions to ballet included La chatte (The Cat) for Dyagilev in 1927.

Orchestral Music

In addition to his symphonies Sauguet wrote a number of concertos. These include the Violin Concerto, Concert d'Orphée, three piano concertos and the so-called The Garden's Concerto, for harmonica and chamber orchestra.

☞ Recommended Recording

Symphony No. 1 "Expiatoire"
Marco Polo 8.223463

Chamber and Instrumental Music

Sauguet's music for smaller groups of instruments or solo instruments makes characteristically French use of wind instruments. Piano music includes the three

Françaises of 1923 and two sets of Pièces poétiques for children.

Scarlatti, Alessandro (1660 - 1725)

Alessandro Scarlatti, a native of Palermo, made his principal career in Naples, where he was instrumental in the development of 18th century Neapolitan opera. He wrote more than a hundred operas and some six hundred cantatas, a considerable amount of church music and a smaller number of purely instrumental works. An important and influential composer, the nature of his compositions particularly with changed fashions in opera and less appetite for cantatas, serenades and oratorios of this period, has led to otherwise unjustified current neglect, in spite of Scarlatti's extreme fecundity.

Scarlatti, Domenico (1685 - 1757)

Sixth of the ten children of Alessandro Scarlatti, Domenico Scarlatti was born in Naples in 1685, the year of birth of Handel and J.S. Bach. After an earlier period in Italy he moved to Portugal and thence, in the service of the Infanta Maria Barbara to Madrid, after her marriage to the Spanish Infante. He remained in the service of Maria Barbara after her husband's accession to the throne and died in Madrid in 1757. He is chiefly known for the large number of short sonatas he wrote for the harpsichord, many of them for his royal pupil and patron.

Keyboard Music

Domenico Scarlatti wrote over 550 single-movement sonatas or 'Exercises' (Esercizi) for the harpsichord, making characteristic but innovative use of the instrument. The Queen also had pianos in her palaces, and some of the sonatas may have been written with these early hammer-action instruments in mind.Scarlatti's earlier compositions included operas, oratorios and other vocal music. He also wrote a relatively small number of sinfonias for instrumental ensemble. K. numbers are based on the catalogue of Scarlatti's sonatas compiled by the American harpsichordist, Ralph Kirkpatrick.

☛ **Recommended Recording**
Keyboard Sonatas K. 1, 9, 11, 87, 96, 132, 135, 141, 146, 159, 198, 208, 247, 322, 380, 435, 466, 474, 481
Naxos 8.550252

Scheidt, Samuel (1587 - 1654)

The German organist and composer Samuel Scheidt was born in Halle in 1587 and represents the first generation of German composers in the Baroque period. He was court Kapellmeister at Halle, first to the Margrave of Brandenburg, and then, when conditions allowed once more in the course of the Thirty Years War, to Duke August of Saxony.

Church Music

Scheidt wrote a large quantity of church music for the German Protestant liturgy. Latin compositions included settings of the Magnificat.

Organ Music

Scheidt's compositions for the organ include a number of pieces based on chorales. He also wrote fantasias, toccatas and dance movements for the instrument.

Ensemble Music

Scheidt also wrote a number of works for instrumental ensemble in various dance forms and published a volume of so-called Canons, suitable for a small group of instruments, demonstrating his skill in this aspect of the art of composition.

Schein, Johann Hermann
(1586 - 1630)

In 1616 the German composer and poet Johann Hermann Schein was appointed Thomaskantor in Leipzig, a position later held by Bach. His importance as a composer lies in the use he made of Italian monody and concerted style in Lutheran church music.

Church Music

Schein, primarily a vocal composer, wrote extensively for the church.

Secular Vocal Music

Schein wrote a number of madrigals and music suitable for either instruments or voices, again demonstrating Italian influence.

Ensemble Music

Schein's compositions also include some twenty Suites for instrumental ensemble.

Schmidt, Franz (1874 - 1939)

A piano pupil of Leschetizky and composition pupil of Bruckner, Franz Schmidt earned his living at first as a cellist in the Vienna Court Opera, where he experienced conflict with Mahler. He later taught composition at the

Vienna Staatsakademie and was director of the Musikhochschule from 1927 to 1931. His work as a composer has something in common with Max Reger, particularly in music for the organ.

Stage Music

Schmidt's opera Notre Dame, based on Victor Hugo, had some success and excerpts, notably an Intermezzo, are heard in concert programmes.

Vocal and Choral Music

Das Buch mit sieben Siegeln (The Book with Seven Seals), based on the Apocalypse, has its own place among modern oratorios.

Orchestral and Chamber Music

Schmidt wrote four symphonies, Variations on a Theme of Beethoven for piano left hand and orchestra and a piano concerto for the left hand, these last, with various chamber works, for the pianist Paul Wittgenstein, brother of the philosopher Ludwig Wittgenstein, who had lost his right arm in the 1914-1918 war.

Organ Music

Schmidt added considerably to the repertoire of organ music, with a series of chorale-preludes, preludes and fugues, toccatas and sets of variations.

Schmitt, Florent (1870 - 1958)

A composition pupil of Massenet and of Fauré at the Paris Conservatoire, Florent Schmitt, in common with a number of his contemporaries, was fascinated by the exotic, an element of orientalism of a kind appearing as a feature in several of his successful compositions.

Orchestral Music

La tragédie de Salomé (The Tragedy of Salome), originally a dance-piece, was revised as a symphonic poem in 1910. An element of exoticism is appropriately apparent in the film-score for Flaubert's Salammbô, with its Carthaginian setting, and in a number of subsequent orchestral works, while his gifts of orchestration are evident in his two symphonies and in a varied series of other compositions.

☛ **Recommended Recordings**

Danse d'Abisag / Habeyssée
"Réves" / Symphony No. 2
Marco Polo 8.223689

La Tragédie de Salomé
Marco Polo 8.223448

Choral Music

Schmitt won early success with his exotic setting of Psalm xlvii in 1904. Other choral works range from settings of fables of La Fontaine to liturgical music, settings of the Mass and other sacred texts.

Chamber and Instrumental Music

Chamber music for various combinations of instruments includes finely judged work for wind instruments, while music for keyboard shows equal variety of conception.

Schnittke, Alfred (1934 -)

Alfred Schnittke's work has won wide acceptance in recent years, particularly since political changes in the former Soviet Union. His early studies in Vienna were followed by formal training at the Moscow Conservatory, where he later taught. His musical language is eclectic, combining a number of styles, contemporary and traditional.

Orchestral Music

Orchestral music by Schnittke includes a number of interesting concertos or works for solo instrument and orchestra. These include concertos for violin, for cello, for oboe and harp, for viola and for piano. A series of Concerti grossi is of significance, with the St. Florian Symphony and In memoriam, for solo viola and orchestra.

Chamber Music

Schnittke's chamber music includes string quartets and sonatas for violin and for cello and piano, with a Sonata for violin and piano in the Olden Style and a Suite in the Old Style for the same instruments.

Schoeck, Othmar (1886 - 1957)

The Swiss composer Othmar Schoeck, son of the painter Alfred Schoeck, contributed extensively to vocal and choral repertoire. Briefly a pupil of Max Reger, he became one of the leading composers of his generation in Switzerland, writing music that is melodic and in vocal settings shows a marked understanding of and respect for the text.

Operas

Operas by Schoeck include Massimilia Doni, based on Balzac, and Penthesilea, based on Kleist.

Orchestral Music

Schoeck's orchestral music includes a cello concerto, a Concerto quasi una fantasia for violin and orchestra and a concerto for French horn.

Vocal and Choral Music

Schoeck's contribution to vocal and choral repertoire is considerable and ranges from a perceptive setting of Walt Whitman in Trommelschläge, for chorus and orchestra, to song-cycles such as Der Wandsbecker Liederbuch, a setting of seventeen poems by the Wandsbeck poet Matthias Claudius, and Das holde Bescheiden, settings of Eduard Mörike.

Schoenberg, Arnold (1874 - 1951)

Arnold Schoenberg has exercised very considerable influence over the course of music in the 20th century, particularly through his development and promulgation of theories of composition in which unity in a work is provided by the use of a determined series, usually consisting of the twelve possible different semitones, their order also inverted or taken in retrograde form, and in transposed versions. Schoenberg's earlier compositions are post-romantic in character, followed by a period in which he developed his theories of atonality, music without a key or tonal centre. Born in Vienna in 1874, he spent his early career in Berlin, until the rise to power of Hitler made it necessary to leave Germany and find safety in America, where he died in 1951. With his pupils Anton Webern and Alban Berg, both of whom he outlived, he represents a group of composers known as the Second Viennese School.

Operas

Schoenberg's most important opera is Moses und Aron, of which he completed only two of the three acts.

Choral and Vocal Music

Gurrelieder, written between 1901 and 1903, is a work of Wagnerian proportions and mood, for solo voices, large chorus and orchestra. Other, later vocal music includes A Survivor from Warsaw, written in 1947, for narrator, male voices and orchestra. Solo songs range from the 1909 settings of Stefan George in Das Buch der hängenden Gärten (The Book of the Hanging Garden) to the cabaret songs he wrote for the Berlin Überbrettl in his earlier years. The Pierrot lunaire, a study of madness, based on German translations of seven poems by Albert Giraud and using Sprechgesang, words half spoken, half sung, was completed in 1912.

Orchestral Music

Schoenberg's music for orchestra includes a violin concerto, a symphonic poem based on Maurice Maeterlinck's medieval drama Pelleas und Melisande and Five Orchestral Pieces.

Chamber Music

In addition to four string quartets and a late string trio, Schoenberg's post-romantic Verklärte Nacht of 1899 is particularly noteworthy.

Schreker, Franz (1878 - 1934)

Trained as a violinist and as a composer at the Vienna Conservatory, Franz Schreker belongs to that group of composers whose careers were eclipsed by the events of 1933 in Germany. Schreker enjoyed very considerable success as a composer of opera, in a style that coupled the late romantic with an element of musical collage, with scenes where different layers of music are juxtaposed or superimposed, all with a mastery of orchestral colour.

Stage Works

Schreker won early success with Der Geburtstag der Infantin (The Birthday of the Infanta), a ballet based on the story by Oscar Wilde. Der ferne Klang (The Distant Sound), an opera staged first at Frankfurt in 1912, has more of Debussy than Wagner about it, dealing with the mystical pursuit by the artist for the distant sound that he has heard. Der ferne Klang influenced Alban Berg, who made a vocal score of the work. Of other operas, Die Gezeichneten (Those marked by the seal) and Der

Schatzgräber (The Treasure-Hunter) are particularly effective, if more conventional than Der ferne Klang.

☞ **Recommended Recordings**

Der Ferne Klang (Complete Opera) (2 CD's)
Marco Polo 8.223270-1

Die Gezeichneten (Complete Opera) (3 CD's)
Marco Polo 8.223328-30

Flammen (Complete Opera)
Marco Polo 8.223422

Schubert, Franz (1797 - 1828)

The son of a schoolmaster who had settled in Vienna, Franz Schubert was educated as a chorister of the imperial court chapel and later qualified as a schoolteacher, briefly and thereafter intermittently joining his father in the classroom. He spent his life largely in Vienna, enjoying the company of friends, but never holding any position in the musical establishment or attracting the kind of patronage that Beethoven had twenty years earlier. His final years were clouded by illness, as the result of a syphilitic infection, and he died in 1828, leaving much unfinished. His gifts had been most notably expressed in song, his talent for melody always evident in his other compositions. Schubert's compositions are generally numbered according to the Deutsch catalogue, with the letter D.

Stage Works

Schubert wrote operas, German operas or Singspiel and incidental music for the theatre. His best known compositions of this kind include the music for the unsuccessful play Rosamunde, Fürstin von Zypern (Rosamunde, Princess of Cyprus), mounted at the Theater an der Wien in December 1823. The ballet music and entracte from Rosamunde are particularly well known.

☞ **Recommended Recording**

Rosamunde: Ballet Music No. 2
Naxos 8.550145

Church Music

Among the various works Schubert wrote for church use particular mention may be made of the second of his six settings of the Mass.

Choral and Vocal Music

Schubert wrote for mixed voices, male voices and female voices, but by far the most famous of his vocal compositions are the five hundred or so songs, settings of verses ranging from Shakespeare to his friends and contemporaries. His song cycles, published in his lifetime are Die schöne Müllerin (The Fair Maid of the Mill) and Die Winterreise (The Winter Journey), while Schwanengesang (Swan-Song) was compiled by a publisher after the composer's early death. Many of these songs by Schubert are very familiar, including Der Erlkönig, the Mignon songs from Goethe and the Songs of Norma from Sir Walter Scott.

Orchestral Music

The Unfinished Symphony of Schubert was written in 1822, but no addition was made to the two movements of the work. Other symphonies of the eight more or less completed include the Great C major Symphony and the charming and classical Fifth Symphony. His various Overtures include two "in the Italian style".

☞ **Recommended Recordings**

Symphonies Nos. 1 & 2
Naxos 8.553093

Symphonies Nos. 3 & 6
Naxos 8.553094

Symphony No. 4 "Tragic" D. 417
Symphony in C Major
Naxos 8.553095

Symphonies Nos. 5 & 8 "Unfinished"
Naxos 8.550145

Symphony No. 9 "Great"
Naxos 8.553096

Chamber Music

Of Schubert's various string quartets the Quartet in A minor, with its variations on the well known Rosamunde theme and the Quartet in D minor, Death and the Maiden, with variations on the song of that name, are the most familiar. The Piano Quintet "Die Forelle" (The Trout) includes a movement of variations on that song, while the great C major String Quintet of 1828 is of unsurpassable beauty. The two Piano Trios and the single movement Notturno date from the same year. Schubert's Octet, for clarinet, horn, bassoon, two violins, viola, cello and double bass was written early in 1824. To the violin sonatas (sonatinas) of 1816 may be added the more ambitious Duo for violin and piano, D. 574, of the following year, and the Fantasy, D. 934, published in 1828, the year of Schubert's death. The Arpeggione Sonata was written for a newly devised and soon obselete stringed instrument, the Arpeggione. It now provides additional repertoire for the cello or viola.

☛ **Recommended Recordings**

Arpeggione Sonata D. 821
Naxos 8.550654

Violin Sonatas (Sonatinas),
D. 348, D. 385 & D. 408 / Fantasy, D. 934
Naxos 8.550420

Piano Trios D. 898 & D. 28
Naxos 8.550131

Piano Trio, D. 929 / Notturno, D. 897
Naxos 8.550132

String Quintet, D. 956 / String Trio, D. 581
Naxos 8.550388

Piano Quintet "Trout"
Adagio and Rondo concertante, D. 487
Naxos 8.550658

Octets D. 872 & D. 803
Naxos 8.550389

String Quartets Vol. 1
"Death and the Maiden", D. 810 & D. 703
Naxos 8.550590

String Quartets Vol. 2
No. 10 in E Flat, D. 87 & No. 13 in A Minor,
D. 804, "Rosamunde"
Naxos 8.550591

Piano Music

Schubert's compositions for piano include a number of sonatas as well as the Wanderer Fantasia and two sets of Impromptus, D. 899 and D. 935. He also wrote a number of dances for piano, waltzes, Ländler and German dances. His music for piano duet includes a Divertissement à l'hongroise, marches and polonaises.

☛ **Recommended Recordings**

Impromptus, D. 899 and D. 935
Naxos 8.550260

Moments musicaux, D. 780
Allegretto, D. 915 / Drei Klavierstücke, D. 946
Naxos 8.550259

Piano Sonatas D. 537 & D. 664
Fantasy (Wandererfantasie)
Naxos 8.550846

Piano Sonatas D. 958 and D. 960
Naxos 8.550475

Piano Sonatas D. 784 and D. 894
Naxos 8.550730

Piano Works for Four Hands:
Lebensstürme, D. 947
Deux marches caractéristiques, D. 886
Divertissement à la hongroise, D. 818
Naxos 8.550555

Schumann, Robert (1810 - 1856)

The son of a bookseller, publisher and writer, Robert Schumann showed early abilities in both music and literature, the second facility used in his later writing on musical subjects. After brief study at university, he was allowed by his widowed mother and guardian to undertake serious study of the piano with Friedrich Wieck, whose favourite daughter Clara was later to become Schumann's wife. His ambitions as a pianist were thwarted by a weakness in the fingers of one hand, but the 1830s nevertheless brought a number of compositions for the instrument. The year of his marriage, 1840, was a year of song, followed by attempts in which his young wife encouraged him at more

ambitious forms of orchestral composition. Settling first in Leipzig and then in Dresden, the Schumanns moved in 1850 to Düsseldorf, where Schumann had his first official appointment, as municipal director of music. In 1854 he had a serious mental break-down, followed by two years in the asylum at Endenich before his death in 1856. As a composer Schumann's gifts are clearly heard in his piano music and in his songs.

Orchestral Music

(a) Symphonies

Schumann completed four symphonies, after earlier unsuccessful attempts at the form. The first, written soon after his marriage and completed early in 1841, is known as "Spring" and has a suggested programme. A second symphony followed in 1846 and the third, the "Rhenish", a celebration of the Rhineland and its great cathedral at Cologne, was written in Düsseldorf in 1850. The fourth of the symphonies was an earlier work, revised for Düsseldorf in 1852. The Overture, Scherzo and Finale, Op. 52, was described by the composer as a "symphonette".

☛ **Recommended Recordings**
Symphonies Nos. 1 & 3
Naxos 8.553082

Symphonies Nos. 2 & 4
Naxos 8.550923

Overture, Scherzo and Finale
Naxos 8.550608

(b) Concertos

Schumann's only completed piano concerto was started in 1841 and completed in 1845. The Cello Concerto of 1850 was first performed four years after Schumann's death, while the 1853 Violin Concerto had to wait over eighty years before its first performance in 1937. The Konzertstück for four French horns is an interesting addition to orchestral repertoire. Schumann's Introduction and Allegro for piano and orchestra was completed in 1853.

☛ **Recommended Recordings**

Cello Concerto
Naxos 8.550938

Introduction and Allegro appassionato Op. 92
Naxos 8.550506

Piano Concerto
Naxos 8.550118

(c) Overtures

The overture to Schumann's only completed opera, Genoveva, unsuccessful in the theatre, is part of concert-hall repertoire, with an overture to Byron's Manfred, again first intended for the theatre. Concert overtures include Die Braut von Messina (The Bride from Messina), based on Schiller's play of that name, Julius Cäsar, based on Shakespeare, and Hermann und Dorothea, based on Goethe. A setting of scenes from Goethe's Faust also includes an overture.

☛ **Recommended Recording**

Overtures: Genoveva / Faust / Manfred
Die Braut von Messina / Julius Cäsar
Hermann und Dorothea
Naxos 8.550608

Chamber Music

Schumann wrote three string quartets in 1842, a fertile period that saw also the composition of the Piano Quintet and a Piano Quartet. Other important chamber music by Schumann includes three piano trios, three violin sonatas and a number of shorter character-pieces that include the Märchenbilder for viola and piano, collections of Phantasiestücke with alternative instrumentation and the cello and piano Fünf Stücke im Volkston, with other short pieces generally suggesting a literary or otherwise extra-musical programme.

☛ **Recommended Recordings**

Piano Quintet, Op. 44
Naxos 8.550406

Adagio and Allegro, Op. 70
Sonata in A Minor, Op. 105
Fantasiestücke, Op. 73 / Romances, Op. 94
Stücke in im Volkston, Op. 102
Naxos 8.550599

Fantasiestücke, Op. 73
Stücke im Volkston, Op. 102
Adagio and Allegro, Op. 70
Naxos 8.550654

Choral and Vocal Music

Schumann wrote a number of part-songs for mixed voices, for women's voices and for men's voices. His choral works with orchestra include Scenes from Goethe's Faust, Das Paradies und die Peri, based on Thomas Moore's poem Lalla Rookh, and Requiem for Mignon, based on Goethe's Wilhelm Meister novel. In his final years he wrote a setting of the Mass and of the Requiem Mass. The solo songs of Schumann offer a rich repertoire, an important addition to German Lieder repertoire. From these many settings mention may be made of the collections and song-cycles Myrthen, Op. 25, Liederkreis, Op. 39, Frauenliebe und-leben, Op. 42, and Dichterliebe, Op. 48, all written in the Year of Song, 1840.

☛ Recommended Recording

Frauenliebe und -leben
Naxos 8.550400

Piano Music

The piano music of Schumann, whether written for himself, for his wife, or, in later years, for his children, offers a wealth of material. From the earlier period comes Carnaval, a series of short musical scenes based on the letters of the composer's name and that of the town of Asch, home of Ernestine von Fricken, a fellow-student of Friedrich Wieck, to whom Schumann was briefly engaged. The same period brought the Davidsbündlertänze (Dances of the League of David), a reference to the imaginary league of friends of art against the surrounding Philistines. This decade also brought the first version of the monumental Symphonic Studies, based on a theme by the father of Ernestine von Fricken, and the well known Kinderszenen (Scenes of Childhood). Kreisleriana has its literary source in the Hoffmann character Kapellmeister Kreisler, as Papillons (Butterflies) have a source in the work of the writer Jean Paul and Noveletten a clear literary reference in the very title. Later piano music by Schumann includes the Album für die Jugend of 1848, Waldszenen of 1849 and the collected Bunte Blätter and Albumblätter drawn from earlier work.

Carnaval, Op. 9
Kinderszenen, Op. 15 / Papillons, Op. 2
Naxos 8.550784

Davidsbündlertänze, Op. 6
Fantasiestücke, Op. 12
Naxos 8.550493

Fantasie Op. 17 / Bunte Blätter Op. 99
Naxos 8.550680

Humoreske, Op. 20
Naxos 8.550469

Kreisleriana Op. 16 / Arabeske Op. 18 /
Faschingsschwank aus Wien, Op. 26
Naxos 8.550783

Piano Works
Intermezzi Op. 4
Impromptus über ein Thema von ClaraWieck
Op. 5 Drei Romanzen Op. 28
Albumblätter Op. 124
Naxos 8.550849

Symphonische Etüden
(Symphonic Studies), Op. 13
Fünf Albumblätter, Op. 99, Nos. 4-8
Arabeske, Op. 18
Naxos 8.550144

Waldszenen, Op. 82 / Kreisleriana, Op. 16
Blumenstück, Op. 19
Naxos 8.550401

Schütz, Heinrich (1585 - 1672)

Schütz was the most important German composer of his generation, a pupil of Giovanni Gabrieli in Venice and later of Monteverdi. He was a member of the court musical establishment of Landgrave Moritz of Hessen-Kassel, later entering the service of the Electors of Saxony in Dresden, employment interrupted briefly by work for the King of Denmark. Schütz lived at a period of great difficulty, and with other musicians suffered from the effects of the Thirty Years War, in which Saxony finally became involved.

Church Music

Schütz wrote a very large amount of church music, Cantiones sacrae and Symphoniae sacrae, the scale of which largely depended on the economic situation of the Dresden court chapel. His Christmas Oratorio exists in more than one version, and he also wrote three settings of the Passion, according to the Gospels of St. Matthew, St. Luke and St. John, with a setting of the Seven Last Words. The church music of Schütz includes settings in German and in Latin.

☛ **Recommended Recordings**

Psalmen Davids
Naxos 8.553044

A Christmas Story
Naxos 8.553514

Secular Vocal Music

Schütz published his first set of Italian madrigals while he was studying in Venice with Gabrieli.

Scriabin, Alexander (1872 - 1915)

A friend and fellow-student of Rachmaninov in Moscow, the Russian composer Alexander Scriabin enjoyed a very different and much shorter career, at first as a concert pianist, with the encouragement of Belyayev, who published his earlier compositions. His interest in philosophy and the theosophical theories of Madame Blavatsky influenced the later form of his composition, particularly the larger scale orchestral works, while his later piano music explores new musical territory. His life was vitiated by a growing self-absorption, coupled with eccentricity of beliefs.

Orchestral Music

Scriabin enjoyed early success with his 1896 Piano Concerto. Of greater significance, however, are the later works, Symphony No. 3 "Le divin poème", Le poème de l'éxtase and Prométhée, Le poème du feu.

☞ **Recommended Recordings**
Symphony No. 1, Op. 26
Prelude for Orchestra (Rêverie) Op. 24
Poèmes Op. 32, Nos. 1 & 2
Naxos 8.553580

Symphony No. 2, Op. 29 / Symphonic Poem
Naxos 8.553581

Symphony No. 3
Naxos 8.553582

Piano Music

Scriabin's earliest piano music was written while he was a student at the Moscow Conservatory, leading to a final series of five sonatas starting in 1911. The remaining seven sonatas cover the years from 1886 until 1907. Other shorter piano pieces include studies, preludes and impromptus, in a style that develops from the influence of Chopin to a sensuous idiom entirely his own.

☞ **Recommended Recording**
Piano Sonatas Vol. 1
Nos. 2, 5, 6, 7 and 9 / Fantasy in B Minor
Naxos 8.553158

Senfl, Ludwig (c. 1486 - 1542/1543)

Senfl occupied an important position as a composer during the period of the Reformation in Germany. Swiss by birth, he was active in Germany, briefly working for the Emperor Maximilian, before securing a position at Munich at the court of the Bavarian Elector.

Church Music

Senfl's music includes Mass settings, settings of the Proper of the Mass, Vespers and motets on Latin texts.

Secular Vocal Music

Senfl wrote a quantity of Lieder for four voices, music of some historical importance, with the changes taking place in the cultural climate of the time.

Sermisy, Claudin de (c. 1490 - 1562)

Claudin de Sermisy occupied a position of contemporary importance in French music, serving the successive Kings of France and the Sainte-Chapelle in Paris in the first half of the 16th century.

Church Music

Church music by Claudin includes a dozen surviving Mass settings and some 110 motets, a St. Matthew Passion, settings of the Magnificat and a four-voice Lamentations for the Holy Week liturgy.

Secular Vocal Music

Claudin made an equally significant addition to the repertoire of French chansons with some 175 works of this kind.

Séverac, Déodat de (1872 - 1921)

Descended from a noble family, Déodat de Séverac studied first in Toulouse, later moving to Paris to study under Vincent d'Indy at the Schola Cantorum, a rival to the academicism of the Conservatoire. There he took organ lessons from Guilmant and worked as assistant to Isaac Albéniz. He spent much of his life in his native south, a region that attracted a number of his contemporaries, artists and poets he had met in Paris.

Operas

Operas by Séverac include Héliogabale, first performed in the arena at Béziers in 1910, preceded in 1909 by Le coeur du moulin (The Heart of the Mill), mounted at the Opéra-Comique in Paris.

Vocal and Choral Music

Songs by Séverac include settings of verse in Provençal as well as of poems by Verlaine, Baudelaire and others. Choral music includes settings of texts in the related language of Catalan.

Orchestral Music

Symphonic poems on the seasons Autumn and Winter were written in 1900, while a symphonic poem based on La Fontaine's fable of the frogs who asked for a king was completed in 1921.

Piano Music

Piano music by Séverac is often pictorial, as in his Chant de la terre (Song of the Earth), described as a Georgic, with his depiction of a rustic idyll, or the festive pieces in En Languedoc.

Shostakovich, Dmitry (1906 - 1975)

Dmitry Shostakovich belongs to the generation of composers trained principally after the Communist Revolution of 1917. He graduated from the St. Petersburg Conservatory as a pianist and composer, his First Symphony winning immediate favour. His subsequent career in Russia varied with the political climate. The initial success of his opera Lady Macbeth of Mtsensk District, based on Leskov, and later revised as Katerina Ismailova, was followed by official condemnation, emanating apparently from Stalin himself. The composer's Fifth Symphony, in 1937, brought partial rehabilitation, while the war years offered a propaganda coup in the Leningrad Symphony,

performed in the city under German siege. In 1948 he fell foul of the official musical establishment with a Ninth Symphony thought to be frivolous, but enjoyed the relative freedom following the death of Stalin in 1953. Outwardly and inevitably conforming to official policy, posthumous information suggests that Shostakovich remained very critical of Stalinist dictates, particularly with regard to music and the arts. He occupies a significant position in the 20th century as a symphonist and as a composer of chamber music, writing in a style that is sometimes spare in texture but always accessible, couched as it is in an extension of traditional tonal musical language.

Stage Works

Katerina Ismailova remains the principal opera of Shostakovich, with the early opera The Nose, based on Gogol, and the ballet The Golden Age. Incidental music for the theatre includes scores for Shakespeare's Hamlet and for King Lear, the same two plays being among the films for which he wrote scores.

Orchestral Music

(a) Symphonies

The fifteen symphonies of Shostakovich range in scope from the First Symphony of 1925, a graduation composition, to the embittered Thirteenth using

Yevtushenko's poems. The Fourteenth, which contains settings of various poems came two years before the Fifteenth and last symphony of 1971. The Fifth Symphony, the immediate post-war Ninth and the Tenth of 1953 are most often heard, while Nos. 2 and 3, with Nos. 11 and 12, have more overtly patriotic suggestions about them.

☞ Recommended Recordings

Symphonies Nos. 1 & 3
Naxos 8.550623

Symphonies Nos. 2 & 15
Naxos 8.550624

Symphonies No. 4
Naxos 8.550625

Symphonies Nos. 5 & 9
Naxos 8.550632

Symphonies Nos. 6 & 12
Naxos 8.550626

Symphony No. 7
Naxos 8.550627

Symphony No. 8
Naxos 8.550628

Symphony No. 10
Naxos 8.550633

Symphony No. 11
Naxos 8.550629

Symphony No. 13
Naxos 8.550630

Symphony No. 14
Naxos 8.550631

(b) Concertos

Shostakovich wrote an early concerto for piano, trumpet and strings, and a second piano concerto, a vehicle for his son Maxim, in 1957. He wrote two violin concertos and two cello concertos.

☞ Recommended Recording

Piano Concertos Nos. 1 & 2
Naxos 8.553126

(c) Suites

Shostakovich arranged concert suites from many of his film and theatre scores.

☞ Recommended Recording

Age of Gold Suite
Naxos 8.553126

Choral and Vocal Music

Choral works by Shostakovich include The Execution of Stepan Razin, a setting of a text by Yevtushenko. His solo songs are generally less overtly political, evidence of a private rather than public voice.

Chamber Music

The fifteen String Quartets by Shostakovich form a remarkable body of work, lucid in texture, often moving in musical content. The intensely felt Viola Sonata of 1975 is the third of his duo sonatas, preceded by the 1934 Cello Sonata and the Violin Sonata of 1968. To these may be added the second Piano Trio and a G minor Piano Quintet, written in 1944.

☞ **Recommended Recordings**

String Quartets Nos. 1, 8 & 9
Naxos 8.550973

String Quartets Nos. 2 and 12
Naxos 8.550975

String Quartets Nos. 3 and 5
Naxos 8.550974

String Quartets Nos. 4, 6 & 7
Naxos 8.550972

Piano Music

The piano music of Shostakovich includes, in addition to two piano sonatas, an ingenious set of Twenty-four Preludes and Fugues, as well as an earlier set of Twenty-four Preludes.

Sibelius, Jean (1865 - 1957)

Sibelius grew to maturity at a time of fervent Finnish nationalism, as the country broke away from its earlier Swedish and later Russian overlords. Brought up in a Swedish-speaking family, Sibelius acquired a knowledge of Finnish language and traditional literature at school and the early Finnish sagas proved a strong influence on his subsequent work as a composer. After early training in Helsinki and later in Berlin, Sibelius made his career in Finland, where he was awarded a state pension. Although he lived until 1957, he wrote little after 1926, feeling out of sympathy with current trends in music.

Stage Works

Sibelius wrote incidental music for Maeterlinck's Pelléas et Mélisande and for Belshazzar's Feast, a play by Procope, with a Prelude and two suites from a score for Shakespeare's The Tempest. His well known Karelia Suite was derived from incidental music for a pageant. His popular Valse triste was originally written for Järnefelt's play Death, and in fact accompanies a death-bed scene.

☞ **Recommended Recordings**

Karelia Suite / Valse triste
Naxos 8.550103

Belshazzar's Feast
Naxos 8.550200

Orchestral Music

(a) Symphonies

Sibelius wrote seven symphonies, an additional eighth apparently completed but destroyed. The first two of these enjoy particular popularity.

☞ Recommended Recordings

Symphonies Nos. 1 & 6
Naxos 8.550197

Symphonies Nos. 2 & 7
Naxos 8.550198

Symphonies Nos. 3 & 4
Naxos 8.550199

Symphony No. 5
Naxos 8.550200

(b) Symphonic Poems etc.

Symphonic poems by Sibelius, their inspiration usually from ancient Finnish legend, include En Saga, the Lemminkäinen Suite, of which the Swan of Tuonela and Lemminkäinen's Return form a part, Pohjola's Daughter and Tapiola. Finlandia was adapted from music provided for Press Pension celebrations in 1899.

☞ Recommended Recordings

Finlandia / The Swan of Tuonela
Naxos 8.550103

Rakastava / Romance / Andante festivo
Naxos 8.550330

En Saga
Naxos 8.550200

(c) Concertos

Sibelius was trained as a violinist. His concerto for the instrument was, however, a technically more demanding work than he could have tackled himself. It now has a place in standard solo violin repertoire.

☞ Recommended Recording

Violin Concerto
Naxos 8.550329

Chamber Music

Chamber music by Sibelius includes a string quartet, "Voces intimae", a sonatina for violin and a number of short pieces for violin and piano.

☞ Recommended Recording

Piano Music
(Finlandia / Kyllikki, Three Lyric Pieces /
The Trees / The Flowers /
Five Characteristic Impressions /
Six Impromptus)
Naxos 8.553661

Sinding, Christian (1856 - 1941)

Remembered by ambitious amateur pianists for his Rustle of Spring, Christian Sinding was a more important figure than this might suggest in the music of his native Norway, where, in his time, he was second only to Grieg. Trained in Leipzig, he fell under the influence of Liszt and Wagner, producing a large quantity of music that enjoyed contemporary popularity.

Orchestral Music

Sinding's orchestral compositions include four symphonies, three concertos for violin, his own original instrument, for which he wrote other pieces with orchestra, and a piano concerto, including his Légende.

Chamber Music

Chamber music by Sinding ranges from piano and string quintets to a series of works for violin and piano and for cello and piano, with a Suite for unaccompanied violin.

☛ **Recommended Recording**
Piano Trios Nos. 2 and 3
Marco Polo 8.223283

Piano Music

Sinding's piano music consists chiefly of shorter genre pieces, of which Rustle of Spring is characteristic. His Sonata, Op. 91, has retained an occasional place in present repertoire.

☛ **Recommended Recording**
Rustle of Spring
Naxos 8.550141

Vocal and Choral Music

Sinding left a large number of songs, principally of Norwegian texts. There are also choral works, some of them celebratory and others unpublished.

Smetana, Bedřich (1824 - 1884)

Smetana holds an important place in the development of musical nationalism in his native Bohemia, where he was born in 1824, the son of a master brewer in the service of Count Waldstein and others. His career was interrupted by a period of self-imposed exile in Sweden, after the political disappointments that followed the turmoil of 1848. He was instrumental in the establishment of Czech national opera and a Czech national style, in particular in his symphonic poems. He was deaf in later life, but continued to compose, an autobiographical element appearing in his string quartets.

Operas

The best known of Smetana's operas is The Bartered Bride, the overture of which makes a brilliant opening to any orchestral concert programme. His other operas have enjoyed less international success.

☛ **Recommended Recording**
The Bartered Bride (orchestral excerpts)
Naxos 8.550376

Orchestral Music

The best known of Smetana's orchestral works is the cycle of symphonic poems Ma vlast (My Country), a set of six works, of which Vltava (River Moldau), which follows the historic course of the river as it flows towards Prague, is the most frequently heard.

☛ **Recommended Recording**
Má Vlast (Complete)
Naxos 8.550931

Chamber Music

Smetana wrote two string quartets, the first with the title "From my life". There is a G minor Piano Trio and two short pieces for violin and piano under the title From the Homeland.

☛ **Recommended Recordings**
String Quartets Nos. 1 and 2
From the Homeland
Naxos 8.550379

Soler, Antonio (1729 - 1783)

The Catalan composer Antonio Soler had his early musical education at Montserrat. In 1752 he joined the Jeronymite order at the Escorial, where he became maestro de capella. He was able to study with Domenico Scarlatti in Madrid and became involved in some controversy with his important book on modulation, Llave de la modulación (Key to Modulation), which laid down the principles of modulation, how to shift from one key to another. His interest in the theory and history of music was considerable, coupled with an enthusiasm for other branches of learning, including mathematics. He was also employed as a consultant on the construction of new organs.

Keyboard Music

Soler is principally known for his many keyboard sonatas, of which he wrote some 120. In some of these typical Spanish rhythms and turns of phrase appear.

Sonatas for Harpsichord Vol. 1
Nos. 1, 15, 18, 19, 43, 54, 85 & 90
Naxos 8.553462

Sonatas for Harpsichord Vol. 2
Nos. 16, 17, 35, 42, 46, 52, 83, 87, 106
& 116 / Rubio No. 92
Naxos 8.553463

Instrumental Music

Soler's six quintets for string quartet and organ, with his six concertos for two organs, form the body of his surviving chamber music.

Vocal and Choral Music

Soler contributed in particular to the Spanish religious villancico, of which he wrote 132. There are settings of the Mass and a setting of the Lamentations for solo soprano with cello, double bass and continuo. He wrote three gypsy villancicos that have particular appeal.

Sor, Fernando (1778 - 1839)

The Catalan composer Fernando Sor is chiefly known for his many compositions for guitar, his own instrument. Although originally opposed to the Napoleonic invasion of Spain, he later accepted a position under the French government and was, in consequence, obliged to seek refuge abroad, in London, and in Paris, where he established himself as a successful performer, teacher and composer.

Guitar Music

Sor published a quantity of music for guitar, some of it pedagogical in purpose and some of it for concert performance. His Méthode pour la guitarre, published in 1830, is among the most important books on guitar technique.

☞ **Recommended Recordings**

6 Divertimenti, Op. 13 / Sonata, Op. 14
Folies d'Espagne and Minuet, Op. 15 (a)
Sonata seconda, Op. 15 (b)
Thème Variée, Op. 15 (c)
Cinquième Fantasie, Op. 16
Naxos 8.553354

24 Exercises, Op. 35, Books I & II /
Society Pieces, Op. 33, Nos. 1 to 3
Naxos 8.553341

Grande Sonate Op. 22 / Divertissement Op. 23
8 Petites Pièces / Grande Sonate Op. 25
Naxos 8.553340

L'Encouragement Op. 34
Divertissement Op. 38 / Six Valses Op. 39
Les deux amis Op. 41 / Six Valses Op. 44 bis
Divertissement militaire Op. 49
Naxos 8.553302

Menuet Op. 11, No. 6 / 8 Etudes
Minuetto Op. 22
Naxos 8.553007

Morceau de Concert, Op. 54
Souvenirs d'une soirée à Berlin, Op. 56
Six Valses et un galop, Op. 57
Fantaisie villageoise, Op. 52
Fantaisie pour guitare seule
Naxos 8.553450

Vocal Music

Sor wrote a number of boleros and seguidillas for voices and guitar, in addition to Spanish, Italian and English songs and duets for voice and piano.

Stage Music

Sor's opera Telemaco nell'isola de Calipso (Telemachus on the Island of Calypso) was staged in Barcelona in 1797. Sor's other theatre music was principally for the ballet, including a successful Cendrillon (Cinderella), a march from which he arranged for guitar.

Spohr, Louis (1784 - 1859)

The name of Louis Spohr remains well known to violinists, brought up to play some at least of his fifteen violin concertos. He was born in Brunswick in 1784 and established himself as a leading virtuoso violinist and as a composer. As a conductor he made use of a baton, a practice unusual at the time and one that alarmed orchestral players in London, who anticipated aggressive intentions. From 1822 until his death in 1859 he was director of music at Kassel, a position initially offered him on the suggestion of Weber. His compositions include a number of works with violin and harp, written for himself and his wife, the harpist Dorette Scheidler.

Orchestral Music

(a) Symphonies

Spohr completed nine symphonies, leaving a tenth unfinished. The later symphonies move from the classical style that he had inherited to music with a programmatic element. They remain relative rarities in the concert-hall today.

(b) Concertos

Spohr wrote fifteen violin concertos, the first completed in 1803 and the last in 1844. The best known of these is probably the eighth, which incorporates an operatic element. Other concertos include two double violin concertos and four concertos for clarinet. The latter are an important and popular part of solo clarinet repertoire and were written for the clarinettist Johann Simon Hermstedt.

    Clarinet Concertos Nos. 1 & 3
    Potpourri Op. 80
    Naxos 8.550688

    Clarinet Concertos Nos. 2 & 4
    Fantasia & Variations Op. 81
    Naxos 8.550689

    Symphonies Nos. 1 and 5
    Marco Polo 8.223363

    Symphonies Nos. 2 and 9
    Marco Polo 8.223454

    Symphonies Nos. 3 and 6
    Marco Polo 8.223439

    Symphony No. 4 / Overtures (Faust / Jessonda)
    Marco Polo 8.223122

    Symphonies Nos. 7 and 8
    Marco Polo 8.223432

    Violin Concertos Nos. 2 and 9
    Marco Polo 8.223510

    Violin Concertos Nos. 7 and 12
    Marco Polo 8.220406

Chamber Music

Spohr wrote some three dozen string quartets, an octet, four double string quartets and seven quintets, in addition to a number of violin duos of principal interest to teachers. The best known of his works for chamber ensemble is the Nonet, scored for flute, oboe, clarinet, horn, bassoon, violin, viola, cello and double bass.

    Piano Trio No. 1 / Piano Quintet, Op. 130
    Naxos 8.553206

    Piano Trios Nos. 2 & 4
    Naxos 8.553205

    Piano Trios Nos. 3 & 5
    Naxos 8.553164

    String Quartets Op. 4, Nos. 1 and 2
    & Op. 15, No. 2
    Marco Polo 8.223253

    String Quartets Op. 11 / Op. 15, No. 1 / Op. 27
    Marco Polo 8.223254

    String Quartets Op. 29, Nos. 1 and 2
    Marco Polo 8.223255

    String Quartets Op. 43 & Op. 45, No. 1
    Marco Polo 8.223257

    String Quartets Op. 45, Nos. 2 and 3
    Marco Polo 8.223258

    String Quartets Op. 58, Nos. 1 and 2
    Marco Polo 8.223256

    String Quartets Op. 74, Nos. 1 and 2
    Marco Polo 8.223259

    String Quartets Op. 84, Nos. 1 and 2
    Marco Polo 8.223251

    String Quartets Op. 84, No. 3 & Op. 93
    Marco Polo 8.223252

    String Quintets Op. 33 Nos. 1 and 2
    Marco Polo 8.223597

String Quintets Opp. 106 and 129
Marco Polo 8.223598

String Quintets Opp. 69 and 91
Marco Polo 8.223599

Stage Works

Operas by Spohr, now generally neglected, include, among the better known, Jessonda. He also composed an opera on the subject of Faust.

Stamitz, Anton (1750 - 1789/1809)

The younger brother of Carl Stamitz, Anton Stamitz, violinist and viola player, was taught by his brother, whom he accompanied to Paris in 1770. There he achieved some success, remaining in France, where he taught, among others, the violinist Rodolphe Kreutzer. There is no record of his activities after 1789, when he was still in the service of the king at Versailles.

Orchestral Music

Like his brother, Anton Stamitz added to the repertoire of the viola with three concertos, in addition to a number of violin concertos.

Chamber Music

Anton Stamitz also left a certain amount of chamber music, although not so prolific as his brother. These works include string quartets and trios, as well as duos for violin and for violin and viola.

Stamitz, Carl (1745 - 1801)

The son of Johann Stamitz, Carl Stamitz was born in Mannheim, where he had his musical training from his father and his father's successors. In 1770 he moved to Paris, subsequently travelling as a virtuoso violinist and later as a viola-player.

Orchestral Music

Carl Stamitz, in a quantity of orchestral music, symphonies and symphonies concertantes, orchestral works with contrasting groups of solo instruments, also added significantly to the concerto repertoire, not least in fifteen authenticated violin concertos and three viola concertos, the last of particular importance in a limited solo repertoire for the instrument.

Chamber Music

Prolific also in his composition of chamber music, Carl Stamitz provided a varied series of compositions for ensembles, ranging from works for wind-band to duos, a number of them involving the viola. His style is very much of its period, stemming from the Mannheim tradition.

Stamitz, Johann (1717 - 1757)

The Bohemian composer Johann Stamitz, a versatile performer on a number of instruments, is chiefly known for his work with the Mannheim orchestra, which he built into what a later visitor, the English Dr Burney, described as an army of generals. He seems to have joined the musical establishment of the Elector Palatine, whose capital was at Mannheim, in 1741, as a violinist, and by 1750 had become director of instrumental music. The Mannheim orchestra became famous for its discipline, evident in particular in the Mannheim crescendo, an effective increase in volume and following decrease that became a feature of the music written for the orchestra, which had other characteristic features, including the ascending melodic figure known as the Mannheim rocket.

Orchestral Music

Music by Johann Stamitz includes symphonies and concertos, the former an important step in the development of the classical form that later came to dominate instrumental music.

Chamber Music

A smaller amount of chamber music by Stamitz consists of trios and sonatas for violin and basso continuo.

Stockhausen, Karlheinz (1928 -)

Stockhausen has been among the leading avant-garde figures in German music since the 1950s. In spite of material difficulties, he studied in Cologne with Frank Martin and was subsequently strongly influenced by attendance at Darmstadt, where summer sessions contributed largely to the development of new music. He went on to study with Messiaen in Paris. Parallel to his work in electronic music, he explored the human element in performance, moving from total serialism, in which every aspect of a piece is controlled by a predetermined serial pattern, to a more flexible approach.

Works

The numbering of Stockhausen's works allows his earlier compositions the numbering of fractions, with his Kontre-Punkte of 1952 as the first whole number, No. 1. A varied and fascinating series of compositions includes Stimmung for electronically treated voices, Mantra, for two pianos, woodblocks and crotales, the result of a visit to the Osaka World Fair, at which his music was featured. Zyklus has an important part in modern percussion repertoire, while work continues on Licht, a project divided into seven days and involving dramatic use of instrumental performance. The size of this work, calculated to reach completion in 2002, is characteristic of the composer's Wagnerian tendencies.

Instrumental and Vocal Music

Of particular interest in the development of Stockhausen's ideas is Gruppen, first performed in 1958, and using three orchestras surrounding the audience. Use of short-wave radio occurs in Hymnen, Spiral and his celebration of the bicentenary of Beethoven's birth, Kurzwellen mit Beethoven (Short-Wave with Beethoven). Aus den sieben Tagen (From the Seven Days), a series of fifteen compositions, is written without notes but with verbal directions to performers, on whose particular imagination and ability he as so often relies. His continuing work Licht (Light) allows a significant dramatic element for solo trumpet in Donnerstag (Thursday), but all in all the comprehensive nature of Stockhausen's work and its development over the last forty years defy succinct summary.

Strauss, Johann I (1804 - 1849)

Founder of the Strauss dynasty of Viennese light music composers, Johann Strauss established his own dance orchestra, enjoying incredible popularity as composer, conductor and violinist in the ball-rooms of Vienna and abroad. He wrote a large quantity of dance music, waltzes, cotillions, galops, quadrilles, polkas and marches. Of these last the Radetzky March enjoyed the greatest popularity.

Strauss, Johann II (1825 - 1899)

The eldest son of Johann Strauss, and not intended by his father for a career in music, Johann Strauss the younger nevertheless established an unrivalled reputation throughout the second half of the 19th century as a composer and purveyor of light Viennese music, involving his two younger brothers in the management and direction of dance orchestras that performed both in Vienna and abroad.

Stage Works

The younger Johann Strauss wrote some sixteen operettas between 1871 and 1897. Of these the best known is Die Fledermaus (The Bat), characteristic in plot and music of Vienna at its most light-hearted. Other operettas are more familiar from dances derived from them, although Der Zigeunerbaron (The Gypsy Baron) remains second in order of popularity to Die Fledermaus.

☞ **Recommended Recording**

Die Fledermaus (2 CDs)
Naxos 8.660017-18

Dance Music

Dance music by the younger Johann Strauss includes waltzes, polkas, quadrilles, marches and other works. Among these the most familiar remains An der schönen, blauen Donau (The Blue Danube), originally a choral waltz-sequence. Strauss, like his father, was extremely prolific as a composer, writing several hundred dances in various forms.

☞ **Recommended Recordings**

Favourite Waltzes, Polkas, Marches Vol. I
Naxos 8.550336

Favourite Waltzes, Polkas, Marches Vol. 2
Naxos 8.550337

Favourite Waltzes, Polkas, Marches Vol. 3
Naxos 8.550338

Favourite Waltzes, Polkas, Marches Vol. 4
Naxos 8.50339

Favourite Waltzes, Polkas, Marches Vol. 5
Naxos 8.550340

Most Famous Waltzes
Naxos 8.550152

Johann Strauss Complete Orchestral Works Vols. I - 52
Marco Polo 8.223201-247, 8.233249, 8.223275, 8.223276 & 8.223279

Strauss, Josef (1827 - 1870)

In spite of ill health, Josef Strauss joined his elder brother, Johann Strauss Jnr, in the provision of dance music, abandoning his profession of engineer. Like his brother and father he wrote waltzes, polkas, quadrilles and marches.

☞ **Recommended Recordings**

Josef Strauss Orchestral Works Vols. I - 3
Marco Polo 8.223561-3

Strauss, Eduard (1835 - 1916)

Eduard Strauss, the third son of Johann Strauss the elder, originally intended for the Austrian consular service, was recruited by his eldest brother into the family music business, to which he contributed until his retirement in 1901. As a composer he was very much less prolific than his brothers and than his father.

Strauss, Oscar (1870 - 1954)

Born in Vienna and a pupil of Max Bruch in Berlin, Oscar Strauss followed the advice of Johann Strauss, who told him to gain experience by conducting in provincial theatres. In Berlin he won some fame in the Überbrettl cabaret, for which Schoenberg also wrote. Returning to Vienna at the turn of the century, he began to write operetta in a series of works that rivalled in popularity those of Lehár. In 1939 he moved to Paris and then to New York and Hollywood, returning after the war to Bad Ischl, where he died in 1954.

Stage Works

Der tapfere Soldat, known in English as The Chocolate Soldier, won particular success in America. Other poppuloar operettas include Der letzte Walzer (The Last Waltz). He wrote film-scores, notably for the film of Schnitzler's La ronde.

Strauss, Richard (1864 - 1949)

Richard Strauss enjoyed early success as both conductor and composer, in the second capacity influenced by the work of Wagner. He developed the symphonic or tone-poem to an unrivalled level of expressiveness and after 1900 achieved great success with a series of impressive operas, at first on a grand scale, but later tending to a more classical restraint. His relationship with the National Socialist government in Germany was at times ambiguous, a fact that protected him but led to post-war difficulties and self-imposed exile in Switzerland, from which he returned home to Bavaria only in the year of his death, 1949.

Operas

Richard Strauss created an immediate sensation with his opera Salome, based on the play of that name by Oscar Wilde. A collaboration with Hugo von Hoffmannsthal followed, with the operas Elektra and the even more effective Der Rosenkavalier in 1911, followed by Ariadne auf Naxos. Der Rosenkavalier (The Knight of the Rose) remains the best known of the operas of Richard Strauss, familiar in excerpt from its famous concert waltz-sequence. From Salome comes the orchestral Dance of the Seven Veils, an important moment in the drama. The late opera Die Liebe der Danae, completed in 1940, may also be known in part from orchestral excerpts.

☞ Recommended Recordings

Salome's Dance
Der Rosenkavalier Waltz Sequence No. 1
Naxos 8.550182

Die Liebe der Danae
Der Rosenkavalier Waltz Sequence No. 2
Naxos 8.550342

Orchestral Music

(a) Symphonic Poems

In the decade from 1886 Strauss tackled a series of symphonic poems, starting with the relatively light-hearted Aus Italien (From Italy) and going on to Don Juan, based on the poem by Lenau, the Shakespearian Macbeth, Tod und Verklärung (Death and Transfiguration), Till Eulenspiegel a study of a medieval prankster, Also sprach Zarathustra (Thus Spake Zarathustra) , based on Nietzsche, a series of fantastic variations on the theme of Don Quixote and Ein Heldenleben (A Hero's Life).

☞ Recommended Recordings

Also sprach Zarathustra
Naxos 8.550182

Aus Italien
Naxos 8.550342

Tod und Verklärung / Don Juan
Till Eulenspiegels lustige Streiche
Naxos 8.550250

Symphony in D Minor / Interludio
Kampf und Sieg
Marco Polo 8.220323

Symphony in F Minor, Op. 12
Marco Polo 8.220358

(b) Concertos etc.

Concertos by Strauss include two for the French horn, an instrument with which he was familiar from his father's eminence as one of the leading players of his time. There is an early violin concerto, but it is rather the Oboe Concerto of 1945, revised in 1948, that has impressed audiences.

Vocal Music

In common with other German composers, Strauss added significantly to the body of German Lieder. Most moving of all, redolent with a kind of autumnal nostalgia that is highly characteristic, are the Vier letzte Lieder (The Four Last Songs).

Stravinsky, Igor (1882 - 1971)

The son of a distinguished Russian singer, Stravinsky spent his earlier years in Russia, either in St. Petersburg or, in the summer, at the country estates of his relatives. He studied music briefly with Rimsky-Korsakov but made a name for himself first in Paris with commissions from the impresario Dyagilev, for whom he wrote a series of ballet scores. He spent the years after the Russian Revolution of 1917 in Western Europe and in 1939 moved to the United States of America. There in the post-war years he turned from a style of eclectic neo-classicism to composing in the twelve-note technique propounded by Schoenberg. A versatile composer, inventive in changing styles, he may be seen as the musical counterpart of the painter Picasso.

Stage Works

Stravinsky made an immediate impression in Paris with his score for L'oiseau de feu (The Firebird), for the Ballets Russes of Dyagilev. There followed the very Russian Petrushka, set in a Russian fair-ground, and the succès de scandale of Le sacre du printemps (The Rite of Spring). After works on a smaller scale in war-time, Stravinsky turned again to ballet for Dyagilev in Pulcinella, based on music wrongly attributed to Pergolesi. Later ballets include Apollon musagète, Le Baiser de la fée, Jeu de cartes and Agon. The Latin opera-oratorio, with a text translated from Cocteau, Oedipus Rex was first staged in 1928, while the opera The Rake's Progress, neo-classical in form and based on the engravings of Hogarth, with a libretto by W.H. Auden and Chester Kallman, was staged in Venice in 1951.

☛ **Recommended Recordings**

Firebird Suite / Petrushka Suite
Naxos 8.550263

The Rite of Spring / Jeu de cartes
Naxos 8.550472

Pulcinella / Danses concertantes
Naxos 8.553181

Orchestral Music

Stravinsky's orchestral music includes symphonies, suites from some of the ballets, and two suites arranged from sets of easy piano pieces. Concertos of various kinds include a 1936 Concerto for piano, wind, timpani and double basses, an Ebony Concerto for jazz band and a Violin Concerto

Chamber Music

Stravinsky's chamber music includes some arrangements of orchestral works, in particular two versions of music from Pulcinella, one for violin and piano and a second for cello and piano, under the title Suite italienne.

Suk, Josef (1874 - 1935)

The son-in-law of Dvořák, composer and violinist, Josef Suk was for long a member of the Czech Quartet. He wrote relatively little chamber music, achieving distinction rather as a composer of orchestral music.

Orchestral Music

The best known of Suk's orchestral works is his Serenade for Strings, written in 1892. Other works, written on a larger scale, in particular the symphony Asrael, in which he mourns the death of his father-in-law and his wife, represent music of greater ambition.

Chamber Music

Suk wrote relatively little chamber music. His Four Pieces, Op., 17, for violin and piano are a standard element in violin recital repertoire.

Sullivan, Sir Arthur (1842 - 1900)

The name of Sir Arthur Sullivan is indissolubly wedded with that of W.S.Gilbert, with whom he wrote a succession of operettas that have remained a popular part of English national repertoire, for long the sole property of the company founded for their performance by Richard D'Oyly Carte, who later built the Savoy Theatre in London for the performance of what became the Savoy Operas. The national institution that Gilbert and Sullivan have become has drawn attention away from Sullivan's more serious work.

Operettas

Operettas with words by Gilbert range from Trial by Jury in 1875 to The Gondoliers in 1889, followed in 1893 by Utopia Limited and, in 1896, by the lesser known The Grand Duke. HMS Pinafore, The Pirates of Penzance, Patience, with its satire on Oscar Wilde, the political satire Iolanthe, The Mikado, Ruddigore and The Yeomen of the Guard, continue to bear witness to the deft and witty music of Sullivan and the comic verbal talents of Gilbert.

Incidental Music
(The Merchant of Venice / Henry VIII /
The Sapphire Necklace / Overture in C)
Marco Polo 8.223461

Macbeth / King Arthur
The Merry Wives of Windsor
Marco Polo 8.223635

Victoria and Merrie England
Marco Polo 8.223677

Suppé, Franz von (1819 - 1895)

Austrian, but Belgian by descent, born in Split, later to be a part of Yugoslavia, Suppé made his career principally in Vienna as a composer and conductor of operetta.

Operettas

Music from the operettas of Suppé is generally familiar through the overtures to Dichter und Bauer (Poet and Peasant), Die leichte Kavallerie (Light Cavalry), Die schöne Galatea (Fair Galatea) and Ein Morgen, ein Mittag und ein Abend in Wien (Morning, Noon and Night in Vienna).

☛ **Recommended Recording**

Overtures
(Ein Morgen, ein Mittag, ein Abend in Wien
Die schöne Galathee / Die Leichte Kavallerie)
Naxos 8.550468

Overtures Volume 1
(Poet and Peasant / Fortune's Labyrinth
Donna Juanita / Carnaval / Boccaccio
The Mistress / Jolly Robbers
The Goal of the Wanderer / Queen of Spades)
Marco Polo 8.223647

Overtures Volume 2
(The Beautiful Galatea / Isabella / The Model
Tantalusqualen / Der Krämer und sein Kommis
Paragraph 3 / Boccaccio / Fatinitza March
Donna Juanita
Marco Polo 8.223648

Overtures Volume 3
(Light Cavalry / Tricoche and Cacolet
Boccaccio March / Titania Waltz / Fatinitza
Humoristische Variationen
Die Heimkehr von der Hochzeit
Herzenseintracht, Polka / Franz Schubert
Triumph-Ouvertüre)
Marco Polo 8.223683

Overtures Volume 4
(Morning, Noon and Night in Vienna
Flotte Bursche / Über Berg, Über Tal, March
Summer Night's Dream
Overture on Mozart's Themes
Zehn Mädchen und Kein Mann / Kindereien
Afrikanreise / Was kommt dort von der Höh'
Solemn Overture)
Marco Polo 8.223730

Svendsen, Johan (1840 - 1911)

A Norwegian composer, conductor and violinist, Svendsen studied in Leipzig. For the last thirty years of his life he concentrated largely on conducting, becoming the leading Scandinavian conductor of his day.

Orchestral Music

Svendsen wrote a number of works for violin and orchestra. Of these the Romance is by far the best known, whether in its original version or in various adaptations that have been made of it, largely to its detriment.

☛ **Recommended Recording**

Romance
Naxos 8.550329

Sweelinck, Jan Pieterszoon

(1562 - 1621)

The Netherlands composer and organist Sweelinck was among the leading musicians of his day, much in demand also as a teacher. He occupies an important position particularly in the development of keyboard music in the early 17th century. He was employed for some 44 years at the Oude Kirk in Amsterdam. Sweelinck was prolific in the provision of church music, with settings of French psalm translations and Latin motets, in addition to secular chansons and Italian madrigals.

Keyboard Music

Sweelinck wrote keyboard music for both secular and sacred use. The first of these includes song-variations for harpsichord and, among other pieces, a tribute to Dowland in Pavana Lachrimae, using John Dowland's most famous melody. In addition to various toccatas and fantasias Sweelinck also provided variations on sacred themes.

☛ **Recommended Recording**

Organ Works
Naxos 8.550904

Szymanowski, Karol (1882 - 1937)

The Polish composer Karol Szymanowskiwas born in the Ukraine, once part of the kingdom of Poland, but studied in Warsaw, much influenced by Chopin and then by Wagner, Richard Strauss, Brahms and Reger. From a well-to-do and cultured family, he read widely, particularly during the years of war, from 1914 to 1917, when he remained on the family estate in the Ukraine, a property destroyed in the civil war. The breadth of his cultural knowledge is reflected in his music and in particular in his settings of literary texts of one kind or another. Musically he is able at times to draw on specifically Polish material, coupled with his own perceptions of Arabic and Persian culture.

Stage Works

The principal opera of Szymanowski is King Roger, a work influenced by the Bacchae of Euripides. Here Dionysus returns to similar effect in medieval Sicily. The ballet Harnasie won some success at its first performance in Prague, followed by performance in Paris.

Orchestral and Vocal Music

A number of Szymanowski's compositions rely on texts of one sort or another, from his Salome, a fashionable subject, in 1906, to Penthesilea, Love-Songs of Hafiz, the third symphony, with its Song of the Night, from Mevlana, Songs of a Fairy-Tale Princess and Songs of the Infatuated Muezzin, to a setting of the Stabat mater and Veni Creator and the 1933 Litany of the Virgin. His purely orchestral works include two violin concertos and three other symphonies, the fourth and last in the form of a sinfonia concertante for piano and orchestra.

Chamber Music

Among the best known of Szymanowski's smaller scale works is Myths, for violin and piano, three pieces, La fontaine d'Aréthuse, Narcisse and Dryades et Pan, a violin sonata, Nocturne and Tarantella and a Romance. His two string quartets are less often performed.

Piano Music

Polish tradition is perpetuated in Szymanowski's twenty Mazurkas. Other piano music includes Masques, Metopes, characteristic titles, and sets of Etudes.

☞ **Recommended Recording**

Piano Works Vol. 1
(Mazurkas Op. 50 / Metopes Op. 29
Four Studies Op. 4 / Piano Sonata Op. 21)
Naxos 8.553016

Orchestral Music and Music for Voice and Orchestra

The last of Szymanowski's four symphonies, a Symphonie concertante with solo piano, was completed in 1932, a vehicle for his own performance, while the Third Symphony, Song of the Night, sets words by the Sufic mystic Mevlâna. Other works for voice and orchestra include settings of poems by Hafiz, Demeter, for female chorus and orchestra, based on the Bacchae of Euripides, a Stabat mater and a Veni Creator, settings of the traditional medieval Latin texts, and a Litany to the Virgin Mary. His orchestral compositions also include two violin concertos.

Vocal and Choral Music

Some of the songs that appear as works for voice and orchestra also exist in a parallel form with piano accompaniment. His settings otherwise range from the literary to the reworking of folk-songs.

Tailleferre, Germaine (1892 - 1983)

One of the lesser known members of the so-called Groupe des Six in Paris in the 1920s, Germaine Tailleferre was associated directly with Auric, Honegger and Milhaud in Cocteau's satirical Les mariés de la Tour Eiffel. Influenced by the clarity and simplicity of Satie, and by her teacher Ravel, she wrote music that later ventured into explorations of new techniques, without ever deserting her original inspiration.

Stage Works

Tailleferre's stage works include the 1921 collaboration with other members of the Six in Les mariés de la Tour Eiffel. Other works for the theatre range from the 1923 ballet Marchand des oiseaux (Bird-Seller) to the 1961 chamber opera Le maître (The Master), based on Ionesco.

Recommended Recording

La Valse des Dépéchés / Quadrille
Marco Polo 8.223788

Chamber Music

Examples of Tailleferre's chamber music are found in her two violin sonatas and violin sonatina, as well as in her Jeux de plein air (Games in the Open Air) for two pianos.

Takemitsu, Toru (1930 - 1996)

Toru Takemitsu is among the most important of those Japanese composers who have written music in the Western tradition, while preserving a fundamental Japanese identity, bringing his awareness of Japanese music and its traditions into a remarkable and very original synthesis. He makes use of Western or Japanese instruments, either separately or together, creating his own very individual sound.

Orchestral Music

Takemitsu's Requiem for strings made a strong impression on audiences who heard it in 1957. November Steps and Aki (Autumn) were scored for biwa, shakuhachi and orchestra.

Chamber and Instrumental Music

Takemitsu won international success with his brief Le son-calligraphie No. 1, the first of three pieces for two string quartets. He has experimented with other instrumental combinations and with the use of prerecorded tape. For this last there is a series of compositions and he also wrote a number of distinguished film-scores.

Tallis, Thomas (c. 1505 - 1585)

The career of the English composer Thomas Tallis spans the troubled period of the reign of Henry VIII, with the sequestration of monastic property, the Protestant régime of his successor, the re-establishment of Catholicism under Queen Mary and the subsequent changes under Queen Elizabeth. These political and religious changes had an obvious effect on music and musicians. Tallis began his career as organist at the Benedictine Priory at Dover, followed by similar service at Waltham Abbey until the dissolution of the monasteries in 1540. He was then organist at Canterbury Cathedral and in 1543 became a Gentleman of the Chapel Royal, a position he retained until his death. Like Byrd, his pupil, he seems to have remained loyal to the old religion, while nevertheless continuing to enjoy royal favour.

Church Music

Tallis wrote a quantity of Latin church music and contributed also to the reformed English liturgy, in some cases adapting earlier Latin compositions. One of his most remarkable achievements is the 40-voice Spem in alium. His setting of the Latin Holy Week liturgy Lamentations represents his work at its height. The composer's name is widely known through the metrical psalm tune known as Tallis's Canon, a setting of God, grant we grace.

☞ **Recommended Recordings**

Lamentation
Naxos 8.550572

Mass for Four Voices / Motets
Naxos 8.550576

Taneyev, Alexander Sergeyevich (1850 - 1918)

Director of the Russian Imperial Chancellery, Alexander Taneyev composed in his spare time, as official duties allowed. His music is thoroughly nationalist in inspoiration and content.

☞ **Recommended Recording**

Symphony No. 2 / Suite No. 2
Marco Polo 8.223133

Taneyev, Sergey Ivanovích (1856 - 1915)

A nephew of Alexander Sergeyevich Taneyev, Taneyev was a pupil of Tchaikovsky at the Moscow Conservatory, studying the piano with the director of the Conservatory, Nikolay Rubinstein. He was the soloist in first Moscow performance of Tchaikovsky's Piano Concerto No. 1, a rôle he repeated in later works by Tchaikovsky for piano and orchestra. He gradually assumed fuller responsibility at the Conservatory, of which he became director in 1885. His pupils included Scriabin and Rachmaninov.

Orchestral Music

Taneyev's orchestral music includes four symphonies and a Suite de concert for violin and orchestra.

☛ **Recommended Recording**

Symphonies Nos. 2 & 4
Marco Polo 8.223196

Chamber Music

Although later works remained unfinished, Taneyev completed six string quartets, two string quintets, two piano quintets and a piano trio. His music, as always, is well crafted, relying on his study of counterpoint, and, while Russian, is, at the same time, representative of the more cosmopolitan tradition that the conservatories had fostered.

Tartíni, Giuseppe (1692 - 1770)

The Italian violinist and composer Tartini made an important contribution to the development of acoustic theory and of the virtuoso violin concerto and solo repertoire. His career centred largely on Padua, where he won international respect also as a teacher, after earlier amatory adventures had necessitated temporary residence elsewhere.

Orchestral Music

Tartini wrote a very large number of concertos for the violin, many of them published in his lifetime.

Chamber Music

The best known of Tartini's many violin sonatas is that known as the Devil's Trill, the result, it was said, of a dream in which the Devil himself played the work. Tartini's technical ability is demonstrated in L'arte del arco, The Art of the Bow, 38 variations on a theme by Corelli. In common with other instrumental composers of the period, he added also to the repertoire of the trio sonata.

Taverner, John (c. 1490 - 1545)

Stories of Taverner's abandonment of music in favour of a career of hostility to English Catholic traditions seem without foundation. He was employed as master of the choristers at Cardinal College (Christ Church), Oxford, in its early heyday, retiring, on Cardinal Wolsey's fall from power, to Boston, where he was held in considerable regard until his death in 1545. The popular if mistaken account of his life is the subject of the opera by Peter Maxwell Davies, *Taverner*.

Church Music

Taverner wrote Latin Mass settings, Magnificat settings and motets. Of the first of these the Western Wynde Mass, using the melody of a popular song of that name, is among the better known. From his Mass Gloria tibi Trinitas came the fragment of a theme that served later generations as the basis of an English genre of consort music, the In nomine.

Instrumental Music

Taverner himself began the tradition of the In nomine, an instrumental arrangement of part of the Benedictus of his Mass Gloria tibi Trinitas.

Tchaikovsky, Pyotr Il'yich (1840 - 1893)

Tchaikovsky was one of the earlier students of the St. Petersburg Conservatory established by Anton Rubinstein, completing his studies there to become a member of the teaching staff at the similar institution established in Moscow by Anton Rubinstein's brother Nikolay. He was able to withdraw from teaching when a rich widow, Nadezhda von Meck, offered him financial support which continued for much of his life, although, according to the original conditions of the pension, they never met. Tchaikovsky was a man of neurotic diffidence, his self-doubt increased by his homosexuality. It is now suggested by some that an impending scandal caused him to take his own life at a time when he was at the height of his powers as a composer. His music is thoroughly Russian in character, but, although he was influenced by Balakirev and the ideals of the Five Russian nationalist composers, he may be seen as belonging rather to the more international school of

composition fostered by the Conservatories that Balakirev so much deplored.

Operas

Two above all of Tchaikovsky's operas have retained a place in international repertoire. Eugene Onegin, based on a work by Pushkin, was written in 1877, the year of the composer's disastrous and brief attempt at marriage. He returned to Pushkin in 1890 with his powerful opera The Queen of Spades.

☛ **Recommended Recording**

Eugene Onegin: Polonaise & Waltz
Naxos 8.550137

Ballets

Tchaikovsky, a master of the miniature forms necessary for ballet, succeeded in raising the quality of the music provided for an art that had undergone considerable technical development in 19th century Russia under the guidance of the French choreographer Marius Petipa. The first of Tchaikovsky's full length ballet-scores was Swan Lake, completed in 1876, followed in 1889 by The Sleeping Beauty. His last ballet, based on a story by E.T.A. Hoffmann, was Nutcracker, first staged in St. Petersburg in December 1892.

☛ **Recommended Recordings**

Swan Lake (complete) (2 CDs)
Naxos 8.550246-247

Sleeping Beauty (complete) (3 CDs)
Naxos 8.550490-492

Sleeping Beauty (Highlights)
Naxos 8.550079

Nutcracker (complete) (2 CDs)
Naxos 8.550324-325

Nutcracker (Highlights)
Naxos 8.550515

Nutcracker (Highlights) / Swan Lake (Highlights)
Naxos 8.550050

Orchestral Music

(a) Symphonies

Tchaikovsky wrote six symphonies. The first of these, sometimes known as Winter Daydreams, was completed in its first version in 1866 but later revised. The second of the symphonies, the so-called Little Russian was composed in 1872 but revised eight years later. Of the other symphonies the fifth, with its motto theme and waltz movement in the place of a scherzo was written in 1888, while the last completed symphony, known as the "Pathétique", was first performed under Tchaikovsky's direction shortly before his death in 1893.

☛ Recommended Recordings

Symphony No. 1
Naxos 8.550517

Symphonies Nos. 2 & 4
Naxos 8.550488

Symphony No. 3
Naxos 8.550518

Manfred Symphony, Op. 58
Naxos 8.550224

Symphony No. 5
Naxos 8.550716

Symphony No. 6
Naxos 8.550782

(b) Fantasy Overtures and other works

Tchaikovsky turned to literary and dramatic sources for a number of orchestral compositions. His first Fantasy Overture after Shakespeare, Romeo and Juliet, was written 1869 and later twice revised. Bunya is a symphonic fantasia inspired by The Tempest and the last of the Shakespearean fantasy overtures, Hamlet, was written in 1888. Francesca da Rimini translates into musical terms the illicit love of Francesca and Paolo, as recounted in Dante's Inferno and Manfred, written in 1885, draws inspiration from the poem of that name by Byron. The Voyevoda is described as a symphonic ballad and is based on a poem by Mickiewicz. Other, smaller scale orchestral compositions include the Serenade for strings, the popular Italian Capriccio, and rather less well known, four orchestral suites. Tchaikovsky thought little of his 1812 Overture, with its patriotic celebration of victory against Napoleon seventy years before, while Marche Slave had a topical patriotic purpose. Souvenir de Florence, originally for string sextet, was completed in 1892 in its final version.

☛ Recommended Recordings

Capriccio Italien / 1812 Overture
Romeo and Juliet / Marche Slave
Naxos 8.550500

Voyevode
Naxos 8.550224

Serenade for Strings / Souvenir de Florence
Naxos 8.550404

Hamlet
Naxos 8.550517

The Tempest
Naxos 8.550518

Francesca da Rimini
Naxos 8.550782

Suites Nos. 1 & 2
Naxos 8.550644

Suites Nos. 3 & 4
Naxos 8.550728

(c) Concertos

The first of Tchaikovsky's three piano concertos has become the most generally popular of all romantic piano concertos. The second concerto is less well known, while the third, started in 1893, consists of a single movement Allegro de concert. Tchaikovsky's single Violin Concerto, rejected as being too difficult by the leading violinist in Russia, Leopold Auer, later found a firm place in repertoire. For solo cello Tchaikovsky wrote the Rococo Variations and the Pezzo capriccioso. Shorter pieces for violin and orchestra include the Sérénade mélancholique and the Valse-scherzo. Souvenir d'un lieu cher, written as an expression of gratitude for hospitality to Madame von Meck, was originally for violin and piano.

☛ **Recommended Recordings**

Piano Concerto No. 1
Naxos 8.550137

Piano Concertos Nos. 1 and 3
Andante and Finale, Op. 79
Naxos 8.550819

Piano Concerto No. 2 / Fantaisie de Concert
Naxos 8.550820

Rococo Variations / Pezzo Capriccioso /
Nocturne
Naxos 8.550519

Violin Concerto / Sérénade mélancholique /
Souvenir d'un lieu cher
Naxos 8.550124

Violin Concerto
Naxos 8.550153

Chamber Music

Tchaikovsky's chamber music includes three string quartets. The slow movement of the first of these has proved very popular both in its original form and in an arrangement by the composer for cello and string orchestra. The Andante funèbre of the third quartet also exists in an arrangement by the composer for violin and piano.

Piano Music

Tchaikovsky provided a quantity of music for the piano, particularly in the form of shorter pieces suited to the lucrative amateur market. Collections of pieces published by the composer include The Seasons, a set of twelve pieces, one for each month, and a number of sets of pieces of varying degrees of difficulty.

☛ **Recommended Recordings**

The Seasons / Chanson triste / Nocturnes etc.
Naxos 8.550233

Piano Music
Polka peu dansante / Romance
Dumka-Russian rustic scene / L'espiègle
Rêverie / Humoresque / Dialogue / Danse russe
Nocturne / Scherzo / Rêverie du soir / Mazurka
Tendres reproches / Capriccioso
Polacca de concert
Naxos 8.550504

Piano Works Vol. I
(Piano Sonata Op. 37 / Six Morceaux Op. 51)
Naxos 8.553063

Vocal Music

Tchaikovsky wrote a considerable quantity of songs and duets, including settings of Goethe's Mignon songs as well as of verses by a number of his contemporaries.

Telemann, Georg Philipp

(1681 - 1767)

Among the most prolific and most famous composers of his generation, Telemann was born in 1681 at Magdeburg and educated at the University of Leipzig, where he founded the University Collegium Musicum and was the city council's preferred candidate for the position of Thomascantor in 1723, when Bach was eventually appointed. Telemann had established himself in Hamburg in 1721 as Cantor of the Johanneum and director of music for the five principal city churches. He remained in Hamburg until his death in 1767, when he was succeeded by his godson, Carl Philipp Emanuel Bach, son of Johann Sebastian Bach. In his long career Telemann wrote a great deal of music of all kinds in a style that extends the late Baroque into the age of Haydn.

Church Music

Telemann's church music includes 46 settings of the Passion and 1043 cantatas, oratorios, Masses, motets and psalms.

Operas

Telemann also wrote operas and other music for the stage, little of it now heard.

Secular Vocal Music

Of the various secular cantatas written by Telemann the best known today is Der Schulmeister.

Orchestral Music

In addition to a number of suites or overtures, Telemann wrote nearly fifty concertos for various solo instruments, including 21 for violin and eight double violin concertos. A Viola Concerto remains a necessary part of an otherwise meagre concerto repertoire, and there are useful concertos for one and for two French horns, for trumpet and for recorder. A number of instrumental compositions were brought together in the Tafelmusik or Musique de Table of 1733.

☞ **Recommended Recording**
Recorder Suite / Viola Concerto
Tafelmusik (excerpts)
Naxos 8.550156

Chamber Music

Telemann was equally prolific in the field of chamber music, providing a quantity of compositions for solo instruments, including a set of a dozen Fantasias for unaccompanied violin, and works for various groups of instruments, duos, trios, quartets and quintets.

☞ **Recommended Recording**
Trio Sonatas in D minor & G major
Naxos 8.550377

Tippett, Michael (1905 -)

Tippett, born in London in 1905, studied music at the Royal College before embarking on an early career as a composer, supported by work with the orchestra and choir of Morley College in South London, tasks that he found socially relevant. His idiosyncratic style developed relatively slowly, to flower in a series of remarkable operas, for which he provided his own libretti. Public recognition came with a knighthood in 1966 and appointment as a Companion of Honour in 1979.

Operas

Tippett's first important opera, The Midsummer Marriage, was staged at Covent Garden in 1955, followed six years later by King Priam, The Knot Garden in 1970 and The Ice Break in 1977, all of them, in one way or another, exploring a world illuminated by Jungian theories of psychology.

Orchestral Music

Well known orchestral music includes a Concerto for Double String Orchestra, a Triple Concerto, Little Music for Strings and a Fantasia Concertante on a Theme of Corelli, as well as four symphonies. Tippett's debt to English tradition is heard in his Divertimento on Sellinger's Round, using an Elizabethan melody.

Vocal and Choral Music

Tippett's A Child of Our Time seemed highly relevant to the state of the world at the time of its completion in 1941. Other remarkable and moving choral works include The Vision of St. Augustine, completed in 1965. Among solo songs or song cycles The Heart's Assurance, settings of poems by Sidney Keyes and Alun Lewis, is of central importance.

Chamber Music

Tippett's chamber music includes four string quartets that reflect developments in his style, with four piano sonatas.

Tomkins, Thomas (1572 - 1656)

The son of a musician employed at the Welsh Cathedral of St. Davids, Thomas Tomkins became master of the choristers and organist at Worcester Cathedral and later served as organist to the Chapel Royal. His career as a church musician was ended by the Civil War and the surrender of Worcester to the parliamentary army in 1646. His brothers Giles, Robert and Nathaniel were also important in the musical life of the country.

Church Music

Thomas Tomkins was primarily a composer of church music, with five service settings and a number of anthems that remain in many cases in English cathedral repertoire. These last include the moving lament for Absalom, When David heard.

Secular Vocal Music

Tomkins added to the repertoire of the English madrigal with works for three, four, five and six parts. The madrigals were published in London in 1622 and include a number of sacred songs with settings of pastoral verses.

Instrumental Music

Tomkins wrote music for instrumental consort, including fantasias and dances, in particular pavanes and galliards.

☛ Recommended Recording

Works for Viols and Voices
Naxos 8.550602

Keyboard Music

The compositions of Tomkins include a relatively small number of keyboard pieces, continuing the tradition, here as elsewhere, of the generation of William Byrd.

Torelli, Giuseppe (1658 - 1709)

Torelli has some importance in the development of the solo concerto and the concerto grosso. He spent much of his career in Bologna as a member of the distinguished musical establishment of San Petronio, where his near contemporary Corelli had once served.

Instrumental Music

Torelli's concerti grossi include an example of the contemporary Christmas concerto, with a pastoral movement recalling the presence of shepherds in the fields near Bethlehem in the Biblical story of the birth of Christ. He made considerable use of the solo trumpet in concertos, sinfonias and sonatas.

☞ **Recommended Recording**
> *Concerto Grosso Op. 8, No.6*
> *Naxos 8.550567*

Tournemire, Charles (1870 - 1939)

A pupil of César Franck and of Widor, Charles Tournemire continued the French tradition of organist-composers. Much of his music is deeply rooted in his Catholic faith, in which he found a refuge and solution to the horrors of contemporary materialism.

Organ Music

For the organ Tournemire wrote his compendious L'orgue mystique (The Mystical Organ), which makes use of plainchant associated with each Sunday of the year, a project that he saw as a counterpart to Bach's work for the Lutheran liturgy. Other organ works include Symphonie-choral, Symphonie sacrée and two Fresques symphoniques sacrées.

Orchestral Music

Tournemire completed eight symphonies, from the first in 1900, the Romantique, to the eighth in 1924, La symphonie du triomphe de la mort (Symphony of the Triumph of Death).

☞ **Recommended Recording**
> *Symphonies Nos. 1 & 5*
> *Marco Polo 8.223476*
>
> *Symphonies Nos. 2 & 4*
> *Marco Polo 8.223478*
>
> *Symphonies Nos. 3 & 8*
> *Marco Polo 8.223808*
>
> *Symphonies No. 7*
> *Marco Polo 8.223877-8*

Turina, Joaquín (1882 - 1949)

A native of Seville, Joaquin Turina won local success before travelling to Madrid, where he met Manuel de Falla and was further influenced by the prevailing currents of musical nationalism. Study in Paris at the Schola cantorum, was followed, in 1914, by a return to Madrid, where he made his subsequent career, in spite of the difficulties he and many others of his background encountered during the days of the republic.

Orchestral Music

Turina won success in 1913 with his symphonic poem Le procésion del Rocio, a work that remains in popular repertory, with the later Danzas fantásticas and the Rapsodia sinfónica for piano and orchestra.

Chamber Music

Turina's chamber music includes La Oración del torero (The Toreador's Prayer), for string quartet or string orchestra, and a number of works that declare their national allegiance and inspiration in their titles, Recuerdos de la antigua España (Memories of Ancient Spain) for lute quartet, and a string quartet de la guitarra.

Piano Music

A similar element is present in piano compositions by Turina, a significant body of work, from the early Suite, Sevilla, representing a recurrent element in his inspiration to the 1943 Por las calles de Sevilla (Through the Streets of Seville).

Vocal Music

Songs by Turina include the interesting Poema en forma de canciones (Poem in the Form of Songs), a cycle of five songs with words by Campoamor.

Guitar Music

Turina wrote music for guitar that is an important part of the repertoire of this essentially Spanish instrument. These works include Sevillana, Fandanguillo, Ráfaga, Sonata and Homenaje a Tárrega.

Tye, Christopher (c. 1505 - ?1572)

The English composer Christopher Tye seems to have spent much of his life at or near Cambridge and at Ely Cathedral.

Church Music

Tye's church music includes Latin and English works, settings of the Mass for the traditional Catholic liturgy and English settings for the reformed liturgy under Edward VI.

☛ **Recommended Recording**
Missa Euge bone / Peccavimus / Omnesgentes
Naxos 8.550937

Instrumental Music

Tye wrote compositions for instrumental consort, including a number of In nomines, following the original example of his contemporary Taverner.

Varèse, Edgard (1883 - 1965)

Preferring the concept of organized sound to that of music, the French-born composer Edgard Varèse exercised a strong influence on the contemporary avant-garde, particularly in the United States, where he spent some time from 1915 until 1928, when he returned to Paris. He returned to America in 1933, eventually finding the necessary backing for his electro-acoustic research.

He enjoyed an earlier career as a conductor of some distinction, but is now remembered chiefly for his experiment in composition and for the influence his work exerted over younger composers.

Works

Varèse made an early impression with his Offrandes for soprano and small orchestra in 1921 and the remarkable Octandre, for wind instruments and double bass, first heard in New York in 1924. Later organized sound included Ionisation for thirteen percussion-players, completed in 1931, and Déserts, with its combination of instrumental performance and recorded tape.

Vaughan Williams, Ralph
(1872 - 1958)

One of the leading English composers of his generation, Vaughan Williams was a pupil of Parry, Charles Wood and Stanford, and later of Bruch and Ravel. In his work as a composer he went some way towards creating a specifically English musical idiom, influenced by his interest in folk-song, but coloured by his own personal vision and language.

Stage Works

The stage music of Vaughan Williams includes the Shakespearean opera Sir John in Love, based on The Merry Wives of Windsor, the masque for dancing Job and the morality The Pilgrim's Progress, based on John Bunyan. Incidental music for the theatre includes music for The Wasps by Aristophanes, of which the Overture is often heard. He also wrote a number of film-scores.

Orchestral Music

(a) Symphonies

Vaughan Williams wrote nine symphonies, the first of these with solo singers, chorus and orchestra A Sea Symphony, with words taken from Walt Whitman, the second "A London" Symphony and the third a "Pastoral" Symphony. The Sixth Symphony, completed in its first version in 1947, seemed to break new ground and was followed by a seventh, the Sinfonia Antartica, that had its origin in a film soundtrack.

☞ Recommended Recordings

Symphonies No. 3 "Pastoral" and No. 6
Naxos 8.550733

Symphony No. 2 "London"
Naxos 8.550734

49th Parallel / Story of a Flemish Farm
Coastal Command
Three Portraits from the England of Elizabeth
Marco Polo 8.223665

(b) Concertos

Compositions by Vaughan Williams for solo instrument and orchestra include the pastoral romance The Lark Ascending, for solo violin, and a Concerto accademico for solo violin and string orchestra. There is an attractive concerto for oboe and two more unusual concertos, one for harmonica and the other for bass tuba. Flos campi uses a solo viola and is scored also for a small choir and chamber orchestra.

(c) Suites etc.

Vaughan Williams made direct use of folk-song in his three Norfolk Rhapsodies, his Fantasia on Greensleeves, for solo flute, harp and strings and in his English Folksong Suite for military band, among other works.

His Fantasia on a Theme by Thomas Tallis for two string orchestras returns to the 16th century for its musical inspiration.

Vocal and Choral Music

Vaughan Williams made a substantial contribution to English choral and vocal repertoire in compositions that include the fine Serenade to Music, completed in 1938. Other compositions range from oratorio to hymn-tune, from folk-song arrangement to the evocative On Wenlock Edge, a setting of poems by A.E. Housman.

Verdi, Giuseppe (1813 - 1901)

Verdi dominated the world of Italian opera from his first considerable success in 1842 with Nabucco until his final Shakespearean operas Otello, staged at La Scala, Milan, in 1887, and Falstaff, mounted at the same opera-house in 1893. His career coincided with the rise of Italian nationalism and the unification of the country, causes with which he was openly associated.

Operas

The best known of Verdi's 28 operas are Nabucco (Nebuchadnezzar), Macbeth, Rigoletto, Il Trovatore, La Traviata, Les Vêpres Siciliennes (The Sicilian Vespers), Simon Boccanegra, Un Ballo in Maschera (A Masked

Ball), La Forza del Destino (The Force of Destiny), Don Carlos, Aida, Otello and Falstaff.

Recommended Recordings

Aida (2 CD's)
Naxos 8.660033-4

Il Trovatore (2 CD's)
Naxos 8.660023-24

La Traviata (Complete Opera) (2 CD's)
Naxos 8.660011-12

La Traviata (Highlights)
Naxos 8.553041

Opera Choruses:
Nabucco / Don Carlos / La Traviata / Ernani
La Battaglia di Legnano / Il Trovatore / Otello
Macbeth / La Forza del Destino / Aida
Naxos 8.550241

Overtures Vol. 1
Aroldo / Il corsaro / Luisa Miller / La traviata
Alzira / Un ballo in maschera
Oberto, conte di San Bonifacio / Aida / Attila
I vespri siciliani
Naxos 8.553018

Overtures Vol. 2
Ernani / Il finto Stanislao / Don Carlo
Giovanni d'Arco / Rigoletto / Nabucco
I masnadieri / Macbeth
La battaglia di Legnano / I due Foscari
La forza del destino
Naxos 8.553089

Overtures and Preludes:
Aida / La Traviata / La Forza del Destino
I Vespri Siciliani / Otello / Nabucco
Naxos 8.550091

Rigoletto (Complete Opera) (2 CD's)
Naxos 8.660013-14

Rigoletto (Highlights)
Naxos 8.553042

Soprano Opera Arias from Don Carlo
La Forza del Destino / Otello
Naxos 8.550606

Tenor Opera Arias from Aida / Don Carlo
Il Trovatore / Macbeth / Rigoletto
Naxos 8.550497

Soprano Opera Arias from Rigoletto
Naxos 8.550605

Church Music

In addition to settings of the Te Deum and the Stabat Mater, Verdi wrote an impressive large scale setting of the Requiem, its origin stemming from the death of Rossini in 1868 and the death of the writer Manzoni. The Requiem is a work of operatic magnificence, none the less moving for its theatrical elements.

The Quattro pezzi sacri (Four Sacred Pieces) were written at various times in Verdi's later years. The first, Ave Maria sulla scala enigmatica, written in 1889, was followed, on publication, by a Stabat mater, the Laudi alla Vergine Maria, on a text from Dante, and a Te Deum for double chorus and orchestra. The Four Pieces were published in 1898.

Victoria, Tomás Luís de

(1548 - 1611)

The greatest Spanish composer of the second half of the 16th century, Victoria was born in 1548 in Avila, where he had his early musical training as a cathedral chorister. He studied further in Rome, continuing in the service of the Jesuit Collegio Germanico before joining the newly formed order of Oratorians. He returned to Spain to a convent chaplaincy in the service of the Dowager Empress Maria, sister of King Philip II, retaining the chaplaincy until his death in Madrid in 1611.

Church Music

Victoria left some twenty settings of the Mass, in addition to a number of Magnificat settings, Lamentations, responsories, anthems, psalms, motets and hymns.

☛ **Recommended Recording**
Missa O quam gloriosum
Missa O magnum mysterium
Naxos 8.550575

Vierne, Louis (1870 - 1937)

Influenced by César Franck and Widor, Louis Vierne belongs to the French tradition of organists, succeeding the latter at the Conservatoire and later becoming organist at Notre Dame. He is an important figure among French organ composers.

Organ Music

Vierne wrote six Organ Symphonies, four collections of Pièces de fantaisie and 24 Pièces en style libre (Pieces in Free Style).

☛ **Recommended Recording**
Organ Symphonies Nos. 3 and 6
Naxos 8.553524

Vieuxtemps, Henri (1820 - 1881)

Henri Vieuxtemps attracted early attention as a prodigy, making his first public appearance as a violinist at the age of six. He later studied with Charles de Bériot and moved with him from Brussels to Paris in 1829. Two years later he embarked on the first of his concert tours, impressing musicians such as Schumann and Paganini. He took composition lessons with Sechter in Vienna and later with Reicha in Paris and wrote violin music for his own use on extended concert tours that took him to the major cities of Europe and, with the pianist Thalberg, to the United States of America. In 1871 he was appointed professor at the Brussels Conservatoire, where his pupils included Eugène Ysaÿe. He died in Algeria in 1881 after eight years of intermittent ill-health that had impeded his teaching and put an end to his playing.

Orchestral Music

Vieuxtemps occupies an important position in the history of the violin concerto, largely fulfilling his aim of infusing the concerto as Viotti had left it with music that made use of the newly developed technical possibilities of the violin. This achievement is demonstrated in his seven Violin Concertos. He also wrote smaller works for solo violin and orchestra, two Cello Concertos and a Duo brillant for violin, cello, piano and orchestra.

Chamber Music

Vieuxtemps wrote a number of pieces for violin and piano. These include operatic fantasias and variations on other well known melodies in a series of twelve Duos concertantes. These and other similar compositions provided topical material for concert tours, including a Souvenir d'Amérique based on Yankee Doodle and a Souvenir de Russie, as well as a Caprice on 16th and 17th century English airs. He also left three String Quartets and a Viola Sonata.

Villa-Lobos, Heitor (1887 - 1959)

Villa-Lobos came to occupy a leading position in the musical life of his native Brazil, a country the varying musical traditions of which he absorbed as a young man by extensive and adventurous travel throughout the region. After a period in Paris, he returned home in 1930, eventually winning official recognition and making a significant contribution to Brazilian music education. His varied compositions include stage-works, choral and instrumental compositions, chamber music, songs and piano music. His instrumental works include a series of Bachianas brasileiras and Chôros, the latter called after the traditional street-music of Rio de Janeiro.

Guitar Music

The Etudes and Preludes written by Villa-Lobos for solo guitar are a familiar part of the repertoire of that instrument.

☛ **Recommended Recordings**

Guitar Concerto
Naxos 8.550729

Preludes / Choro No. 1 Como Pode o Peixe
Nesta Rua / Samba Leie
Naxos 8.550226

Amazonas / Erosão / Gênesis
Dawn in a Tropical Forest
Marco Polo 8.223357

Chôros Nos. 8 and 9
Marco Polo 8.220322

Dança frenética / Danças africanas
Dança dos mosquitos / Rudepoema
Marco Polo 8.223552

Discovery of Brazil
Marco Polo 8.223551

Pequena Suite / Capriccio, Op. 49
Prelúdio, Op. 20 / Elégie, Op. 87
Bachianas brasileiras Nos. 2 and 6
Assobio a jato
Marco Polo 8.223527

Piano Trios Nos. 1 and 3
Marco Polo 8.223182

Piano Trio No. 2 / Cello Sonata No. 2
Marco Polo 8.223164

String Quartets Nos. 1, 8 and 13
Marco Polo 8.223389

String Quartets Nos. 2 and 7
Marco Polo 8.223394

String Quartets Nos. 3, 10 and 15
Marco Polo 8.223393

String Quartets Nos. 4, 6 and 14
Marco Polo 8.223391

String Quartets Nos. 5, 9 and 12
Marco Polo 8.223392

String Quartets Nos. 11, 16 and 17
Marco Polo 8.223390

Symphony No. 6 / Rudá :Dio dámore
Marco Polo 8.223720

Viotti, Giovanni Battista

(1755 - 1824)

A pupil of Pugnani, Giovanni Battista Viotti could claim to represent the continuing tradition of Italian violin-playing that started in the last quarter of the 17th century with Corelli. Pugnani had been a pupil of Somis, who had been a pupil of Corelli. Viotti made his first concert tour abroad with his teacher in 1780, moving thereafter to Paris, where he made a strong impression with his playing, entered the service of Marie-Antoinette and concerned himself with operatic administration. The Revolution in 1792 caused him to seek refuge in London, where he played at the concerts organized by Salomon, performances in which Haydn was involved during his two visits to London in the 1790s. Political exile from London took him for eighteen months to Germany and on his return to London at the beginning of the new century he occupied himself chiefly with the wine trade, rarely playing in public. The failure of his business was followed by appointment in 1819 as director of the Paris Opéra, a position he was compelled to relinquish two years later, when he returned to stay with friends in London, dying there in 1824. His career as a performer was relatively short, but his influence on violin-playing was very considerable, witnessed notably by the younger generation of players that included Rode, Kreutzer and Baillot.

Orchestral Music

Viotti's orchestral music consists principally of his 29 violin concertos, in a style that develops from the compositions of the early 1780s to the romantic lyricism of the later concertos, works that strongly influenced the concertos of younger violinist-composers.

Chamber Music

Viotti's chamber music includes fifteen Quatuors concertants, a number of trios for two violins and cello, duos, many of them for two violins, and works for solo violin. These exhibit, in general, the particular features of Viotti's style of playing, with the violin usually enjoying prominence.

Vivaldi, Antonio (1678 - 1741)

The Italian composer and violinist Antonio Vivaldi was born in Venice in 1678 and after his ordination in 1703 embarked on an intermittent career in the service of the Ospedale della Pietà, an institution for the education of orphan, illegitimate or indigent girls, an establishment with a formidable musical reputation. His later career brought involvement in opera. As a composer Vivaldi was prolific, with some 500 concertos to his credit, in addition to a quantity of works for the church and for the theatre. He left Venice in 1741 in the apparent hope of

finding new patrons in Vienna, where he died shortly after his arrival in the city.

Church Music

The surviving church music of Vivaldi includes the well known Gloria, in addition to a number of settings of psalms and motets.

☛ **Recommended Recording**

Gloria / Beatus vir
Naxos 8.550767

Operas

None of the fifty odd operas of Vivaldi remain in standard repertoire.

Concertos

The most famous of all Vivaldi's concertos are I quattro stagioni (The Four Seasons), characteristic compositions to which the composer attached explanatory programmatic sonnets. These four concertos, for solo violin, string orchestra and harpsichord, form part of a collection Il cimento dell'armonia e dell'invenzione (The Contest of Harmony and Invention), one of seven collections of such compositions published in the composer's lifetime. In addition to concertos for solo violin, Vivaldi also wrote concertos for many other solo instruments, including the flute, oboe, bassoon, cello and viola d'amore, and for groups of solo instruments.

☛ Recommended Recordings

Cello Concerti, Vol. 1
(RV 398, 399, 404, 406, 412 & 419)
Naxos 8.550907

Cello Concerti, Vol. 2
(RV 400, 401, 408, 413, 422 & 531)
Naxos 8.550908

Cello Concerti, Vol. 3
(RV 402, 403, 407, 409, 418, 423 & 424)
Naxos 8.550909

Cello Concerti, Vol. 4
(RV 405, 411, 414, 416, 417, 420 & 421)
Naxos 8.550910

Concerti Op. 3 L'estro armonico
Nos. 1, 2, 4, 7, 8, 10 & 11
Naxos 8.550160

Famous Concerti
Naxos 8.550384

Flute Concerti
Naxos 8.550385

Oboe Concerti Vol. 1
(RV 450, 452-454, 534-536)
Naxos 8.550859

Oboe Concerti Vol. 2
(RV 447, 451, 455, 457, 461 & 463)
Naxos 8.550860

The Four Seasons
Concerto alla rustica RV. 151
Naxos 8.550056

Violin Concerti, Op. 8
(Il cimento dell'armonia e dell'invenzione),
Nos. 5-12
Naxos 8.550189

Wind Concerti
Naxos 8.550386

Wind Concerti (for Double Winds)
(RV 122, 533, 537, 538, 539, 545 & 560)
Naxos 8.553204

Chamber Music

Vivaldi wrote a number of sonatas and trio sonatas, many of them designed for one or two violins and basso continuo. He also wrote a series of chamber concertos, compositions similar in approach to the solo and multiple concertos, but scored for smaller groups of instruments.

☛ Recommended Recording

Trio Sonatas Op. 1, Nos. 11 & 12
Op. 5, No. 5
Naxos 8.550377

Wagner, Richard (1813 - 1883)

Wagner was a remarkable innovator both in harmony and in the structure of his work, creating his own version of the Gesamtkunstwerk, dramatic compositions in which the arts were brought together into a single unity. As a man he was prepared to sacrifice his family and friends in the cause of his own music and his overt anti-semitism has attracted unwelcome attention to ideas that are remote from his real work as a musician. In the later part of his career Wagner enjoyed the support of King Ludwig II of Bavaria and was finally able to establish his own theatre and festival at the Bavarian town of Bayreuth. He developed the use of the Leitmotiv (leading motif) as a principle of musical unity, his dramatic musical structure depending on the interweaving of melodies or fragments of melody associated with characters, incidents or ideas in the drama. His Prelude to the love tragedy Tristan und Isolde led to a new world of harmony.

Operas & Music Dramas

Wagner won his first operatic success in Dresden with the opera Rienzi, based on a novel by Edward Bulwer-Lytton. This was followed a year later, in 1843, by Der fliegende Holländer (The Flying Dutchman), derived from a legend recounted by Heine of the Dutchman fated to sail the seas until redeemed by true love. Tannhäuser,

dealing with the medieval Minnesinger of that name, was staged in Dresden in 1845. Wagner's involvement in the revolution of 1848 and subsequent escape from Dresden led to the staging of his next dramatic work, Lohengrin, in Weimar, under the supervision of Liszt. The four operas that form the tetralogy The Ring, Das Rheingold, Die Walküre (The Valkyries), Siegfried and Götterdämmerung (The Twilight of the Gods), is a monument of dramatic and musical achievement that occupied the composer for a number of years. Other music dramas by Wagner include Tristan und Isolde, Die Meistersinger von Nürnberg (The Mastersingers of Nuremberg), and the final work, Parsifal.

☛ Recommended Recordings

Tannhäuser / Lohengrin
The Flying Dutchman (Orchestral excerpts)
Naxos 8.550136

The Flying Dutchman (2 CD's)
Naxos 8.660025-26

The Ring-Orchestral Highlights
Naxos 8.550211

Tristan und Isolde / Die Meistersinger
Parsifal / Götterdämmerung (Orchestral excerpts)
Naxos 8.550498

Orchestral Music

The best known of Wagner's orchestral compositions is the Siegfried Idyll, an aubade written for the composer's second wife, Cosima, illegitimate daughter of Liszt and former wife of Wagner's friend and supporter Hans von Bülow.

Songs

At the root of Wagner's drama of forbidden love, Tristan und Isolde, was his own affair with Matilde Wesendonk, wife of a banker upon whose support he relied during years of exile in Switzerland. The five Wesendonk-Lieder are settings of verses by Matilde Wesendonk.

☞ **Recommended Recording**

Wesendonk-Lieder
Naxos 8.550400

Walton, William (1902 - 1983)

William Walton represents a period in English music between Vaughan Williams and Benjamin Britten. After a period as a chorister at Christ Church, Oxford, he later failed to complete his graduate studies and was for a time dependent on the patronage and encouragement of the Sitwell family. He spent his later years on the island of Ischia.

Orchestral Music

Walton composed two symphonies, the first of which was completed in 1935 and has become part of the standard orchestral repertoire. His Violin and Cello Concertos are now frequently performed while his Viola Concerto is the most important 20th century work for that instrument. Among his most popular works are the two orchestral suites from Façade, originally designed to accompany chanted poems by Edith Sitwell, and the Overtures Portsmouth Point and Scapino, together with the coronation marches, Crown Imperial and Orb and Sceptre. Walton wrote music for a number of films, some of which has been adapted for concert performance including music for Henry V.

☞ **Recommended Recording**

Symphony No. 2 / Viola Concerto
Naxos 8.553402

Choral Works

The oratorio Belshazzar's Feast, its biblical text adapted by Osbert Sitwell, remains an imposing element in English choral repertoire.

Weber, Carl María von (1786 - 1826)

Carl Maria von Weber, a cousin of Mozart's wife Constanze, was trained as a musician from his childhood, the son of a versatile musician who had founded his own travelling theatre company. He made a favourable impression as a pianist and then as a music director, notably in the opera-houses of Prague and Dresden. Here he introduced various reforms and was a pioneer of the craft of conducting without the use of violin or keyboard instrument. As a composer he won a lasting reputation with the first important Romantic German opera, Der Freischütz.

Operas

The opera Der Freischütz (The Marksman), first staged in Berlin in 1821, blends many of the ingredients typical of German Romanticism, simple peasant virtues mingling with the magic and latent evil of the forest, where the hero's magic bullets are forged at midnight. The grand heroic-Romantic opera Euryanthe is better known for its overture as is the opera Oberon, written for London in 1826.

Orchestral Music

Weber's two concertos and the concertino for clarinet were written for the clarinettist Heinrich Baermann. Weber also wrote two piano concertos and a Konzertstück for piano and orchestra for his own use, as well as a useful Horn Concertino and Bassoon Concerto. His Aufforderung zum Tanze (Invitation to the Dance) is well known in an orchestral version of a work originally written for piano.

☞ Recommended Recordings

Clarinet Concertos Nos. 1 & 2 / Concertino
Naxos 8.550378

Invitation to the Dance
Naxos 8.550081

Piano Concertos Nos. 1 and 2
Polonaise brillante, Op. 72
Konzertstück, Op. 79
Naxos 8.550957

Symphonies Nos. 1 & 2
Dances and Marches from Die Drei Pintos,
Turandot & Silvana
Naxos 8.550928

Chamber Music

Weber's chamber music includes a Clarinet Quintet and a Grand Duo Concertant for clarinet and piano, successors to the concertos and concertino for Baermann.

☞ Recommended Recording

Grand Duo Concertant Op. 48
Quintet Op. 34 / Variations Op. Posth & Op. 33
Naxos 8.553122

Piano Music

Aufforderung zum Tanz (Invitation to the Dance) is a charming programme piece following the progress of an invitation to dance, as a young man escorts his partner to the dance-floor and engages in polite conversation. Weber's other piano compositions include four sonatas for the instrument.

☛ **Recommended Recordings**

Piano Works Vol. 1
Sonata, Op. 24 / Variations Opp. 2 & 40
Invitation to the Dance, Op. 65
Naxos 8.550988

Piano Works Vol. 2
Sonata, Op. 39 / Variations Opp. 6 & 55
Grande Polonaise, Op. 21
Naxos 8.550989

Piano Works Vol. 3
Sonata, Op. 49 / Variations, Opp. 5, 7, 9
Momento capriccioso, Op. 12
Naxos 8.550990

Piano Works Vol. 4
Sonata, Op. 70 / Variations, Op. 28
Les Adieux, Op. 81 / Rondo brillante
Polacca brillante
Naxos 8.553006

Webern, Anton von (1883 - 1945)

Webern, with Alban Berg, was a pupil of Arnold Schoenberg in Vienna, moving in style to atonalism and then serial technique, writing music of brief concision and often of extreme delicacy. His influence on later composers has been very considerable.

Orchestral Music

Webern's sensitive technical command is shown in his Orchestral Variations of 1940, while his innovative approach to the past is demonstrated in his version of a Bach fugue, Fuga (Ricercata).

Weelkes, Thomas (1576 - 1623)

Weelkes served briefly as organist at Winchester College before his appointment to a similar position at Chichester Cathedral, from which he was eventually dismissed for drunkenness and profanity of language. He was for a time associated with the Chapel Royal. His achievement as a composer lies in his madrigals and in music he wrote for the Church of England.

Church Music

Weelkes wrote a number of service settings that remain in continued use. His anthems include the well known Hosanna to the Son of David. The sacred madrigal,

When David heard, treats with the deepest feeling King David's lament for the death of his son Absalom.

☞ **Recommended Recording**
Anthems
Naxos 8.553209

Madrigals

Weelkes published a number of collections of madrigals, following the musical fashions of the turn of the century, the first collection published in 1597. These include On the plaines Fairie traines, Though my carriage be but careless. As Vesta was from Latmos hill ascending was his contribution to the collection in honour of Queen Elizabeth, The Triumphs of Oriana.

Weill, Kurt (1900 - 1950)

Kurt Weill was an important figure in German musical life during the period of the Weimar Republic. He left Germany in 1933 and later became a citizen of the United States of America, turning his musical attention to compositions for Broadway.

Stage Works

Weill collaborated with Bertold Brecht in Die Dreigroschenoper (The Threepenny Opera), a topical derivative of The Beggar's Opera set in contemporary Germany, with music strongly influenced by the jazz of the period. Other collaborations with Brecht included Aufstieg und Fall der Stadt Mahagonny (The Rise and Fall of the City of Mahagonny). His work for Broadway is now attracting revived attention.

Orchestral Music

Weill arranged an instrumental suite from Der Dreigroschenopfer, the Kleine Dreigroschenmusik.

Weiss, Silvius Leopold (1686 - 1750)

Weiss was a leading lutenist in the time of J.S. Bach, whom he met during the former's visit to Leipzig and later in Dresden, where Weiss was a member of the court chapel. He wrote a considerable quantity of music for the lute.

Lute Music

Weiss left some six hundred compositions for lute, described as Sonatas and Partitas. These form a major part of the repertoire of the instrument.

☞ **Recommended Recording**
Sonatas for Lute
Naxos 8.550470

White, Robert (c. 1538 - 1574)

Robert White was trained as a singer at Trinity College, Cambridge, and later served as Master of the Choristers at Ely Cathedral. He seems later to have been employed at Chester Cathedral and finally at Westminster Abbey.

Church Music

White's church music includes settings of a number of Latin texts, with two versions of the Holy Week Lamentations. He also wrote anthems for the English liturgy.

☛ **Recommended Recording**

Lamentation for 5 voices
Naxos 8.550572

Widor, Charles-Marie (1844 - 1937)

Widor occupies an important position in the idiosyncratic tradition of French organ music, serving as organist at St Sulpice in Paris for 64 years. His organ pupils included Tournemire, Vierne, Albert Schweitzer and Marcel Dupré, with composition pupils such as Honegger and Milhaud. His works include chamber music, choral and vocal works and orchestral works, with symphonies that also involve the organ.

Organ Music

Much of Widor's organ music calls for the full resources of the great instruments made for major Paris churches by Cavaillé-Coll. Of particular interest are Widor's ten Organ Symphonies, including the eighth, the Symphonie gothique. Some movements from the symphonies have won a special position in virtuoso repertoire, in particular the famous Toccata that ends Symphony No. 5 and the Marche pontificale of Symphony No. 1.

Orchestral Music

Three of Widor's five symphonies include the organ in their instrumentation, the Third Symphony, Symphonie antique and Sinfonia sacra. His symphonic poem La nuit de Walpurgis (Walpurgis Night) is scored for chorus and orchestra and the Ouverture espagnole suggests the interest in Spain that led Widor to establish a house in Madrid for the use of French musicians. He left two piano concertos and a Fantaisie for piano and orchestra, with a cello concerto.

Chamber Music

Widor left a quantity of meticulously crafted chamber music, including piano quintets, trios and violin sonatas.

☛ **Recommended Recording**

Piano Trio in B Flat / Piano Quintet in D Minor
Marco Polo 8.223193

Piano Music

Widor's piano music consists largely of shorter pieces, many with descriptive titles.

Operas

While the name of Widor is not immediately associated with opera, he nevertheless had some success with his Les pêcheurs de Saint-Jean (The Fishermen of St John) at the Opéra-Comnique in 1905.

Vocal and Choral Music

Widor contributed to sacred choral and vocal repertoire and to the repertoire of French secular song.

Wiener, Jean (1896 - 1982)

Jean Wiener became a jazz enthusiast after his study at the Paris Conservatoire and in the 1920s formed a jazz piano duo with Clément Doucet. He was of some signifance in the promotion of new music, both by his friends of the Groupe des Six and by composers such as Schoenberg, Berg and Webern. His compositions involve the use of jazz, encompassed with French wit and elegance.

Piano Music

Characteristic piano music by Wiener includes Chicken Reel - Histoire sans paroles, Sonatine syncopée and Touchez pas au Grisbi (Don't touch Grisbi), from the successful film-score, one of some three hundred such works.

Wieniawski, Henryk (1835 - 1880)

A pupil of Massart at the Paris Conservatoire, the Polish violinist Henryk Wieniawski began his career as a virtuoso in earnest in 1851, spending some three years in Russia giving concerts and writing music for his own use. After further concert tours he accepted an invitation from Anton Rubinstein to join the staff of the St Petersburg Conservatory, where he served from 1860 until 1872. Exhausting concert tours of the United States of America were followed by appointment as successor to Vieuxtemps at Brussels Conservatory, where he taught until 1877. At the same time he continued his concert tours, brought to an end only by ill-health and his death in Moscow in 1880.

Violin Music

Wieniawski's compositions were principally for his own use. They include two important violin concertos as well as a number of pieces designed to display his technical and romantic musical accomplishments. His *Souvenir de Moscou*, *Souvenir de Posen* and *Le carnaval russe* may be considered a concession to Russian audiences, while the *Reminiscences of San Francisco* were no doubt designed as a compliment to the audiences of that city.

☛ Recommended Recording

Violin Showpieces
Opp. 4, 6, 7, 11, 15, 16, 17 & 23
Op. 12, No. 2 / Op. 19, Nos. 1-2
Naxos 8.550744

Wilbye, John (1574 - 1638)

The English madrigalist Wilbye spent the greater part of his life in the service of the Kytson family at Hengrave Hall near Bury St. Edmunds.

Madrigals

Wilbye followed the example of Thomas Morley as a composer of madrigals, publishing collections of his work in 1598 and 1609 and contributing one madrigal to the 1601 collection in honour of Queen Elizabeth, The Triumphs of Oriana, the six-voice The Lady Oriana. Well known madrigals by Wilbye include Sweet hony sucking bees, Weep O mine eyes and Happy, O happy he.

Willaert, Adrian (c. 1490 - 1562)

Among the most important composers of his generation, the Flemish musician Willaert was employed at the court of the Dukes of Ferrara and from 1527 as maestro di cappella at St. Mark's in Venice, director of one of the most distinguished musical establishments of the time.

Church Music

Willaert, as might be expected, wrote a quantity of church music, Mass settings and motets, the latter of more importance, evidence of his sure command of contrapuntal technique.

Chansons & Madrigals

In addition to his Latin church music Willaert also wrote French chansons and Italian madrigals.

Wolf, Hugo (1860 - 1903)

The Austrian composer Hugo Wolf carried still further the expressive power of the German Lied. His later life was clouded by illness, depression and final insanity, after a period of intense activity as a composer.

Songs

Collections of songs by Wolf include the 53 Mörike songs of 1888, the settings of Eichendorff, a group of twenty songs published in 1889, 51 Goethe songs completed in 1889, the Spanisches Liederbuch of the same year, and the two collections of the Italienisches Liederbuch, the first written in 1891 and the second in 1896. These, with the many other songs written between 1888 and 1897, form a remarkable body of work in which the texts set were given prominence in performance and served as the real and acknowledged inspiration for the music.

Xenakís, Iannís (1922 -)

The Romanian-born composer Iannis Xenakis, of Greek parentage, settled finally in Paris in 1947, taking out French citizenship. After earlier scientific training in Athens, he was largely self-taught as a composer, in Paris receiving encouragement from Messiaen. There is a close connection between mathematics and music in his work and with architecture.

Works

In addition to the theoretical writings and teaching of Xenakis, there are a varied series of compositions, from the orchestral Metastasis of 1954, Pithoprakta and Achoripsis, to the Empreintes of 1975 and the 1979 Pleïades, for percussion. Other instrumental music includes works for harpsichord, amplified or, in Khoai, unamplified.

Zelenka, Jan Dísmas (1679 - 1745)

The Bohemian composer Jan Dismas Zelenka played the double bass in the royal orchestra in Dresden, whence he was despatched for study in Italy, eventually returning to spend the rest of his life in the Saxon capital. It was expected that he would succeed Heinichen as court Kapellmeister, but the position went, instead, to Hasse, and Zelenka remained, now as Church Composer, a position of much less importance. He won the admiration of distinguished contemporaries, such as Johann Sebastian Bach, for his use of counterpoint, his harmonic imagination and originality, and made some use of Bohemian folk elements.

Orchestral Music

Zelenka's orchestral compositions include a set of five Capriccios, among other compositions in the musical idiom of his time.

Vocal and Choral Music

Much of Zelenka's surviving work is in the form of sacred vocal music, settings of the Mass or of movements from the Mass, of psalms and of canticles.

Zemlinsky, Alexander von

(1871 - 1942)

Friend, teacher and later brother-in-law of Schoenberg, Alexander Zemlinsky won growing importance in the Viennese musical world at the beginning of the twentieth century. He taught Alma Mahler, who discussed with her husband, with reference to Zemlinsky, the relationship between physical ugliness and spiritual beauty. His earlier career was at the Vienna Volksoper, in Prague and in Berlin. 1933 forced his departure for Vienna, then Prague and finally the United States of America, where he died in 1942.

Stage Works

Mahler promised, before his resignation, to stage the ballet Das gläserne Herz at the Vienna Court Opera, a work based on Hofmannsthal from which an orchestral suite was later derived. His two operas based on Oscar Wilde, Eine florentinische Tragödie (A Florentine Tragedy) and Der Zwerg (The Dwarf), based on Wilde's Birthday of the Infanta, won contemporary success.

Orchestral Music

In addition to three symphonies, Zemlinsky wrote a Lyric Symphony, for soprano, baritone and orchestra, based on Rabindranath Tagore and, in 1934, a Sinfonietta.

Chamber Music

Chamber music by Zemlinsky includes four string quartets and a clarinet trio.

Vocal and Choral Music

Choral works by Zemlinsky include settings of Psalms, while his songs deserve attention in their continuation of an older German tradition in the context of the Vienna of the Second Viennese School.

Zimmermann, Bernd Alois

(1918 - 1970)

Zimmermann occupies a special position in German music of the twentieth century, his musical language and techniques relatively original. For much of his career he taught at the Cologne Musikhochschule, drawing, in his music, on his own wide cultural background and his own roots in Catholic teaching and tradition.

Operas

Die Soldaten has been considered by many to be the most improtant German oepra since Berg's Lulu.

Orchestral Music

Zimmermann's orchestral works include concertos for violin, for oboe, for atrings and for orchestra, with Canto di speranza (Song of Hope) for cello and orchestra.

A

A is the note of the musical scale used generally for tuning (= French, Italian, Spanish: la). Notes in English are given letter names, A,B,C,D,E,F & G.

Accelerando

Accelerando (Italian: becoming faster) is a term in general use to show that the music should be played at an increasing speed.

Accompaniment

An accompaniment is an additional part for a performer of any kind that is less important than another, which it serves to support and enhance. The piano is often used to provide an accompaniment to a solo singer. In instrumental works for, say, violin and piano the rôles may be reversed.

Adagio

Adagio (Italian: slow) is an indication of tempo and is sometimes used to describe a slow movement, even when the indication of speed at the start of the movement may be different. The diminutive form adagietto is a little faster than adagio.

Air

Air (= Italian: aria) appearing sometimes with the earlier English spelling ayre, means a tune or melody, for voice or instrument.

Alla

The Italian alla means "in the manner of" (= French: à la) and may be found in titles like that of Mozart's 'Rondo alla turca', Rondo in the Turkish Style.

Allegro

Allegro (Italian: cheerful, lively) is generally taken as fast, although not as fast as vivace or presto. Allegretto is a diminutive, meaning slightly slower than allegro. These indications of speed or tempo are used as general titles for pieces of music headed by instructions of this kind. The first movement of a classical sonata, for example, is often 'an Allegro', just as the slow movement is often 'an Adagio'.

Allemande

An allemande is a German dance (the word itself is French) in 4/4 time, often the first dance in a baroque dance suite, where it is frequently followed by a courante, a more rapid dance. The allemande, which appears in earlier English sources often as alman, almain or with similar spellings, is generally moderate in speed.

Alto

The alto (= Italian: high) is the lower female or unbroken male voice, or male falsetto of similar range. The alto clef (see Clef) is a sign written on the musical stave to show that the middle line of the stave is middle C. It is now used for much of the music written for viola and other instruments of similar range. Female alto soloists are usually described as contralto rather than alto.

Andante

Andante (Italian: walking) is a word used to suggest the speed of a piece of music, at walking pace. The diminutive andantino is ambiguous and means either a little faster or a little slower than andante, more often the former.

Anthem

An anthem is a short vocal composition. In the Church of England the word indicates such a composition often using a non-liturgical text (i.e. not part of the official service). A full anthem is for full choir, without soloists, while a verse anthem makes contrasting use of solo singers. Both these forms flourished in the Church of England from the late 16th century.

Arabesque

The word 'arabesque' originally indicated a decorative pattern in Arab style found in painting or architecture. Its most common use in music has been as a descriptive title of short decorative piano pieces of the 19th or early 20th century. There are two well known Arabesques by the French composer Debussy.

Arco

Arco (Italian: bow) is used as an indication to string-players that they should use the bow, rather than pluck with the fingers (see pizzicato).

Aria

An aria is a song or air. The word is used in particular to indicate formally constructed songs in opera. The so-called da capo aria of later baroque opera, oratorio and other vocal compositions, is an aria in which the first section is repeated, usually with additional and varied ornamentation, after the first two sections. The diminutive arietta indicates a little aria, while arioso refers to a freer form of aria-like vocal writing.

Assai

Assai (Italian: very) appears often in indications to performers of the speed of a piece of music, as in allegro assai, very fast, or allegro assai moderato, very moderately fast.

Atonal

Atonal music is music that has no specific tonality, is not in a specific key and therefore has no specific 'home' note or chord. The word atonality refers technically to various forms of 20th century music not in a key.

Aubade

An aubade is a morning-song. A well known example is the Siegfried Idyll, a work written by Richard Wagner to be played for his second wife Cosima on the morning of her birthday.

B

B is a note in the musical scale (= German: H; French, Italian, Spanish etc.: si).

Badinerie

Badinerie (French: teasing), indicates a piece of music of light-hearted character. The best known badinerie is the lively last movement of Bach's Suite in B minor for flute, strings and continuo.

Bagatelle

Bagatelle, used as the title of a short light-hearted piece of music, was employed most notably by Beethoven in a series of such compositions for piano. The descriptive title was thereafter used by a number of other composers.

Bagpipe

The bagpipe is an ancient instrument, at least in its most primitive form, and is still found in a number of countries. It is a reed instrument, with the reed sounded by air expressed from a leather bag. It generally makes use of a single pipe that can be fingered to produce different notes, with additional drones, pipes that produce single notes, a marked feature of bagpipe music and of its imitations for other instruments. The sophisticated and more versatile French musette, a bagpipe operated by bellows, gave its name to a baroque dance suite movement, marked, usually in the bass, by the continuing sound of a drone, a repeated single note.

Ballad

Ballad, derived from the late Latin verb 'ballare', to dance, came to be used primarily to describe a folk-song of narrative character or a song or poem written in imitation of such a folk-song. The title Ballade was used by Chopin to describe four piano-pieces of otherwise concealed narrative content, apparently based on narrative poems of ballad type by the patriotic poet Mickieiwicz, while Brahms in one of his Ballades transfers into music an old Scottish narrative ballad.

The Ballade of French music and poetry of the 14th and 15th centuries denotes a different and fixed literary and musical form.

Bar

In written Western music the bar-line came to be used, a vertical line through the stave, to mark metrical units or bars (= measures). By the later 17th century the bar-line had come to be used immediately preceding a strong beat, so that a bar came to begin normally with an accented note. The double bar or double bar-line marks the end of a section or piece.

Barcarolle

A barcarolle is a boating-song, generally used to describe the boating-songs of gondoliers in Venice, imitated by composers in songs and instrumental pieces in the 19th century. Chopin wrote one such Barcarolle for piano, and Mendelssohn provided four shorter piano pieces of this kind. At the end of the century and in the early 20th century the French composer Gabriel Fauré wrote thirteen Barcarolles. There is a particularly well known barcarolle in Offenbach's opera The Tales of Hoffmann (Les contes d'Hoffmann).

Baritone

The word 'baritone' describes a type of male voice of middle range. The word is also used to specify pitched and valved brass instruments of lowish register and as an adjective to distinguish the rare lowest member of the oboe family, also known as a bass oboe, sounding an octave (eight notes) lower than the normal oboe.

Baroque

Once used as a term of critical disapproval, the word 'baroque' is now used in music to designate a period of musical history from about 1600 to about 1750, although any such periodisation in history can only be a rough guide. In musicology the term was borrowed from the history of art and architecture. In music the baroque era may conveniently be divided into three fifty-year periods, Early Baroque, Middle Baroque and Late Baroque. The first of these is typified by the Italian composer Monteverdi, the Middle Baroque by composers such as Henry Purcell in England or Lully in France and the Late Baroque by Johann Sebastian Bach, Handel and Vivaldi.

Bass

The word 'bass' describes the lower register and lower sonorities in music. In vocal music it indicates the lowest type of male voice, and in instrumental music is generally used to indicate the bottom part. As an adjective it is used to describe instruments of lower register, such as the bass clarinet. In common speech the word bass may indicate the double bass, the largest and lowest instrument of the string family, or, in brass bands, an instrument corresponding to the orchestral tuba, the bass of the brass family.

Bass-baritone

A bass-baritone is a male singer with a range that includes both bass and baritone registers, described by Wagner, who wrote for this kind of voice, as a high bass.

Basso contínuo

The basso continuo or continuo is the figured bass commonly used in music of the baroque period. It was the normal practice to make use of a bass instrument of some kind, for example a cello or bass viola da gamba and a chordal instrument, a keyboard instrument or plucked string instrument, the part of the latter indicated by numbers added to the music for the bass instrument, showing the chords as a basis for improvised accompaniment or 'filling in' and embellishing of harmonies.

Bassoon

The bassoon is a double-reed wind instrument (= German: Fagott; Italian: fagotto). It is the bass of the woodwind section in the modern orchestra, which can be augmented by the use of a double bassoon of lower range.

Beat

The beat or pulse in a piece of music is the regular rhythmic pattern of the music. Each bar should start with a strong beat and each bar should end with a weak beat. These may be known as the down-beat (strong, at the beginning of a bar) and the up-beat (weak, at the end of a bar). Up and down describe the gestures of a conductor, whose preparatory up-beat is of even greater importance to players than his down-beat.

Berceuse

A berceuse is a cradle-song or lullaby, in lilting triple or compound time. The most famous example of the use of this title is by Chopin, who wrote one Berceuse, followed by Liszt.

Bewegt

Bewegt (German: agitated) is used as a tempo indication meaning something the same as the Italian 'agitato', although mässig bewegt is used as the equivalent of allegro moderato.

Bolero

The bolero is a Spanish dance, popular in Paris in the time of Chopin and in Latin America. One of the best known examples of the dance in art music is Ravel's ballet music Boléro, music of mounting intensity described by the composer as an orchestrated crescendo.

Bourrée

A bourrée is a duple-rhythm French dance sometimes found in the baroque dance suite, where it was later placed after the sarabande, with other lighter additional dances.

Brass

The brass section of the orchestra includes metal instruments where the sound is produced by forcing air through a cup-shaped or conical mouthpiece. The brass section usually consists of trumpets, trombones and tuba and French horns.'

Brio

Brio (Italian: vivacity, fire or energy) appears as an instruction to performers as, for example, in allegro con brio, fast with brilliance and fire, an indication used on a number of occasions by Beethoven.

C

C is a note in the scale (= French: ut; Italian: do).

Cadence

A cadence usually consists of two chords that provide musical punctuation at the end of phrases or sentences.

Cadenza

A cadenza, based often on an extended and embellished final cadence, at least in classical concertos, is a passage originally improvised by a performer in which virtuoso ability might be shown. Cadenzas are now more often written by the composer, although some modern performers continue to improvise. In classical concertos the cadenza often leads to the last section of a movement.

Camera

Camera (Italian: room,chamber) is found principally in the phrase 'sonata da camera', chamber sonata, to be distinguished in music of the baroque period from the sonata da chiesa, church sonata. The secular sonata da camera generally consists of dance movements.

Canon

A canon in music is a device in counterpoint in which a melody announced by one voice or instrument is imitated by one or more other voices or instruments, entering after the first has started, in the manner of a round. The word canon may describe the device as it occurs in a piece of music or a complete composition in this form, like Pachelbel's well known Canon.

Cantabile

Cantabile (Italian: in singing style) appears often at the beginning of movements as in andante cantabile - at walking speed and in a singing style.

Cantata

A cantata is generally a choral work of some length that also uses solo voices, usually with instrumental accompaniment. The texts used may be sacred or secular. Some cantatas use solo voices without chorus or choir.

Cappella

Cappella, meaning chapel, is found particularly in the phrase 'a cappella' for unaccompanied choral singing. The words chapel, cappella and Kapelle, indicate a musical establishment rather than a place, as in the English Chapel Royal, the musicians of the monarch. The spelling capella may also be found.

Capriccio, caprice

Capriccio (Italian: caprice; = French: caprice) appears in a variety of musical meanings, used differently at different periods and by different composers. In the later 16th century and 17th century it generally indicated a fugal composition (see Fugue), but later came to signify dances or dance suites or any composition that allowed a relatively free play of fancy, as in the Capriccio espagnol (Spanish Caprice) of Rimsky-Korsakov or the Capriccio italien (Italian Caprice) of Tchaikovsky.

Cassation

The word 'cassation' is of disputed origin and was used principally in the third quarter of the 18th century in South Germany to describe a piece of music akin to a divertimento or serenade, music intended primarily for entertainment. Mozart uses the word to describe three of his own serenades.

Celesta

A celesta (= French: céleste) is a small keyboard instrument developed in the later 19th century and using hammers that strike metal bars to give a ringing sound. Tchaikovsky used the celesta, then a new instrument, in his Dance of the Sugar-Plum Fairy in his Nutcracker ballet.

Cello

The word cello is now in very general use instead of the longer word violoncello, a diminutive of the word violone, indicating the big viol, the double bass of the bowed viol family. The cello normally plays the bass line of the string section in an orchestra, its register the approximate equivalent of the lowest male voice.

Cembalo

The word 'cembalo' is usually used to indicate the harpsichord.

Chaconne

A chaconne (= Italian: ciaconna; earlier English: chacony) is in origin a dance popular in Spain in the early 17th century. It came to signify a form in which there are a series of variations over a short repeated bass or chordal pattern. Famous examples of the form are found in Bach's Chaconne for unaccompanied violin in his D minor Partita or the earlier Chacony in G minor by Henry Purcell.

Chamber music

Chamber music is music for a small ensemble of instruments, intended for performance in a room or chamber, as opposed to a church or larger building.

Chamber orchestra

A chamber orchestra has come to indicate an orchestra smaller in size than the usual symphony orchestra.

Chanson

A chanson is a French song. The word is used to indicate songs from the troubadour compositions of the Middle Ages to the art-songs of the 19th and 20th centuries.

Chant

(see Plainchant and Gregorian Chant)

Chapel

The word chapel (= Latin: cappella, capella; French: chapelle; German: Kapelle) signifies, in the ordinary sense, a place of worship. In music it may be used to indicate a group of musicians employed by the church or by the court, as in the English Chapel Royal, the group of musicians employed by the English monarch, or, in later continental terminology, any musical establishment.

Choir

A choir is a group of singers. The word is generally used to indicate such a group in a church, or the part of the church in which such a group is normally placed.

Chorale

A chorale is a German Lutheran hymn-tune, a number of which were composed or arranged by Luther himself and adapted in later centuries to various harmonies, the most famous of all by Johann Sebastian Bach. The word is also used in America to signify a choir or chorus.

Chorale prelude

The chorale prelude, an introduction to a chorale, was developed in 17th century Germany as an organ composition based on a chorale melody. The form is found in the later 17th century in the work of Buxtehude and in the early 18th century most notably in the 45 chorale preludes of Johann Sebastian Bach.

Chord

A chord is the simultaneous sounding of two or more notes. The adjective is chordal. The study of harmony involves the correct placing of chords with relation to each other.

Chorus

A chorus is a group of singers. The word is also used to indicate a refrain in a song.

Chromatic

Chromatic notes are those that do not belong to the diatonic scale. If an ascending scale is taken from the note C, in the form C, D, E, F, etc., chromatic notes would be C# (C sharp), D# (D sharp), etc., notes not found in the diatonic scale of C major, which has no sharps or flats.

Clarinet

A clarinet is a woodwind instrument with a single reed, as opposed to the oboe, which has a double reed. The clarinet was developed from the year 1800 onwards from the earlier chalumeau, which played notes only in the lower register. The new instrument added notes in the higher register. Clarinets are built in different keys, most commonly in B flat and in A.

Clarino

Clarino was the word often used in the 17th and 18th centuries for trumpet. Now the word describes the upper register of the trumpet, much used in the baroque period, when the trumpet, lacking valves, could only produce successive notes in the highest register, an art that later fell into temporary disuse.

Classical

In the most general meaning of the word, classical music may designate fine music or serious music. More technically the word may refer to a period in the history of music, the later 18th century, the age of Haydn, Mozart and Beethoven. The classical may be differentiated from the so-called romantic, the relatively experimental and less formally restricted kinds of music that became current in the 19th century.

Clavichord

The clavichord is a small early keyboard instrument with a hammer-action. The strings are struck by a tangent, a small oblong strip of metal, eliciting a soft sound. The limited dynamic range of the clavichord make it unsuitable for public performance, but it was historically much favoured by composers such as Carl Philipp

Emanuel Bach, second son of Johann Sebastian Bach and a leading keyboard-player in the middle of the 18th century.

Clef

The five lines generally used in musical notation have no precise meaning without the addition at the left-hand side of a clef, a sign that specifies the note to be indicated by one of the lines, from which other notes may be gauged. The so-called treble clef, familiar to pianists and violinists, otherwise known as a G clef, is used to show that the second line from the bottom is G. The so-called bass clef, otherwise known as an F clef, shows that the second line from the top is the F below middle C. C clefs are used on any line to show the position of the note known as middle C. Most frequently found are the alto clef, a C clef on the middle line of the stave (the group of five lines) and the tenor clef, a C clef on the second line from the top. The alto clef is the principal clef used for the viola, the tenor of the string family, while the tenor clef is used for the upper register of instruments like the cello and the bassoon. In plainchant, with its four-line stave, there are C clefs and F clefs which may appear on any line.

Coda

A coda (Italian: tail) is the ending of a piece of music. This may be very short, but in a composition on a large scale may be extended. The diminutive codetta may be used to indicate the closing part of a section of a composition.

Coloratura

Originally signifying colouring, the word coloratura is generally used to describe vocal music that is extensively ornamented and calls for ability in a very high register. A typical part for a coloratura soprano is that of the Queen of the Night in Mozart's opera The Magic Flute (Die Zauberflöte).

Concertante

A concertante part in a piece of music is a part that calls for some element of solo performance, as in a classical concerto. The word is found in the phrase Sinfonia concertante, which is used to indicate an orchestral composition with two or more solo instruments, a title used from the late 18th century onwards.

Concertino

The concertino is the small group of solo instruments used in a concerto grosso in contrast to the whole body of the orchestra, consisting of ripieno players (see Concerto grosso). A concertino may also be a small concerto (see Concerto).

Concerto

A concerto is a piece of instrumental music that contrasts a solo instrument or a small group of solo instruments with the main body of the orchestra. In the earlier 17th century the word had a more general significance, but in the early 18th century it came to mean primarily a work as described above.

Concerto grosso

The concerto grosso developed towards the end of the 17th century, particularly with the works in this form by Corelli, followed by Handel and many other composers. A small group of soloists, often two violins, cello and harpsichord, the concertino, is contrasted with the whole string orchestra, the concerto grosso, with its less skilled ripieno players. The concerto grosso may involve wind instruments as well as strings. The form has been revived by some 20th century composers, at least nominally.

Consort

Consort, used in earlier English, indicates a group of instruments, as, for example, a consort of viols in the late 16th and early 17th centuries. A broken consort is a consort of mixed instruments, strings and wind.

Continuo

A continuo part, a regular feature of much instrumental music in the 17th and 18th centuries, was played by a keyboard-player or performer on a chordal instrument such as a lute or harp, reading from the bass line of a composition, generally with numbers to indicate the choice of chords, which would then be filled out, with other melodic and contrapuntal embellishments. The continuo or basso continuo was a necessary part of instrumental music, but gradually fell into disuse towards the end of the 18th century, while remaining an important element in the accompaniment of operatic recitative.

Contralto (see Alto)

Cor anglais

The cor anglais is the English horn, a tenor oboe that sounds a fifth lower than it is written.

Cornet

The cornet is a valved brass instrument, resembling a trumpet but with a wider bore. It was used in the second quarter of the 19th century before the full development of the valved trumpet, but is now principally found in brass bands.

Cornetto

The cornetto or cornett is a wind instrument made of wood or ivory, or nowadays reproduced in fibre-glass. It has a cup-shaped mouthpiece, like brass instruments, but finger-holes, like a recorder, and was much used in the 17th and earlier 18th centuries, often to support or even replace treble voices. The bass of the cornetto family is the serpent, once found in village church bands in England and now revived.

Counterpoint

Counterpoint is the combination of two or more melodic lines, the second or later additional melodies described as counterpoints to the first. If harmony is regarded as vertical, as it is in conventional notation, signifying the simultaneous sounding of notes in chords, counterpoint may be regarded as horizontal. The adjective from counterpoint is contrapuntal. The phrase modal counterpoint is used to indicate 16th century counterpoint or Palestrina counterpoint and the phrase tonal counterpoint is used to indicate the later baroque counterpoint of Johann Sebastian Bach and his contemporaries.

Countertenor

A countertenor voice is that of a male alto. Sometimes a distinction is made between the two, the second indicating the English falsetto tradition and the first a natural voice of similar range.

Courante

The French courante, a triple-time dance movement found frequently in the baroque dance suite, generally follows the allemande, the opening German dance. It is sometimes not distinguished from the Italian corrente, although the corrente is generally simpler in texture and rhythm than its French counterpart.

Crescendo

Crecendo (Italian: growing, becoming louder) is frequently used as a dynamic instruction to performers.

Cycle

A song cycle is a set of songs intended to be performed as a group, as in Schumann's Dichterliebe (The Poet's Love) or Schubert's Winterreise (Winter Journey). The 19th century Czech composer Smetana wrote a cycle of symphonic poems, Ma Vlast (My Country).

Cymbals

Cymbals (= Italian: piatti, German: Becken, French: cymbales) are pairs of round metal plates, generally made of an alloy of tin and copper, which may be struck together. A single cymbal may be suspended and struck with a hard or soft stick. The instrument is of ancient origin, but its more modern use occurs first principally in the later 18th century, as part of the Turkish music used, for example, by Mozart in The Abduction from the Seraglio (Die Entführung aus dem Serail). It found much fuller and more varied use in the 19th and 20th centuries.

D

D is a note of the scale (= Italian, French: re).

Da capo

Da capo (Italian: from the beginning), abbreviated to the letters D.C. at the end of a piece of music or a section of it, means that it should be played or sung again from the beginning (De capo al fine) or from the beginning up to the sign (Da capo al segno). A da capo aria, often found in the later baroque period, is an aria in three sections, the third an ornamented repetition of the first.

Decrescendo

Decrescendo (Italian: growing less) is used as a direction to performers, meaning becoming softer.

Diminuendo

Diminuendo (Italian: becoming less) is used as a direction to performers to play softer.

Divertimento

A divertimento is an instrumental composition intended for entertainment, usually in a number of movements. The term is used particularly in the second half of the 18th century. Haydn described his first string quartets as Divertimenti and the title is also used by Mozart and other composers of the period.

Divertissement

The French word divertissement (= Italian: divertimento) is used in English principally to indicate the additional dance entertainment that is often a part of classical ballet. A well known example would be the series of characteristic dances that entertain the heroine towards the end of Tchaikovsky's Nutcracker.

Double bass

The double bass is the largest and lowest of the instruments of the string section of the orchestra. It has generally four or five strings and its music sounds an octave (eight notes) lower than it is written. If, as often in music before 1800, the double bass plays the same music as the cello, the sound will be an octave lower.

Double bassoon

A double bassoon plays an octave lower than the bassoon.

Drum

The form of drum generally found in the orchestra is the kettledrum or, in incorrect Italian, timpani, since the Italian singular timpano seldom appears in English usage. Other smaller and larger drums may also be used, including the snare-drum, a smaller instrument with a vibrating strip that can be switched on or off, and the bass drum. Timpani are tunable, nowadays usually by means of pedals that loosen or tighten the drum-skin.

Duet

A duet is a piece of music written for two performers. On the piano such a piece would involve two players on one instrument.

Duo

A duo is a piece of music for two performers. Written for the piano such a piece would need two performers and two pianos.

Dynamics

Dynamics are the levels of sound, loud or soft, in a piece of music.

E

E is a note of the scale (= Italian, French: mi).

Elegy

An elegy (= French: élégie) is a lament, either vocal or instrumental.

English horn

The English horn is more generally known in England as the cor anglais. It is the tenor oboe.

Ensemble

The word ensemble is used in three senses. It may refer to the togetherness of a group of performers: if ensemble is poor, the players are not together. It may indicate part of an opera that involves a group of singers. It can also mean a group of performers.

Entr'acte

As the word suggests, an entr'acte (= German: Zwischenspiel) is music between the acts of a play or opera.

Etude

An étude is a study, intended originally for the technical practice of the player. Chopin, Liszt and later composers elevated the étude into a significant piece of music, no mere exercise.

Exposition

The exposition in sonata-allegro form is the first section of the movement, in which the principal thematic material is announced. In the exposition of a fugue (a fugal exposition) the voices (= parts) enter one by one with the same subject: the exposition ends when all the voices have entered.

F

F is a note of the scale (= Italian, French: fa).

Fagott

Fagott (German) or fagotto (Italian) is the bassoon, the bass of the woodwind section in the orchestra (see Bassoon).

Fanfare

A fanfare is a flourish of trumpets or other similar instruments, used for military or ceremonial purposes, or music that conveys this impression.

Fantasy

Fantasy (= French: fantaisie; Italian: fantasia; German: Fantasie) is a relatively free form in the 16th and 17th centuries, in which a composer may exercise his fancy, usually in contrapuntal form. In later periods the word was used to describe a much freer form, as in the written improvisations for piano of this title by Mozart, or Beethoven's so-called Moonlight Sonata, described by the composer as Sonata quasi una fantasia, Sonata like a Fantasia.

Fiddle

A fiddle is a violin, but the word is used either colloquially or to indicate a folk-instrument. The Australian composer Percy Grainger, who objected to the use of words of Latin origin, used the word fiddle for violin, middle-fiddle for viola and bass fiddle for cello, as part of his eccentric vocabulary of 'blue-eyed English'.

Flat

The word "flat", indicated by a sign derived from the letter b, shows that a note should be lowered by a semitone. In a more general sense music that is flat may simply be out of tune, its pitch below the accepted pitch.

Flautist

A flautist is a player of the flute.

Flute

The word flute may indicate a variety of wind instruments without reeds. The modern orchestra makes use of transverse flutes, augmented as necessary by a smaller transverse flute known as a piccolo and very occasionally by a larger instrument, the alto or bass flute, pitched a fourth lower. The straight flute is known in English as a recorder (= French: flûte à bec; German: Blockflöte; Italian: flauto dolce) but was not used in the orchestra after the later Baroque period.

Follía, La

The Italian La Follia, (= Spanish: Folía; French: Folie d'Espagne) is a well known dance tune popular from the 16th century or earlier and found in the work of composers such as Corelli (1653 - 1713), who used the theme for a set of variations forming a violin sonata, or later by Rachmaninov (1873 - 1943) in his incorrectly named Variations on a Theme of Corelli.

Forte

Forte (Italian: loud) is used in directions to performers. It appears in the superlative form fortissimo, very loud. The letter f is an abbreviation of forte, ff an abbreviation of fortissimo, with fff or more rarely ffff even louder.

Fortepiano

The word fortepiano, with the same meaning as pianoforte, the full name of the piano, with its hammer action and consequent ability to produce sounds both loud and soft, corresponding to the force applied to the keys, is generally used to indicate the earlier form of the piano, as it developed in the 18th century. A Mozart piano, for example, might be called a fortepiano. The instrument is smaller, more delicately incisive in tone than the modern instrument, and is in some respects more versatile.

Fugue

Fugue has been described as a texture rather than a form. It is, in essence, a contrapuntal composition. The normal fugue opens with a subject or theme in one voice or part. A second voice answers, with the same subject transposed and sometimes slightly altered, usually at the interval of a fifth, while the first voice continues with an accompaniment that may have the character of a countersubject that will be used again as the piece progresses. Other voices enter one by one, each of them with the subject, the third in the form of the first entry, the fourth in the form of the answer in the second voice. A fugue may have as few as two voices (the word voice does not necessarily imply singing in this context) and seldom more than four. The subject announced at the beginning provides the chief melodic element in a fugue. When all the voices have entered, the so-called fugal exposition, there will be an episode, a bridge that leads to a further entry or series of entries answering each other, now in different keys. The fugue, as it had developed by the time of Johann Sebastian Bach, continues in this way, often making use of stretto (overlapping entries of the subject) and pedal-point (a sustained note, usually below the other parts) as it nears the end. The fugue became an important form or texture in the Baroque period, reaching its height in the work of J. S. Bach in the first half of the 18th century. Later composers continued to write fugues, a favourite form of Mozart's wife Constanze, with Beethoven including elaborate fugues in some of his later piano sonatas and a remarkable and challenging Grosse Fuge (Great Fugue) as part of one of his later string quartets. Technically the writing of fugue remains an important element in the training of composers.

G

G is a note of the musical scale (= French, Italian: sol)

Galliard

The galliard is a courtly dance of the late 16th and early 17th century in triple metre usually following a slower duple metre pavan. The two dances are often found in instrumental compositions of the period, sometimes in suites.

Galop

The galop is a quick dance in duple metre, one of the most popular ballroom dances of the 19th century. The dance appears as a parody in Offenbach's operetta Orpheus in the Underworld in a can-can.

Gamba

Gamba (Italian: leg) is in English used colloquially to designate the viola da gamba or leg-viol, the bowed string instrument popular from the 16th until the middle of the 18th century and held downwards, in a way similar to that used for the modern cello, as opposed to the viola da braccio or arm-viol, the instrument of the violin family, held on the arm or shoulder.

German dance

The German dance (= German: Deutsche, Deutscher Tanz) describes generally the triple metre dances of the late 18th and early 19th centuries, found in the Ländler and the Waltz. There are examples of this dance in the work of Beethoven and of Schubert.

Gigue

The gigue (= Italian: giga; English: jig) is a rapid dance normally in compound duple metre (the main beats divided into three rather than two). The gigue became the accepted final dance in the baroque instrumental suite.

Giocoso

Giocoso (Italian: jocular, cheerful) is sometimes found as part of a tempo instruction to a performer, as in allegro giocoso, fast and cheerful. The same Italian adjective is used in the descriptive title of Mozart's opera Don Giovanni, a dramma giocoso.

Giusto

Giusto (Italian: just, exact) is found in tempo indications, as, for example, allegro giusto, as in the last movement of Schubert's Trout Quintet, or tempo giusto, in strict time, sometimes, as in Liszt, indicating a return to the original speed of the music after a freer passage.

Glissando

Derived from the French glisser, to slide, the Italianised word is used to describe sliding in music from one note to another. On the harp or the piano this is achieved by sliding the finger or fingers over the strings or keys, and can be achieved similarly on bowed string instruments, and by other means on the trombone, clarinet, French horn and pedal timpani among others.

Glockenspiel

The glockenspiel is a percussion instrument similar in form to the xylophone, but with metal rather than wooden bars for the notes. The instrument appeared only gradually in the concert-hall and opera-house and is found in Handel's oratorio Saul and elsewhere. Mozart made famous use of the glockenspiel in The Magic Flute (Die Zauberflöte), where it is a magic instrument for the comic bird-catcher Papageno. It is now a recognised if sparingly used instrument in the percussion section of the modern orchestra.

Gong

The gong is a percussion instrument originating in the East. In the modern orchestra it is usually found in the form of the large Chinese tam-tam. The gong appears in Western orchestral music in the late 18th century, and notable use of sets of gongs of varying size is found adding exotic colour to Puccini's oriental operas Madama Butterfly and Turandot.

Grave

Grave (Italian: slow, solemn) is used as an indication of tempo and mood, meaning slow and serious.

Grazioso

Grazia (grace) forms the Italian adjective grazioso, used as an indication of expression and of tempo, particularly in the 18th century.

Gregorian chant

Plainchant, the modal chant of early Christian and continuing Catholic worship and its derivatives, is often known as Gregorian chant, after Pope Gregory the Great , St. Gregory, to whom the attempt at standardisation of the chant in the late 6th century is attributed.

Guitar

The modern concert guitar is a plucked string instrument generally with six strings. The instrument has a long history, in one form or another. In more recent times it became popular in Vienna in the early 19th century with the work of the Italian composer and guitarist Mauro Giuliani and in Paris with the Catalan Fernando Sor. In Spain it was, of course, the national instrument. The player Andrés Segovia had a strong influence on the form of the modern guitar, the repertoire of which now includes fine concertos by the composers Joaquín Rodrigo, Manuel Ponce, Villa-Lobos, Castelnuovo-Tedesco and others.

H

The letter H is used in German to denote the English note B, while B in German signifies the English B flat. In the use of the letters of a word to form a musical motif, the presence of H allows a complete musical version of the name BACH (B flat - A - C - B = German: B - A - C - H), used by various composers, including Liszt. The Russian composer Dmitry Shostakovich uses a musical cryptogram derived from the first letters of his name in German, DSCH, which becomes D - Es (= E flat) - C - H. This occurs in a number of his works as a kind of musical signature.

Habanera (= Havanaise)

The Habanera is a Cuban dance from Havana, later introduced to Spain. One of the most famous examples is found in Bizet's Spanish opera Carmen, where Carmen herself sings a seductive Habanera. Ravel includes a Habanera in his Rapsodie espagnole and also wrote a Vocalise en forme de habanera, while Debussy makes use of the characteristic rhythm of the dance.

Harmonica

The Western harmonica or mouth-organ is an invention of the early 19th century, inspired by the ancient Chinese bamboo mouth-organ, the sheng. The 20th century chromatic harmonica, of which Larry Adler has been a leading exponent, has inspired a number of composers, including Vaughan Williams, who wrote a Romance for harmonica and orchestra.

Harmoniemusik

Harmoniemusik is music for wind band. In its more limited sense the term is used to signify music for wind bands or wind ensembles in the service of the nobility from the middle of the 18th century to the end of the third decade of the 19th century, and their popular counterparts. The Harmonie, the band itself, which varied in number from a duo to the often found sextet or octet or to a much larger number of players, had its counterpart in France and in England, as well as its successors among emigrants to the United States of America.

Harmonium

The harmonium, developed in the early 19th century from experiments in the last quarter of the century before, is a keyboard instrument that produces its sounds by means of air from bellows passing through free reeds, metal tongues that are made to vibrate. The instrument has a relatively small classical repertoire, its use either domestic or as a cheap substitute for the church organ. Dvořák wrote Bagatelles for two violins, cello and harmonium, and Schoenberg made some use of the harmonium in chamber arrangements of works of his own and in versions of two waltzes by Johann Strauss.

Harmony

Harmony describes the simultaneous sounding of two or more notes and the technique governing the construction of such chords and their arrangement in a succession of chords. Following the convention of writing music from left to right on a horizontal set of lines (staff or stave), harmony may be regarded as vertical, as opposed to counterpoint, which is horizontal. In other words harmony deals with chords, simultaneous sounds, and counterpoint with melody set against melody.

Harp

The harp is an instrument of great antiquity, represented from as early as 3000 B.C. in Sumeria. The form of the instrument has varied, but the modern double-action harp, a development of the early 19th century, is in general orchestral use. The strings are tuned in flats, starting from a bottom C flat, with seven pedals, each of which can change a given set of strings to a natural or a sharp. The C pedal, therefore, in its three positions, can make all the Cs on the instrument flat, natural or sharp. Other forms of harp survive. The Aeolian harp, with strings of the same length and pitch but of different thicknesses, was to be placed by an open window, its sounds produced by the wind blowing through the strings. Various forms of Celtic harp are still in use.

Harpsichord

The harpsichord is a keyboard instrument with strings running from front to back of its wing-shaped horizontal box and soundboard. Unlike the piano and the earlier clavichord with its hammers that strike the strings, the harpsichord has a mechanism by which the strings are plucked. The instrument seems to have existed in a simple form in the 14th century and assumed considerable importance from the early 16th until the fuller development of the pianoforte towards the end of the 18th century. Variations of dynamics on the harpsichord are possible through the use of stops that activate different lengths of string and by the use of a muting buff stop and of the two manuals often found on the instrument. In addition to its ubiquitous use in the music of the baroque period, the harpsichord has also been used by modern composers, since its revival at the end of the 19th century.

Heldentenor

The heroic tenor or Heldentenor is a tenor with a quality of voice suited to the heroic rôles of 19th century French Grand Opera and of the music-dramas of Wagner, as in the part of Tannhäuser in Wagner's opera of that name.

Horn

The horn takes its name from the horn of an animal, the original form of this wind instrument in ancient times. The instrument was long associated with hunting and as a means of military signalling. The instrument now generally known as the French horn developed in France in its familiar helical form, but in one form or another the horn had come to be a frequent instrument in music for the church, the theatre and the chamber by the early 18th century. The natural horn was able to play the notes of the harmonic series, modified by the use of the right hand in the bell of the instrument, and in different keys by the use of different crooks that changed the length of the tube and hence the length of the air column. The valve horn was developed in the first quarter of the 19th century, its two and later three valves making variations possible in the length of tube and hence in the pitch of the fundamental and harmonic series stemming from it, but the natural horn continued in use at the same time. The double horn was developed in the late 19th century and is now in common use. Concertos for the French horn include the four concertos by Mozart. In the classical orchestra the two horns played a largely sustaining part. The modern orchestra normally has four French horns. The hunting associations of the horn led to its evocative use in Romantic music, as in Weber's opera Der Freischütz, and in the same composer's opera Oberon, in which the horn has a magic rôle to play.

Hornpipe

The hornpipe is a rapid British dance that exists in various metres, triple, duple and quadruple. In its earlier English form it is found in the keyboard suites and stage music of the English composer Henry Purcell, and in keyboard and orchestral movements by Handel. It later came to be popularly associated particularly with sailors in the so-called Sailors' Hornpipe derived from a fiddle-tune.

Humoresque

Schumann was the first composer to use the title Humoreske for a relatively long work for piano, the humour of the title used rather in the sense of a mood of one sort or another. The word later came to indicate very much shorter pieces, such as the well known G flat Humoresque by Dvořák, one of a set of eight.

Hymn

A hymn is a song of praise, whether to a god, saint or hero. The plainchant hymn has a place in the Divine Office. In Protestant Christian worship, where the hymn assumed considerable importance, after the chorales of Martin Luther and his followers, the metrical homophonic form dominated.

I

Impressionism

Impressionism was a term at first used mockingly to describe the work of the French painter Monet and his circle, who later made use of the word themselves. It was similarly used to describe an element of vagueness and imprecision coupled with a perceived excess of attention to colour in the early music of Debussy, who did not accept the criticism or the label, although his harmonic innovations and approach to composition have points in common with the ideals of Monet.

Impromptu

The word impromptu was first used as a title for a musical composition in 1822 by the Bohemian composer Voříšek for six piano pieces, to be imitated by Schubert's publisher in naming a set of four piano Impromptus, to be followed by four more, perhaps so named by the composer. Chopin used the title for four compositions in this seemingly improvised form, and there are further impromptus by other composers from that period onwards, generally, but not always, for a single instrument.

Improvisation

Improvisation was once a normal part of a performer's stock-in-trade. Many of the greatest composer-performers, from Bach to Mozart and Beethoven, were masters of improvisation, but in the 19th century this became a less common part of public performance, although it remained and remains a necessary skill for a church organist, traditionally required to provide a musical accompaniment of varying length to liturgical ritual. In baroque music the realisation of a figured bass, the improvisation of a keyboard part from a given series of chords, was a necessary musical accomplishment, while the improvisatory element in the addition of ornaments to a melodic part remained normal in opera and other kinds of solo performance.

Instrumentation

Instrumentation is generally used to mean orchestration, the art of writing music for instruments, or, alternatively, the actual scoring of a particular composition.

Interlude

In the theatre an interlude performs the same function as an entr'acte, music between acts or scenes, designed to bridge a gap. It may also be used to indicate music played or sung between two other works or two sections of a work.

Intermezzo

Earlier signifying a comic interlude inserted between the acts of an opera seria, the 19th century intermezzo was often either a musical interlude in a larger composition or a piece of music in itself, often for solo piano. In this second sense it is used by Schumann and later by Brahms in their piano music, while both Mendelssohn and Brahms use the word as a movement title in chamber music.

Interval

In music an interval is the distance in pitch between two notes, counted from the lower note upwards, with the lower note as the first of the interval. The violin, for example, is tuned in intervals of a fifth, G to D, D to A and A to E, the double bass in fourths, from E to A, A to D and D to G. Harmonic intervals occur simultaneously, as when a violinist tunes the instrument, listening carefully to the sound of two adjacent strings played together. Melodic intervals occur between two notes played one after the other.

Intonation

Intonation is the exactness of pitch or lack of it in playing or singing. Collective intonation is that of a group of instruments, where slight individual variations in pitch can be lost in a generally more favourable effect.

Invention

The two-part Inventions of Johann Sebastian Bach are contrapuntal two-voice keyboard compositions, and the word is often understood in this sense, although it had a less precise meaning in earlier music.

Istesso tempo

L'istesso tempo, the same speed, is found as an instruction to the player to return to the previous speed of the music.

J

Jig

The jig (= French: gigue; Italian: giga), a lively dance in compound time, became the usual final dance of the baroque dance suite.

Jota

The jota is a traditional Spanish dance, transmuted into an orchestral composition by the Russian composer Glinka in his Jota aragonesa.

K

Kapelle

Chapel (= German: Kapelle; Italian: cappella; French: chapelle) is a musical establishment, generally of a king, prince or other ruler.

Kapellmeister

The Kapellmeister is the director of music (= Italian: maestro di cappella; French: maître de chapelle) of a musical establishment, either of a king or prince, or of an opera-house or municipality. The term Kapellmeistermusik has a pejorative implication, suggesting music that is correct but uninspired, a criticism widely if inaccurately applied to a number of 19th century composers now subject to re-evaluation.

Key

Keys on a musical instrument are the levers which when depressed produce a particular pitch of note. The word may be applied to keyboard instruments such as the piano, the organ and the harpsichord, or to the metal keys on woodwind instruments such as the flute, oboe, clarinet and bassoon.

The key in which a piece of music is written indicates the scale used and the key note or home note, on the chord of which it must end. Not all music is in a key, since attempts have been made in the 20th century to extend music beyond the supposed limitations of key or tonality. It is, in any case, only the very simplest music that remains in one key throughout. Contrast is usually sought by changes of key during a composition, which will end in the key in which it began, although mode may change from major to minor (that is, a symphony in C minor may end with a movement in C major, after intervening movements in other keys). The Fifth Symphony of Beethoven, for example, is in C minor and opens with a movement in that key, followed by a slow movement in A flat major, a C minor third movement with a Trio section in C major and a last movement in C major.

Key signature

The key signature is the sharps or flats, or absence of either, at the beginning of a piece of music, indicating the sharps, flats and naturals belonging to the key of the music. Since a major or minor scale, the two now in common use, has a fixed order of tones and semitones (whole steps and half steps), these can only be preserved when there is a change of key note by the addition of sharps or flats. In the major scale, for example, there are semitones or half steps between the third and fourth degrees and seventh and eighth degrees of the scale. In the scale of C major, played on the white notes of the piano, these semitones fall between E and F and between B and C, a fact apparent from the piano keyboard, where there is no black key between the notes that form these pairs. To keep the same pattern in the scale of G, the note F must be raised to F sharp, so that there is still a semitone between the seventh and eighth notes of the scale. Major key signatures can be calculated on the same system. Each key with an extra sharp starts on a key note a fifth higher, while the keys with flats are in a descending order of fifths. C major itself has no sharps or flats, G has one sharp, D two, A three, E four, B five, F sharp six and C sharp major seven, each new sharp the seventh note of the scale. Descending in fifths, F has one flat, B flat two flats, E flat, three, A flat four, D flat five, G flat six and C flat seven, each new flat the fourth note of the scale.

Konzertmeister

The leader of an orchestra (that is, the principal first violin) is known in German as a Konzertmeister and in the United States as a concertmaster, the latter term now finding more general favour in other English-speaking countries, apart from Great Britain, where the word leader is still preferred.

L

Lament

Dirges or laments are an important element in primitive musical practice in mourning the dead or at other moments of parting. One of the most important and influential laments of Western music is Monteverdi's Lament of Arianna (= Ariadne), abandoned by Theseus on the island of Naxos, where she became a follower of the god Dionysus. This is the only surviving part of a lost opera of 1608. The lament was much imitated, not least by the English composer Henry Purcell in the lament sung by Dido, betrayed by her lover Aeneas, in the short opera Dido and Aeneas.

Lamentations

The Lamentations of Jeremiah form part of the Catholic liturgy of Holy Week, the week before Easter, traditionally chanted, but from the middle of the 15th century providing material for polyphonic setting.

Ländler

The Ländler is an Austrian country dance in a slow triple metre, a precursor of the waltz.

Larghetto

Larghetto is a diminutive form of Largo (Italian: broad, wide, large) usually a direction of tempo, meaning slow. Larghetto is slowish, not as slow as Largo.

Largo

Largo (Italian: broad, wide, large and consequently slow) is used as a frequent instruction to performers. Handel's Largo, an aria from his opera Serse, is in fact marked Larghetto, although this does not seem to affect its speed in popular performance.

Legato

Legato (Italian: smooth) is used as an instruction to performers. It is the opposite of staccato, which indicates a shortening and consequent detaching of notes.

Leggero (Leggiero)

Leggero means light (= French: léger) and is used as a direction to performers.

Legno

Legno, wood, appears in the phrase 'col legno', with the wood, an instruction to string players to hit the strings with the back of the bow. Examples of col legno are found in the Danse macabre of Saint-Säens and at the opening of Holst's The Planets.

Leitmotif

The leitmotif (= German: Leitmotiv) is particularly associated with the music-dramas of Wagner, although the practice has a longer history. The leading motive is a theme or part of a theme, associated in the work of Wagner with a character, idea or event, and forming in his music-dramas an essential element in their construction.

Lento

Lento (Italian: slow; = French: lent, lentement) is used in instructions to performers. Negatively some French composers, notably Couperin, use the direction sans lenteur, without slowness.

Libretto

The libretto, the little book, is the text of an opera or similar vocal work, originally issued in a small printed book.

Lied

Lied, (German: song), Lieder in the plural, is used more specifically to indicate songs in the great German tradition of song-writing exemplified by the work of Schubert, Schumann, Brahms, Hugo Wolf, Richard Strauss and others. It should not be confused with Leid, sorrow, as in Kreisler's Liebesleid, the sorrow of love.

Loure

The loure is a French dance of the 17th and 18th centuries, the name derived from a bagpipe used in Normandy. The dance is usually in 6/4 time and has been described as a slow gigue. Examples are found in Bach's E major Partita for unaccompanied violin and in the fifth of his French Suites.

Lute

The lute, a plucked string instrument popular from the Middle Ages until the 18th century and now revived, came originally from the East, its name derived from the Arabic 'ud. It existed in many different forms and in its Western form is usually pear-shaped, with a flat belly and central soundhole or rose. Its neck has frets, pieces of gut tied to mark the notes on the fingerboard, and its peg-box is generally bent back to form a right angle with the neck. The number of strings has varied, although the six-string lute was common. The lute was one of the most popular instruments in the time of Shakespeare, when the leading performer was John Dowland, who wrote songs with lute accompaniment. In the first half of the 18th century Johann Sebastian Bach wrote for the instrument, of which one of the leading exponents and composers was Sylvius Leopold Weiss. A player of the lute is a lutenist, or, less commonly, lutanist. The meaning of luthier, originally a maker of lutes, has been extended to cover makers of all string instruments.

Lyre

The lyre, the symbol of a musician in Western cultural tradition, is an ancient instrument, found in characteristic form in ancient Greece, where it was the instrument of Apollo. Similar instruments, with strings stretched from a cross-bar to a lower sound-box, to be held in the left arm and plucked with the right hand, are found in other cultures.

M

Madrigal

Originally a form of vocal composition of 14th century Italy, the madrigal became, in the 16th and 17th centuries, a favourite form of part-song, stemming first from Italy. In England the madrigal became popular in the last two decades of the 16th century in adaptations of Italian compositions and in new works by English composers.

Maestoso

Maestoso (Italian: majestic) is used to suggest a majestic manner of performance, either in mood or speed.

Magnificat

The Magnificat is the canticle drawn from the biblical words attributed to the Mother of Christ, My soul doth magnify the Lord. It forms part of the evening service of Vespers, in the Divine Office of the Catholic liturgy, and thus appears in composed settings. As part of the evening service of the Church of England it has similarly been subjected to musical treatment. There are notable settings in the early 17th century by Monteverdi and a hundred years later by Johann Sebastian Bach and by Vivaldi, among many others.

Major

Major (= Latin: greater) is used in musical terminology to describe a form of scale that corresponds to the Ionian mode, the scale on the white notes of the keyboard from C to C. The intervals between the first note or tonic (key note) and the second, third, sixth and seventh degrees of the major scale are described as major (that is, C to D, a major second; C to E, a major third; C to A, a major sixth; C to B, a major seventh). A major chord or major triad consists of a bottom note with a note a major third above, and, optionally, a note a perfect fifth above the bottom note. In this way the chord or triad C - E - G is described as major.

Malagueña

A malagueña is a Spanish dance from the region of Málaga. The word is later used to indicate a form of Spanish gypsy song. There is an example of the mood and rhythm of the Malagueña in Ravel's Rapsodie espagnole.

Mandolín

The mandolin, a plucked string instrument similar to the lute, exists in various forms. It has fixed metal frets and metal strings in pairs. The prevalent method of playing is tremolando, the notes rapidly repeated with a plectrum. It has been used in opera, notably in Verdi's Otello and in Falstaff, and in the concert-hall in Mahler's Seventh and Eighth Symphonies.

Manual

The manual is a keyboard for the hands, the word used for instruments such as the organ or harpsichord that often have more than one keyboard. It is opposed to the pedal-board found generally on the organ and much more rarely on the harpsichord or fortepiano.

Marímba

The marimba is a form of resonating xylophone occasionally used in the Western orchestra in compositions of the 20th century.

Mass

The Mass, the Eucharist of Catholic worship (= Latin: Missa; Italian: Messa; French & German: Messe), has long provided texts for musical setting. The Ordinary of the Mass, the normally recurrent parts of the liturgy, consists of the Kyrie eleison (Lord have mercy), Gloria (Glory be to God in the highest), Credo (I believe), Sanctus (Holy, holy, holy), Benedictus (Blessed be he who comes in the name of the Lord) and the Agnus Dei (Lamb of God). These are the texts most often set. The Proper of the Mass changes from day to day, according to the season or the occasion. The texts of the Proper are less often set, except for texts that may be used with some frequency.

Mazurka

The mazurka is a Polish dance, transformed by Chopin in some fifty piano pieces in this form.

Measure

A measure is, in English, a bar, in the sense of the music written between the vertical bar-lines written on the stave to mark the metrical units of a piece of music.

Mélodie

The French art-songs of the 19th and 20th centuries are known as mélodies, the counterpart of the German Lieder.

Melodrama

A melodrama is a drama with musical accompaniment and interludes, although the word has come to have a different popular meaning in English. In the technical sense of the word, Bizet's collaboration with Alphonse Daudet in L'Arlésienne is a melodrama, and the word is used to describe the grave-digging scene in Beethoven's opera Fidelio.

Meno

Meno (Italian: less) is used in musical directions to qualify other words as in meno mosso, with less movement.

Mesto

Mesto (Italian: sad) is used in directions to performers as an indication of mood, as in the slow movement of the Horn Trio of Brahms, which is marked Adagio mesto.

Metamorphosis

Metamorphosis, change of shape, is used particularly to describe the process of thematic metamorphosis, the transformation of thematic elements used by composers such as Liszt, a procedure unkindly satirised by one contemporary critic as the life and adventures of a theme.

Metronome

The metronome is a device, formerly based on the principle of the pendulum, but now controlled more often by electronic means, which measures the equal beats of a piece of music, as a guide to players. The metronome mark of 60 indicates one beat a second, 120 is twice as fast and 240 twice as fast again. The principle was based on the work of Galileo, but the most frequently found clockwork metronome was devised in Vienna by Beethoven's contemporary and briefly his collaborator Count Maelzel.

Mezzo

Mezzo (Italian: half) is found particularly in the compound words mezzo-forte, half loud, represented by the letters mf, and mezzo-piano, half soft, represented by the letters mp. Mezzo can serve as a colloquial abbreviation for mezzo-soprano, the female voice that employs a generally lower register than a soprano and consequently is often, in opera, given the parts of confidante, nurse or mother, secondary rôles to the heroine, usually a soprano. The instruction mezza voce directs a singer to sing with a controlled tone. The instruction can also occur in instrumental music.

Minor

Minor (= Latin: smaller) is used in musical terminology to describe a form of scale that corresponds, in its natural form, to the Aeolian mode, the scale on the white notes of the keyboard from A to A. Two other forms of the minor scale are commonly used, the melodic minor and the harmonic minor. The melodic minor scale is a form of minor scale that uses the natural minor form descending, but sharpens the sixth and seventh degrees ascending. The harmonic minor scale uses the natural minor with a sharpened seventh degree ascending and descending. The intervals between the first note or tonic (key note) and the third, sixth and seventh degrees of the natural minor scale are described as minor (that is, C to E flat , a minor third; C to A flat, a minor sixth; C to B flat, a minor seventh). C to D flat forms a minor second. A minor chord or minor triad consists of a bottom note with a note a minor third above, and, optionally, a note a perfect fifth above the bottom note. In this way the chord or triad C - E flat - G is described as minor.

Minstrel

The word minstrel has been used loosely to indicate a musical entertainer, providing his own accompaniment to his singing. The medieval minstrel, a secular musician, flourished between the 13th and 15th century, generally as an itinerant singer.

Minuet

A minuet (= French: menuet; German: Menuett; Italian: minuetto) is a triple metre French dance popular from the second half of the 17th until at least the end of the 18th century. It appears as an occasional element of the baroque instrumental suite and later as a movement in the pre-classical and classical symphony and allied forms, gradually replaced by the scherzo. The minuet usually has a complementary trio, a contrasting section in similar metre.

Miserere

Miserere (Latin: have mercy) is the first word of Psalms 50, 54 and 55, and the word appears on numerous occasions in Latin liturgical texts. There is a famous setting of Psalm 50 (= 51 in the Hebrew and English Psalter) by the early 17th century Italian composer Gregorio Allegri, the property of the Papal Chapel, written down from memory by Mozart at the age of fourteen, during his visit to Rome in 1770.

Missa

The Latin word Missa, the Catholic Mass or Eucharist, is found in the title of many polyphonic settings of the liturgical texts. The phrase Missa brevis, short Mass, was at first used to indicate a Mass with shorter musical settings of the Ordinary. It later came to be used on occasion for settings that included only the first two parts of the ordinary of the Mass, the Kyrie and the Gloria. Mass titles, particularly in the 16th century, are often distinguished by the musical material from which they are derived, sacred or secular, as in Missa Adieu mes amours, or Missa Ave Regina. The Missa Papae Marcelli, the Mass of Pope Marcellus, is the setting of the Mass written by Palestrina, supposedly to preserve polyphony from condemnation by the Council of Trent.

Mode

Modal scales are found in various forms. Plainchant, the traditional music of the Catholic liturgy, makes use of eight modes, the church modes, with names derived from very different, earlier Greek modes. The first church mode is the Dorian, the third the Phrygian, the fifth the Lydian and the seventh the Mixolydian. These are the so-called authentic modes, their range from D to D, E to E, F to F and G to G respectively. Each authentic mode has an associated plagal mode using the same final note, but within an octave range that starts a fourth below the final and extends a fifth above it. These plagal modes take the Greek prefix hypo-, as in Hypodorian, Hypophrygian, Hypolydian and Hypomixolydian. Theorists later distinguished two further pairs of authentic and plagal modes, the Aeolian, A to A, and the Ionian, C to C. The Locrian mode, B to B, is inaccurately named, but was early distinguished as Hyperaeolian. Early polyphony, reaching a height of perfection in the 16th century, is modal, and its techniques continue to be studied as modal counterpoint, a necessary element in the training of a musician. These listed modes and a variety of other modes may be distinguished in folk-music, while composers of the 20th century have constructed their own synthetic scales or modes.

Moderato

Moderato (Italian: moderate) is used as an indication of the speed to be adopted by a performer. It may be used to qualify other adjectives, as allegro moderato, moderately fast.

Molto

Molto (Italian: much, very) is often found in directions to performers, as in allegro molto or allegro di molto, molto vivace or molto piano.

Mosso

Mosso (Italian: moved, agitated) is generally found in the phrases più mosso, faster, and meno mosso, slower.

Motet

A motet is generally a choral composition for church use but using texts that are not necessarily a part of the liturgy. It is the Catholic equivalent of the anthem of the

Church of England. Motets appear in very different forms from the 13th century onwards.

Motif

The word motif, coined from French, is used in English instead of the German Motiv, or English and American motive. It may be defined as a recognisable thematic particle, a group of notes that has a recognisable thematic character, and hence longer than a figure, the shortest recognisable element.

Moto

Moto (Italian: motion, movement) is found in the direction 'con moto', with movement, fast. A moto perpetuo is a rapid piece that gives the impression of perpetual motion, as in the Allegro de concert of Paganini or the last movement of Ravel's Violin Sonata.

Movement

A movement is a section of a more extended work that is more or less complete in itself, although occasionally movements are linked together, either through the choice of a final inconclusive chord or by a linking note, as in the first and second movement of Mendelssohn's Violin Concerto.

Mute

Mutes (= Italian: sordino; French: sourdine; German: Dämpfer) are used to muffle the sound of an instrument, by controlling the vibration of the bridge on a string instrument or muffling the sound by placing an object in the bell of a brass instrument.

N

Nachtmusik

Nachtmusik (German: night-music) is best known from Mozart's Eine kleine Nachtmusik, A Little Night Music, a serenade.

Natural

A natural is a note that is neither a sharp nor a flat. The adjective is used to describe the natural horn or natural trumpet, without valves.

Neoclassical

Neoclassical style in music indicates a 20th century eclectic return by some composers to various styles and forms of earlier periods, whether classical or baroque. The style is exemplified in the score for the ballet Pulcinella by Stravinsky or by the same composer's opera The Rake's Progress.

Nocturne

A nocturne is a night-piece, music that evokes a nocturnal mood. It was developed as a form of solo piano music by the Irish pianist and composer John Field in the early 19th century, leading to its notable use by Chopin. The title has been used more recently by other composers for both instrumental and vocal compositions.

Nonet

A nonet is a composition for nine performers.

Notation

Notation is the method of writing music down, practices of which have varied during the course of history. Staff notation is the conventional notation that makes use of the five-line staff or stave, while some recent composers have employed systems of graphic notation to indicate their more varied requirements, often needing detailed explanations in a preface to the score. Notation is inevitably imprecise, providing a guide of varying accuracy for performers, who must additionally draw on stylistic tradition.

Note

A note in English is either a single sound or its representation in notation. American English refers to a single sound as a tone, following German practice.

O

Obbligato

Obbligato (Italian: obligatory) is often used virtually as a noun in English, in spite of its derivation. It is used to indicate an additional instrumental part that cannot be omitted, particularly when a solo instrument adds an accompanying melody in some baroque vocal forms. There is, for example, a well known violin obbligato to the mezzo-soprano aria Laudamus te, in the B minor Mass of Bach.

Oboe

The oboe is a double-reed instrument, an important part of the woodwind section of the modern orchestra. The mechanism of its keys underwent considerable development in the 19th century. In earlier times it formed an important part of the outdoor military band, but the Western symphony orchestra normally uses a pair of instruments. The oboe d'amore is the alto of the oboe family, used in the baroque period, and the tenor is found in the cor anglais or, in the mid-18th century, in the oboe da caccia. The tone of the instrument, much affected by different methods of cutting the reeds, can impart a characteristic sound to a whole orchestra.

Octave

The octave is an interval of an eighth, as for example from the note C to C or D to D. The first note can have a sharp or flat providing the last note has the corresponding sharp or flat (i. e. C sharp to C sharp).

Octet

An octet is a composition for eight performers.

Ondes Martenot

The ondes Martenot, an electronic instrument invented by the French musician Maurice Martenot, produces single sounds by means of a keyboard that controls the frequencies from an oscillator. It has a wide range and offers the possibility of glissando. It became popular among French composers, including Milhaud, Honegger, Koechlin, Schmitt, Ibert, Jolivet, Messiaen and Boulez. Varèse also wrote for it, as he did for the less versatile electronic instrument, the theremin.

Opera

An opera is a drama in which most of the actors sing all or most of their parts. The form developed at the end of the 16th century in Italy, from where it spread to other regions of Europe, although it never became a regular part of London musical life until the early 18th century. Internationally Italian opera has proved immensely important and popular, while opera in France underwent independent development in the later 17th century under the Italian-born composer Lully. The 19th century brought particular developments in German romantic opera and in the innovative music-dramas of Wagner. The word opera covers a wide variety of musico-dramatic forms, from the Orfeo of Monteverdi to The Threepenny Opera (Dreigroschenoper) of Kurt Weill and Berthold Brecht of 1928, derived from the English anti-heroic Beggar's Opera two centuries earlier.

Opéra bouffe

Opéra bouffe is the French term for comic operetta of composers such as Offenbach in 19th century France.

Opera buffa

Opera buffa is Italian comic opera, particularly in the form it took in early 18th century Italy.

Opéra comique

French opéra comique originally purely comic and later more sentimental in mood, included spoken dialogue, interspersed with songs.

Opera seria

Opera seria was the form of Italian serious opera that held sway from the reforms of the early 18th century for a hundred years. It came to be governed by strict rules as to subject and structure, and underwent reform in the interests of greater realism in the second half of the 18th century with the composer Gluck.

Operetta

Operetta is light opera, a development largely of the 19th century, exemplified in the work of Offenbach in France and Johann Strauss the younger in Vienna.

Opus

Opus (= Latin: work) is generally used in the listing of a composer's works by opus numbers, usually abbreviated to Op. Since the Latin plural opera would lead to unnecessary confusion it is best avoided, although the alternative opuses remains an unsatisfactory substitute. Opus numbers are not always a guide to the date of composition or even to the date of publication.

Oratorio

Oratorio has its origin in the musical performances used by the followers of St. Philip Neri, the Oratorians, a religious order founded in 1575, although it has a possible remoter origin in the liturgical drama of the Middle Ages. Forms of oratorio change, but it remains primarily a work in which religious texts often with a narrative content are set for performance by singers and instruments. The oratorio underwent various developments throughout Europe, with the 17th century composer Carissimi and his successors in Italy, Charpentier in France, and later with Telemann and others in Germany and, above all, Handel in the English oratorio of the early 18th century.

Orchestra

The orchestra, the dancing-place of the ancient Greek theatre, came, in the early 18th century, to have its modern meaning as a group of instrumental performers of varied number, although this meaning still met with objections at the time. The size and composition of the orchestra has differed from century to century, but during the course of the 17th century the string section developed as a five-part and later as a four-part section, with first and second violins, violas and cellos and double basses, the last two playing the same part, although the double basses would sound an octave lower. In the later 18th century it became usual to have in the orchestra an additional pair of French horns and a pair of oboes, doubling flute as necessary, with a bassoon doubling the bass. By the end of the 18th century a larger ensemble that included when necessary a pair of trumpets and drums was usual. In the 19th century clarinets, already used by Mozart and Haydn, became a regular part of the woodwind section, in addition to flutes, oboes and bassoons. The brass section came to include trombones, instruments earlier used for special purposes only, as well as trumpets, to be extended to instruments of lower range during the century. The 20th century has brought an extension of the percussion section. The number of players involved in a full symphony orchestra has grown very considerably, with over sixty string players, and a possible forty or more wind and percussion players. This compares with Mozart's Salzburg orchestra of 23 string players and a dozen or so wind-players and the orchestras of less prosperous princedoms, which might employ much smaller forces, a dozen or less string players and four or five wind players.

Orchestration

Orchestration is the art of arranging music for the orchestra or the way in which this is done.

Organ

The organ is a keyboard instrument in which the sound is produced by air passing through pipes of various size and construction to give a wide variety of pitches and timbres. The instrument has its probable Western origin in the Hellenistic period, with the water-organ of Alexandria. Varying in size and mechanical efficiency, the organ had by the later 17th century given rise to an important school of performance, leading directly to the achievement of Johann Sebastian Bach in the first half of the 18th century. Technical developments have taken

place since then, giving still greater versatility to the king of instruments.

Ostinato

Ostinato (Italian: obstinate) indicates a part that repeats the same rhythm or melodic element. The basso ostinato or ostinato bass occurs in the ground bass of baroque arias where a melody is set over a repeated bass pattern. Ostinato is used by the Bavarian composer Carl Orff in his instrumental teaching methods, where it may form a basis for improvisation by pupils.

Overture

The overture (= French: ouverture; German: Ouvertüre; Italian: sinfonia) is an introductory piece, often designed to initiate an opera or other dramatic work. The late 17th century French overture of Lully opens with a slow section in dotted (uneven) rhythm, followed by a fugal section, before the return of the slow opening. The Italian overture provides the origin of the symphony, with two fast movements framing a central slow movement. The word Ouvertüre or Ouverture is sometimes used to mean an orchestral suite, as in the four orchestral suites of Johann Sebastian Bach. In the 19th century the overture became also a possible independent composition, a concert movement, often with literary or geographical associations, or an occasional connotation. Early examples of these occur in Mendelssohn's Overture A Midsummer Night's Dream, originally intended as a concert overture, or in the programmatic overtures of Berlioz.

P

Pantomime

Although a pantomime in Britain has come to indicate a children's Christmas entertainment, making use of traditional and topical elements in a mixture of fairy-story, comic routine and popular song, the word originally indicated a performance entirely in mime, in this sense having a long history. In this second and original sense pantomime is sometimes found as part of a descriptive title of a musical work or part of a work originally so intended.

Part

A part may indicate the line or music intended for a particular performer. Earlier choral music, for example, was written in separate part-books, one for each part, as is the modern practice with orchestral parts, rather than in the full vocal score now usual. The art of part-writing or, in American, voice-leading, is the art of writing simultaneous parts according to the established rules of harmony. A part-song is a vocal work in which different voices are used, as distinct from a song in which all sing the same melody.

Partita

Partita is another word for suite, used, for example, by Johann Sebastian Bach in the title of a set of keyboard suites or in the three Partitas for unaccompanied violin.

Passacaglia

The passacaglia is a baroque dance variation form on a short melodic formula usually occurring in the bass. It is similar in form to the chaconne, in which a recurrent bass pattern forms the basis of the composition, implying a recurrent harmonic progression. The two forms are sometimes confused by composers.

Famous examples of the passacaglia include Johann Sebastian Bach's C minor Passacaglia for the organ. Something of the form appears in the last movement of the Fourth Symphony of Brahms, and passacaglias occur in Berg's opera Wozzeck and in Britten's opera Peter Grimes.

Passion

The four accounts of the suffering and death of Christ, as given in the first four books of the New Testament, were customarily sung during the Catholic rites of Holy Week to plainchant, with a division of parts where direct speech is involved. It became customary in the 15th century to allow the singing of the parts of the crowd (= Latin: turba) in the biblical narrative in polyphonic settings, with a gradual extension of the polyphonic element in the next century. The best known settings of the Passion are the surviving Lutheran settings by Johann Sebastian Bach of the accounts of the Passion in the Gospels of St. Matthew and of St. John.

Pastorale

Pastorale is a musical expression of a genre familiar in European literature from Hellenistic times or earlier, an idealisation of the rural, in literary form, in the lives and loves (often fatal) of shepherds and shepherdesses, and then, by extension, of the country in general. The word may be used as the title of a piece of music suggesting a rural idyll. In Italy it was associated particularly with the dance-form, the Siciliano, used to suggest the scene of shepherds in the fields near Bethlehem at the birth of Christ. Such pastoral movements formed part of the Christmas concertos of Corelli and his contemporaries and imitators. Adjectivally used, the Pastoral Symphony of Beethoven, in true Wordsworthian fashion, offers emotions experienced on a visit to the country, recollected in what passed for tranquillity in his life.

Pavan

The pavan (= French: pavane), a stately duple metre dance of the 16th and early 17th centuries, appears in various English spellings, paven, pavin and other forms. Coupled with the quicker triple metre galliard, it was among the most popular dances of the time. The origin of the word is attributed either to the Italian town of Padua or to the peacock (= Italian: pavone). Well known examples include the English composer John Dowland's Lachrimae, or Seaven Teares Figured in Seaven Passionate Pavans or Ravel's nostalgic Pavane pour une infante défunte, (Pavan for a Dead Infanta).

Pentatonic

The pentatonic or five-note scale is formed by the black notes of the keyboard, or the white notes C, D, E, G and A - two whole tones, a minor third and a whole tone. This form of scale is the basis of folk melodies in many countries, from China to Scotland, and occasionally occurs, in passing at least, in the work of 20th century composers. It is an important element in the educational music of Carl Orff and in the choral method of the Hungarian composer Zoltán Kodály.

Percussion

The percussion section of the orchestra includes all instruments that are played by being struck, including the piano and celesta. Originally consisting of a pair of kettledrums or timpani, appearing normally with a pair of trumpets, in the orchestra of the later 18th century, a military importation, the percussion section was significantly enlarged with the allegedly Turkish fashion of the later 18th century, involving the occasional use of bass drum, cymbals and triangle in an imitation of the Janissary band. Liszt shocked audiences by including a triangle in the orchestration of a piano concerto, dubbed a triangle concerto by a hostile critic, and gradually other percussion instruments were added for occasional effects, including even, by Erik Satie, the typewriter.

Performance practice

Performance practice or performing practice (= German: Aufführungspraxis) indicates the attempt to perform music in the way envisaged originally by the composer. The second half of the 20th century has brought a significant interest in musicology and the technology and scholarship necessary to the construction of copies of earlier instruments and to the study of methods of performance on these instruments. The study of performing practice extends from the study of music of the earliest periods to that of relatively recent periods of the 19th and early 20th centuries.

Philharmonic

The adjective Philharmonic and noun Philharmonia are generally used as adopted titles by orchestras or by music-loving societies of one sort or another. The words have no other technical meaning.

Phrase

A phrase in music, on the analogy of syntactical use, is a recognisable musical unit, generally ending in a cadence of some kind, and forming part of a period or sentence. Phrasing in performance has a less precise use, indicating the correct grouping of notes, whether as phrases in the technical sense or in smaller distinct units, corresponding to the various possible syntactical uses of punctuation.

Piano

Piano (Italian: soft) is generally represented by the letter p in directions to performers. Pianissimo, represented by pp, means very soft. Addition of further letters p indicates greater degrees of softness, as in Tchaikovsky's Sixth Symphony, where an excessive ppppp is used.

Pianoforte

The pianoforte, known generally as the piano, was developed during the 18th century. A keyboard instrument, it is distinguished from the harpsichord by its hammer action, with hammers striking the strings when keys are depressed. Dynamic change is possible by applying more or less force to the keys. The instrument underwent a number of technical changes during the century and in the years following became the most popular instrument of domestic entertainment.

Piano trio

Piano trio, piano quartet and piano quintet indicate works for the piano with varying numbers of string instruments. The piano trio is scored for piano, violin and cello, the piano quartet for piano, violin, viola and cello, and the piano quintet for piano, two violins, viola and cello.

Piccolo

The piccolo (Italian: small) is the small flute, pitched an octave higher than the ordinary flute. Adjectivally the word may be applied to other instruments or groups, as in coro piccolo, small chorus. The violino piccolo, a smaller violin, is used by Johann Sebastian Bach in the first Brandenburg Concerto, where it is to be tuned a third higher.

Pitch

The pitch of a note is the frequency of its vibrations. The exact pitch of notes has varied over the years and nowadays differs to some extent between continent and continent or even between orchestra and orchestra.

Earlier pitches were generally lower, but not necessarily standardised. Perfect pitch is the ability to distinguish the pitch of a note, according to generally accepted nomenclature. Relative pitch is the ability to distinguish the pitch of one note with relation to another, given note.

Più

Più (Italian: more) is found in directions to performers, as in più forte, louder, or più lento, slower.

Pizzicato

Pizzicato (Italian: plucked) is a direction to performers on string instruments to pluck the strings. A return to the use of the bow is indicated by the word 'arco', bow. Pizzicato notes on the violin, viola and cello are normally plucked with the index finger of the right hand. The great violinist Paganini, however, introduced the technique of left-hand pizzicato for occasional use, notably in one of the variations of his 24th Caprice, where it produces a very special effect.

Plainchant

Plainchant is the traditional monodic chant of the Catholic and Eastern Christian liturgies. In Western Europe plainchant was largely but not completely standardised under Pope Gregory the Great at the end of the sixth century. This form of chant is free in rhythm, following the words of the liturgical texts, and is modal, using the scales of the eight church modes. In its long history it has undergone various reforms, revisions and attempts at restoration.

Poco

Poco (Italian: little) is found in directions to performers, as in poco allegro, although un poco allegro, a little fast, would be more accurate. Poco, in fact, is commonly used meaning un poco, a little.

Polacca

Polacca, Polish, appears often in the phrase Alla polacca, in the Polish manner, as in the last movement of the first Brandenburg Concerto of Johann Sebastian Bach.

Polka

The polka, a Bohemian dance, became one of the most popular ball-room dances of the 19th century, its title a possible reference to Poland. It is used by Smetana in his Czech opera The Bartered Bride and elsewhere and in William Walton's jeu d'esprit Façade.

Polonaise

The polonaise is a Polish dance in triple metre. Although the title is found in French Suite No. 6 of Johann Sebastian Bach and elsewhere in the earlier 18th century, the form is best known from the piano pieces written by Chopin a hundred years later, works that elevated the original dance to a higher level, while capturing the current spirit of Polish nationalism.

Polyphony

Polyphony is the writing of music in many parts or in more than one part, with reference in particular to contrapuntal practices. Monody or monophony are possible opposites.

Post Horn

The post horn is a relatively simple kind of horn once played by postilions as a signal of the departure, arrival or approach of a coach. Mozart made brief use of the instrument in his Post Horn Serenade, and its sound was imitated by various composers, including Johann Sebastian Bach in his harpsichord Capriccio on the Departure of His Beloved Brother, which includes a Postilion Aria and a fugue on the sound of the post horn.

Postlude

A postlude is played at the end of a piece and indicates, in particular, the additional piano phrases that may appear at the end of a song, after the singer has stopped. The word is more widely used to describe the closing section of a work or to indicate a piece of music to be played as the conclusion of some ceremony, the opposite of a prelude.

Prelude

A prelude (= Latin: praeludium, praeambulum; French: prélude; German: Vorspiel) is a movement or section of a work that comes before another movement or section of a work, although the word also has been used for short independent pieces that may stand alone, or even for more extended works, such as Debussy's Prélude à l'après-midi d'un faune.

Presto

Presto (Italian: quick) is used frequently as a direction to performers. An even faster speed is indicated by the superlative prestissimo or even il più presto possibile, as fast as possible.

Programme music

Programme music is music that has a narrative or descriptive extra-musical content. Music of this kind has a long history, but the term programme music was coined by Liszt, whose symphonic poems principally attempt to translate into musical terms works of literature, such as Goethe's Faust or Dante's Divina Commedia. It seems preferable that the term should be limited to instrumental music for concert use and should not include either incidental music or ballet music.

Psalm

Psalms are the texts included in the biblical Book of Psalms and retaining an important place in the services of the Catholic Divine Office, sung to plainchant. The biblical texts are not metrical and therefore use a relatively simple form of chant that can be expanded by the use of a longer reciting note, the final syllables sung to a short syllabic formula. After the Reformation of the early 16th century metrical versions of the Psalms became current, with texts that could be sung to hymn-tunes. Harmonized settings of the biblical and metrical Psalms have been current in Protestant churches and chapels since the 16th century.

Q

Quadrille

The quadrille was one of the most popular ball-room dances of the 19th century, generally in a brisk duple metre.

Quarter-tone

Divisions of the tone smaller than a semitone are occasionally found in art-music, particularly in the 20th century. Quarter-tones occur in the solo violin part of the Second Violin Concerto of Belá Bartók.

Quartet

A quartet is a composition for four players or the name for a group of four players.

Quintet

A quintet is a composition for five players or the name for a group of five players.

Quodlibet

A quodlibet (Latin: what you please) is a light-hearted composition generally containing a combination of well known tunes. There is an example in Johann Sebastian Bach's Goldberg Variations, where the composer combines the theme of the variations with two popular songs of the time.

R

Rallentando

Rallentando (Italian: becoming slower) is a direction to a performer to play gradually slower.

Recitative

Recitative is used in vocal works, particularly opera and oratorio, usually for a solo voice, in relatively free rhythm. In this respect recitative is distinct from the formal aria. Recitative might be accompanied by basso continuo, harpsichord or other chordal instruments and a bass instrument (recitativo secco or dry recitative), or accompanied by a larger number of instruments (recitativo accompagnato, accompanied recitative). Recitative is often used for narrative or for the forwarding of the plot in opera.

Recorder

The recorder (= German: Blockflöte; French: flûte à bec; Italian: flauto dolce), the straight flute, exists in a variety of sizes, the principal of which are the descant or soprano, the treble or alto, the tenor and the bass, the first and third of which have a range upwards from C and the second and fourth of which have a range upwards from F, with similar fingering. Other sizes of recorder include the smallest, the sopranino, an octave higher than the treble and the great bass, an octave lower than the tenor. An even larger family of recorders existed in the later 16th century. The earlier recorder was used in consort music, while it was used rather as a solo instrument in music in the later 17th and early 18th centuries, with sonatas for the instrument by Handel and solo parts in the second and fourth of the Brandenburg Concertos of Johann Sebastian Bach. The revival of the instrument in the 20th century has led to a number of new solo works for recorder.

Reed

Reeds, made either from traditional material or from plastic or metal, are used to produce a musical sound from their vibration by means of an air column. The clarinet uses a single reed, fastened to a hollow mouthpiece, while the oboe and bassoon use a double reed, one side vibrating against the other. The reed-pipes of the organ are generally made of metal, with a thin vibrating tongue to produce the sound. Similar laminae are used in the mouth-organ and harmonica. Some instruments, like the bagpipes or the crumhorn, use covered double reeds, set inside an air chamber.

Register

The register of a voice or instrument is a distinct part of its range. The clarinet, for example, has a distinctive lower register known, from the origin of the instrument, as the chalumeau register, and an upper register of more flute-like timbre.

Registration

Registration is the choice of stops used by an organist or harpsichordist, a much more elaborate matter for the former.

Requiem Mass

The Catholic Mass for the Dead opens with the words Requiem aeternam dona eis, Domine (Eternal rest grant unto them, O Lord), leading to the use of the word Requiem for the Mass for the Dead. Important settings of the Requiem include that by Mozart and the large scale settings of the Requiem by Berlioz and by Verdi. Brahms set a collection of Lutheran texts to form his German Requiem, while Fauré set a liturgical text that used parts of the burial service.

Rhapsody

The title rhapsody (= French: rapsodie) came into general use in music of the mid-19th century, notably with the Hungarian Rhapsodies of Liszt. It implies a work free in form and inspiration, often an expression of national temperament, as in the Slavonic Rhapsodies of Dvořák and the Rapsodie espagnole of Ravel.

Rhythm

Rhythm, an essential element in music in one way or another, is the arrangement of notes according to their relative duration and relative accentuation.

Rigaudon

The French folk-dance, the rigaudon, is occasionally found in instrumental dance suites of the 17th and 18th centuries. It was normally in a brisk duple metre.

Ritardando

Ritardando (Italian: becoming slower) abbreviated often to rit., is often used as a direction to players.

Ritenuto

Ritenuto (Italian: held back) directs a player to slow down at once.

Ritornello

The ritornello, a recurrent phrase or passage, is a feature of baroque form, where an aria may be punctuated by re-appearances of a short instrumental phrase. It became a frequent element in baroque solo concertos by composers such as Vivaldi, and works with operatic connotations.

Rococo

Rococo, a term borrowed, as are so many other terms in musicology, from architecture and the visual arts, is used in particular to describe the light decorative French style as found in the work of Couperin and Rameau in the first half of the 18th century.

Romanticism

Romanticism in cultural history is a word that defies precise definition. In music it is most commonly applied to a period or the predominant features of that period, from the early 19th century until the early 20th. Features of romanticism in music include an attention to feeling rather than to formal symmetry, expressed in a freer use of traditional forms, an expansion of the instrumental resources of music and an extension of harmonic language. Music also reflected other preoccupations, influenced particularly by the arts of literature and painting, and their preoccupation with the remote and exotic, whether historical or geographical, or both. Early German romantic opera, for example, is found in Weber's Der Freischütz, with its plot involving woodmen and huntsmen and the mysterious midnight magic of the forest.

Rondo

Rondo (= French: rondeau) form involves the use of a recurrent theme between a series of varied episodes, often used for the rapid final movement of a classical concerto or symphony.

Rubato

Rubato, (Italian: stolen), is a direction to allow a player a measure of freedom in performance. The phrase tempo rubato is also found.

S

Saltarello

The saltarello is a rapid Italian dance in triple metre, examples of which survive from the Middle Ages. The rhythm and energy of the dance are similar to those of the tarantella. A well known example appears in the final movement of Mendelssohn's 'Italian' Symphony.

Sarabande

The sarabande is a slow dance in triple metre, generally found in the baroque instrumental suite. The dance seems to have been Latin American in origin, imported from Latin America to Spain in the 16th century.

Saxophone

The saxophone, a single-reed instrument, was invented in the middle of the 19th century by Adolphe Sax. It is used widely in jazz, and has never been a permanent member of the symphony orchestra. Notable use is made of the saxophone by Ravel in his Boléro and in his orchestration of Mussorgsky's Pictures at an Exhibition, and other composers have used the instrument for special effects.

Scale

A scale is a sequence of notes placed in ascending or descending order by step.

Scherzo

A scherzo is a light-hearted movement found from the early 17th century in various forms, but used by Beethoven as an alternative to the minuet in symphonies, sonatas and other instrumental forms. Chopin expanded the form very considerably. The diminutive scherzino or scherzetto is occasionally found, while scherzando occurs as a direction to performers. The scherzo, like the minuet, is generally used to frame a trio section of contrasted material.

Score

A musical score is written music that shows all parts. A conductor's score, for example, may have as many as thirty different simultaneous instrumental parts on one page, normally having the woodwind at the top, followed below by the brass, the percussion and the strings. A distinction is made between a vocal score, which gives voice parts with a simplified two-stave version of any instrumental parts, and a full score, which includes all vocal and instrumental parts generally on separate staves. To score a work is to write it out in score. A symphony, for example, might be sketched in short score, on two staves, and later orchestrated or scored for the required instruments.

Seguidilla

The seguidilla or seguidillas is a fairly quick triple-metre Spanish dance. There is a famous imitation of the form in Carmen's seguidilla in the first act of Bizet's opera Carmen.

Semi-opera

The term semi-opera has been coined to describe the English dramatic works of the later 17th century that combined spoken drama with a significant element of music, as in Purcell's King Arthur, with a text by Dryden, or in the same composer's The Fairy Queen, an adaptation of Shakespeare's A Midsummer Night's Dream.

Sempre

Sempre (Italian: always) is found in directions to performers, as in sempre piano, always soft.

Senza

Senza (Italian: without) is found in directions to performers, particularly in phrases such as senza sordino, without mute.

Septet

A septet is a composition for seven players or the name for a group of seven players.

Serenade

A serenade (= German: Serenade, Ständchen) is often similar in form to the divertimento. Etymologically a piece for evening performance, usually outdoors, the counterpart of the morning Aubade, the title came to have a much more general meaning, although it often suggests a piece of music in honour of someone or something, an extension of the traditional performance of a lover beneath the window of his mistress.

Serialism

Serialism is the important 20th century compositional technique that uses, as a basis of unity, a series of the twelve semitones of the octave in a certain order, which may then be taken in retrograde form, in inversion and in retrograde inversion, and also in transposition. The technique, an extension of late romantic chromaticism, was formulated by Arnold Schoenberg in the 1920s followed by his pupils Alban Berg and Anton Webern, and thereafter by many other composers. Problems arise for the listener in the difficulty of hearing the series, however visually apparent from the written score.

Sextet

A sextet is a composition for six players or the name of a group of six players.

Sharp

A sharp, represented by the sign #, added before a note, raises its pitch by a semitone. In general terms music that is sharp may be simply out of tune, at too high a pitch.

Siciliana

The siciliana or siciliano (= French: sicilienne) had its probable origin in a Sicilian shepherd dance or song. It came to be associated in the later 17th century with the pastoral, particularly in the Christmas Concerto of the period. The siciliana is normally in compound dotted rhythm and is slow and sometimes melancholy in mood.

Side-drum

The side-drum or snare drum is military in origin. It is a small drum, played with two wooden sticks, with a band of gut strings or wires that can be stretched across the under-surface of the drum to add a rattling effect when it is struck.

Sinfonia

Sinfonia (Italian: symphony) in earlier usage indicated a passage or piece of instrumental music, sometimes an introductory piece, leading later to the Italian overture, known as the sinfonia before the opera, the origin of the Italian symphony.

Sinfonia concertante

The sinfonia concertante is a concerto that uses two or more solo instruments. The title was used in the later 18th century by Mozart, Haydn and their contemporaries, and has occasionally been used by composers since then.

Sinfonietta

A sinfonietta is a small symphony. The word is sometimes used to indicate a small orchestra.

Singspiel

A Singspiel is a German form of play with music. The word is used to indicate a stage work that makes some use of spoken dialogue, even in a context of primarily musical interest. Examples are found in Mozart's The Magic Flute and in Beethoven's only opera, Fidelio.

Sonata

The title sonata originally designated music that was to be played rather than sung. The baroque sonata developed in two parallel forms. The first, the sonata da chiesa or church sonata, was generally of four movements in the order slow-fast-slow-fast, the faster movements fugal in character. The second, the sonata da camera or chamber sonata, was in essence a dance suite. Sonatas of this kind might be played by a melodic instrument with basso continuo or with a realised keyboard part, or in the form of trio sonatas, with two melody instruments and basso continuo, therefore normally involving four players.

The classical sonata, instrumental music again generally in several movements, might involve one or more instruments. There was in particular a development of the solo keyboard sonata, from Carl Philipp Emanuel Bach to Beethoven. Duo sonatas, generally using a keyboard instrument and a melody instrument, developed from an earlier form in which the melody instrument predominated to a form in which the keyboard assumed greater importance, with an optional accompaniment from a melody instrument. Greater degrees of equality between the two were achieved in the later violin sonatas of Mozart and the violin sonatas and cello sonatas of Beethoven.

The 19th century brought an expansion of the sonata and greater freedom in the treatment of existing forms, often with more considerable technical demands on performers, as in the violin and piano sonatas and cello and piano sonatas of Brahms.

Sonata-form

Sonata-form, otherwise known with similar inaccuracy as first movement form or sonata-allegro form, developed during the second half of the 18th century as a principal form in instrumental music, from Haydn onwards. The form is based on a triple division of a movement into exposition, development and recapitulation. The first section normally contains two contrasting subjects, the first in the tonic key and the second in the dominant key or in the relative major of a minor key movement. The section ends with a coda or codetta. The middle section, the development, offers varied treatment of themes or parts of themes that have already been heard. The recapitulation brings back the first and second subjects now in the tonic key. The movement ends with a coda. The form is used for all kinds of instrumental music, from sonatas to symphonies, and is expanded and varied in a number of ways.

Sonatina

A sonatina is a little sonata, simpler in structure and shorter in length than a sonata.

Soprano

The soprano is the highest kind of female voice. The word may be used as an adjective to describe instruments of higher range, such as the soprano saxophone, or to qualify the word clef, the soprano clef, now little used, puts a C clef on the bottom line of the stave.

Sostenuto

Sostenuto (Italian: sustained) is a direction to performers to play smoothly.

Spinet

The spinet is a small form of harpsichord.

Staff

The staff or stave (plural: staves) indicates the set of lines used for the notation of notes of different pitches. The five-line stave is in general use, with a four-line stave used for plainchant. Staves of other numbers of lines were once used. The system, with coloured lines for C and for F, followed principles suggested first by Guido of Arezzo in the 11th century. Staff notation is the system of notation that uses the stave.

Stop

The stop on an organ is the device that brings into operation a particular set of pipes.

Stretto

In a fugue stretto is the device by which a second voice enters with the subject overlapping a first voice, rather than starting after the completion of the subject by the first voice. The word is sometimes used to indicate a faster speed, particularly at the climax of a movement.

String

String instruments are chordophones, instruments that sound by the vibration of a string of a certain tension. The string section of the modern orchestra uses first and second violins, violas, cellos and double basses. A string trio consists of violin, viola and cello; a string quartet consists of two violins, viola and cello and a string quintet either of two violins, two violas and cello, as in the case of Mozart's work in this form, or of two violins, viola and two cellos, as in the case of Schubert's famous C major String Quintet and the Quintets of Boccherini. Other numbers and combinations of string instruments are possible in other ensembles.

Study

A study (= French: étude; German: Etüde) is a piece of music originally designed primarily for the technical development of the player. Studies came, however, to be compositions of considerable musical distinction, as in the case of the Etudes of Chopin or of Debussy.

Subject

A subject is a theme or group of themes.

Suite

A suite is an instrumental piece consisting of several shorter pieces. The baroque suite generally contains a series of dance movements, in particular the allemande, courante, sarabande and gigue. Later suites of all kinds exist, some formed by extracts of a larger work, an opera, ballet or incidental music.

Symphony

Originally indicating a generally instrumental section or composition, as in the case of the brief instrumental introduction to Monteverdi's opera Orfeo, the symphony came to be the principal serious orchestral form of the later 18th century and thereafter. This later form of the symphony (= Italian: sinfonia) has its immediate origin in the three-movement Italian overture to opera found in the work of Alessandro Scarlatti in the late 17th and early 18th century. The Italian overture opens with a fast movement, followed by a slow movement and a final fast dance-movement in triple metre. The function of the symphony as an overture continued into the second half of the 18th century, to be replaced more generally by its new function as an isolated orchestral form. The classical symphony of Haydn and Mozart is generally in four movements, opening with a sonata-form allegro, followed by a slow movement, a minuet and trio and a rondo finale. With Beethoven the symphony grew in size and ambition, an example followed later by Brahms,Bruckner and others. In the 19th century and into the 20th century the symphony, now much expanded, remained the most respected and demanding form that a composer might tackle. A symphony may loosely be defined as an orchestral composition generally in several movements.

T

Tafelmusik

Tafelmusik (German: table-music; = French: musique de table), indicates music used to accompany banquets. Telemann provides a well known example in three sets of Musique de Table, more commonly seen now under the German title, Tafelmusik.

Tambourine

The tambourine is a small single-headed hand-drum with jingles in its wooden frame. It is an instrument of some antiquity, but first found an occasional place in the symphony orchestra only in the 19th century, when it came to be used for exotic effects, as in the Capriccio espagnol and Sheherazade of Rimsky-Korsakov, where it gives a touch of the Spanish and the Middle Eastern respectively.

Tam-tam

The tam-tam is a gong, an instrument of Chinese origin in its Western orchestral form. It is first found in this context towards the end of the 18th century, when it is used for dramatic effect. Gustav Holst makes use of the tam-tam in Mars, from The Planets, and sets of gongs of a more obviously oriental kind are used by Puccini in his operas Madama Butterfly and Turandot.

Tanto

Tanto (Italian: so much) is occasionally found in tempo indications, as in allegro ma non tanto, similar in meaning, if slightly weaker than allegro ma non troppo, allegro but not too much.

Tarantella

The tarantella is a folk-dance from the Southern Italian town of Taranto. A 6/8 metre dance of some rapidity, it has been connected, by a process of false etymology, with the tarantula spider and either the effects of its bite or a means of its cure. There are well known examples in piano pieces by Chopin and by Liszt.

Te Deum

The Te Deum (Latin: We praise Thee, O Lord) is a canticle sung in thanksgiving and forming a part of the Divine Office, where it appears after Matins on Sundays and major feast days. It later formed part of the Church of England morning service. Well known examples are found in two settings by Handel, the Utrecht Te Deum and the Dettingen Te Deum , with more elaborate settings in the 19th century from Berlioz and Bruckner.

Temperaments

Temperaments are the various alterations of strict tuning necessary for practical purposes. Equal temperament, now in general use, involves the division of the octave into twelve equal semitones, a procedure that necessitates some modification of intervals from their true form, according to the ratios of physics. Equal temperament, exemplified in Johann Sebastian Bach's 48 Preludes and Fugues for the Well-Tempered Clavier, won gradual acceptance in the 18th century, replacing earlier systems of tuning. It has been plausibly suggested that the system of equal temperament was borrowed from China, where its mathematical basis was published towards the end of the 16th century.

Tempo

Tempo (Italian: time) means the speed at which a piece of music is played. Sometimes the exact tempo is given at the beginning of a piece of music with the number of beats to a minute, as measured by a metronome. More often tempo indications give the performer more latitude, although the Hungarian composer Belá Bartók, for example, gives exact timings, often of each section of a work. In much earlier music the tempo is implicit in the notation or in the type of music.

Tenor

The tenor voice is the highest male voice, except for the falsetto or otherwise produced register of the male alto and male soprano. In the Middle Ages the word had a different meaning. The tenor part of a vocal composition was the thematic basis, borrowed often from plainchant. The tenor voice came to assume the principal rôles in opera, largely replacing the castrato by the later 18th century. Various forms of tenor voice are demanded, particularly in opera, where the strong Heldentenor, (heroic tenor), met the requirements of Wagner, while other composers made use of lighter-voiced lyric tenors. The word tenor is also used adjectivally to describe instruments with a pitch lying between bass and alto, as, for example, the tenor trombone or, in earlier times, the tenor violin. The tenor clef, a C clef placed on the second line from the top of the five-line stave, is used for the upper registers of the cello and bassoon and for the tenor trombone.

Ternary form

Ternary form is a tripartite musical structure, three-part song-form, in which the third part is an exact or modified repetition of the first. Standard examples of ternary form can be heard in the minuet and trio movements of Haydn and Mozart or in the more expanded scherzo and trio movements of Beethoven.

Theme

A theme is a complete tune or melody which is of fundamental importance in a piece of music. Thematic metamorphosis or thematic transformation describes a process used by Liszt and others in which a theme may undergo transformation to provide material to sustain other movements or sections of a work, where new and apparently unrelated themes might otherwise have been used.

Theremin

The theremin, an electronic instrument invented by Léon Thérémin, a scientist of French origin who lived and worked in Russia, has the original feature of being played without the performer touching it. Frequencies and dynamics are controlled by the movement of the player's hands in the air, with pitch varying according to the distance of the right hand from an antenna and dynamics varying by the similar use of the left hand.

Time

Time, unlike the word tempo, which means speed or pace, is used in music for the metrical divisions or bar-lengths of a piece of music. These are indicated by two numbers at the beginning of a work or at the introduction of a changed time by two numbers that form a time-signature. The higher of the two numbers shows how many beats there are in a bar, while the lower number shows what kind of note it is. In this way a duple time-signature of 2/4 means that each bar consists of two quarter notes or crotchets or their equivalent in notes of shorter or longer duration. An indication of compound time such as 6/8 shows that there are six quavers or eighth notes in each bar, although in faster speeds these will be in two groups of three. Prime higher numbers such as five or seven necessitate asymmetrical groupings of notes.

Timpani

Timpani, kettledrums, unlike most other drums, have a definite pitch, tuned nowadays by pedals, but in earlier times by taps that served the same purpose, tightening or slackening the skin to produce higher or lower notes. In the later 18th century pairs of timpani were generally used in conjunction with pairs of trumpets, both instruments being of military origin. Beethoven made novel use of the timpani, as in his Violin Concerto, where they play an important part. Other composers made still greater use of the timpani, most eccentrically Berlioz, who calls for sixteen timpani and ten players in his Grande Messe des morts (Requiem).

Toccata

A toccata is an instrumental piece, often designed to display the technical proficiency of a performer and found particularly in keyboard music from the 15th century onwards. There are notable examples in the organ music of Johann Sebastian Bach, with some toccatas containing a series of movements.

Tombeau

Tombeau (French: tomb, tomb-stone) is a title used by French composers in tributes offered to predecessors or contemporaries. Ravel had recourse to this baroque title in his 1914 Tombeau de Couperin.

Tone poem

A tone poem (= German: Tondichtung) is a symphonic poem, an orchestral composition that seeks to express extra-musical ideas in music. The term Tondichtung was preferred by Richard Strauss, a master of the form.

Transcription

Music may be transcribed or arranged for instruments other than those for which it was originally designed. Well known transcriptions are found among the short pieces arranged for violin and piano by the famous violinist Fritz Kreisler.

Transposition

Music may be transposed when the original key is changed, a process all too necessary in accompanying singers and for whom a transposition of the music down a tone or two may be necessary. Some instruments are known as transposing instruments because the written notes for them sound higher or lower than the apparent written pitch, when they are played.

Transverse flute

The orchestral flute (= Italian: flauto traverso) is transverse, held horizontally, as opposed to the recorder, which is held vertically.

Treble

The treble voice is a voice in the higher register. The word is generally used for the unbroken voice of boys, although the register may be similar to that of the female soprano. Treble instruments are instruments of higher register and the G clef in use for this register is commonly known as the treble clef. Originally the treble or triplum was the third part added above a duplum or second additional part, lying above the lowest part, the tenor of the medieval motet.

Tremolo

Tremolo (Italian: trembling) indicates the quick repetition of a note, particularly in string-playing. This is impossible on the keyboard with a single note, but tremolo effects can be achieved by playing in rapid alternation two notes of a chord.

Triangle

The triangle is now part of the orchestral percussion section. It is an instrument of indefinite pitch made from a steel bar bent into the shape of an equilateral triangle and is played by being struck with a steel beater or, for softer effects, a wooden stick. It was used occasionally in opera in the earlier 18th century, but came into its own with the Turkish music of, for example, Mozart's opera The Abduction from the Seraglio (Die Entführung aus dem Serail). Its appearance in Liszt's E flat Piano Concerto in 1853 caused some amusement among hostile critics. Tremolo effects are occasionally demanded.

Trill

A trill is a musical ornament made by the more or less rapid alternation of a note and the note above, in the classical period generally starting on the latter.

Trio

A trio is a composition designed for three players or the name of a group of three players. The word also indicates the central contrasting section framed by a repeated minuet or scherzo.

Trio sonata

The trio sonata, the most popular of middle and late Baroque instrumental forms, is a sonata for two melody instruments and basso continuo, usually a bass instrument and a chordal instrument, and consequently usually calls for four players. Trio sonatas are found at their best in the work of Corelli at the end of the 17th century. These consist of two sets of a dozen church sonatas (sonate da chiesa) and two sets of a dozen chamber sonatas (sonate da camera). There are distinguished later examples by Telemann, Handel and Johann Sebastian Bach, although the six organ Trio Sonatas by Bach interweave three strands of melody, one for each hand and one for the feet, and are, of course, for one player.

Trombone

The trombone made its first appearance in the middle of the 15th century. It is a brass instrument with a cup-shaped mouthpiece and a slide that enables the player to shorten or lengthen the tube and hence the notes of a particular harmonic series. The early trombone was known in English as a sackbut. The instrument had ceremonial associations and in the later 18th century was only occasionally used in the orchestra, notably by Mozart in his masonic opera The Magic Flute (Die Zauberflöte) and in his Requiem Mass. With Beethoven the trombone becames an accepted if not indispensable part of the orchestra.

Troppo

Troppo (Italian: too much) is found in tempo indications, warning a player not to overdo an effect, as in allegro ma non troppo, allegro but not too much.

Troubadour

Troubadours were the court poets and composers of Southern France in the 12th and 13th centuries. The trouvères flourished particularly in the 13th century to the north of the country. Their surviving music forms an important body of secular song from this period.

Trumpet

The trumpet has a long remoter ancestry. The modern trumpet, a standard member of the brass section of the orchestra, differs from its predecessors in its use of three valves, by which the length of the tube can be changed to produce the notes of the harmonic series from different fundamentals. Baroque trumpeters came to specialise in the use of the upper or clarino register of the valveless natural trumpet, a register in which adjacent notes were possible. Experiments during the 18th century led to the short-lived keyed trumpet, which could play adjacent notes in the lower register as well. This was used by Haydn in his 1796 Trumpet Concerto. The valve trumpet came into relatively common use in the second quarter of the 19th century. Trumpets are built in various keys, although the B flat and C trumpets are now most often found.

Tuba

The tuba provides the bass of the orchestral brass section, with varying numbers of valves to allow the shortening and lengthening of the tube. It was developed in the second quarter of the 19th century.

Tubular bells

Tubular bells, tuned metal tubes suspended from a vertical frame, are used in the percussion section of the modern orchestra for special effects, making their earlier appearance primarily in opera.

Tuning-fork

The tuning-fork, an English invention of the early 18th century, is a two-pronged metal device used to give a note of fixed pitch when it is struck against a hard surface. Its musical use is for the tuning of other instruments to a standard pitch.

Turca

Alla turca (Italian: in the Turkish manner) is found in descriptive titles of music towards the end of the 18th century and thereafter, as in Mozart's well known Rondo alla Turca, Rondo in the Turkish Style. Turkish music, at that period, was superficially imitated, principally by the use of triangle, cymbals and bass drum, added to a supposedly typical melody of martial character, derived remotely from the Janissary band.

Tutti

Tutti (Italian: all) is used in orchestral music to distinguish the part of a solo instrument from that of the rest of the section or orchestra. In English this Italian plural adjective has come to be used as a noun, as in the phrase 'an orchestral tutti', meaning a passage played by the whole orchestra, or at least not specifically by solo instruments.

Twelve-note composition

Twelve-note composition is composition by the use of the twelve semitones of the octave in a predetermined order or series, which may be inverted, written in retrograde form or in retrograde inversion, and transposed. The system of composition, developed by Arnold Schoenberg in the early 20th century, has had a strong influence over the course of music of the 20th century (see Serialism).

U

Unison

Unison is the simultaneous sounding of the same note by two or more singers or players. Unison songs are not in different parts, with all singers singing the tune together.

V

Variations

Variation form involves the repetition of a theme in changed versions. It is possible to vary the melody, its rhythm and its harmony, or to vary by addition. Early variation forms include the chaconne and the passacaglia, originally dances based on variations on a simple repeated bass or chordal pattern. Later examples of variations include Elgar's well known Enigma Variations and the Handel, Haydn and Paganini Variations of Brahms.

Verismo

Verismo (Italian: realism) is used in connection with the attempts at realism in late 19th century Italian opera, particularly with Mascagni's opera Cavalleria rusticana, followed by Leoncavallo's Pagliacci.

Vespers

Vespers is the evening service of the Divine Office, elements of which have proved suitable for more elaborate setting than the normal plainchant. Particularly notable in this respect is the 1610 compilation by Monteverdi for his published Vespers in Honour of the Blessed Virgin.

Vibraphone

A vibraphone is a form of metallophone with resonators below its horizontally arranged metal bars and a mechanism to allow a vibrato effect, giving the instrument a characteristic resonance. It has been used for special effects by a number of 20th century composers.

Vibrato

Vibrato is a technique of vibration used on various instruments and by singers, at one time used sparingly or not at all, but tending to over-use from performers anxious to conceal poor intonation.

Viol

Viols are bowed string instruments usually held downwards and therefore described as viole da gamba, (leg-viols), as opposed to instruments like the violin and its predecessors, held horizontally and described as viole da braccio, (arm-viols). Viols are made in various sizes, generally with six strings and with frets, lengths of gut tied round the neck and fingerboard of the instrument to show the position of the notes. Viols were the most important bowed string instruments from the 15th century, but were gradually superseded by instruments of the violin family, leaving only one form of double bass as a survivor. The revival of interest in earlier music has brought a marked revival in the fortunes of the viol, most recently in cinematic attention to the famous 17th century player and composer Marin Marais. In the 16th and 17th centuries consorts or chests of viols, sets of matched instruments of different size and range, were much in use, often as a means of domestic music-making. The viol is often incorrectly referred to in English as a gamba, an etymological solecism.

Viola

The viola (= German: Bratsche; French: alto) is the tenor of the modern violin family, with a range that extends a fifth below that of the violin and starts an octave above that of the cello. Violas are built in various sizes and were at one time used for both the alto and tenor registers. Experiments were made, starting in the later 19th century, to produce an instrument of sufficient size to provide the desired resonance while remaining small enough to be manageable, and more recently a larger instrument, played downwards like a cello and not held horizontally like a violin, has been devised. Violas take the tenor part in the string section of the modern orchestra and in string quartets, while the solo concerto and duo sonata repertoire of the instrument, starting in the early 18th century, has been considerably enlarged in the 20th.

Viola d'amore

The viola d'amore, used principally in the 17th and 18th centuries, is a bowed instrument generally with seven bowed strings and seven sympathetic strings, tuned to vibrate in sympathy with the playing strings. The instrument has a peculiar resonance of its own and has a small but interesting modern repertoire.

Violin

The violin, a bowed instrument with four strings, is used to provide the soprano and alto parts in the string section of the modern orchestra and the string quartet. It was developed in something approaching its modern form in the 16th century, gradually coming to occupy an unrivalled position because of its remarkable acoustical properties and its versatility. Particular distinction was added by the great violin-makers of Northern Italy and of the Austrian Tyrol, while the later 18th century brought gradual changes of construction of both bow and instrument to provide greater resonance.

Violone

The violone is the double bass of the viol family, although the word was once occasionally used with less accuracy to indicate the cello or any large viol.

Virginal

The virginal is a small harpsichord of varied shape and size. The word was used very generally in England in the 16th and 17th centuries for instruments of this type, with a keyboard and a mechanism by which quills plucked the horizontally stretched strings. The etymology of the word is uncertain, although it allowed obvious scope for Elizabethan and Jacobean punsters.

Vivace

Vivace, lively, is commonly used as an indication of tempo.

Vocalise

A vocalise is a vocal work, whether an exercise or not, that has no words. There is a well known and frequently transcribed Vocalise by Rachmaninov, and vocalisation is also called for in an orchestral context with the chorus parts of Neptune in Holst's suite The Planets.

Voice

Voice is used technically in music to indicate a particular musical line, even if this is intended for an instrumentalist and not a singer. The American 'voice-leading' is the equivalent of the English 'part-writing', writing different parts or lines of music for simultaneous performance.

W

Waltz

The waltz (= French: valse; German: Walzer), a dance in triple time, became the most popular of all ball-room dances in the 19th century, typified in Vienna by the compositions and performances of the Strauss family. As a purely instrumental form, the waltz provided an apt vehicle for composers from Chopin to Ravel.

Woodwind

The woodwind section of the modern orchestra includes flutes, oboes, clarinets and bassoons and related instruments, although flutes are generally no longer made of wood. These instruments are all aerophones, blowing instruments, the sound produced by blowing across an aperture in the case of the flute, by the vibration of a single reed in the case of the clarinet and by the vibration of double reeds in the case of the oboe and the bassoon.

X

Xylophone

The xylophone, a percussion instrument with sets of horizontally arranged wooden bars to be struck by wooden sticks is used by composers from the 19th century onwards for special effects, as in the Danse macabre of Saint-Saëns, with its dancing skeletons, and in Puccini's opera Madama Butterfly.

CLASSICAL MUSIC USED IN FILMS

L'ACCOMPAGNATRICE

Mozart:
Laudate Dominum
Naxos 8.550495

Schubert:
Der Hirt auf dem Felsen
Naxos 8.553113

Schumann:
Von fremden Ländern, from Kinderszenen
Naxos 8.550784

Einsame Blumen, from Waldszenen
Naxos 8.550401

ACE VENTURA PET DETECTIVE

Mozart:
Eine kleine Nachtmusik, 2nd & 3rd mvts.
Naxos 8.550026

THE ADVENTURES OF PRISCILLA, QUEEN OF THE DESERT

Verdi:
Sempre libera, from La Traviata
Naxos 8.553041

THE AGE OF INNOCENCE

J. Strauss Jr:
Blue Danube
Naxos 8.550152

J. Strauss Sr:
Radetzky March
Naxos 8.550900

Beethoven:
Piano Sonata No. 8, 2nd mvt.
Naxos 8.550045

AMADEUS

Mozart:
Piano Concerto No. 20, 2nd mvt.
Naxos 8.550434

Requiem
Naxos 8.550235

Gran Partita, Adagio
Naxos 8.550060

Symphony No. 25, 1st mvt.
Naxos 8.550113

Symphony No. 29, 1st mvt.
Naxos 8.550119

LES AMANTS DE PONT-NEUF

J. Strauss Jr:
The Blue Danube
Naxos 8.550152

Britten:
Variations on a theme of Frank Bridge
Naxos 8.550823

Shostakovich:
String Quartet No. 3
Naxos 8.550974

AMERICAN GIGOLO

Mozart:
Clarinet Concerto, 2nd mvt.
Naxos 8.550345

ANNA

Chopin:
Waltz, Op. 69 No. 1
Naxos 8.550365

ANONIMO VENEZIANO

A. Marcello:
Oboe Concerto in D Minor, 2nd mvt.
Naxos 8.550556

ANTONIA'S LINE

Bach:
Cello Suite No. 1, 1st mvt.
Naxos 8.550677

APOCALYPSE NOW

Wagner:
Ride of the Valkyries, from Die Walküre
Naxos 8.550211

ANOTHER WOMAN

Satie:
Gymnopédie No. 3
Naxos 8.550305

Bach:
Cello Suite No. 6
Naxos 8.550678

AU REVOIR LES ENFANTS

Schubert:
Moment musical No. 2
Naxos 8.550259

AUTUMN SONATA

Chopin:
Prelude, Op. 28 No. 2
Naxos 8.550366

Schumann:
Aufschwung
Naxos 8.550493
Piano Concerto, 3rd mvt.
Naxos 8.550118

Bach:
Sarabande from Cello Suite No. 4
Naxos 8.550678

Handel:
Recorder Sonata, Op 1 No. 11
Naxos 8.550700

BABETTE'S FEAST

Mozart:
La ci darem la mano, from Don Giovanni
Naxos 8.550866

BADLANDS

Orff:
Carmina Burana
Naxos 8.550196

BARRY LYNDON

Handel:
Sarabande from Harpsichord Suite No. 11
Naxos 8.550416

Schubert:
Piano Trio No. 2, 2nd mvt.
Naxos 8.550132

BEYOND BEDLAM

Fauré:
Requiem - Libera me
Naxos 8.550765

BREAKING AWAY

Mendelssohn:
Saltarello from Symphony No. 4
Naxos 8.550055

BRIEF ENCOUNTER

Rachmaninov:
Piano Concerto No. 2
Naxos 8.550117

CARRINGTON

Schubert:
String Quintet, 2nd mvt.
Naxos 8.550388

CASINO

Bach:
St. Matthew Passion, Wir setzen uns
Naxos 8.553198

CHARIOTS OF FIRE

Allegri:
Miserere
Naxos 8.550827

CHILDREN OF A LESSER GOD

Bach:
Concerto for 2 violins in D Minor, 2nd mvt.
Naxos 8.550194

CLEAR AND PRESENT DANGER

Dvořák:
Symphony No. 9, 2nd mvt.
Naxos 8.550271

A CLOCKWORK ORANGE

Beethoven:
Symphony No. 9, 4th mvt.
Naxos 8.550181

Rossini:
William Tell Overture
Naxos 8.550236

Elgar:
Pomp and Circumstance No. 1
Naxos 8.550229

Purcell:
March from Funeral Music for Queen Mary
Naxos 8.553129

COLONEL CHABERT

Beethoven:
Piano Trio No. 5, 2nd mvt.
Naxos 8.550948

Schumann:
Davidsbündlertänze Nos. 2 & 17
Naxos 8.550493

Mozart:
Clarinet Trio, 3rd mvt.
Naxos 8.550439

COLONEL REDL

J. Strauss Sr:
Radetzky March
Naxos 8.550900

Schumann:
Träumerei, from Kinderszenen
Naxos 8.550784

Liszt:
Liebestraum No. 3
Naxos 8.550647

J. Strauss Jr:
The Blue Danube / Roses from the South
Emperor Waltz / Wiener Blut
Naxos 8.550152

Chopin:
Impromptu No. 4
Naxos 8.550647

UN COEUR EN HIVER

Ravel:
Violin Sonata, 2nd mvt.
Naxos 8.550276
Piano Trio, 1st mvt.
Naxos 8.550934

CRIES AND WHISPERS

Chopin:
Mazurka, Op. 17 No.4
Naxos 8.550358

Bach:
Cello Suite No. 5, Sarabande
Naxos 8.550678

CRIMES AND MISDEMEANOURS

Bach:
English Suite No. 2
Naxos 8.553012

CRIMSON TIDE

Catalani:
Ebben?, from La Wally
Naxos 8.550606

DANGEROUS LIAISONS

Handel:
Largo from Serse
Naxos 8.553751
Allegro from Organ Concerto No. 13
Naxos 8.550069

THE DEAD POETS SOCIETY

Beethoven:
Piano Concerto No. 5, 2nd mvt.
Naxos 8.550121
Symphony No. 9, 4th mvt.
Naxos 8.550181

Handel:
Allegro from Water Music
Naxos 8.550109

DEATH AND THE MAIDEN

Schubert:
String Quartet No. 14, 1st mvt.
Naxos 8.550590

DEATH IN VENICE

Mahler:
Symphony No.5, Adagietto
Naxos 8.550528

DEER HUNTER

Myers:
Cavatina
Naxos 8.551172

DIE HARD

Bach:
Brandenburg Concerto No. 3, 1st mvt.
Naxos 8.550046

DIE HARD 2

Sibelius:
Finlandia
Naxos 8.550103

DIVA

Catalani:
Ebben?, from la Wally
Naxos 8.550606

DR JEKYLL AND MR HYDE (1931)

Bach:
Toccata and Fugue in D Minor
Naxos 8.553859

Ich ruf zu dir, from Orgelbüchlein
Naxos 8.553032

Schumann:
Aufschwung
Naxos 8.550493

THE DOORS

Orff:
Carmina Burana, beginning
Naxos 8.550196

DRIVING MISS DAISY

Dvořák:
Song to the Moon, from Rusalka
Naxos 8.551172

E LA NAVE VA

Verdi:
Overture to The Force of Destiny
Naxos 8.553089

THE ELEPHANT MAN

Barber:
Adagio
Naxos 8.551149

ELVIRA MADIGAN

Mozart:
Piano Concerto No. 21, 2nd mvt.
Naxos 8.550434

EXCALIBUR

Orff:
Carmina Burana, beginning
Naxos 8.550196

Wagner:
Siegfried's Funeral March from Götterdämmerung
Naxos 8.550211

Prelude to Tristan and Isolde
Naxos 8.550498

EXOTICA

Schubert:
Impromptu, Op. 90 No. 4
Naxos 8.550260

EXPOSED

Tchaikovsky:
Violin Concerto, 3rd mvt.
Naxos 8.550153

Bach:
Courante from Partita No. 4
Naxos 8.550693

FANTASIA

Dukas:
The Sorcerer's Apprentice
Naxos 8.551148

Ponchielli:
Dance of the Hours from la Gioconda
Naxos 8.550081

Schubert:
Ave Maria
Naxos 8.551172

Mussorgsky:
Night on the Bare Mountain
Naxos 8.550051

Stravinsky:
Rite of Spring
Naxos 8.550472

Beethoven:
Symphony No. 6
Naxos 8.553474

Bach:
Toccata and Fugue in D Minor
Naxos 8.553859

Tchaikovsky:
Waltz of the Flowers from Nutcracker
Naxos 8.550515

FATAL ATTRACTION

Puccini:
Con onor muore, from Madame Butterfly
Naxos 8.553152
Un bel di, from Madame Butterfly
Naxos 8.553152

FAUSTRECHT DER FREIHEIT

Shostakovich:
Piano Concerto No. 2, 2nd mvt.
Naxos 8.553126

FEARLESS

Górecki:
Symphony No. 3, 3rd mvt.
Naxos 8.550822

Beethoven:
Für Elise
Naxos 8.550647
Piano Concerto No. 5, 3rd mvt.
Naxos 8.550121

FIVE EASY PIECES

Mozart:
Symphony No. 40, 1st mvt.
Naxos 8.550299

Chopin:
Prelude Op. 28, No.4
Naxos 8.550366

FORBIDDEN GAMES
Traditional:
Romance d'amour
Naxos 8.551171

FOUR WEDDINGS AND A FUNERAL
Mendelssohn:
Wedding March
Naxos 8.550790

Handel:
Arrival of the Queen of Sheba
Naxos 8.551147

FRANCES
Beethoven:
Symphony No. 7, 2nd mvt.
Naxos 8.550180

Mozart:
Piano Sonata No. 11, 1st mvt.
Naxos 8.550258

FRANKIE AND JOHNNY
Debussy:
Clair de lune
Naxos 8.550253

THE FRENCH LIEUTENANT'S WOMAN
Mozart:
Piano Sonata No. 15, 2nd mvt.
Naxos 8.550448

GALLIPOLI
Albinoni:
Adagio
Naxos 8.550014

Bizet:
Duet from the Pearl Fishers
Naxos 8.553030

Paganini:
Centone di Sonate No. 3
Naxos 8.553141

GODFATHER 3
Mascagni:
Intermezzo from Cavalleria Rusticana
Naxos 8.550240

GOODBYE AGAIN
Brahms:
Symphony No. 3, 3rd mvt.
Naxos 8.550280

THE GREAT DICTATOR
Brahms:
Hungarian Dance No. 5
Naxos 8.550110

GREEN CARD

Mozart:
> Clarinet Concerto, 2nd mvt.
> Naxos 8.550345

> Flute & Harp Concerto
> Naxos 8.550159

> Flute Concerto No. 1
> Naxos 8.550074

THE GREY FOX

Flotow:
> M'appari from Martha
> Naxos 8.551172

GREYSTOKE THE LEGEND OF TARZAN, LORD OF THE APES

Elgar:
> Symphony No. 1, 1st mvt.
> Naxos 8.550634

> Pomp and Circumstance March No. 4
> Naxos 8.550229

Boccherini:
> Minuet
> Naxos 8.551142

HANNAH AND HER SISTERS

Bach:
> Piano Concerto No. 5, 2nd mvt.
> Naxos 8.550423

Puccini:
> Sola perduta, from Manon Lescaut
> Naxos 8.550606

HARD TARGET

Beethoven:
> Piano Sonata No. 23, 3rd mvt.
> Naxos 8.550045

HEARTBURN

Handel:
> Arrival of the Queen of Sheba
> Naxos 8.551147

HEAT AND DUST

J. Strauss Jr:
> Tales form the Vienna Woods
> Naxos 8.550152

HEAVENLY CREATURES

Puccini:
> Humming Chorus, from Madame Butterfly
> Naxos 8.553152

> E lucevan le stelle, from Tosca
> Naxos 8.553153

HENRY V

Canteloube:
> Baïlero from Chants d'Auvergne
> Naxos 8.551171

HOT TO TROT

Mouret:
Rondeau from Suite No. I
Naxos 8.551153

HOWARDS END

Beethoven:
Symphony No. 5, 3rd mvt.
Naxos 8.550177

THE HUNT FOR RED OCTOBER

Sibelius:
Finlandia
Naxos 8.550103

HUSBANDS AND WIVES

Mahler:
Symphony No. 9, 1st mvt.
Naxos 8.550535-36

IMMORTAL BELOVED

Beethoven:
Symphony No. 5, 1st mvt.
Naxos 8.550177

Symphony No. 6, 4th mvt.
Naxos 8.553474

Symphony No. 7, 2nd mvt.
Naxos 8.550180

Symphony No. 9, 4th mvt.
Naxos 8.550181

Für Elise
Naxos 8.550647

Piano Sonata No. 14, 1st mvt.
Naxos 8.550045

Piano Sonata No. 8, 2nd mvt.
Naxos 8.550045

Violin Concerto, 1st mvt.
Naxos 8.550149

I'VE HEARD THE MERMAIDS SINGING

Delibes:
Flower Duet, from Lakmé
Naxos 8.551171

JEAN DE FLORETTE

Verdi:
Overture to The Force of Destiny
Naxos 8.553089

J'EMBRASSE PAS

Bach:
Cello Suite No. 1, 1st mvt.
Naxos 8.550677

JESUS OF MONTREAL

Pergolesi:
Stabat Mater
Naxos 8.550766

JFK

Mozart:
Horn Concerto No. 2, 3rd mvt.
Naxos 8.550148

JOUEUR DE VIOLON

Bach:
Chaconne from Partita No. 2 for Solo Violin
Naxos 8.550570

Beethoven:
Violin Sonata No. 9, 2nd mvt.
Naxos 8.550283

Mozart:
String Quartet No. 19, 1st mvt.
Naxos 8.550543

KALIFORNIA

Beethoven:
Symphony No. 8, 2nd mvt.
Naxos 8.553475

KEINER LIEBT MICH

Mozart:
Queen of the Night, Aria from Die Zauberflöte
Naxos 8.553438

KIKA

Granados:
Spanish Dance, Op. 37 No. 5
Naxos 8.553037

KIND HEARTS AND CORONETS

Mozart:
Il mio tesoro, from Don Giovanni
Naxos 8.550383

THE LADYKILLERS

Boccherini:
Minuet
Naxos 8.551142

THE LAST ACTION HERO

Mozart:
Overture to The Marriage of Figaro
Naxos 8.550185

THE LAW OF DESIRE

Shostakovich:
Symphony No. 10, 2nd mvt.
Naxos 8.550633

THE LIVING DAYLIGHTS

Mozart:
Symphony No. 40, 1st mvt.
Naxos 8.550299

Borodin:
String Quartet No. 2, 3rd mvt.
Naxos 8.550850

LORENZO'S OIL

Mozart:
Ave verum corpus
Naxos 8.550495

Barber:
Adagio
Naxos 8.551149

Mahler:
Symphony No. 5, Adagietto
Naxos 8.550528

Elgar:
Cello Concerto, 2nd mvt.
Naxos 8.550503

A. Marcello:
Oboe Concerto, 2nd mvt.
Naxos 8.550556

LOVE AND DEATH

Prokofiev:
Troika, from Lt. Kijé Suite
Naxos 8.550381
March from Love for Three Oranges
Naxos 8.550381

MADAME SOUZATSKA

Beethoven:
Piano Sonata No. 23, 3rd mvt.
Naxos 8.550045

Schumann:
Piano Concerto
Naxos 8.550118

MAN TROUBLE

Bach:
Et resurrexit, from B Minor Mass
Naxos 8.550586

Chopin:
Nocturne in E Flat, Op. 9 No. 2
Naxos 8.550356

MANHATTAN

Gershwin:
Rhapsody in Blue
Naxos 8.550295

MAURICE

Tchaikovsky:
Symphony No. 6, 3rd mvt.
Naxos 8.550782

Bach:
Goldberg Variations
Naxos 8.550078

Allegri:
Miserere
Naxos 8.550827

MEETING VENUS

Wagner:
Pilgrims' Chorus, from Tannhäuser
Naxos 8.551171

Overture to Tannhäuser
Naxos 8.550136

A MIDSUMMER NIGHT'S SEX COMEDY

Mendelssohn:
Intermezzo & Scherzo, from A Midsummer Night's Dream
Naxos 8.550055

Piano Concerto No.2, 2nd mvt.
Naxos 8.550681

MISERY

Beethoven:
Piano Sonata No. 14, 1st mvt.
Naxos 8.550045

Tchaikovsky:
Piano Concerto No. 1, 1st mvt.
Naxos 8.550137

MR. JONES

Beethoven:
Symphony No. 9
Naxos 8.550181

MRS. DOUBTFIRE

Rossini:
Factotum, Aria from The Barber of Seville
Naxos 8.553436

MONA LISA

Puccini:
Love Duet from Madame Butterfly
Naxos 8.553152

A MONTH IN THE COUNTRY

Mendelssohn:
Violin Concerto, 2nd mvt.
Naxos 8.550055

MOONRAKER

Chopin:
Prelude, Op. 28 No. 15
Naxos 8.550366

J. Strauss Jr:
Tritsch Tratsch Polka
Naxos 8.550337

Leoncavallo:
Vesti la giubba, from I Pagliacci
Naxos 8.660021

MOONSTRUCK

Puccini:
Che gelida manina, from La Bohème
Naxos 8.553151

Love Duet from La Bohème
Naxos 8.553151

THE MUSIC LOVERS
Tchaikovsky:
1812 Overture
Naxos 8.550500
Piano Concerto No. 11, 1st & 2nd mvts.
Naxos 8.550137

MY BEAUTIFUL LAUNDRETTE
Waldteufel:
The Skaters
Naxos 8.553337

MY DINNER WITH ANDRÉ
Satie:
Gymnopédie No. 1
Naxos 8.550305

MY GEISHA
Puccini:
Un bel di, from Madame Butterfly
Naxos 8.553152

MY LEFT FOOT
Mozart:
Un' aura amorosa, from Cosi fan tutte
Naxos 8.553172

Schubert:
Trout Quintet, 4th mvt.
Naxos 8.550658

NATURAL BORN KILLERS
Mussorgsky:
Night on Bare Mountain
Naxos 8.550501
Orff:
Carmina Burana
Naxos 8.550196
Puccini:
Madame Butterfly, Humming Chorus
Naxos 8.553152

NEW YORK STORIES
Ketèlbey:
In a Persian Market
Naxos 8.553515

A NIGHT AT THE OPERA
Verdi:
Anvil Chorus, from Il Trovatore
Naxos 8.550241

NIJINSKY
Debussy:
Prélude à l'après-midi d'un faune
Naxos 8.550262

Rimsky-Korsakov, Scheherazade
Naxos 8.550726

Stravinsky:
The Rite of Spring
Naxos 8.550472

NIKITA

Mozart:
Eine kleine Nachtmusik, 1st mvt.
Naxos 8.550026

ORDINARY PEOPLE

Pachelbel:
Canon
Naxos 8.550104

OUT OF AFRICA

Mozart:
Clarinet Concerto, 2nd mvt.
Naxos 8.550345

PETER'S FRIENDS

Offenbach:
Can Can from Orpheus in the Underworld
Naxos 8.550924

Puccini:
Un bel di, from Madame Butterfly
Naxos 8.553152

PHILADELPHIA

Giordano:
La mamma morta, from Andrea Chénier
Naxos 8.551171

PICNIC AT HANGING ROCK

Beethoven:
Paino Concerto No. 5, 2nd mvt.

PLATOON

Barber:
Adagio for Strings
Naxos 8.551149

PRETTY WOMAN

Verdi:
Duet from La Traviata
Naxos 8.551041

PRINCE OF THE TIDES

Haydn:
Symphony No. 104, 3rd mvt.
Naxos 8.550287

PRIZZI'S HONOR

Rossini:
Overture to The Barber of Seville
Naxos 8.550236

RAGING BULL

Mascagni:
Intermezzo from Cavalleria Rusticana
Naxos 8.550240

REVENGE OF THE NERDS III

Verdi:
Triumphal March from Aida
Naxos 8.553596

RICHARD III (1996)

Charpentier:
Fanfare from Te Deum
Naxos 8.550581

ROLLERBALL

Bach:
Toccata and Fugue in D Minor
Naxos 8.553859

Albinoni:
Adagio
Naxos 8.550014

Shostakovich:
Symphony No. 5, 4th mvt.
Naxos 8.550632

A ROOM WITH A VIEW

Puccini:
O mio babbino caro, from Gianni Schicchi
Naxos 8.550606

Firenze, from Gianni Schicchi
Naxos 8.551156
Doretta's Dream, from La Rondine
Naxos 8.550605

ROSEMARY'S BABY

Beethoven:
Für Elise
Naxos 8.550647

ROXANNE

J. Strauss Jr:
The Blue Danube
Naxos 8.550152

SCHINDLER'S LIST

Bach:
English Suite No. 2, Bourrée
Naxos 8.553012

Gade:
Tango Jalousie
Naxos 8.550950

Lehár:
Meinen Lippen sie Küßen so heiß
Naxos 8.550941

SERPICO

E lucevan le stelle, from Tosca
Naxos 8.553153

SEVEN

Bach:
Air from Suite No. 3
Naxos 8.550245

THE SEVEN YEAR ITCH

Rachmaninov:
Piano Concerto No. 2
Naxos 8.550117

SHADOWLANDS

Gauntlett:
Once in Royal David's City
Naxos 8.550589

THE SHINING

Bartók:
Music for Strings, Percussion and Celesta
Naxos 8.550261

THE SILENCE OF THE LAMBS

Bach:
Goldberg Variations
Naxos 8.550078

SLAUGHTERHOUSE 5

Bach:
Brandenburg Concerto No. 4, Presto
Naxos 8.550048

Piano Concerto No. 5, 2nd mvt.
Naxos 8.550423

SLEEPING WITH THE ENEMY

Berlioz:
Symphonie Fantastique, 2nd mvt.
Naxos 8.550093

SNEAKERS

Chopin:
Waltz No. 14
Naxos 8.550365

Smetana:
String Quartet No. 1 in E Minor (Allegro vivo - Appassionato)
Naxos 8.550379

SOMEONE TO WATCH OVER ME

Delibes:
Flower Duet from Lakmé
Naxos 8.551171

SOMEWHERE IN TIME

Rachmaninov:
Paganini Rhapsody, Var. 18
Naxos 8.550117

SOPHIE'S CHOICE
Schumann:
Kinderszenen
Naxos 8.550784

THE SPY WHO LOVED ME
Bach:
Air from Suite No. 3
Naxos 8.550245

STREETFIGHTER
Bizet:
Habanera from Carmen
Naxos 8.550727

STRICTLY BALLROOM
J. Strauss Jr:
The Blue Danube
Naxos 8.550152

SUNDAY, BLOODY SUNDAY
Mozart:
Soave sia il vento, from Così fan tutti
Naxos 8.553172

SWING KIDS
Beethoven:
Archduke Piano Trio, 1st mvt.
Naxos 8.550949

THROUGH A GLASS DARKLY
Bach:
Cello Suite No. 2, Sarabande
Naxos 8.550677

TIE ME UP! TIE ME DOWN!
Gade:
Tango Jalousie
Naxos 8.550995

TO BE OR NOT TO BE
Chopin:
Military Polonaise
Naxos 8.550360

TOUS LE MATINS DU MONDE
Marais:
Tombeau - Le Badinage - Sonnerie etc
Naxos 8.550750

TORRENTS OF SPRING
Chopin:
Etude, Op. 10 No. 6
Naxos 8.550364

Bach:
Concerto for 2 Violins in D Minor, 2nd mvt.
Naxos 8.550194
Mozart, Overture to Don Giovanni
Naxos 8.550185

TRADING PLACES

Mozart:
Overture to the Marriage of Figaro
Naxos 8.550185

TRUE LIES

J. Strauss Jr:
The Blue Danube
Naxos 8.550152

TRUE ROMANCE

Delibes:
Flower Duet from Lakmé
Naxos 8.551171

TURNING POINT

Prokofiev:
Balcony Scene, from Romeo and Juliet
Naxos 8.550380

THE UNTOUCHABLES

Leoncavallo:
Vesti la giubba, from I Pagliacci
Naxos 8.660022

WALL STREET

Verdi:
Questa, o quella, from Rigoletto
Naxos 8.553042

WAYNE'S WORLD

Tchaikovsky:
Romeo and Juliet
Naxos 8.550500

WHERE ANGELS FEAR TO TREAD

Donizetti:
Mad Scene from Lucia di Lammermoor
Naxos 8.550605

WHITE NIGHTS

Bach:
Passacaglia in C Minor
Naxos 8.553859

WHO FRAMED ROGER RABBIT

Liszt:
Hungarian Rhapsody No. 2
Naxos 8.550327

THE WITCHES OF EASTWICK

Puccini:
Nessun dorma, from Turandot
Naxos 8.550497

THE YOUNG POISONER'S HANDBOOK

Alfvén:
Roslagsvår, from The Prodigal Son
Naxos 8.553115

Ravel:
Bolero
Naxos 8.550172

2001: A SPACE ODYSSEY

R. Strauss:
Also sprach Zarathustra
Naxos 8.550182

J. Strauss Jr:
The Blue Danube
Naxos 8.550152

2000 LEAGUES UNDER THE SEA

Bach:
Toccata and Fugue in D Minor
Naxos 8.553859

List of Illustrations

About the Author

Keith Anderson was born in England in 1929. He was educated at Lancing College, with a scholarship in classics and music, and after military service in a number of orchestras studied at Wadham College, Oxford, where he took a degree in Literae Humaniores, followed by a degree in English Literature at London University and a subsequent degree in Music at Durham. After a brief period in Madrid, he moved to Turkey, where he remained for seven years, teaching and finally employed as a translator and broadcaster by the Turkish Ministry of Information. In 1961 he returned to Britain in the aftermath of the military coup d'état, taught for a time in Scotland and then resumed musical studies, in particular with Alexandre Moskowsky of the Hungarian Quartet. From 1966 until 1973 he was a Lecturer in Music at a College of Education for mature students in Leeds, while continuing work as a free-lance violinist, more particularly in Baroque music, as an examiner, and as an Open University tutor and lecturer. In 1973 he moved to the Chinese University of Hong Kong as a member of the University Ensemble and served for three years also as chairman of the Music Department, followed by a number of years teaching in Hong Kong, principally at the Conservatory, the Academy for Performing Arts and the Hong Kong Baptist College, coupled with practical work as a player and conductor, and with an equally busy career as a writer, broadcaster and editor. He has served as chief editor for Naxos, Marco Polo and associated labels of HNH International since the foundation of the company.